CREATE A BRAND THAT INSPIRES

CREATE A BRAND THAT INSPIRES

HOW TO SELL, ORGANIZE AND SUSTAIN INTERNAL BRANDING

Wolfgang Giehl
and
F. Joseph LePla

authorHOUSE®

AuthorHouse™
1663 Liberty Drive
Bloomington, IN 47403
www.authorhouse.com
Phone: 1-800-839-8640

Published by AuthorHouse 04/23/2012

ISBN: 978-1-4670-3952-9 (sc)
ISBN: 978-1-4670-3951-2 (hc)
ISBN: 978-1-4670-3950-5 (e)

Library of Congress Control Number: 2011917216

To William Rodgers for inspiring us through his leadership and editorial recommendations.

William Rodgers received his master of science in management from the Massachusetts Institute of Technology Sloan School of Management and served on the research staff at Harvard Business School while doing doctoral work in marketing. He was president of Hamilton Consultants of Cambridge, Massachusetts, a marketing strategy consultancy with an emphasis on brand consulting and affiliated with a number of well-known marketing professors at leading US business schools such as Tuck School, Harvard, Wharton, and Northwestern University. William Rodgers died on March 19, 2009, in Charlestown, Massachusetts.

CONTENTS

You can focus your internal branding efforts on a few things that will assure its success. Making brand part of your normal management and employee processes will ensure adoption and acceptance.

PREFACE

It takes strength to compete. If companies are not strong, they are bound to fail. Strength cannot be bought; one must become strong. A well-known and well-regarded brand helps to make a company strong. Internal branding—especially in the service industries—is the essential underpinning of successful brands that have longevity, great competitive strength, and high financial value. Driven by a shared, authentic corporate culture and guided by a convincing, dedicated top management, employees will build brand value with all their actions and interactions, empowering the brand every day.

Because of this belief, Wolfgang Giehl was co-author of the first book on this topic, *Focus Internal Branding,* in Germany in 2004. The book attracted the interest of William Rodgers, who recognized potential in a fusion of European and American brand knowledge. We thank Will for his initiative in kicking off the translation and update of this book. We also owe him a debt for bringing Joe LePla into the authors' team, giving us the rewarding experience of co-writing from opposite sides of the globe. All of us are deeply saddened that Will didn't see the finished collaborated work; William Rodgers died in March 2009 at only 64 years old.

Create A Brand That Inspires: How to Sell, Organize, and Sustain Internal Branding—A Best Practice Study was developed into a completely new manuscript and structured according to the three core challenges for brand management: selling the brand internally to senior management, organizing the brand on all management levels, and living the brand within each company's community. This makes this study a rewarding read not just for managers but also for executives and team leaders. We've provided up-to-date case studies and practical information regarding how to develop a successful internal branding initiative.

We never cease to learn, especially from our customers, among whom we also include our students. We would like to thank them for keeping this topic alive and for their continued pronounced interest. We also appreciate the contributions of the Advanced Learning Institute (Chicago, IL), which has offered a series of 2-day seminars providing case examples of organizations in various stages of internal branding. We were avid students ourselves, listening to presentations by practitioners from such companies as Nationwide Insurance, IBM, and Boeing in recent sessions.

We also wish to thank Lynn Parker and Beth Woolley for editing and proofing; Jen Travis, Lynn Parker, Briana Marrah, and Beth Woolley for seminal work around the online brand experience, social branding, and branding and brand communities; Beth Woolley for the brand relationship model diagram; and Bob Zammit for his help as an editor, as a style authority, and with word spackle. Finally, we'd like to thank Rachel Sabre Olmsted for keeping things on track and expending the tremendous energy necessary to pull all of the legal reviews and permissions together to make this study printable.

Internal branding is a relatively new field with not much written about how it really works. There remain friendly debates about even its dimensions and definition. Although we've gained more understanding of internal branding mechanics, one thing is certainly true: Only by tasting can you know a flavor. There always remains what we call the secret of your brand. That certain magic one can't describe; one has to live it. We hope our readers will find success with their internal branding endeavors.

Wolfgang Giehl
Bonn, Germany

F. Joseph LePla
Seattle / Washington, USA

INTRODUCTION
Internal Branding's Evolution

The practice of internal branding is not as new as it seems. The United States Marine Corps (established in 1775) has a distinctive brand that causes its troops to act differently than the regular US Army, and that distinction is recognized by friends and foes alike. The product of the US Marines is a result of extensive troop training on how to consistently live the brand. Other examples of internal branding from the last century include Texaco's brand service and dress code, which were tied to an advertising campaign that said, "You can trust your car to the man who wears the star"; IBM's branding of its computer service people (blue suits, white shirts); and GM's Mr. Goodwrench quality program. Disney may have been one of the first corporations to embark on a large-scale internal branding effort with its original Disneyland theme park, and Mayo Clinic set its brand strategy of physician collaboration to find answers in the first decade of the last century.

So why did internal branding only recently become popular as a term and as an area garnering greater attention? First, the term *brand* only became popular in the mid-1900s for packaged consumer goods like Jell-O or Tide. The *brand manager* at Procter and Gamble, General Mills, or Quaker Oats at that time was really a marketer. The brand manager's job focused on visual brand identity and sales.

Now people believe that brand is applicable to most industries. Internal branding has been used by organizations that range from restaurants to government agencies and from exclusive hotels to banks and health care providers. Health care, particularly in its completely privatized incarnation in the United States, relies on the personal relationships between patient, physician, and health care staff. Therefore it is one of the industries at the forefront of internal branding innovation with lessons that can be applied to both business-to-business (B2B) and business-to-consumer (B2C) industries.

Even the concept of what can be a brand has stretched to include movie stars, countries, nonprofits, and nongovernmental organizations. Still, many companies think only in terms of visual branding, messaging, and advertising and not in terms of how they are delivering the brand through their interactions.

The concept of integrated branding, introduced in the early 1990s, describes the process of aligning company structure, corporate culture, business strategy, employee actions, visual brand, and communications to create compelling customer experiences. Internal branding activities are the actions an organization undertakes to create this alignment.

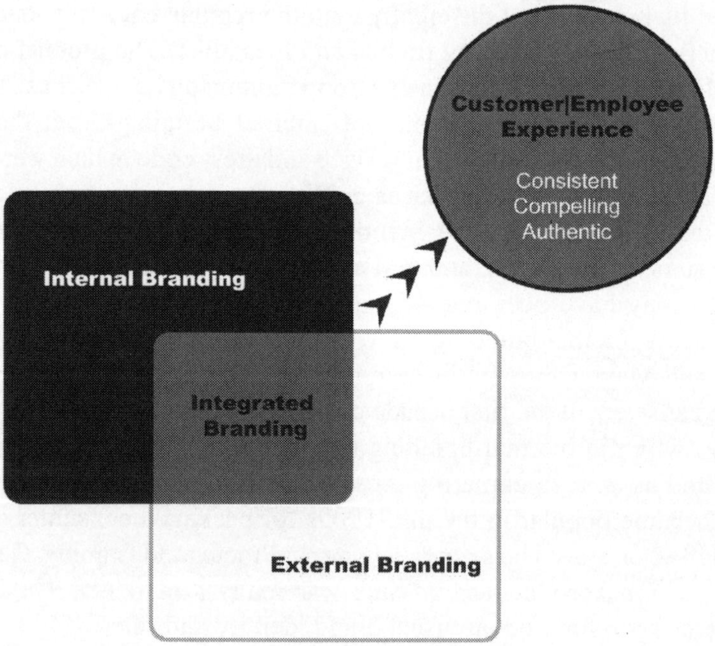

Internal branding integrates strategic, tactical and staff decision making, external sales, marketing, and social networking with an organization's core value.

Internal branding fuels revenue growth and profitability through its positive impact on both the customer and employee experience through:

Customers

- A service or product price premium
- Developing strong brand communities
- More distinctive product or service offerings
- Favorable word-of-mouth recommendations
- Greater customer loyalty

Employees

- Higher employee morale and engagement
- Ability to hire better candidates at lower costs
- Improved job acceptance-versus-offers
- Reduced employee turnover
- Reduced worker's compensation costs
- Reduced sick days

Finally, with the rise of social networks and communities, the world has evolved to a point that the object of internal branding is not a unidirectional customer experience but a conversation that results in shared brand building. Whether you manage a global, national, or even local brand in this new social world, helping the chief executive officer (CEO), managers, and employees express your brand and participate in your brand community have become the keys to success. Because employees play an integral role in online communities, this change increases the need for strong internal branding to equip your CEO, managers, and employees to live the corporate culture and explain the brand's promise.

SECTION I

Selling Internal Branding to Your Organization

CHAPTER 1

Branding Your Organization in an Online World

Internal branding is the process of aligning culture, infrastructure, leadership, and metrics. It empowers employees to live the brand through how they do their jobs, their internal and customer interactions, and personal expression.

Perhaps the world is getting smaller, but its impact on each of us is anything but small. Sometime around the end of the twentieth century, we gained the ability to instantly communicate with people anywhere in the world, and they with us. Through the web, people are now able to have relationships with anyone else who is plugged in from Surinam to Sri Lanka. This single change is having a greater impact on how organizations brand themselves than has anything else that has occurred in the last hundred years.

Where communications, such as advertising and public relations, used to be enough to build brand preference, these channels have been all but lost in the fire hose of information we experience each day. A weekday edition of the *New York Times* contains more information than the average person in 17th century England would have encountered in an entire lifetime.[i] And now, the web has libraries of data available at our fingertips.

The Need for New Brand Constructs

By embracing this worldwide network of websites, blogs, and social networking sites, we have tapped into a new world in which brand identification turns into helping customers build their identities and brand experiences are seen as part of more encompassing brand community. We need to replace our old branding constructs with principles that take these changes into account. The new reality is that successful brands will be based more on individual employee expression and online group conversations that companies have little or no control over.

What does this mean for managing branded customer experiences? We need new ways of thinking that allow employees to more authentically connect with customers. What does this mean for branding your organization? On the downside, it will be much more difficult to influence customer opinions from the top. On the upside, potential customers can learn a lot more about why they should buy your products than they could in the past. If your brand is to thrive in this environment, you will need to have all of your ducks in a row. You will need to back up what you say with what you do and back up what you do with a deep understanding of your organization's true value.

In this new world, teaching people how to embrace change is a necessity. How your organization and employees represent your brand will evolve rapidly with every online conversation. As part of this process, companies will find themselves redefining roles from the CEO on down to empower corporate culture, brand alignment, and social expression.

The most frequent mistake that brand and marketing managers make is to assume that delivering high quality is the same as having a strong brand. Quality without a differentiated strategic direction won't get everyone on the same page and put scarce resources where they are needed most. It won't result in an ownable customer experience.

While management approaches such as Lean and Six Sigma improve company processes and quality, they don't deal with differentiation. If my company and one down the street provide the same service and adopt the same Lean practices, how does the customer choose between them? Brand is a definable and compelling set of differences in business approach and culture that lead to customer loyalty and relationships. Effective internal branding will give Lean and Six Sigma initiatives even more impact by focusing process development on activities that build brand difference. In turn, Lean and Six Sigma will provide a more functional and clearer-thinking organization in which brand building can thrive.

How ready are you to build your brand? Here are some questions to help you assess your current brand-building capabilities. This will provide you with the information to answer each one of these questions and translate your answers into action.

- Do you have a clear and actionable brand promise?
- Does the promise include actionable brand tools such as a strategic role, a guiding principle, culture norms, a story, and a personality?
- Do you use your brand to develop strategy?
- Have you hired employees who buy into your brand?
- Are employees brand ambassadors?
- Are brand goals integrated into employee performance expectations?
- Does human resources use change management principles?
- Do your employee social media guidelines integrate your brand approach?

People Make the Difference

Whether you work in a product or service business, a for-profit or not-for-profit, it is ultimately people who make the difference. Your employees, from research and development (R&D) to customer support, create and deliver your uniquely branded experience. It's your employees who form the unbreakable relationships between you and your customers. In short, your employees must live your brand for sustainable success. But a well-defined brand only creates a framework and direction for employee behaviors and specific actions; living the brand is ultimately the way to energize the talents and enthusiasm of employees as they forge their own unique takes on your brand.

What does effective internal branding look like? It aligns all employees—including those in the back office and in supporting roles as well as those on the front lines—with your brand promise. It arms all employees with actionable brand tools, which are the compass that enables them to deliver consistent customer experiences. It supports and builds the corporate culture into something that is rewarding to employees and that delivers the company's brand experience.

Research on the interrelation between family and work demonstrate that company culture can influence productivity.[ii] An employee's work environment is a key consideration in creating company loyalty. Many companies benefit from a positive culture, while others suffer from negative cultural consequences. In October 2009, France Telecom deputy CEO Louis-Pierre Wenes resigned after a number of employees committed suicide. 24 workers committed suicide in the space of 18 months; some left notes blaming the company's culture and management style for increasing pressure and misery at work.[iii]

This study takes that premise one step further. Culture does more than build employee identification with the company. Culture is a key delivery system for your brand experience to both other employees and customers.

Business-to-Business Branding Is as Important as Consumer Branding

With 3 of the top 5 brands being B2B brands in a recent Interbrand study,[iv] it's clear that people don't have two separate modes for making business choices versus personal choices. In a recent study conducted by DHL, the company found that its customers, particularly in its supply chain business, chose it because of the trust they had in the brand. The DHL brand reassured customers that they were getting the right information and that such information would be easy to understand. These customers felt that using DHL's products reflected positively on their professionalism.[v]

We've also seen no difference between companies that offer services as products versus those that offer more tangible products. We think that internal branding is critical to service brands because it helps services to create compelling points of difference. Throughout, when we refer to *product* we'll be using the term to include companies that offer a service as their product. When we talk about *customer service*, we'll be talking about the way in which customers are treated by the company.

Key Measures of Effectiveness

Do you already have a strong brand? See how your organization measures up.

- Clarity is at the heart of an effective brand.
  - ✓ Can employees talk in a compelling and consistent way about the value you bring to your customers and constituents?
  - ✓ Do they understand the difference between providing a quality experience and a branded experience?
  - ✓ Do they know how to act in ways that demonstrate and build brand value?
  - ✓ Do customers have a good understanding of where you are going?
- Authenticity breaks through the noise and builds long-term relationships.
  - ✓ Do employees believe that their managers and senior team are walking the talk?
  - ✓ Do a significant percentage of employees feel deeply connected to your organization?
  - ✓ Have employees emotionally bought into your story in a way that shines through in their conversations?

- ✓ Would you sacrifice short-term profitability to keep your promise?
- Transparency demonstrates that you are trustworthy.
  - ✓ Do leaders and managers keep their promises to employees?
  - ✓ Does the company keep its promises to customers?
  - ✓ Do you communicate with employees with frequency about all aspects of the organization?
  - ✓ Are your leaders engaged with your brand community online and off?
- Accountability allows you to see progress.
  - ✓ Do you measure employee brand competency?
  - ✓ Do you measure aided and unaided brand/value awareness?
  - ✓ Do you measure any gap between what customers value and how well you perform?
  - ✓ Do you measure the strength of your company culture and brand community?
  - ✓ Do you take action based on what you measure?

Case Study: Encouraging Employee Brand Action [Ballard Power Systems]

A small firm in British Columbia called Ballard Power Systems received a visit from engineers and purchasing staff of one of the major US automobile manufacturers. The auto company's delegation took a tour of Ballard's facilities and then met the researchers in the lab to discuss the progress of their mutual technical projects and to search for more solutions. After a while, the meeting was interrupted for a lunch break.

One of the Ballard technicians chose to be absent during lunch. When the visitors returned to the laboratory, this technician showed them a rough model of the idea that had been discussed just that morning. He had quickly constructed the model in the workshop during the lunch break.

"That would have taken us 3 weeks," said one of the Americans, "including the 2 weeks to reserve time in the workshop."[vi]

That evening, the same technician did not attend dinner. Instead, he built the actual device and, by midnight, was far enough along that he was able to connect it to a test bench. The test results were ready in time for the meeting with the visitors the next morning. In 24 hours, the employee created results that the visiting team claimed would have taken anywhere from 7 weeks to 3 months in their own company.

People who have studied Ballard point to the energy and self-direction of the company's employees and their identification with the company as the decisive reasons for its extraordinary success.

Ballard exemplifies an important aspect of internal branding. Every company has a unique approach to developing and delivering its products or customer service. Employees who are aligned with that unique approach make a huge difference in how compelling a brand and its products are to customers. One result of this alignment is strong and lasting customer relationships. Companies that then extend this approach to their marketing benefit from the additional leverage of a brand that is completely integrated inside and out.

Companies that do internal branding well, like Ballard, are deliberate in their efforts to align employee behavior with company strategy and goals. They nurture a company culture that supports employee behavior based on their unique, branded approach to delivering products or customer service. While they may set up practice and procedure guidelines that are customer-directed, they also empower employees to use brand-informed judgment to better serve the customer. Employees understand the promise they are keeping and can then apply their knowledge of that promise to all decisions and actions.

What typifies Ballard's brand approach and culture? Ballard's brand promise is "to be an R&D leader in fuel cells resulting in application-specific product quality and performance." Another part of their promise includes "hiring employees who have a deep knowledge of fuel cell technology."[vii] They translate this approach to employee action by encouraging employees to invent and innovate.[viii] Internal branding works better in companies that practice a flatter management style instead of a centralized command-and-control style. That's because employee empowerment taps into each worker's creativity and allows decisions to be made with the best information closest to the problem. Empowerment has the added benefit of allowing a company to respond quickly to change.

Employee empowerment is reflected in two key aspects of Ballard's organizational style: role models who are inspirational (the confidence and sincerity of the Ballard founders is contagious) and fewer bureaucratic or hierarchical restrictions.

Ballard also employs other brand tools. Cultural norms are building blocks of organizational culture.[ix] These can be defined as a shared set of actionable values. Here are some of Ballard's cultural norms:

- *Helping society*: The company works on technology intended to solve environmental problems.
- *Goal achievement*: The company has regularly been able to increase the performance of its products.
- *Success you can see and feel*: Results are used as models for demonstration and presentation of effective practices.
- *Making a difference*
- *The essential importance of each person's work*
- *Employee ownership*: Ballard employees at all levels are shareholders in the company.
- *Pride*: Ballard employees consider it an honor to work for their company.
- *Flexibility*: The company allows flexible working hours and habits; the result is what counts.

---

i Suzuki, *The David Suzuki Reader,* 226

ii "Firmen profitieren von Familienförderung."

iii Abboud, "France Telecom Talks with Unions on Suicide Spate."

iv "Best Global Brands 2008," accessed September 26, 2009, http://www.interbrand.com/en/best-global-brands/best-global-brands-2008/best-global-brands-2008.aspx

v "McKinsey & Company/MCM Marketing Centrum Münster," unpublished raw data.

vi Koppel, *Powering the Future*, 154

vii "Business Focus," accessed September 30, 2009, http://www.ballard.com/About_Ballard/Corporate_Direction/Business_Focus.

viii "Careers," accessed September 30, 2009, http://www.ballard.com/About_Ballard/Careers/

ix LePla, Davis, and Parker, *Brand Driven*, 111

CHAPTER 2

Understanding Internal Branding

The Brand Promise and How to Keep It

We define an organization's brand as resulting from the promise it keeps. In order to make and keep that promise, an organization's internal branding and external brand expression must be two sides of the same coin. When we use the term *brand*, our primary focus is the organization's brand—also known as the umbrella brand or master brand—not specific product brands.

How employees demonstrate and express your brand is critical to company success. Whatever business goals you set and employee behaviors you measure will be what are experienced by your customers. Behaviors are specific and repeatable actions that can be identified. They are how you live your brand in your corporate culture.

Employees and customers have slightly different relationships with your brand. Employees' views of the brand are more likely to be influenced by the company's reality through their everyday working experiences. This means that, even when negative things like internal cost cutting are happening, the customer view of the brand can remain more or less intact. If a crisis occurs, as in the case of the employee suicides at France Telecom, a company can reinforce the external identity without losing too much brand equity.

But if your external brand communications don't align with how you act over time, your brand will suffer. While it used to take time for unaligned communications and actions to be perceived as such by customers, this customer perception lag has been greatly reduced in this time of instant communications and social communities.

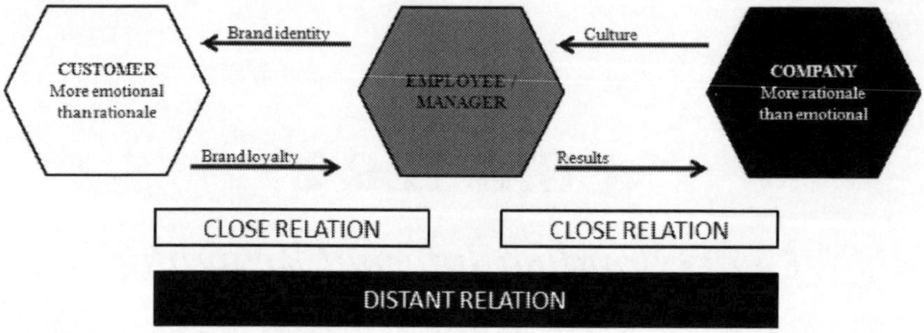

The same alignment is needed for an employer brand. It's essential for employees to value the same things about the brand's product and services as customers do for long-term success. That doesn't mean that the organization shouldn't pay attention to creating an attractive working environment, but treating the working environment as if it were a separate brand leads to employee confusion and separates employees from customers. Without customers, there would be no brand.

Brands Are About Becoming and Being

Internal branding is a process of becoming what you desire to be. The process of becoming begins with understanding what a company can own over time, how it's organized, how employees are empowered, and how to build a strong brand community.

While there are several brand models in use, most will share several common elements.

- A brand promise composed of brand tools and expressed in brand messaging.
- Brand tools that summarize the core concepts of the brand so that employees can live them.
- Brand messaging that can be expressed as positioning statements, message platforms, and story.

Box 1—The Process of Becoming

Brand Environment
What you do well
What your community values
What you can own over time

Internal branding building blocks
Brand culture (Delivered via brand tools)
Corporate culture
How you are organized
How you lead
The products you develop
How you deliver customer service
How you measure performance

Brand Experience
What is demonstrated
What is lived
What is expressed

Employee/Customer experience

Brand Community

Box 1 dispels two common myths about branding. First, branding is synonymous with marketing communications or corporate identity. Marketing communications is what you say about the experience you deliver, not the experience itself. For communications to be effective, they must express what employees live and deliver. The second myth is that an internal branding effort doesn't have to seamlessly connect with what customers experience. Your brand is your brand, whether you are viewing it from the standpoint of being an employer, an employee, a customer, or another interested party.

And it all starts with internal branding, which is the engine that drives the multitude of ways your brand is experienced. This is especially important for service companies, because employees are providing the value that customers buy; in the end it is always personal commitment coupled with an understanding of how to live the brand that makes the difference.

Five Components of an Internal Branding Initiative

The goal of internal branding is to help all employees understand how their roles positively impact the customer experience and company success. There are five components in a typical internal branding

, these components help you to define, live, and promise:

2. Culture and Leadership
3. Brand Management
4. The Change Plan
5. Brand Measurement

Brand Tools

Brand tools are what the organization uses to guide all decision making, behavior, and communications. These tools can have different names and be used in many different ways. In the Brand Tools at a Glance table below, we'll describe some tools and how they are used. If you are currently living your brand to any extent, it's important to continue building from your current tool or tools. If you aren't currently using tools, it's important to decide on which tools to use and then stick with them.

Many companies have just one tool, such as values they use in everything from defining culture and individual behavior to messaging. Others prefer specific tools for specific brand functions. The brand promise is the cumulative effect of all brand tools working together. We'll also refer to specific tools that the authors have found helpful in living the brand. In case studies, we'll use the term each company uses internally when known.

This table may help you decipher the alphabet soup of brand tool terminology. Many tools are used in more than one way, depending on the company.

Brand Tools at a Glance

Name	Use
Strategic role, über strategy, brand essence, corporate value proposition	Defines the organizing strategy and value that forms the basis for the brand category and product, service, and communications development

Guiding principle, values, brand essence, corporate value proposition	What the brand does differently from others, guiding how employees integrate the brand into their actions
Cultural norms, personality, values	Tools that define the way the organization and employees behave
Mission, vision	What the company does or wants to do
Story, positioning, elevator statement	The core value messages of the brand
Brand heritage	The history of the brand

In companies with the most successful brands, their top-level business strategy is also a brand tool, sometimes called a strategic role or über strategy. The strategic role is a benefit-based category that describes why a prospective customer must consider the company.

For automotive manufacturer Volvo, that über strategy or strategic role is about "ensuring the safety of drivers and passengers." They have consistently demonstrated safety through their more than 75 year history of safety firsts, including the shoulder harness and the rear blind-spot-viewing camera. A recent innovation is an infrared sensor that will activate the car brakes if a front-end collision is imminent and the vehicle is traveling at 18 miles per hour or slower. They believe that this may result in a 50 percent decline in collisions. "Ensuring the safety of drivers and passengers" succinctly defines Volvo's value in a way that energizes employees. The company's resulting actions demonstrate to customers why they must consider Volvo when shopping for a new car.

In addition to the strategic role, other brand tools that we'll talk about extensively, and that make up the promise, include an organization's guiding principle, story, brand heritage, personality, and cultural norms. Each tool has a distinct role in empowering employee action and customer interactions and in building a healthy corporate culture.

The guiding principle is a company's unique approach to its strategic role. It's not a message but rather every employee's context for making on-the-job decisions. For Salal Credit Union, the guiding principle is "Connecting" coupled with a strategic role of "Money management made easy." "Connecting" means that every Salal Credit Union employee looks for ways to form relationships with its members. For investment boutique Freestone Capital Management, it's "Be invested," which is its unique approach to its role of "Investment boutique for alternative thinkers." "Be invested" means that employees will invest in completely understanding client needs and literally be invested in the company's own investments.

The story organizes the compelling points of the brand, including a version of its strategic role and why it's unique. It can be thought of as a value proposition for the company's brand. The story can have many lengths and is often presented as a series of bullet points that are easier for employees to put into their own words. It's also often included on the home page and the "About Us" sections of websites or wherever a company description is necessary.

Here's Freestone's story:

> Freestone is not your typical wealth management firm. We are an investment boutique for alternative thinkers. This means we think differently and challenge the norm in order to deliver alternative investment strategies that preserve your capital through diversification for up and down markets. It also means we eliminate conflicts; we are both independent and are invested in our own approach, making us truly invested in our clients' success. And finally, it means we have a boutique structure that is designed to give you the attention you deserve in all facets of your wealth management needs.[x]

Here's the bulleted version that staff can then personalize:

- We are an investment boutique for alternative thinkers. We think differently and challenge the norm in order to deliver alternative investment strategies that preserve your capital through diversification for up and down markets.
- We are independent and are invested in our own approach, making us truly invested in our clients' success.

- We are structured to give you the attention you deserve in all facets of your wealth management needs.

Culture and Leadership

Company culture is something that starts on an organization's first day in business, but to be most effective, it needs to be defined and managed. Organizations understand their culture by looking at why the company was founded and the types of decisions and events that are important to how it became what it is today. This roots and history building block is your brand heritage.

In addition to brand heritage, the corporate culture includes the language, values, corporate structure, expression, and events unique to the company. It's essential that the CEO and senior management team continually demonstrate, talk about, and define the corporate culture as part of the internal branding process. An organization that has a culture that employees understand and embrace has a competitive advantage in the market. Cultural fluency creates a foundation for a strong online brand community, which we believe to be the next major shift in brand management and company marketing.

Two brand tools that can help managers build the culture are cultural norms and personality. Cultural norms are the behaviors that employees cite when they take action. An example is, "Since we reward initiative, I've decided to institute this program before the next planning cycle." While cultural norms typically start by employees observing and emulating senior management, after a while, they take on lives of their own. You can discover what norms exist by querying employees with such questions as, "What are the ways you do things that have helped you succeed in our culture?"

The brand personality is a series of traits that set the standard for how employees treat each other and the world as well as the tone and manner of company communications. The Beryl Companies have reinvented the health care call center and help more than 450 hospitals and health systems in the United States build better relationships with their customers. Their personality, which includes the traits friendly, collaborative, results-oriented, passionate, and reliable, is used for hiring and is built further through unique staff activities that encourage engagement and team building.[xi] What bubbles to the surface for Beryl is the feeling that customers can trust them with very important patient communications and engagement.

Brand Management

It's really important to set up a governance and management system prior to starting an internal branding initiative. We don't recommend treating internal branding as a series of one-off, unrelated tactics such as building a website, holding an employee brand event, or conducting an employee marketing campaign. Rather, use a systematic approach that begins by determining where the brand work will live and who will be its sponsor.

We've found that a cross-functional brand team with a global brand manager at the helm is the most effective way to manage internal branding. While we commonly see internal branding initiatives managed by marketing, sales, or human resources, the downside to such an approach is siloed thinking. For more information on brand management styles, we recommend picking up *Strategic Brand Management* by Kevin Lane Keller.

The Change Plan

Branding is an evolving process. Every day, it's added to by your employees, customers, and other members of your brand community.

When you start an internal branding process for the first time, the change plan describes how the organization will move employees from point A to point B. While it will cover the logistics of internal branding, the change plan should be most concerned with the becoming process. Although all change happens on a bell curve that ranges from early adoption to lagging far behind,[xii] there are ways to speed up the process for all employees. Business health expert Barbara Grant, a principal consultant of Seattle-based MGS Consulting, says about change, "People don't pay attention to what's ended, so they have trouble moving on."[xiii] This involves acknowledging the good aspects of the organization that you are leaving behind. When you recognize that people need to move through the emotional part of any change beginning with denial and ending with acceptance, you will be in the right zone to develop the elements and messaging for your internal branding process.[xiv]

Brand Measurement

The very best internal branding will fail if it isn't tied to clear measurements. Your brand team and senior leaders need to come to consensus on what success looks like. We've observed several actions that are associated with employee commitment. Employee commitment in turn results in less turnover, greater word-of-mouth recommendation, positive brand awareness, and greater productivity. These include:

- participation in online discussion about the brand,
- willingness to recommend the organization to others as a place to work or to buy products from,
- willingness to work for a brand for less money than for competitors,
- giving a brand high ratings in terms of overall opinion and day-to-day company experiences,
- buy-in to a brand's future business direction, and
- an ability to accurately explain the brand promise and apply it to work.

Case Study: Living by Cultural Norms [The Four Seasons Hotels and Resorts]

Chairman and CEO Isadore Sharp opened the first Four Seasons hotel in downtown Toronto in 1960. That began a series of successful openings with a brand formula of spacious rooms equipped for both business and relaxation with a friendly staff to "make every guest wish a reality."[xv] The Four Seasons was the first to introduce 24-hour-a-day, 7-days-a-week room service, twice daily housekeeping, complimentary bath amenities, terry cloth robes, hairdryers, and multiple, two-line telephones in both the guest room and the bathroom.

"Early in the company's history, we decided to focus on redefining luxury as service, and that became our strategic edge," explains founder Sharp.

> And, in order to deliver on that promise, we needed to harness the 'best of the best' employees who are dedicated, committed, and inspired to deliver great service. They are

> the standard-bearers for the intuitive, highly personalized service we aspire to provide.
>
> The Four Seasons is dedicated to perfecting the travel experience through continuous innovation and the highest standards of hospitality. From elegant surroundings of the finest quality to caring, highly personalized 24-hour service, Four Seasons seeks to embody a true home away from home for those who know and appreciate the best. The deeply instilled Four Seasons culture is personified in its employees—people who share a single focus and are inspired to offer great service.[xvi]

Sharp focused on creating a cultural norm of the Golden Rule (Do unto others as you would have them do unto you) with the expectation that each employee would then treat the guests in a similar manner. In addition to the Golden Rule, the Four Seasons uses other cultural norms (known as *core principles*) that include: offering only experiences of exceptional quality; recognizing people as its greatest assets; instilling a sense of dignity, pride, and satisfaction in everything we do; working together cooperatively; and respecting each other's contributions and importance.

These principles help the Four Seasons define "who we are and inform the decisions we make."[xvii] Four Seasons' cultural norms demonstrate its commitment to hire only people who genuinely like people. The Four Seasons has the recruitment and retention of new talent down to a fine art.

As we mentioned earlier, one test of a strong brand is whether the management team will put its brand promise before short-term profitability. According to a former general manager, "if there was anything wrong with employee morale, then there was a *big* problem . . . to miss a quarterly number was not desirable, but it happens." To ensure that the culture and cultural norms were alive and well, employees fill out an annual questionnaire consisting of 200 to 300 questions as part of their formal review process. No problem is too small to escape the immediate consideration of senior management. Because senior managers also walk the walk, they treat employees as they would want to be treated.

The Four Seasons' cultural norms drive rapid dissemination of service innovations. A doorman who noticed that joggers often drank water upon their return to the hotel decided to greet each jogger with a bottle of water ("do unto others," "experiences of exceptional quality"). The concept went over extremely well and was translated into a best practice ("respecting each other's contributions," "working together cooperatively") to all Four Seasons within one week of the decision.[xviii]

Leaders also talk the talk—positive reinforcement is frequent and immediate for employees who live the brand. The company celebrates extraordinary service with tickets to the theater, dinner, employee-of-the-month recognition, and cash bonuses.

Management and staff share and nurture stories of extraordinary service and, in time, can become legends themselves. Take for example the delivery of a common cup of coffee to a popular satellite radio talk show host by the general manager of the Four Seasons of Boston. Through a couple of miscues by the Four Seasons' staff, this celebrity did not get the cup of coffee he anticipated during a stay. He vented his frustration on national radio. The general manager of the Boston hotel, hearing the newscast in the morning, managed to bring down, while dressed in the uniform of the service staff, coffee and sundry treats to him and his staff while they were broadcasting live. According to a well-placed source, it left the host momentarily speechless, and the event turned into an internal brand legend.

The coffee story may reveal a bit of the difference between the Four Seasons and other super luxury hotels. While the Four Seasons has a dynamic, entrepreneurial approach to luxury with an emphasis on exemplary service, others, such as the Ritz Carlton, have a very methodical approach to achieving customer satisfaction. These internal branding differences translate into different customer experiences.

The results for the bottom line have been significant. Four Seasons has expanded to 75 hotels in 31 countries and has received more AAA Five Diamond awards than any other hotel company; it has done so every year since 1986, and it received 21 awards in 2007. The *2007-2008 Zagat Survey of the World's Top Hotels, Resorts, and Spas* listed Four Seasons as number 2 in the top hotel chains category; 18 Four Seasons hotels made the Condé Nast Traveler Top 100 in 2006; and the Four Seasons was the Best Hotel Group Worldwide according to *Gallivanter's Guide* in 2007. The Four Seasons is also only 1of 18 firms that have been on the list every year since the launch of *Fortune Magazine's* Top 100 Companies to Work for in America in 1988.

---

[x] S. Svenson, in discussion with the authors, October 2009.

[xi] "Our Culture," accessed September 26, 2009, http://www.beryl.net/about-us/our-culture

[xii] Rogers, *Diffusion of Innovations,* 209

[xiii] Barbara Grant (consultant, MGS Consulting), in discussion with the authors, August 2009.

[xiv] Bridges, *Managing Transitions*, 56

[xv] "About Us," Four Seasons, accessed July 7, 2009, http://www.fourseasons.com/about_us/

[xvi] Ibid.

[xvii] Ibid.

[xviii] Ibid.

CHAPTER 3

Selling Internal Branding to Your Senior Team

One of the most frequent questions we hear is "How do I sell the need for internal branding to my senior team?"

The challenge is that internal branding is typically treated as an afterthought to external branding campaigns. We believe this stems from a lack of executive-level knowledge of the role that internal branding plays in brand value creation—an employee role that has only become more vital with the growth of social networking.

As with your public image, your brand exists whether or not you choose to manage it. It is built by employee and customer experiences every day. What happens if you don't have a strong brand?

Box 2—The Warning Signs of a Weak Brand

- Weak Corporate Culture
- Internal Silos and Turf Wars
- Low Employee Morale
- Brand Tools That Employees Can't Act upon
- Business Strategies at Odds with Brand Value
- Brand Architecture That's Confusing to Employees and Customers
- Duplicative Products
- Declining Market Share
- Stodgy Reputation

Begin with the Basics

If you aren't clear about what makes your organization distinct, you aren't ready to embark on internal branding. The basis of any brand is the ability to tell the world in one simple concept why customers must consider you and why partners must work with you. If you don't know this, then you need to define your brand promise using your brand tools before going any further.

The brand environment is at the intersection of what you do well, what your customers value, and what is ownable over time. Each organization has certain things that it does well because of the experiences of its executives and what they choose to value. Your approach must be focused on what your customers, influencers, and fans (your online community) value.

Finally, what you choose as the strategic role of your brand must be something that is ownable. *Ownable* means that, when prospective customers think about your business category, they associate you with a specific value within that category. By understanding that value you can continue to create and improve products or deliver customer service that exemplifies the value and therefore stand out in the marketplace. Mayo Clinic has been about "The patient comes first" since its inception. You can discover these components of your brand through internal and customer research. This is the door to developing a promise that employees understand and can act upon.

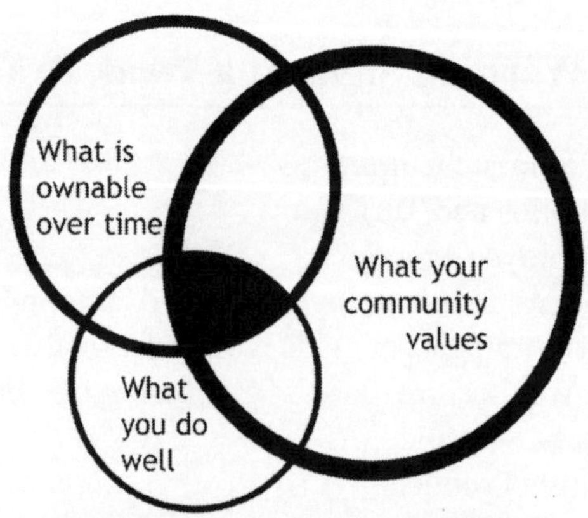

BRAND INTERSECTION

Your brand promise must also be something that you can apply in every division and department of the organization. If you believe that branding is only a marketing function or if you leave it up to marketing to do the heavy lifting, you will typically not create strong internal branding practices. Without them, you will find that your strategic planning, your product and services development, and even your quality initiatives will not fully leverage your value.

Washington state health care provider Group Health uses a brand team drawn from all parts of its organization to keep this more than 8,500 employee organization with more than 26 medical centers aligned with its brand. Its promise is about better health engagement and using innovation to help its members get there. One of the advantages that Group Health has over its competition is that it integrates health care and coverage. This means it is able to provide health care services in the United States that typical providers cannot; these include one of the first integrated, electronic patient records systems that allows physicians to see almost every procedure or interaction a patient has had and gives patients immediate access to their medical records.

To support its promise of "Innovation for better health" with staff, Group Health employees ask "What's next for the patient's health?," its guiding principle. These brand tools require coordination, and the organization has used a brand team with a working understanding of brand concepts to make this happen. The team has included key people from the health system, health plans, the physician group, sales, marketing, advertising, community relations, the research arm, the community foundation, and the CEO. "I believe the brand team has enabled us to enhance the effectiveness of our brand and speed up its adoption throughout the organization," explains Lin MacMaster, vice president of marketing. Our efforts with staff have contributed to significantly increased member satisfaction and are one of the reasons we received the highest member satisfaction among commercial health plans in the Northwest region as ranked by J.D. Power and Associates.[xix]

Why should you do the hard work of internal branding to get employees aligned to your brand? If you don't, how will you keep people working in the same direction? How will you keep them building compelling and ownable value?

A key part of building Group Health's brand has been helping their leaders and staff consistently deliver on the brand's promise. The organization has adopted four staff brand behaviors to support the brand promise:

- Demonstrate caring.
- Promote continuous improvement.
- Collaborate for better results.
- Represent Group Health well.[xx]

Group Health is working on making every staff member a brand ambassador with the ability to foster customer loyalty. That's why staff members are evaluated on these brand behaviors through an annual 360 degree input and feedback process. It reminds all of them of the crucial role they play in shaping the way their customers—and potential customers—experience Group Health.

Siloed employee performance goals without an actionable, unified focus can't generate sustainable business or continued healthy profit margins. Failing to align employees with the brand makes it much more difficult to implement strategies and achieve goals. By challenging employees with well-defined brand tools, you will create a shared sense of purpose and emotional engagement.

Internal Branding Creates Sustainable Success

Senior management can create business school-perfect strategic plans and metrics, but without strong internal branding practices, these strategies will fall short of their full potential. Internal branding equips CEOs for one of the most difficult tasks they face: getting employees to align emotionally and cognitively to better deliver company value. Lack of employee alignment can often be traced back to a lack of brand clarity and commitment at the most senior levels.

A clear brand and effective internal branding campaign has the added benefit of replacing a "What's in it for me" attitude with company-oriented loyalties. It's very difficult for managers to maintain fiefdoms if they are held accountable for on-brand actions.

Internal Branding Creates Value-Centric Employees

If creating a compelling marketplace promise isn't enough to move your team to embark on internal branding, consider this: internal branding gives employees a strong reason to work for you beyond simply earning a paycheck. Research tells us that when employees understand the promise they are delivering, they feel more satisfied with their work.[xxi] When a company's value isn't clearly understood or demonstrated, employees are much less committed to their employers. In fact, when brand value is clear, employees are even willing to trade some remuneration for being able to work for the specific company. We frequently see data about employees' willingness to take from 5 percent to 20 percent less in pay in order to work for a strong brand.[xxii] It follows that satisfied employees create satisfied customers.

Effective internal branding is instrumental in connecting the dots between value and what each employee does to create that value. Valuing the employee relationship also helps you understand how to use brand to recruit prospective employees. A strong brand and culture also allows you to mobilize your workforce to become a good referral source for new employees. According to John Sullivan, professor of management at San Francisco State University, employee referrals have a better return on investment than recruiter-based hires "due to markedly better rates in offer acceptance, voluntary turnover, and on-the-job-performance."[xxiii]

Internal Branding Turns Corporate Culture into an Organizational Asset

Another way to explain the value of internal branding is to talk about its effect on company culture. The 1990s and 2000s witnessed the rise of companies that traded on their internal culture as a creative force for driving product development. Companies such as Ben & Jerry's, Yahoo!, Google, and Zappos.com have all harnessed the power of culture to competitive advantage. Zappos.com's purchase was attributed by Amazon to its culture.[xxiv]

Internal Branding Paves the Way to Market Leadership

As we've explained, companies that have strong brands also have a clear promise, clear goals, and deep customer relationships. Internal branding allows employees to focus on creative ways to build even more value and innovate in ways that meet new market needs, as we saw in the Ballard, Group Health, and Four Seasons examples. Brand focus helps these companies enhance their product lines, invent new offerings, and make customer service more distinctive (i.e. they become market leaders, maintaining competitive advantage and higher margins over the long term).

A growing part of internal branding activities is the online community of employees and followers that develops when employees are emotionally and cognitively aligned. Amy Davis of Mayo Clinic talks about word-of-mouth being the primary marketing vehicle for their organization. According to Davis:

> We know that 95 percent of patients say good things about Mayo Clinic after visits, and an average of 46 others heard good things. Further, 90 percent recommended Mayo Clinic, and of 20 so advised, an average of 7 actually came. With an average of 500,000 patients per year, this means that the number of people hearing something positive in a given year was 21,850,000.[xxv]

Case Study: Employees as the Brand Difference [The Beryl Companies]

The Beryl Companies, based in Dallas, Texas, is an organization that uses its internal branding activities to create a high-level differentiation in what many consider to be a commodity market: health care call centers. Beryl works with a list of over 450 hospitals and health systems throughout the United States that reads like a who's who of American health care and manages over 3 million patient calls for their customers annually.

Beryl's call advisors represent these hospitals to patients in phone and web experiences for everything from referring a physician to signing up for classes to following up after a hospital procedure to enquire about a patient's health. Because of how important these calls are to the patient and how Beryl services serve to extend each hospital's brand, it's very important for call advisors to be both knowledgeable and caring. The Beryl brand promise is that, in the competitive world of US health care, it will help its clients "Own the health care consumer." This means helping hospitals form long-term relationships with their patients. The unique way it does this is through telephone and web relationships that are characterized by a caring and personal touch. Call advisors are encouraged to go out of their away to help patients and each other.

For CEO Paul Spiegelman, this makes the care and feeding of staff one of his most important jobs. Spiegelman calls and considers staff his coworkers, which reinforces the team culture that is vital to keeping employees engaged. He calls this process "The Circle of Growth."

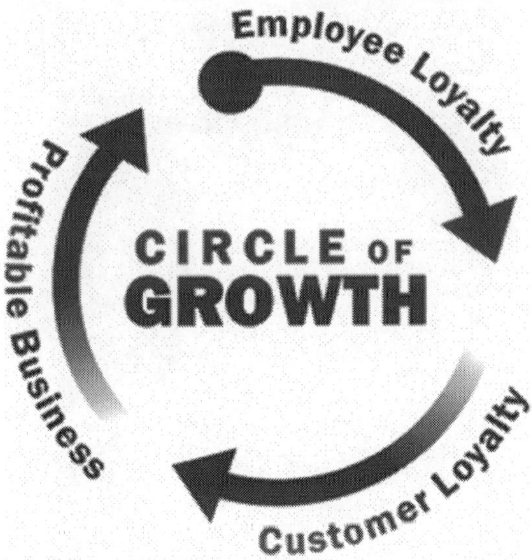

Beryl's Circle of Growth Philosophy. Image used with permission from Beryl Companies.

Spiegelman believes that paying attention to his coworkers' needs will generate deep loyalty. In turn, this will generate customer loyalty. Beryl has dedicated a senior management position to making sure this happens. Says Lara Morrow, Queen of Fun and Laughter, "We believe that our workforce is our family, and we have a lot of fun while getting it done for our clients."

Fun includes year-round contests that frequently use games and challenges to encourage staff to get to know clients better. For instance, one contest was modeled after *The Great Race* reality TV show and encouraged coworkers to virtually race around the country to discover clues at client websites. The winning team received a free trip to New York City and was treated to a client visit to get a firsthand view of one of the brands that Beryl represents.

Beryl's Paul Spiegelman is always up for a challenge and uses the CEO position to build culture in unexpected and fun ways.
Image used with permission from Beryl Companies.

The result of all of this work has been a very low rate of call advisor turnover. In fact, many call advisors have made their way into the ranks of middle management as a result of Beryl's support for ongoing education. Beryl has been consistently recognized as one of the Best Companies to Work for in America.[xxvi] Low turnover results in a more experienced call advisor team, which serves to further reinforce Beryl's Circle of Growth.

Beryl has taken its coworker-based branding to its customers through their online experiences as well. Based on a campaign called "The Face of Beryl," the opening flash sequence on their home page features the faces of Beryl coworkers, which then transform into photos of patients being helped.

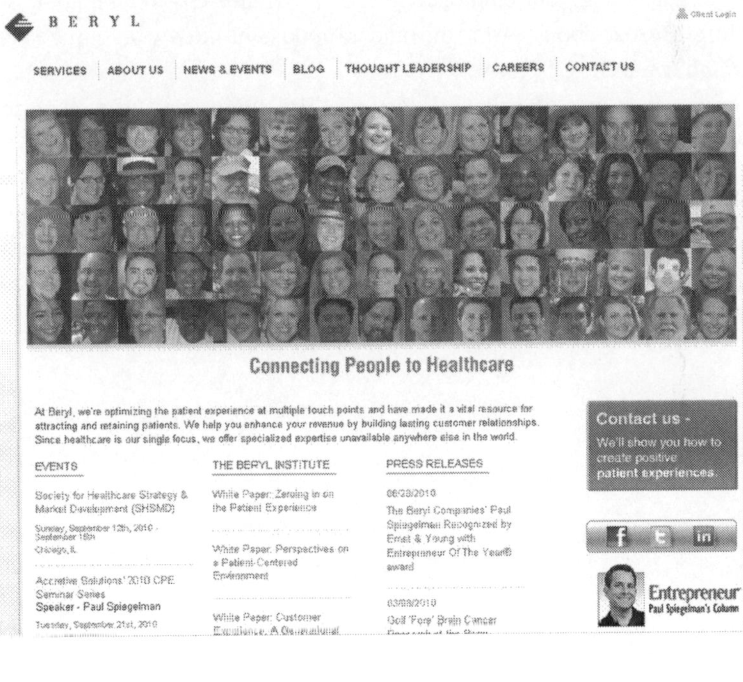

[xxvii]

---

xix Lin MacMaster (vice president marketing, Group Health), in discussion with the authors, October 2009.

xx Jay Gusick (executive director, brand, communications and public relations, Group Health), in discussion with the authors, October 2009.

xxi "Best Employer Canada," accessed July 2, 2009, http://was2.hewitt.com/bestemployers/canada/pages/index.htm

xxii Parker LePla, "Client Research 2004-2009," unpublished raw data, last modified December 2009, word

xxiii John Sullivan and M. Burnett, "Updating Your Employee Referral Programs: ERE Community Q&A," *Dr. John Sullivan Blog*, November 30, 2008, http://drjohnsullivan.com/articles-mainmenu-27/recruiting-tools-mainmenu-37/223-updating-your-employee-referral-program—ere-community-qaa

xxiv "Jeff Bezos about Amazon and Zappos,"http://www.youtube.com/watch?v=-hxX_Q5CnaA

xxv Davis, *Bringing the Brand to Life,* Presentation at the American Advanced Learning Institute, Washington, D.C., April 26-28, 2006

xxvi "2007 Best Small and Medium Companies to Work for in America," Great Place to Work Institute, accessed July 2, 2009, http://www.greatplacetowork.com/what_we_do/lists-us-sme-2007.htm

xxvii "Beryl," accessed July 2, 2009, http://www.beryl.net/

CHAPTER 4

Branding the Organization

Start with Tools That Explain and Train

Internal branding is an organization-wide endeavor. It starts with a brand promise that consists of a set of brand tools to help employees learn how to live the brand. It shapes corporate culture while aligning employee performance with top-level business and brand strategies. Although what companies call it may vary, in the most effective brands, the brand promise defines the relationship between the organization and its customers in a highly compelling yet clearly understandable way. The boundaries set by the brand promise determine the playing field for a company's strategic planning, the markets it enters, and its unique approach to branding its goods and services.

Few companies begin their lives with a defined brand promise or well-defined culture. For start-ups, these can be inferred from your initial business strategy and the personal backgrounds of your management team. In the case of established companies that are in the process of becoming brand driven, the best way to determine the brand promise is through customer and employee research to find out and build on the value that currently exists.

The brand promise is defined by a few brand tools that align and build the brand over time. These are the strategic role, guiding principle, personality, story, and cultural norms.

Box 3—Brand Tools Criteria

Brand tools must be:

- ✓ actionable (if employees can't use them as a compass, they aren't tools),
- ✓ differentiating (tools need to move all parts of the organization to better deliver on an ownable promise),
- ✓ focused on the customer (brand tools work to build customer interactions with the organization),
- ✓ few (in the course of a hectic work day, complex brand promises will be forgotten), and
- ✓ based in reality (tools have to reflect what you do well and what your customers value).

Aligning Internal Branding with Strategy and Offerings

A brand promise results in a distinctive culture, a style of operations, and specialization within the markets that the organization serves. The brand promise consists of one or more brand tools that help the company and its employees live the brand. The strategic role brand tool for HSBC has been to be "The world's local bank," which has resulted in a strategic plan that calls for a strong presence in each country it operates in. HSBC lists the parameters for this role as:

- largest international emerging markets bank,
- widespread international network,
- uniquely cosmopolitan customer base, and
- considerable financial strength.[xxviii]

In contrast, ING is primarily an online bank whose strategic role is "Creating high-performance vehicles for people saving for retirement."[xxix] This brand appeals to everyday people around the world who are looking for ways to save for retirement with safe but higher-than-average returns.

While both are banks, they have two entirely different ways of capturing and sustaining their customer base. As a result, their external and internal branding look very different. HSBC stresses ubiquity of branches in many countries and a long tradition of internationalism. ING stresses higher interest rates for savings accounts and money market funds. HSBC internal branding supports its local service focus, while ING emphasizes one culture and people who are behind the scenes but friendly when reached through customer service.

Internal branding is guided by brand strategy, which is based on brand promise, culture, and business strategy. Both HSBC and ING take deposits, sell CDs, and write mortgages and car loans. For its expression of internal branding, HSBC relies on the staff in the local branches who see many of its customers once per week or more. ING relies more heavily on the quality of its website and on the telephone capabilities of its customer service representatives.

An Organizational View of Internal Branding.

Internal Branding Leverage Points

Garnering the level of brand success experienced by both of these companies demands that you understand how internal branding helps organizations shape customer experience. *An Organizational View of Internal Branding* (above) provides a basic understanding of how the employee conveys brand value from the company to the customer. One important difference from many business school models is an increased emphasis on the brand promise as an influencer of business strategy.

We outline the leverage points that will allow you to significantly improve brand effectiveness.

Experience with Your Goods and Services

How employees perceive your products is critical to how they champion your brand. If you offer something that employees also use, they will be demoralized if their experience doesn't reflect your communicated brand. Employees can also have negative brand experiences secondhand as they listen to others' brand stories.

To support positive brand experiences for employees, we recommend benchmarking employees' brand experiences in the same manner as customers'. Once you have benchmarks, you can monitor and act on them over time. We recommend the additional step of creating a cultural norm about continuous improvement that includes fixing negative employee experiences. Employees who can tell improvement stories are a powerful branding force.

The Brand Promise

The brand promise directs and gives substance and scope to all business strategy. In fact, when organizations have done the best job of brand management, their brand and top-level business strategies are the same thing. This is very clearly illustrated by HSBC, whose promise of "The world's local bank" translates into strategies that build the business while strengthening brand differentiation.

If the discipline of tying strategic planning to the brand promise isn't practiced, organizations miss out on the brand's full potential. A fuzzy brand strategy results in less compelling products, teams that work at cross-purposes, overlapping products, and conflicting or confused employee loyalties—not to mention senior teams that can't bring a clear and focused approach to creating the organization's future.

Corporate Culture

Organizations that practice internal branding have a better sense of who they are. That's because they make deliberate choices to codify organizational style and culture,[xxx] thought leadership, brand tools, and brand expression. Many organizations fail to establish a single point for brand governance and therefore suffer from multiple, de facto brand directions and a lack of enterprise-wide buy-in.

Sub-Brand Definition

Sub-brands aren't just about product nomenclature. In combination with your master brand (usually your organization's name and promise), they are the frame for how customers interact with you. See chapter 9 for more information on brand architecture.

There are 3 types of sub-brands:

- offerings that represent future areas of growth,
- offerings that need to be named and featured in order to compete in a market, and
- offerings that enhance your reputation.

The natural impulse of companies with new products is to give them a distinctive brand name in the mistaken belief that this will result in better customer visibility. The reverse is typically true. Customers want simplicity and don't have the time to sort out a confused brand structure. Only create sub-brands for offerings and services that will be either major revenue producers (donation producers in nonprofits) or will result in a major reputation boost. Clear sub-branding is essential to internal branding, because it creates greater employee clarity.

Group Health has a research arm that has changed the course of how medicine is practiced and how people live their lives. Because it was known as the Center for Health Studies, the connection to Group Health wasn't clear to outsiders or staff. While it garnered national attention, little of that awareness attached to Group Health. The organization subsequently changed its name to Group Health Research Institute and clearly explained how it contributed to Group Health's promise of better health through innovation as demonstrated in the *Helmet Safety* advertisement. This gave a morale boost to staff members, who were proud to be associated with the Institute and impressed employers and individual members who saw it as a sign of Group Health's thought leadership and commitment to excellent health care.

Helmet Safety. Used with permission from Group Health Research Institute.

Brand Touchpoints

The brand is what the customer experiences, not necessarily what the company or organization intends to deliver. A brand is created in every interaction with employees, customers, and other stakeholders. It is also judged to be good or not at each of these touchpoints (or places where a brand is experienced, including any interaction with an employee or other customers as happens in an online brand community). Touchpoints are very complicated for service brands—such as health care, logistics, or hospitality—in which there are more places for customers to experience the brand and therefore greater challenges to ensure that people are experiencing it consistently.

Contrast the simplicity of Dannon Yogurt branding (employees play almost no role in direct customer services) to Ritz-Carlton branding (the brand is tested by each guest multiple times a day). Most of the branding for Dannon is created by customers eating the yogurt, by its packaging, and to a lesser degree, by its online presence and its foundation's efforts that support healthy lifestyles and good nutrition. Ritz-Carlton, by contrast, has 2,192 guests a day (800,000 per year) each interacting with up to 5 or 6 employees each day. Mail and logistics group Deutsche Post DHL manages more than 1 million customer contacts per hour. These are huge numbers of touchpoints across their systems.

Given the number of interactions, and the chances for something to go wrong, Ritz, DHL, and other service organizations have a greater need to monitor all aspects of the user experience.

Customer touchpoint mapping is the process of identifying all customer interactions with your brand, creating a consistent delivery plan for every touchpoint, measuring results, and making continuous improvements. Touchpoint mapping includes identifying the touchpoint, describing the process accompanying each touchpoint, and then evaluating how well that touchpoint meets a customer's needs while delivering the brand.

For instance, if you have a coffee company whose brand is based on their coffee experience being a daily ritual, you would map its touchpoints around making and drinking its coffee either at the coffee shop or at home. You would place more importance on elements that contribute to the ritual, such as the making or drinking, and place less on such things as the grocery store purchasing process.

We also recommend creating a narrative about each touchpoint based on customer segments. For instance, for a medical provider, you could describe a young mother named Jane and her experience choosing a doctor:

> Jane talked to a customer support person at the clinic to discuss the merits of various physicians and care teams. The customer support person couldn't give much detail on why she should consider one team over another for her family.
>
> She then went online to check out the doctor. Not only did she find an attractive photo of her physician, but she was also able to learn about her whole medical care team. There was even a short video of the physician explaining his beliefs about family care. She had been about to schedule a meet-and-greet appointment to get a better feel for the team, but the website was so comprehensive that she almost felt she could skip this step.

The combination of naming, process description, evaluation, and narrative can bring touchpoints to life while creating a high level of experience consistency.

Few companies monitor customer touchpoints as well as the Ritz-Carlton. With more than 17,000 "Ladies and Gentleman of the Ritz-Carlton" serving customers, President and Chief Operations Officer (COO) Horst Schulze is emphatic about using its Malcolm Baldridge National Quality Award process to strive for 100 percent customer loyalty, 100 percent employee pride and joy, and zero customer difficulties. The feedback loop from customer to employee is strengthened during daily check-ins relative to the Ritz-Carlton credo and semiannual reviews. They conduct surveys on customer loyalty and employee pride and joy via a process owned by the human resource director, the operations director, the quality director, the finance director, and functional leaders. All guests are entered into a Guest Recognition CLASS database to have their likes/dislikes, previous difficulties, family interests, personal interests, and preferred credit cards tracked with daily updates on service quality indicators.

Internal and External Branding Processes

Aligning all employees with the brand is a process that requires coordination among division and department leaders, especially those in marketing, sales, and human resources. The team driving internal branding needs to work closely with the teams responsible for external branding. We often see budget allocations for external branding campaigns, while educating employees is an afterthought. In our experience, one of the most critical factors in long-term brand success is fully engaging employees before any external campaign is introduced.

Process alignment is most effective when it starts with the basics. These basics include defining department and employee brand performance metrics and redesigning recruiting, orientation, and training from a brand promise perspective. While it's popular in some organizations to use contests and other rewards to encourage employee participation, there is no substitute for integrating brand action into each employee's job description. When it's part of the job, employees and their managers won't be tempted to relegate brand to something that gets done when they have the time.

It's important for senior management to codify its culture, brand tools, and visual and verbal corporate identity rather than delegate this job to marketing. Marketing, public relations, and sales then have powerful brand experiences to communicate. Volvo's "For Life" campaign has a lot more impact precisely because Volvo employees live the brand of safety.[xxxi]

The Employee Experience

One of the reasons for the increase in internal branding interest is the growth of venues where employees act as brand intermediaries. Customers now have unprecedented access to employees, which blurs the lines between private and public activities of a company. The net of this trend is that all employees have now become a voice in the world with all of the opportunities and perils that represents.

Alignment and buy-in are also important for senior management recruitment. New CEOs and other C-suite officers have a much greater ability to damage a long-standing and successful brand; RCA lost its dog association during one CEO's tenure, and Dell Computer lost its momentum when Michael Dell stepped down. On the plus side, a senior manager who has bought into your brand as a precondition for employment can further the organization's understanding and use of its brand.

Case Study: Tying Senior Management Action to Brand Results [REM Medical]

REM Medical's vision is to become the national quality sleep care provider. It currently provides sleep care specialty services through clinics that offer sleep disorder diagnosis, testing, and treatment in the southwestern United States. Its mission is to enable people to lead happier and healthier lives with better nights' sleep.

What sets REM Medical apart from the competition is the fact that a physician is involved from diagnosis through testing, treatment plan, and patient compliance. Further, patients feel that the REM Medical team is personally concerned about their well-being, and the team follows up to make sure the proper care was given during treatment.

REM Medical turned this into a brand promise by creating a new health category that also doubles as their strategic role: "Physician-led sleep care." This role telegraphs to referring physicians and prospective patients how they are different. Most sleep labs just have technicians and no single person overseeing the coordination of each patient's care. In contrast, a clinic that delivers sleep care requires specialists, and REM Medical is the first health care system of its type to have sleep care specialists overseeing care. Therefore, referring physicians can be confident that their quality of care is upheld when they outsource sleep disorder diagnosis and treatment, and patients can know that they are being treated by the best.

REM Medical's Brand Tools

Once CEO Russell Benaroya and President/COO Eric Page arrived at these brand tools with their senior management team, they set financial metrics to continue their journey to becoming a national brand. They determined that their first step was to greatly increase the number of new patients in their existing clinics. They quickly realized that, while having volume and financial goals were good, increasing patient volume was directly related to staff actions.

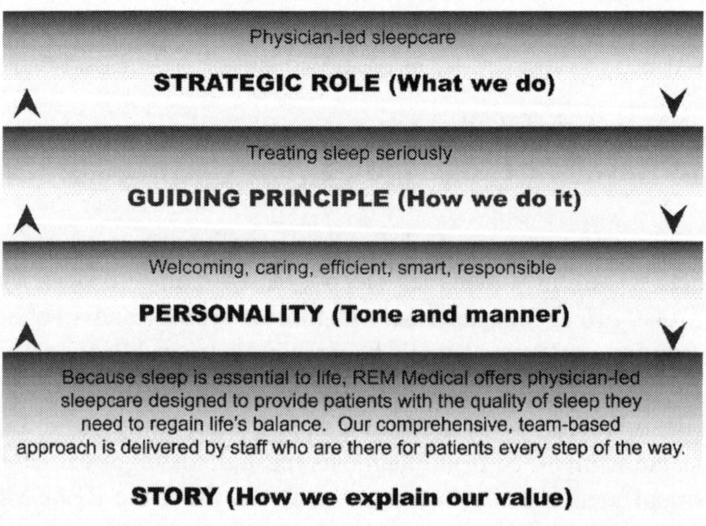

Health care employees are motivated more by helping people than by personal financial goals. Benaroya and Page's decision to lead with brand metrics rather than financial metrics resulted in much greater engagement, because it gave employees incentives around something that they cared about—their patients getting a good night's sleep. The guiding principle of "Treating sleep seriously" gives employees the power to improve the service they provide. Personality traits of being welcoming and caring help employees focus on the much-needed emotional support that their sleep-deprived patients require. But Benaroya and Page also took the brand another step further by building brand goals and manager bonuses directly into their strategic growth plan outlined in the image titled *REM Medical Strategic Planning.*

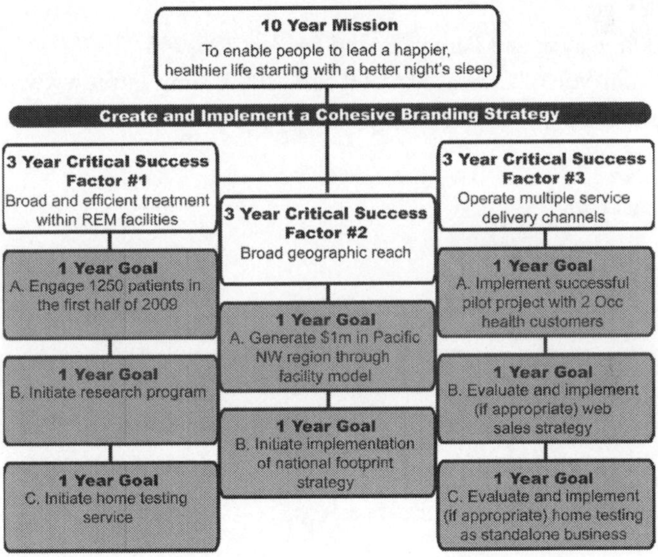

REM Medical Strategic Planning.

Integrated Brand and the REM Medical Strategic Plan

"The lesson we learned from this is clear," explains Benaroya. "Business or financial metrics result in siloed thinking with managers asking themselves, 'How come I am doing this one little thing?' Making the connections clear between actions and our brand promise created highly motivated people."

Adds Page, "If you ask people if they'd rather meet a revenue goal or bring sleep care to 100 new people, the answer is obvious. What our brand did was allow us to show how the business goal met the brand goal."

---

xxviii HSBC home page accessed October 3, 2009, http://www.hsbc.com/1/2/home

xxix ING home page, accessed October 3, 2009, http://www.ing.be/private/index.jsp

xxx LePla, Davis, and Parker, *Brand Driven,* 127-145

xxxi "About Volvo," accessed October 3, 2009, from http://www.volvocars.com/us/top/about/values/Pages/safety.aspx

CHAPTER 5

The Rise of the Employee Ambassador

Employees, Public Opinion, and Brand Communities

Once upon a time, before 1994, there was a clear boundary separating a company's employee and customer relationships. The web has eliminated that boundary. In so doing, it has given the world access to what once was private behind the scenes. Now, every employee has the potential to be a company intermediary and brand standard-bearer on any given day, and the words they say or write may be searchable and retrievable forever.

Customers can easily pierce your corporate veil with just a few mouse clicks. Customers can *friend* your CEO on Facebook or discover that your director of operations is also a Deadhead in their spare time by Googling them. Meanwhile, disenfranchised employees can read blogs from a company hate site that purports to tell the truth about unfair practices, further reinforcing erroneous beliefs.

The traditional command and control model for employee and customer branding is being swept away. It is being replaced by brand communities both online and offline; the company, its employees, its customers, and company followers all play a role in building and protecting—or destroying—your brand.

What is the impact of every employee being a brand ambassador? On the down side, you have much less control over public communications. It's just not possible to regulate what employees do on the web. This leaves you vulnerable to all kinds of employee mayhem.

This was the experience of Domino's Pizza when two employees filmed a prank in their Conover, North Carolina, restaurant's kitchen that violated health code standards. "In a few days, thanks to the power of social media, they ended up with felony charges, more than a million disgusted viewers, and a major company facing a public relations crisis."[xxxii] By Wednesday afternoon, the video had been viewed more than a million times on YouTube. References to it were in 5 of the 12 results on the first page of a Google search for "Domino's," and discussions about Domino's had spread throughout Twitter.

"We got blindsided by two idiots with a video camera and an awful idea," said Domino's spokesman, Tim McIntyre, who added that the company was preparing a civil lawsuit. "Even people who've been with us as loyal customers for 10, 15, 20 years, are second-guessing their relationship with Domino's, and that's not fair."[xxxiii]

The *New York Times* reinforced this view, "In just a few days, Domino's reputation was damaged. The perception of its quality among consumers went from positive to negative," according to the research firm YouGov, which conducts online surveys of about 1,000 consumers every day regarding hundreds of brands.[xxxiv]

The Decline of Credible Information

A second downside concerns the nature of web information. In the Internet age, the public is less sure who to believe and what institutions to trust. Information has turned into "my opinion" versus "your opinion." According to a Pew Trust research study, "49 percent of US respondents fear they are seeing false or inaccurate news reports online."[xxxv] People's trust in corporate institutions is also low. The Edelman 2006 Trust Barometer concluded that only 49 percent of Americans and 38 percent of Europeans exhibited a high amount of trust in large companies.[xxxvi]

Online information is further compromised by the use of page linking that drives search engine relevancy. According to Chris Dellarocas of the Publius Project:

> Links constitute the true currency of reputation on the web. Even the most malicious online content will remain largely unnoticed unless others choose to link to it. Links are all the

> more important since search engines, that ultimate arbiter of online relevance, use a page's link counts as the primary determinant of that page's ranking within a set of search results.[xxxvii]

At the same time, having access to volumes of information, rather than helping, has made it even more difficult for companies to build authentic reputations as people respond negatively to being overexposed to information.

Finally, it has become easier for the public to evaluate advertising claims by going directly to employees or reading customer-generated product reviews. This has contributed to the downfall of advertising as the premier brand-building medium. If your advertising doesn't accurately represent what you deliver, that fact is going to be broadcast over and over again in cyberspace.

People want a more accurate and authentic view of who you are. Direct word-of-mouth reports have always been a preferred mode for gaining information for business and consumer purchases. Customers most often get information about a product or service by asking a friend or family member. In 2007, 86.9 percent of respondents to a Marketing Sherpa study indicated that "they would trust a friend's recommendation over a review by a critic, while 3.8 percent said they would trust user reviews over a critic."[xxxviii]

Developing an Employee Brand Community

It pays to be proactive rather than restrictive and defensive when it comes to social media. If you can't control what employees say, then what's called for is a way of educating to empower employees. That requires clear guidelines. If you think of brand building as a conversation with employees rather than as a policing action, you'll be on the right track. Employees will benefit from guidelines that help them understand the legal and appropriate etiquette for online networking. But just as importantly, they need to understand and be able to put your brand promise into the context of their lives to authentically tell others about it.

It's essential for organizations to get up to speed quickly on social branding and online brand communities. Whether you use it or not, social media is already having a significant impact on your company's success. Social branding is becoming a key component of internal branding. For more on this topic, see chapter 11.

The Cultural Experience: A Prerequisite for Effective Ambassadors

The founders of Four Seasons, Ritz-Carlton, Infosys, the Beryl Companies, and Southwest Airlines all had strong, innovative visions that transformed their respective industries. They all believed in the trickle-down theory of internal branding to generate and promote brand recognition. It can be summed up as "Treat the employee as number one so that the employee in turn treats the customer as number one." Customer satisfaction leads to essential repeat business that reinforces the brand and that, in turn, reinforces employees acting according to the brand.

When you walk into the Beryl Companies headquarters in Dallas, you know that something is different right away. First, there is a reader board welcoming you by name and signaling to employees who the visitors are so they can play a role in that person's brand experience. Then there is a flat-screen TV that prominently displays employee anniversaries with Beryl. Inside, instead of the typical call center austerity, the atmosphere is rich and engaging; employee recognition and after-work activities figure prominently. Beryl doesn't just talk about valuing its employees, it does everything it can to demonstrate it.

Many of the best-known organizations that excel at internal branding share a common culture of trust and transparency. Some, like Forrester or Ritz Carlton, may be more autocratic while others, like Mayo Clinic, may be participatory, and still others, like McKinsey, may be meritocracies—all empower their employees. The way Southwest Airlines defines and directs its culture figures prominently in employee action—"Warrior Spirit, a Servant's Heart, and a Fun-LUVing Attitude"[xxxix]—as it focuses on its mission of the "Highest quality of customer service delivered with a sense of warmth, friendliness, individual pride, and company spirit."[xl]

Skills for Effective Brand Ambassadors

Helping employees become brand ambassadors may make you feel like you are herding cats, but the upside is that you will have created a powerful force for building your brand. When employees speak with their own voices, they tap into the power of peer-to-peer recommendations and garner the support that a strong brand community can give in times of trouble (for more information on brand ambassadors, see chapter 12). For your brand ambassadors to be most effective, though, they need to be prearmed with knowledge.

Brand Promise

Have employees internalized your brand promise? Can they speak to it passionately from their own work experiences? The next step after defining your promise is to get employees to connect to that promise on a deep level. Can they speak to it every day? Worn out quality phrases like "We provide the highest quality service you can find" and "Customers tell us we're the best" don't cut it for prospective customers who really want to know why you are better. With the advent of social brands and brand communities, companies have a great opportunity to demonstrate their value.

Business Direction

In brand equity testing over the past decade, we've learned that deep customer relationships are associated with customers understanding where you are headed with future products. Therefore, the first step in improved customer understanding of your business direction is employee education. Can your employees explain how your products are evolving and where you are going? Can they talk about what's in it for the customer to stay with you over the long-term?

Personal Stories

In a comprehensive study of business leaders, researchers analyzed business strategy deployment at 40 banks, hospitals, manufacturers, and utilities. They found that storytelling was one of the leading factors in whether or not each organization reached its goals.[xli]

In addition to whatever they are doing now, the employee ambassador's job description must include being a storyteller. This means they help employees develop a competency in telling your brand story and how that story is played out in their work lives.

By *personal stories,* we mean one or more stories that employees can tell with conviction from their personal work experience. The stories can relate to any experiences they have had that demonstrate how the organization is living its brand promise. Building this competency requires training, role playing, and a performance measurement that becomes part of year-end evaluations. It's a good idea to have a process to capture stories for later repurposing. By making the story personal, employees will speak with a level of conviction that will persuade others. Be careful when using employee stories in communication; they must be authentic and may not always represent the reality of company-wide service levels.

Here's a story told by a DHL Express employee on the company's intranet. In 2007, this employee participated in a company competition that asked employees to contribute stories about their personal commitment to customer-oriented behavior:

> On a Friday evening of the day before Mother's Day, 5 parcels with flowers came in late to our department after the delivery trucks had left. If I had left them there, they wouldn't have been delivered until Monday—too late for Mom and with 3-day-old wilted flowers as well! After I left work for the day, I delivered the 5 parcels using my own car. This prevented customer complaints. I paid for the 50 km worth of gas and wasn't paid for the time I spent.[xlii]

AAA Northern California, Nevada, and Utah believes that employee stories help make the connection between values-based behaviors and the resulting member experience. For them, stories create a vital connection with the customer at an emotional level. AAA features employee story posters within operations centers to demonstrate the employee/customer connection.

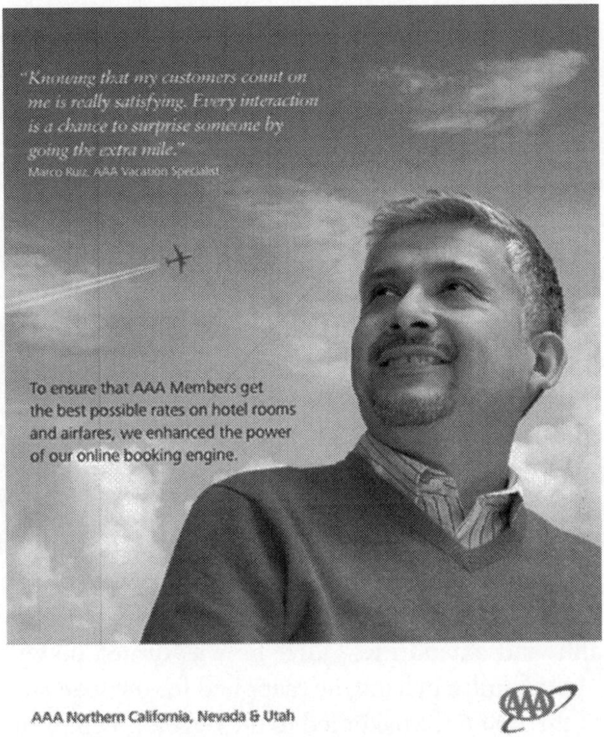

AAA Marketing Collateral. Used with permission from AAA Northern California, Nevada, and Utah.

Box 4—A Brand Community Checklist

Here are things that equip the employee ambassador to represent your brand in online communities:

- ✓ Employee Online Guidelines (including sections on legal, online etiquette, and brand tools)
- ✓ Cultural Norm Alignment to Empower Employees
- ✓ Brand Promise Workshop
- ✓ Understanding of Future Product Direction
- ✓ Storytelling Workshop
- ✓ Social Media Use Tutorial

Case Study: Using Employee Storytelling to Bring Your Brand to Life [Medtronic]

Minnesota-based Medtronic is an example of how one company has developed a culture around storytelling to accomplish its goals. Medtronic is a leader in medical technology, providing lifelong solutions for people with chronic disease. Founded in 1949, its 2006 revenue was 11.3 billion, and it has 36,000 employees. It was named in Fortune's annual list of "America's Most Admired Companies" for the 9th consecutive year and ranked number 1 in its industry sector in 2006.[xliii]

The concept for Medtronic started with its founder, Earl Bakken, seeing *Frankenstein* when he was 11 years old and being fascinated by the way electricity sparked life into the monster's inanimate body. Bakken, the inventor of the first wearable, battery-powered, transistorized cardiac pacemaker, sat down and wrote the company's brand promise, "To apply biomedical engineering to alleviate pain, restore health, and extend life," after he was turned down for a bank loan. With that promise in hand, he reapplied for the loan and got it. The invention of the first pacemaker led to the development of increasingly sophisticated electronic devices that are credited with savings millions of lives and improving countless others.

Medtronic's primary internal branding goal was to create a culture around storytelling so that employees understand the impact they have on the people they serve and can feel proud of the work they do because their values align with those of the company.[xliv]

Employees in medical technology manufacturing can feel far removed from the people who use their products. But stories make employees much more aware of the effect Medtronic's equipment has on real lives. Storytelling also reminds employees about the values of the company, reconfirming why they work there and giving them something tangible to believe in. Medtronic looks for every opportunity to communicate these things.

Additionally, Medtronic uses stories to reinforce its guiding principle of "Customers come first." Medtronic also uses both positive and negative stories to reinforce how employees can build its brand. For instance:

- A salesman drives miles at night to deliver equipment needed immediately to treat a patient.
- An engineer, excited about new technology, bores the doctor he's taken to dinner and loses a sale.
- The founder goes out of his way to listen and talk to patients who have benefitted from Medtronic's products and shares those stories within the company.

As a part of orientation, new employees hear the CEO explain the company's birth, evolution and mission, and resulting Medtronic breakthroughs. Their employee holiday party features patients telling their stories. Leadership sessions often feature stories. According to Medtronic's Paul Erdahl, "Stories spread the glue of the mission through the organization."[xlv]

Medtronic illustrates the point that it's not enough to just *have* a story. Medtronic has created an infrastructure for telling stories inside the organization that gives employees an opportunity to connect with the end results of their work: improving lives. They make sure leaders hear patient stories so they can continue to communicate the impact being made to the rest of the organization. Their promise is refreshed with every new story employees tell.

What are the results of the Medtronic storytelling culture? 87 percent of employees indicate that the Medtronic mission is consistent with their personal values; 92 percent believe the work they do supports the mission.

xxxii Clifford, "Video Prank at Domino's Taints Brand."

xxxiii Ibid.

xxxiv Ibid.

xxxv Susannah Fox, "Trust and Privacy Online: Why Americans Want to Rewrite the Rules," *Pew Internet and American Life Project*, August 20, 2000, http://www.pewinternet.org/Reports/2000/Trust-and-Privacy-Online/Summary/Findings.aspx

xxxvi "Annual Edelman Trust Barometer," http://edelmaneditions.com/wp-content/uploads/2010/12/edelman-trust-barometer-2006.pdf

xxxvii Chris Dellarocas, "Is the Lack of Web Link And Search Engine Accountability the Elephant in the Room of Online Reputation?," *Publius Project*, November 28, 2008, http://publius.cc/printpdf/lack_web_link_and_search_engine_accountability_elephant_room_online_reputat

xxxviii McCarthy, *Entertainment Habits Survey Results,* 7

xxxix "Southwest Cares," accessed October 2, 2009, http://www.southwest.com/about_swa/southwest_cares/our_people.html

xl "Southwest Airlines Safety Commitment," accessed October 1, 2009, http://www.southwest.com/about_swa/safety_commitment.pdf

xli Denning, *The Leader's Guide to Storytelling,* 20-21

xlii "DHL Company Story Contest," DHL, accessed from DHL corporate intranet.

xliii "Fortune Global Most Admired Companies 2006," *Fortune Magazine,* http://money.cnn.com/magazines/fortune/globalmostadmired/top50/

xliv "Mission and Culture," accessed October 2, 2009, http://www.medtronic.com/careers/mission-culture/index.htm

xlv Clark, *Around the Corporate Campfire*, 137

CHAPTER 6

Building Organizational Cultures That Build Competitive Advantage

In chapter 1, we talked about the four tests of clarity, authenticity, transparency, and accountability that determine whether you are doing effective internal branding. The driver of these traits is corporate culture. Culture provides the behavioral glue that causes employees to act in ways that build strong relationships.

In this chapter, we'll talk about the cultural behaviors that provide brands with competitive advantage. We'll also examine how to manage cultural norms and personality traits to take behavior well beyond scripted greetings and questions, job role definitions, and standards of dress. While some organizations focus on values rather than on cultural norms, we find that values still have to be translated into cultural norm behaviors, so it's important to take this additional step.

What Behaviors Should You Adopt?

Although every company is different, there are behaviors that are more aligned with particular industries than with others. We think of these as über behaviors, or defining behaviors for an organization or organization type. All investment bankers need to look professional and act credibly, because they are placing large amounts of clients' money at risk. In contrast, workers at a Disney park need to smile and like working with children, since theirs is a child's world, and families come from far away and at great expense to be there.

Here are a few über behaviors we've observed:

- "We're fun": Because of employee behavior at Homewood Resorts, customers come away with the feeling that Homewood Resort employees care a lot about you having a good time, whether it's bringing out more wine at happy hour or ferrying lodgers to different places in the neighborhood.
- "We're friendly": At Starbucks, employees make an effort to learn first names and engage customers who are waiting for service. Friendly conversations with customers can fill in for what otherwise might be a frustrating wait.
- "We care": This is the standout behavior at many health care providers, such as sleep disorder specialist REM Medical in Arizona. REM Medical is often a last resort for sleep-deprived patients who are at the end of their emotional ropes.
- "We go the extra mile": Clothier Nordstrom frequently demonstrates in action that it will do something unexpected for its customers, such as shopping the store based on a customer request and bringing clothes back to the customer.
- "We are efficient and no-nonsense": Swiss Railways exudes a serious, "Let's get the business done" approach. The infrastructure is not fancy; everything is aimed at getting each package delivered on time.

Über behaviors help these companies compete by differentiating their brands, and in many situations, the behavior is their competitive edge.

But you can't just decide to focus on behaviors that you don't demonstrate. First, you don't know if a given trait will be valued by your customers. Second, simply stating a behavior, as many organizations do in their missions, isn't enough. Shaping your culture to make you more competitive is a management process that focuses on employee and team skill-building.

Base Behaviors on the Facts

If you are starting with no cultural knowledge or if you only have a basic employee dress code and service guidelines, how can you build a more strategic culture? Start by fielding a questionnaire to the following groups: senior management, department heads, and employees who aren't managers but who demonstrate leadership skills. Ask each of these groups 6 questions:

1. "If a prospective employee asked you how to get ahead at the company, what would you say?" (cultural norms)
2. "What are the ways we do things around here? If someone makes an important decision, what do they say about the way the company operates to justify this behavior?" (cultural norms)
3. "What kinds of behaviors are rewarded here?" (cultural norms, personality)
4. "What is our business style if stated as personality traits?" (personality)
5. "What would customers or constituents say are the behaviors that make us important to them?" (cultural norms, personality, über behavior)
6. "What would customers say are the behaviors that harm our relationships with them? (cultural norms, personality, über behavior)

After finding out what staff members think, also field questions 4 through 6 to existing customers. Unless you are a very well-known brand, don't bother asking these questions of noncustomers; they won't know enough about you to answer intelligently. These answers will give you a very good idea of all current cultural behaviors and provide you with the building blocks for becoming more competitive.

Here is a sample set of cultural norms that you might discover from these questions:

- We'll drop everything and help each other when it serves a higher purpose.
- There are different rules for senior management.
- Learn from mistakes; don't point fingers.
- Everyone is valued and should be heard.
- No one gets fired for making the safe choice.
- Everyone needs to be heard before we can make a decision.

- Everyone is on a first-name basis.
- Many things are important, but we have to make 15 percent after-tax profits first and foremost.
- Clients can trust us to always come through.

What does this list tell you about this company's culture? Do any of these norms exist in your organization? Which would cause you to say "This isn't a place where I could work"? What might be an über behavior that this company could build from these norms?

The company described above could successfully create an über behavior of "We're here for you," but only if it understands and puts limits on the cultural norm of "Many things are important, but we have to make 15 percent after-tax profits" and eliminates the cultural norm of "There are different rules for senior management." If we uncovered this situation, we'd also recommend that it add a norm of "Meeting our customer needs is more important than short-term gains."

Imagine the difference between a company that is clear about its cultural norms and one that isn't. The company that doesn't manage its cultural norms is going to be faced with many unnecessary and demoralizing internal conflicts. It won't enjoy the competitive advantage of a distinguishing über behavior that allows it to thrive.

Refining Culture to Be More Effective

How can you change your culture once you understand where you want to go? As with any change, we recommend that you do your research homework so that you base the change on real data. Then, determine the optimal set of cultural norms for delivering your brand promise. What are the ones you use most often? What's missing?

Finally, recognize that defining change is only the first step to living your brand. You want a change management plan that engages employees and demonstrates what effective results look like. Depending on your organizational structure, this might include regular discussions at weekly departmental meetings. For others, it could mean an internal communications campaign and a series of all-hands meetings and workshops. We know that effective cultural changes happen when leaders are clear about direction and employees are given power and then rewarded for making it happen.

Change management requires planning and a long-term commitment to being successful. There are many good texts on the subject of change management. One we'd recommend is *Managing Transitions* by William Bridges.

Case Study: Making a City Extraordinary through Internal Branding [City of Olympia Public Works]

The City of Olympia is the capital of Washington State and a bustling college town on the Puget Sound in the northwest part of the United States. The city's 300–person Department of Public Works was realigned into 5 lines of business, each with separate responsibilities for delivering on the city's goals. While this reorganization streamlined areas of responsibility, it also shifted employees to new areas and accentuated cultural and work area differences. How could they create alignment within each line of business with the overall department goals and with the city's vision so that each employee could understand and live their part in delivering the larger promise? The answer was "Through the organization's brand tools, including its cultural norms, all aimed at increasing the department's effectiveness in meeting customers' needs."

The City of Olympia Public Works brand promise is "Supporting systems for an extraordinary Olympia through integrating sustainability into vital community services." Its values are innovation, respect, and effectiveness. The lines of business include those responsible for water, waste, transportation, administration, and technical services. Its commitments are examples of its values in action and establish cultural norms for the organization. These include listen, seek first to understand and then to be understood, welcome and reward feedback, celebrate both taking risks and success, and others pictured in the following cultural norms posters from City of Olympia Public Works.

Cultural norms poster used with permission from City of Olympia Public Works.

Each line of business first came up with a clear definition of its role in delivering City of Olympia Public Works' and the city's vision. For example, Waste ReSources' role is "To create opportunities to eliminate waste." Then, the organization rolled out the brand through internal branding activities, including training, communications, hiring, and measurement. All of the internal branding activities were designed to help employees learn to use the brand promise and cultural norms as a filter for decisions.

Training

The City of Olympia Public Works brand promise and cultural norms provide a common language for getting things done. For example, the city launched a new leadership development series—"Open Door Series: Unleash your inner extraordinary"—to train employees on how to use the brand as the connective tissue in everything they do. This year-long training, with 1-day sessions per month, helps leaders practice using their missions and roles to make decisions in support of the department's goals. It also helps them to identify and prioritize internal shifts in processes to better deliver on those goals.

Communications

To communicate and remind people of each line of business vision and mission, the City of Olympia Public Works department created custom posters for each group. The goal was to provoke conversations about the brand. Water Resources' strategic role is "Passionate caretakers of tomorrow's water" as illustrated in the *Water Resources* poster.

Water Resources poster used with permission from City of Olympia Public Works.

Other communications included toolkits to help supervisors talk about their promise tools in their staff meetings, web pages for employees, and a series of videos demonstrating each department's promise in action. Every quarterly staff roundtable meeting starts with a slide on the mission and strategic role with content within linked to each.

Employees were also taught to be storytellers who connect the dots between City of Olympia Public Works projects and what the community understands about the project. The city created a series of posters that connected workers and their stories with the rest of the workforce.

Image from City of Olympia Public Works Plan 2008.
Used with permission from City of Olympia Public Works.

City of Olympia Public Works also tells the story about how every employee's efforts impact the city as a whole. Whenever they get feedback from a citizen about something the organization has done, those stories are posted and celebrated so that every employee can see how living the brand makes a difference in people's lives.

Hiring

One way City of Olympia Public Works is measuring how well its cultural norms have impacted its effectiveness is in hiring. With more than 600 applicants for an external relations position, the hiring team asked questions that reflected the mission, vision, and values. The result was a hire that perfectly mirrored the organization. A recruitment video that talks about the mission is now available on the city's website. They even rewrote the rejection letter based on values and got calls from recipients that it was the best rejection letter they'd ever received. The language is now the city standard.

Measurement

In City of Olympia Public Works' strategic plan, Transportation links its metrics back to its promise of "Shaping the community through better transportation choices." In each case, the measurement is some metric that actually demonstrates the city department is living its promise. In 2008, the City of Olympia Public Works measured how it was putting sustainability into action by measuring:[xlvi]

- greenhouse gas emissions,
- sewer spill volumes,
- accident rates,
- whether federal drinking water quality standards were exceeded,
- water conservation rates,
- pavement condition,
- mobility improvements,
- waste produced and recycled rates,
- project estimates costs, and
- the stabilization of rates.

As a result of the clarification of the City of Olympia Public Works brand promise, employees have a better reason to get up and come to work every day: they understand their part in achieving an extraordinary City of Olympia. Now, employees can understand their part in living the promise. That makes it personal; employees now ask themselves,

"What I can do to live the mission?" The results are paying off with residents; the city saw more than a 50 percent increase in the distribution of water-saving kits the year after they began internal branding.

According to Bonnie Herrington, creative brand manager of City of Olympia Public Works, the key is to balance everyday actions with future goals: "Realize it is critical to develop 'promise' ambassadors at *all* levels of the organization. You must always be looking strategically toward the future yet remain grounded in the present."

The leadership team has the basis for cross-area collaboration and continues to work on reducing barriers to solutions that flow across lines of business, to solutions needed to address the most complex problems facing the city—involving long-term issues related to sustainable planning, transportation, and environmental impacts. Most importantly, each line of business has a strategic way to engage and impact customer behavior. The department also has a clearer voice with the city council and is able to demonstrate how the entire department, as well as each line of business, is delivering on the city's goals.

[xlvi] "Public Works Business Plan 2008," accessed October 2, 2009, http://olympiawa.gov/documents/PublicWorks/business_plan/2008_Business_Plan.pdf

SECTION II

Organizing Internal Branding

CHAPTER 7

Integrating Internal Branding into the Organization

Even if you do everything else right, internal branding won't bring the change you want if it is treated as a one-time program. Programs have an end point and must battle with other company needs for budget. For internal branding to be effective, it requires the organization to shift thinking about it as a task to embrace it as the normal course of business.

The roads to successful brand living are as unique as each organization's management style. Each road begins with the vision of the people involved. Brand managers have a lot of influence over what the brand becomes and whether it survives as a core aspect of the organization beyond their tenures.

Box 5—Attributes of Brand Management

Brand commitment and a strong business strategy focus are two important attributes of brand management. Here are some other brand management ideas from brand leaders:

"Find the balance between consistency, creativity, and innovation," –Bonnie Herrington, creative brand manager, City of Olympia Public Works[xlvii]

"Leadership must have a clear understanding of the brand focus and vision—if not, every other brand action will be for naught. Our CEO, Thomas Trompeter, always incorporates our guiding principle of 'We go the extra step,' into his newsletter message, which shows not only his understanding of that principle but acts as a constant, subtle reminder to staff." –Diana Olsen, marketing and community relations manager, HealthPoint[xlviii]

"Senior managers get tired of seeing the same brand messages every day. It's the job of your brand management team to keep them committed and excited about the brand and to fight against the tendency to drift." –Pam McCoy, director, marketing and brand strategy, Milliman Care Guidelines[xlix]

"The important things in brand management are shared goals, agreements, and implementation planning with various internal partners to create a consistent focus on standards and benefits." –Virginia Vovchuk, director of brand strategy and design, AAA Northern California, Nevada, and Utah[l]

"We focus on two parallel tracks—one is branding employee/customer touchpoints; the other is teaching every staff member to use our brand of "Am I being personal and accountable?" in each moment." –Lynn Ostrowski, director of brand and corporate relations, Health New England[li]

The first step in integrating your brand is to set up the right internal branding structure. You need:

- a sponsor,
- an owner,
- a cross-departmental team,
- a reporting cycle, and
- benchmarks.

Sponsors and Owners

A sponsor is a high-level executive on the senior management team. The sponsor's job is to provide authority for the project and actively sell it as a senior management responsibility to leaders and to everyone else. An owner is the person who is responsible for making sure the work gets done. While the owner will delegate much of the work, they are the-buck-stops-here individual and will be extensively involved in project planning and measurement. The owner is typically a midlevel manager in larger companies.

A best practice for successful internal branding is for the CEO to be its sponsor. The owner doesn't necessarily have to be a direct report of the CEO, but that helps.

The best owners demonstrate passion and commitment to building the brand. While the obvious choice is someone in human resources or marketing, the danger in that is creating the perception that internal branding is a human resources or marketing task rather than something that is required of all managers and employees. Internal branding, like strategic development, is an activity that requires an organization-wide commitment, which is difficult to achieve in our siloed working world.

The internal branding manager should preferably also own the external brand work, making them the global brand manager. Managing the organization as an integrated brand is essential to long-term success. If branding is the promise that you keep, employees are the ones who demonstrate the promise to your customers. At the same time, your communications need to reflect the compelling value of that promise.

Brand Managers and Brand Teams

The brand manager is responsible for seeing that the work gets done and that the CEO and other senior managers are kept informed and understand the importance of the work. In some organizations, this person is called the global brand manager because they have authority over all aspects of company and product branding. Having specific product brand managers without a global brand manager doesn't make sense; brands operated in this way won't work in coordination, tend not to build the corporate brand, and lack the continuity brought by a global manager. As mentioned previously, the best practice is to create a cross-departmental brand group that helps the global brand manager make decisions, heads task forces that create deliverables, and oversees communications.

Depending on the size of the organization, the brand manager position may not be full-time. When it isn't, there is an opportunity to rotate ownership every few years to keep the work fresh.

Actionable Benchmarks and Reporting

Benchmarks are essential, because when organizations don't embark on the branding journey with an eye to measuring and learning from progress, results are spotty. A strong, managed brand creates several benefits for the organization. These benefits, which include loyalty, a premium valuation, and willingness to recommend, are also the ones that you should use to measure how your internal branding is doing.

With employee research, we recommend measuring beliefs, motivations, and cultural norms. These are the levers that help employees create new on-brand actions. Often research is conducted for the purpose of measuring employee satisfaction, but employee satisfaction by itself doesn't provide actionable insight. Seek to measure how well employees have integrated brand tools into their work lives. "What do you do differently based on living the brand?" might be a question to ask. In addition, determine to what degree employees feel that the company is delivering on its brand promise so you can compare those answers to what customers perceive.

You can work with brand benchmarks in two dimensions. The first has to do with the value that a customer ties to a brand and the second is the performance of the brand based on what customers and other stakeholders value. Value tells you what should be true; performance tells you what is true.

Value

The highest form of value are associations—that which immediately comes to mind when seeing a brand name or logo. When I say DHL, what comes to mind? When I say FedEx, what comes to mind? When what comes to mind is a benefit, this is a value high-water mark because it is top-of-mind, and the customer doesn't need a prompt—other than the company name—to remember it.

The best way to determine what's truly valued is with open-ended questions. Open-ended questions let respondents put the way they think about your value in their own words. Giving employees or customers a list of answers to choose from ensures that you aren't going to find out what they really care about. If the associations employees make with your brand name are more than "The place where I work" but rather speak to the heart of what makes your brand different, then you have a very strong brand. When employees have such clarity, you will have a much easier time delivering a compelling, differentiated customer experience. Your ultimate goal is to have employees mention your brand tools as associations.

What does it mean when we don't see brand tools occurring as associations? There could be three explanations. The first is that employees don't know what the brand tools are. The second is that they haven't had enough communications that tie brand value to what they know about the company. The third is that they don't believe that the company lives its brand. It is vital to understand which of these is the case with your brand so that you can take the right corrective action.

Performance

In order to measure performance, you'll need to establish what customers value, what you do well, and what is ownable, and then turn that value into brand tools. Once that is done, you can then measure an employee's absolute belief about the importance of a particular value and then how well your organization performs on that value.

For instance, if the company has determined that its strategic role brand tool is "Finding families for children" (the strategic role for Holt International), it would ask employees, "On a scale of negative 5 to positive 5, how important is it that any company in our category focuses on finding families for children? Then it would ask, "On that same scale, how well does our company deliver on finding families for children?" The difference between the two averaged scores (absolute value minus performance) is the brand gap. A small gap (less than .5) or a positive gap is always better. When you have conducted this research with both employees and customers, you will have a good indication of whether you have an employee communications problem or your company really isn't living its brand in a certain area and needs to change what it is doing.

Brand Equity

While value and performance dimensions are ways to determine whether your employees are living your brand, there is a third set of measurements that you can use for a faster check when you don't have the time or budget to conduct in-depth research. The Brand Equity Score is a measurement system designed to provide a broad numeric measurement to see how well employees are living your brand. It includes questions regarding experience, opinion, role, direction, and service and product quality. Together, these questions can show you whether employees feel they have a strong relationship with the company and whether that aligns with your customers' reality. At Health New England (HNE), they include brand equity questions in every customer survey they conduct.[lii]

Another approach to internal branding benchmarking is the employee/supervisor survey. At Four Seasons, an extensive employee survey is used to evaluate a specific location's general manager. They ask employees to evaluate the general manager's adherence to the Golden Rule of treating others as you would have others treat you. Because the survey is used as an input to decisions about salary and promotion, it has teeth. Because it reveals the employees' perspectives of their environment, it drives adherence to the Golden Rule. Without the tie to the general manager's career development and compensation, the survey would lose its impact; without the tie to the core brand promise, the survey would lose its ability to improve the brand.

To say this another way, there are certain prerequisites for a healthy workforce in any industry. Employees must feel like they are treated fairly, like they are earning competitive wages; they must be engaged in their work and empowered. But focusing on these in the abstract without attaching them to the core brand value of what the organization uniquely delivers to customers misses an opportunity. Employees should be ambassadors for creating more of what makes your organization successful. A vanilla quality culture will not create long-term profitability; customers are ultimately the ones who make your brand great.

Southwest Airlines is a good example of how to use internal branding and external communications to create one, integrated experience. When Southwest Airlines launched its ad campaign "Southwest Is a Symbol of Freedom," it matched the promotion with an internal campaign, "At Southwest, Freedom Begins with Me." The internal campaign focused on 8 employee freedoms derived from working at Southwest Airlines. [liii] They included the freedom to pursue good health, to create financial security, to travel, to make a positive difference, to learn and grow, to create and innovate, to work hard and have fun, and to stay connected. [liv] The external ad campaign was very successful and continued with variants of "You Are Now Free to Move about the Country" externally and "You Are Now Free to Be More Productive" internally. With this realization of the connectedness of internal and external branding, it's a lot easier to figure out how employee branding can support the overall brand strategy.

Finally, you can also measure workforce statistics as a way of inferring your program's effectiveness. These include employee turnover, the ratio of acceptances to job offers, and the per employee labor costs versus peer averages.

Case Study: Forging a Worldwide Brand Experience [DHL]

In 1969, three Californians—Adrian Dalsey, Larry Hillbloom, and Robert Lynn—had an idea that resulted in the world's largest express and logistics service, DHL (created using the first initial of their surnames). The idea was to take shipping documents from San Francisco to Honolulu by plane. Customs procedures could start before the ships arrived, and waiting times in the harbor were significantly reduced. Shipping companies saved a fortune.

A new industry was born: international air express service, the fast delivery of documents and shipments by aircraft. This meant a radical change in the way global business was done. DHL was the first air express service in Eastern Europe and China and an early adopter in using technology to expedite package delivery. It went worldwide in the 1980s, and today the brand is one of the pillars of the Deutsche

Post, the world's leading postal and logistics services group with about 470,000 employees and generated revenue of more than 51 billion euros in 2010. DHL is the global umbrella brand for its global mail, express, freight, forwarding and supply chain solutions.

Anything that DHL does in terms of its internal branding is a big undertaking. For instance, in 2005, DHL introduced its new corporate uniform that had to be distributed to employees in more than 220 countries and territories worldwide. More than 1.4 million items of clothing were distributed.

Decisions Around Internal Branding

DHL uses its size to take advantage of its brand's visual identity. For DHL, this means people notice its 250 aircraft, 75,000 vehicles, and around 275,000 employees delivering on-brand performance.

DHL recognized that consistent visual branding is important but, that the employees are the actual power behind the brand.[lv] Between 2003 and 2005, DHL conducted more than 5,000 customer interviews and 200 face-to-face employee interviews worldwide to determine how they were seen, how they saw themselves and as input for how they wanted to be seen. This resulted in the first description of DHL's brand identity and promise, which was carefully aligned in 2009 and reinforced with the new group's business strategy called "Strategy 2015," which was presented by CEO Frank Appel in March 2009.

[lvi]

DHL's global service brand is based on a promise of performance. The brand rests on a set of brand attributes and benefits, condensed into three brand values: personal commitment, proactive solutions, and local strength worldwide. These are demonstrated as the personal commitment of the employees, the constant search for solutions that anticipate customer needs instead of merely reacting to problems, and the combination of in-depth knowledge of local markets with a worldwide network.

DHL has defined each brand value in actionable ways based on what they learned from their brand environment research.

- Personal Commitment: As individuals, we all care about our customers; we foster reliable relationships and take responsibility to make things easy for them.
- Proactive Solutions: DHL proactively offers high-quality solutions to address particular customer needs.
- Local Strength Worldwide: We provide a strong network with global coverage based on locally comprehensive services.[lvii]

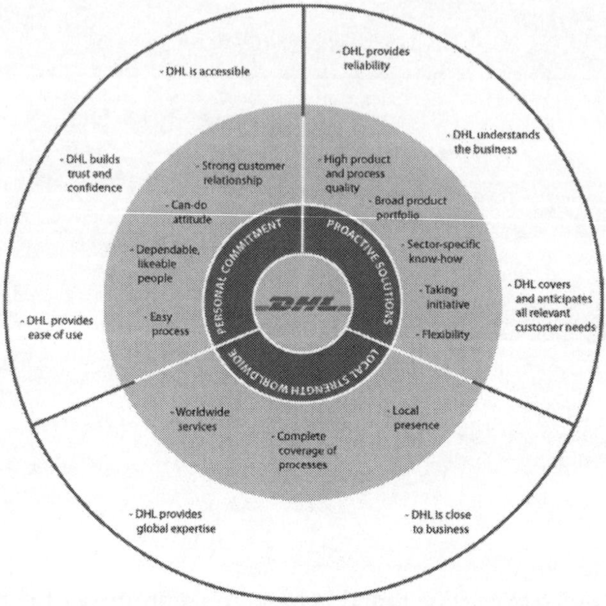

The DHL brand diagram as it was originally developed in 2006. Since then brand values, attributes and benefits have been progressively updated to reflect changes in the business strategy, logistics markets and customer expectations.

The core features translate into employees providing helpful services and determining customer needs beyond the mere basics. DHL likes to talk about this as "Service provided by a friend." This is supported by the central message of the DHL internal branding, which is that everyone counts ("We are the brand").

In order to create a consistent customer experience, DHL has precise guidelines for all staff. The *DHL Brand Book* is a brand sourcebook that defines its brand tools and attributes and how to bring them to life every day. For example, for the service attribute of reliability—more than 40 specific behaviors tie it to performance, generating customer experience consistency.

DHL explains its brand promise through its brand values while also explaining how these translate into a more competitive and compelling customer experience based on customer stories. For personal commitment, here's a story from a US customer: "He comes for the pickup, and I'm not ready; I'm nearly frantic. He says, 'No problem.

I can swing back,' or he'll help me finish packing it up. I'll never give that up."[lviii]

Beyond behaviors, continued visual uniformity is an essential element of brand building. Guidelines create global consistency around dress, packaging design, vehicles, documents and forms.

The company seeks to hire people who take initiative and are flexible. They then extensively train each employee so they know the best mode of delivery inside out, regardless of whether they are dealing with urgent express documents or the supply chains of a company that outsources its logistics. Special brand training sessions are customized to specific employee levels with 15 minute, 60 minute, and whole-day sessions.

Refining the Brand

Whether in corporate design, service quality, or advertising, when it comes to living the image of the brand, DHL leaves nothing to chance. As Christoph Baumgarten, former DHL corporate brand manager explained: "To mold the identity of a brand and its distinctive features is fruitless tinkering if the brand identity cannot be brought to life and turned into a positive customer experience. Brand building is the responsibility of our entire network."[lix]

On a country by country basis, DHL identifies those barriers that damage customer loyalty or brand appeal. As a second step, it identifies elements that turn occasional customers into regular customers. The result of this purchasing decision analysis is an understanding of factors that impact the brand experience. Favorable purchasing factors that also complement the brand are then introduced into staff performance targets.

As a result of the internal branding activities, since the 2006 DHL global brand campaigns have placed a strong focus on DHL people, portraying them as brand heroes dedicated to keeping the brand promise and making DHL customers more successful.

DHL 2009 "Brand Heroes" Campaign. DHL material based on DHL research, unpublished raw data.

A special internet website, the DHL Brand World (www.dhl-brandworld.com) was launched in 2009 as the central platform for internal and external brand communications. It is an essential part of the organization's integrated brand strategy. Acknowledging the importance of interactive digital media for the brand community, it provides information about the brand to internal and external audiences and serves to bring emotional resonance to the brand experience.

DHL believes that its continuous integrated branding efforts have resulted in its recognition as one of the top 100 global brands in the Millward Brown BrandZ 2009 ranking. Ranked 68th, with a brand value of 9.7 billion US dollars, it's ahead of many of its competitors.[lx]

---

xlvii Bonnie Herrington (creative brand manager, City of Olympia Public Works), in discussion with the authors, October 2009.

xlviii Diana Olsen (marketing and community relations manager, HealthPoint), in discussion with the authors, December 2009.

xlix Pam McCoy (director, marketing and brand strategy, Milliman Care Guidelines), in discussion with the authors, August 2009.

l Virginia Vovchuk (director of brand strategy and design, AAA Northern California, Nevada, and Utah), discussion with the authors, November 2009.

li Lynn Ostrowski (director of brand and corporate relations, Health New England), in discussion with the authors, October 2009.

lii Ibid.

liii Miles and Mangold, "Positioning Southwest Airlines through Employee Branding."

liv "Benefits," accessed October 2, 2009, http://www.southwest.com/html/about-southwest/careers/benefits.html

lv "Markenwelten—marken und ihre macher, Weltmarke DHL."

lvi Appel, "Group Strategy 2015."

lvii DHL, "DHL material based on DHL research," unpublished raw data.

lviii Ibid.

lix "Markenwelten—marken und ihre macher, Weltmarke DHL."

lx "BrandZ Ranking," accessed October 2, 2009, http://www.millwardbrown.com/Sites/mbOptimor/BrandZ/default.aspx

CHAPTER 8

Defining the CEO Role

Employees won't live the brand unless their leaders do. This is a central tenet of all internal branding. The CEO is at the center of any integrated brand. How CEOs define their role will impact everything from the brand promise to the consistency of the brand experience delivered. The CEO is in the best position to see how it all fits together and to give the brand its voice. That gives the CEO the ability to flag on-brand actions for others while discouraging actions that aren't on-brand. As more people use social media, the CEO will be called upon to be the online brand community leader. How a CEO responds to this challenge will have growing significance on a CEO's effectiveness.

Internal Branding as a Core CEO Function

According to a study by Catherine Good,[lxi] the impact of brand strategy on business management is increasing. She states, "Compared to the past, when brand management was restricted to an operative function, the CEOs, marketing, and communications managers now stress the strategic importance of brand management." This is further supported by the growth of the global brand manager position and brand teams that report directly to the CEO.

Good concludes that the assumption that the CEO must stand behind the brand is now a given and that CEO support is especially critical for service companies.[lxii] Such brand innovators as Apple take this a step further and tie the CEO's brand to major product introductions—such as when Steve Jobs introduced the iPhone.

The Implications of Shifting Brand Management from Tactical to Strategic

Good further points out that brand experts David A. Aaker and Erich Joachimsthaler track this shift in their book *Brand Leadership: The Next Level of the Brand Revolution*[lxiii] and note how the classic brand product management system is being gradually replaced by one that looks at branding from both internal and external points of view. The brand leadership model directly concerns the CEO, because it drives brand management actions to drive revenues as well as to build brand meaning. The Classical Brand Management Systems versus The Brand Leadership Model demonstrates the important differences between these models.

[lxiv]

	CLASSIC BRAND MANAGEMENT SYSTEM	BRAND LEADERSHIP MODEL
From Tactical to Strategic Management		
Perspective:	Tactical and reactionary	Strategic and visionary
Status of the brand manager:	Inexperienced and with a short time horizon	Higher in the org. and longer-term horizon
Conceptual model:	Brand image	Brand equity
Focus:	Short-term financial figures	Brand equity figures
From a Limited to a Broader Focus		
Product-market focus:	One product, one market	Multiple brands and markets
Brand structures:	Simple	Complex brand architectures
Number of brands:	Focus on individual brands	Focus on a category
Regional focus:	National	Global
Communications role of the brand manager:	Coordinator with limited options	Team leader with many communications options
Communications focus:	External	Internal and external
From Turnover to Brand Identity as the Strategy Driver		
Strategy driver:	Turnover and marketshare	Brand identity

The Classical Brand Management Systems versus The Brand Leadership Model.

Defining the CEO's Management Style

The other big success factor, in addition to embracing brand as strategy, is each CEO's management style. How CEOs live the brand is highly dependent on style. While there are several CEO style models out there, researchers Raymond Miles and Charles Snow describe four main roles for the CEO in their seminal book *Organizational Strategy, Structure, and Process.*[lxv] This model can give you a useful starting point for building the CEO brand approach. In Good's 2008 doctoral dissertation,[lxvi] she sets up the premise that the four roles outlined by Miles can have a significant impact on how employees perceive a company's brand.

According to Good, Miles and his research team defined four roles—*defender, analyst, prospector,* and *reactor*—that explain how CEOs "define their company's scope—how they configure the technology, structures, and processes required to implement their chosen strategy."[lxvii] We've found that these roles can be useful shorthand for helping you understand how to fit the puzzle pieces of CEO and internal branding together in organizations.

What are these CEO roles? Three of the four roles are points on a spectrum that ranges between flexibility and stability.

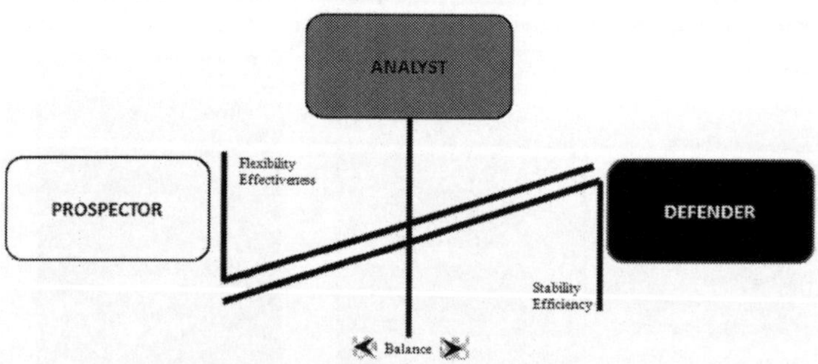

Three CEO Roles on a Spectrum

As the most flexible, prospectors leverage new product and market opportunities while valuing flexibility. They tend to make frequent product line changes and don't rely on a single product for success. Prospectors encourage more participative rather than command-and-control management models, pushing decisions lower in their organizations when possible. They invest in persons and groups that scan the company's market environment for potential opportunities. Their top management is dominated by marketing and R&D experts who are results-oriented. Prospectors' organizations can suffer from limited profitability and overcommitment of resources. Prospectors can quickly adapt to changes in competitive conditions; however, their organizations rarely achieve a similar level of efficiency to that of a defender.[lxviii]

As brand champions, prospectors are great at picking up and embracing the brand flag, but they have a difficult time sticking with it. You will hear these CEOs contest their own brand messages. They will also find new, exciting initiatives that pique their interest and command their attention. And integrated branding will be one in a long line of company initiatives. Managers and employees will feel like brand is the new initiative du jour.

We've discovered a couple of CEO strategies that are effective for keeping these leaders focused. The first is to tie your brand to a really big vision. A big vision, like doubling your customer base in 5 years, is something that will capture the prospector CEO's extra energy and need for challenge. By tying brand results and metrics to achieving this vision, you will meet this CEO's needs.

A second prospector strategy is to constantly reinvent your brand by making it the instrument for guiding change. This branding approach is becoming more necessary for all businesses as online relationships and global competition accelerate market change. An agile brand strategy can encompass everything from the way you deliver products to what media you use to create brand experiences. Apple has been very good at reinventing its brand experience with the iPod, iTunes, and the iPhone while staying true to its core brand of innovation for knowledge workers.

When working with prospectors, it's important to emphasize to the organization what doesn't change in your brand equation while keeping people excited about new directions.

On the other end of the spectrum, defenders focus on making what already exists better and more efficient. They can drive competitors out of the market through product excellence and through production, process, and delivery efficiencies. A good example of a defender was the Eastman Kodak Company (through various CEOs), which held a lock on film market share for many decades. Defenders are most effective in highly stable, unchanging markets and are vulnerable to major market shifts.[lxix]

Defenders often do a fantastic job of building a brand and are very willing and even anxious to ensure that employees get it right. With a defender CEO, you can build very strong internal alignment and a high level of brand tool use. Unfortunately, defenders can be too rigid in brand compliance and resistant to new ways to energize your brand. They tend to downplay innovations based on your strategic role and prefer to dwell on product features (e.g., with Kodak it was about film rather than about being in the image business; therefore, they didn't see image digitalization as a threat until the digital camera market was well past inception). Large companies with established products attract defenders and, if public, find their opinions reinforced by their board of directors.

Defenders don't need a lot of encouragement to model and champion the brand once it's established. What they do need is more encouragement to empower employees to meet customers' future needs. One brand strategy for a defender CEO is to help them see how encouraging new product discovery can create an even more defensible overall brand. One way to do this is to institute an annual "state of the organization" analysis and visioning session for senior leadership in which all ideas and concepts are welcome. This exercise can free a defender CEO and team from their constraints and cause them to question and rethink revenue streams that have grown organically rather than through conscious management. This exercise is most effective if the organization is very clear about its strategic role and uses it as a compass for guiding the visioning process.

Analyst CEOs lie between these two extremes. The analyst is a unique combination of prospector and defender. An experienced analyst attempts to combine the strengths of both, minimizing risk while maximizing profit-making chances. Analysts tend to be slower in making product changes than prospectors, but they are less committed to stability and efficiency than defenders are. Analysts seek balance. They take advantage of new product and market opportunities and, at the same time, care for the traditional core business. Marketing and technology types dominate top management and are closely followed by production managers. Since two structures are combined in the same organization, the main risks lie in inefficiency on the one hand and ineffectiveness on the other.[lxx]

The analyst is best adapted for the brand champion role. Their brand vulnerability is not building the brand at a deep level. One strategy for analyst CEOs is to ensure that the CEO gives the brand team a mandate to build out brand visioning and employee living-the-brand programs. By having permission to push both sides of the stability/flexibility equation, the brand team will meet this CEO's needs and develop effective internal branding.

While the defender, the prospector, and the analyst generate consistent action, the reactor CEO takes actions that result in inconsistent strategies and instability. Reactor organizations have confused business strategies, poorly adapted processes and infrastructure, and an inability to shift with market changes.[lxxi]

With reactors, it's best to stick to the basics, such as a consistent communications theme and basic, if generic, brand tools around service and reliability. Anything too strategic will get lost, and any claim that is too specific will be disproved by inconsistent management actions.

Aligning with the CEO's Personality

A CEO's personality also has an impact on your brand and influences a CEO's management style. What's the relationship between the CEO's personality and your brand? In start-up companies, the CEO's personality is usually the organization's brand personality. That's because the CEO has both a strategic and cultural role as the company head. While strategy determines business actions, CEO personality determines the tone and manner of communications, the types of people who will succeed in the organization, and initial cultural norms. If you understand this as the company is developing, you can compensate for CEO shortcomings by balancing their strong suits. For instance, if you have a high-energy, highly innovative, and intuitive CEO like Sir Richard Branson of Virgin, you might want to cultivate the additional personality trait *methodical* so the organization values the importance of legwork.

Forrester Research CEO George Colony enjoyed the challenge of predicting the future of information technology and brought tremendous enthusiasm to the task. "I went to a dinner party recently where we played a parlor game, and as part of it, everyone was asked to choose one word to describe him. I chose 'fun.' That might rub some people the wrong way, but I find that I've got to have fun at whatever I'm doing or my level of effectiveness goes down. I adore working. I'd pay to do what I do."[lxxii] His enthusiasm was contagious; more staff became part of his family-like network of insightful people working together to foretell the future. Colony has described his ideal job candidate as "the kid who lipped off in third grade."[lxxiii]

When a new CEO comes into an existing company, a best practice is to review and tweak the organization's brand personality and other brand tools based on the new CEO's approach. Managing this shift will ensure a smooth transition while enhancing the brand by adding the new CEO's distinctiveness. In a company with an integrated brand and a committed CEO, the CEO aligns their vision with that of the organization—they become one and the same. William D. Green, chairman and CEO of Accenture puts it this way:

> Accenture has been governed by its core values. They shape the culture and define the character of our company. They guide how we behave and make decisions. Through the years, these simple, yet powerful values have continually guided our decision making as well as our interactions with our clients and each other.[lxxiv]

Box 6—CEO Brand Mindset Necessities

The CEO must:

- see the focus set by the strategic role, guiding principle, and personality as an opportunity, not a limitation;
- be the chief brand ambassador—online and offline—of the organization;
- set an example by demonstrating on-brand behavior and understand the need to focus on distinctive behaviors that will be identified with the company;
- be on a mission to explain "the way we do things around here" to firmly establish cultural norms inside the company; and
- demand that brand actions be tied to business strategy and top- and bottom-line results.

The CEO's Role with Senior Management

The brand-savvy CEO understands that internal branding is most effective when all initiatives are flavored by the brand. This is particularly important in midsize and large companies, because senior leaders are in charge of company initiatives that extend throughout the organization. It is easy for competing initiatives to derail internal branding if the CEO doesn't help leaders understand how all work is informed by the brand promise. The best result of a successful brand-neutral initiative can only be that it improves the organization in a generic sense. If it doesn't focus on unique brand strengths in addition to generic quality improvement, it will fail to deliver a more compelling and distinctive customer experience.

For example, if a company embarks on a Lean program (originally Toyota's continuous improvement process) to improve its effectiveness and its competitor across the city does the same Lean work, quality will improve but differentiation won't. If you're the CEO, you need to have an understanding of how to insert brand strategy into all goal-setting and strategy-building conversations. This can be as simple as asking the question, "How does this initiative help us deliver more of our brand promise?"

Forrester Research CEO George Colony wants his speeches and presentation settings to be letter-perfect in keeping with his company's brand values. One executive relates that he accompanied Colony to a presentation on Kiawah Island, and no sooner had the small plane touched down then Colony went to the meeting room to check out the audio and video equipment himself. This was before dinner. He practiced his speech at that time and fixed a few accessories in the room. The flowers were in the sight line, and he had them moved. He made some adjustments to the audio. This attention to quality and detail is his way of reinforcing Forrester's brand promise of "Strong delivery of compelling material."

CEOs who believe in branding don't just leave the customer experience to third-party research. They frequently mystery shop their company's service centers or call their own call centers to see for themselves. Many CEOs who support internal branding also give pop quizzes to employees on the firm's brand promise and, like Colleen

Barrett (former president of Southwest Airlines), take the pulse of the employees through open-door policies and luncheons.

In summary, it's impossible to imagine a workforce that can live its brand without strong CEO brand commitment. You can help your CEO by understanding their leadership type and adjusting your brand emphasis accordingly. The most effective CEOs lead the work around the ongoing interpretation of your brand tools, including giving substance to your organization's cultural norms. CEOs who "get it" understand that flagging on-brand behavior is more than unnecessary minutia but rather part of helping people understand the big picture. This might look like Marvin Bower of McKinsey insisting that all consultants (they were all male in the early days) wear hats, or Forrester's George Colony's concerns about how a presentation room is set up and his insistence that analysts rehearse their presentations multiple times.

Case Study: The CEO Builds a Brand from the Ground Up [Nestlé Nespresso]

Nestlé Nespresso SA[lxxv] is a Swiss company and a wholly owned subsidiary of the Nestlé Corporation. It sells portioned coffee systems worldwide. At the time Gerhard Berssenbrügge took the reins in 2001, Nespresso had revenues of 2,000,000 Swiss francs. By 2006, revenues had increased to 1.16 billion Swiss francs, and their products were marketed in 38 countries.

[lxxvi]

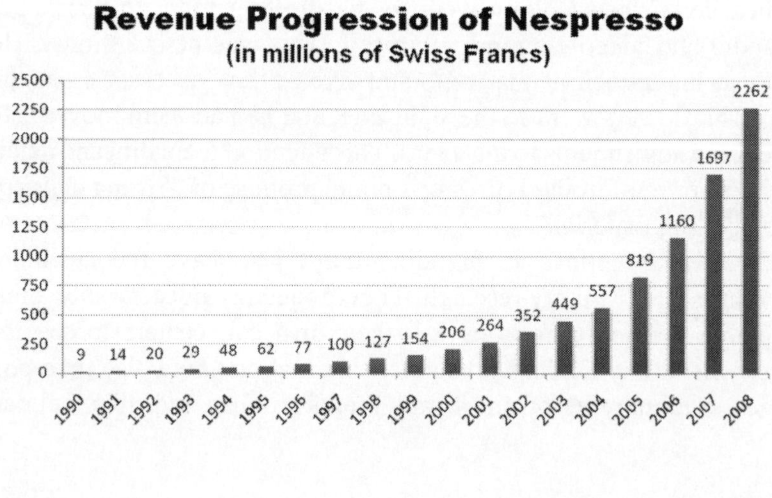

Shortly after taking up his position, Berssenbrügge mapped out his vision for the company, defining the Nespresso brand. We think that Berssenbrügge is a good example of an analyst CEO who could both initiate and build a sustainable brand. Since that time, the firm has consistently achieved profitable growth. By 2010, Nespresso aims to generate 2 billion Swiss francs in annual revenues. Within 3 to 5 years, Berssenbrügge intended that the company have a stronger global presence, a wider offering, and a better-known brand.

Berssenbrügge saw international and product range expansion as a necessity for becoming competitive. He also saw branding as paramount for Nespresso. "The development of the Nespresso brand is central," he stated in an interview in *Prange*.[lxxvii] His vision was to make Nespresso "preferred and respected as the leading quality coffee company for portioned coffee and become an icon for *perfect coffee* worldwide." As Olivier Quillet, their international marketing director, expressed it, "The reference, not the preference" of the portioned coffee market.[lxxviii] Similar to the Coca-Cola bottle, they designed the coffee capsule and the *N* to achieve the status of cult symbol and become the epitome of quality.

Nespresso's Distinctive Visual Identity.
Image used with permission from Nestlé Nespresso.

Berssenbrügge believed Nespresso was not a product but an experience. The Nespresso brand essence states, "The main purpose of Nespresso is to offer the consumer 'the ultimate coffee experience.'"[lxxix]

Nespresso demonstrated that it could and did deliver this through multiple, independent blind tests.[lxxx] Nespresso's goal is to never allow a situation in which others are making a better coffee than it is.[lxxxi] Nespresso is regarded as the number one coffee brand in Switzerland. As per the company's own research, the brand enjoys 40 percent unaided and 90 percent aided awareness among the Swiss. According to surveys by Brand Asset Valuator, brand awareness increased from 70 percent in 2000 to 96 percent in 2005.[lxxxii]

Berssenbrügge describes himself as the "godfather of the brand." In his blueprint, he ranks brand management as one of his top three goals—alongside focusing on employees and the brand promise.

Berssenbrügge doesn't see a need to pursue projects that don't contribute to the consumer experience of the ultimate cup of coffee, because Nespresso does not fall within that defined concept. Berssenbrügge lives the values of the Nespresso brand. As the chief brand ambassador, he exerts his personal influence on the brand's definition, its strategy, and its cultural norms, which he believes has contributed to its standout success.

[lxi] Good, "Führen durch Marken."

[lxii] Ibid.

[lxiii] Aaker and Joachimsthaler, *Brand Leadership,* 7-8

[lxiv] Good, "Führen durch Marken."

[lxv] Miles and Snow, *Organizational Strategy, Structure and Process*, 31-94

[lxvi] Good, "Führen durch Marken."

[lxvii] Ibid.

[lxviii] Ibid.

[lxix] Miles and Snow, *Organizational Strategy, Structure and Process,* 31-49

[lxx] Ibid.

[lxxi] Ibid.

[lxxii] Schwartz, "Life/Work: Issue 40."

[lxxiii] Poss, "Wisdom in the Forrester Style," 95.

[lxxiv] "Our Core Values," accessed January 5, 2010, http://www.accenture.com/us-en/company/overview/values/Pages/index.aspx

[lxxv] Good, "Führen durch Marken."

[lxxvi] "The Nestlé Creating Shared Value Report," last modified March 2008, http://www.nestle.com/Common/NestléDocuments/Documents/Library/Documents/Corporate_Social_Responsibility/Nestlé-CSV-Report-Mar2008-EN.pdf

[lxxvii] Good, "Führen durch Marken."

[lxxviii] Good, "Führen durch Marken."

[lxxix] "Our Commitment to Our Consumers," accessed October 3, 2006, 2009. http://www.nespresso.com/mediacenter/index.php?page=international-press-detail&id=17

[lxxx] Labhart, "Das Geheimnis des Schäumchens."

[lxxxi] Seidel, "Wenn Kunden Gern Teuer Trinken."

[lxxxii] Coppetti, "Young and Rubicam's Brand Asset Consulting," unpublished raw data.

CHAPTER 9

Using Brand Architecture to Focus Your Internal Branding

Chances are, if your company has more than one product line, you are confusing your customers. That's because product brands grow in organic ways that often don't fall into neat, understandable categories for customers. Therefore, the way companies organize their brands often bears little resemblance to what matters to customers. When a company's brand architecture is an exact duplicate of its organizational chart, it won't deliver a compelling brand experience.

Figuring out your brand architecture is worth the time and energy. Architecture is an internal branding essential, because it defines the relationship between brand value and how your company and products are named and organized. Clear brand architecture will bear fruit in better product decisions, employee clarity, customer clarity, and greater revenue generation.

What Is Brand Architecture?

Brand architecture shapes how customers perceive company value. It determines what you choose to give evocative or descriptive names, how many brands you offer, how you relate your brands to each other, and how you talk about the complementary value of your corporate and product brands. For instance, IBM focuses on its master brand (IBM) and gives its product brands a lesser role in its marketing. In IBM's case, this emphasis on the master brand makes it easier for staff to present a common face and value to the world, which fulfills its brand promise of "Global innovation."

For brand architecture to be effective, it must be structured from the customer's point of view rather than the company's. The best architecture is one that makes it simple and easy for customers to understand and purchase products. Brand architecture defines your organization in a rational, value-based, customer-facing structure that creates a clear product naming methodology.

Another purpose of the architecture is to guide future investment and strategy. Organizing your brands won't do any good if you then find yourself creating new brands for every product you develop or acquire. Brand architecture helps you ask and answer the questions, "Where do new products fit?" and "How will prospective offerings reinforce our master brand or sub-brand value propositions?"

It's also useful to focus employees on what's important about a given product and how that relates to the bigger, company-wide picture. You can define what's important in a brand value proposition that provides you with the key customer-based assets of the product brand, thereby helping you build new product value and keeping the product aligned with your corporate brand.

Brand Architecture Clarifies Product Delivery for Employees and Customers

Global logistics brand DHL likens itself to a physical version of the internet, providing customers with smart gateways to physically move goods around the world. It uses sub-branding to create clearly defined global market segments.

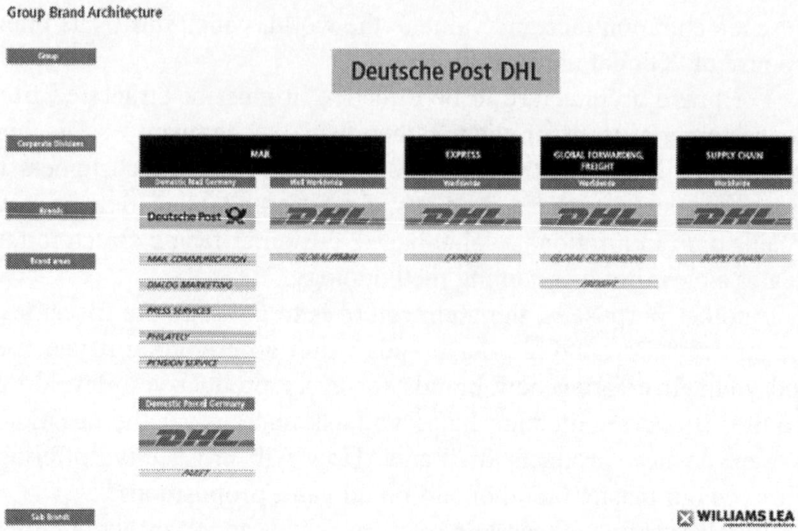

The names of its brand areas are descriptive and customer-facing; making what could be very complex simple:

- DHL Express offers international express services for parcels and covers more than 220 countries and territories.
- DHL Freight provides partial and full-load overland goods delivery throughout Europe.
- DHL Global Forwarding offers project logistics services in the air and ocean freight markets worldwide.
- DHL Supply Chain specializes in contract logistics services and customized supply chain solutions for a wide range of industries.
- DHL Global Mail provides mail and communication services with direct connections to more than 200 countries and domestic mail services in key markets.[lxxxiii]

Box 7—Brand Architecture Lexicon

Understanding the components of typical brand architecture will help you define your own. An emphasis on building a strong master brand is essential to most architectures:

- ✓ Master Brand: The primary named brand that holds a shared value across all products.
  Example: Honda is a brand that stands for reliability and excellent handling; this is true whether you buy a Civic or an Accord.
- ✓ Sub-Brand: A product brand, typically with an evocative name, that is always in relationship to a master brand.
  Example: Honda Civic. The Honda name tells you why to look at any of its branded products; the Civic is for people who want a smaller or lower-priced offering.
  Sub-brands are growth engines, offerings that are sold separately, in a competitive market with other named brands, and to be most effective, have profit and loss responsibilities.
- ✓ Descriptive Product/Service Name: Descriptive name that explains the basic value of the product/service without explanation.
  Example: Honda Civic sedan. The sedan is a four-door car.
- ✓ Ingredient Brand: Named brand that provides supporting value to other brands, often expressed as an icon.
  Example: Honda Civic sedan with XM Satellite radio. The ingredient is not the reason to buy the brand, but it is an added feature or benefit that enhances value.

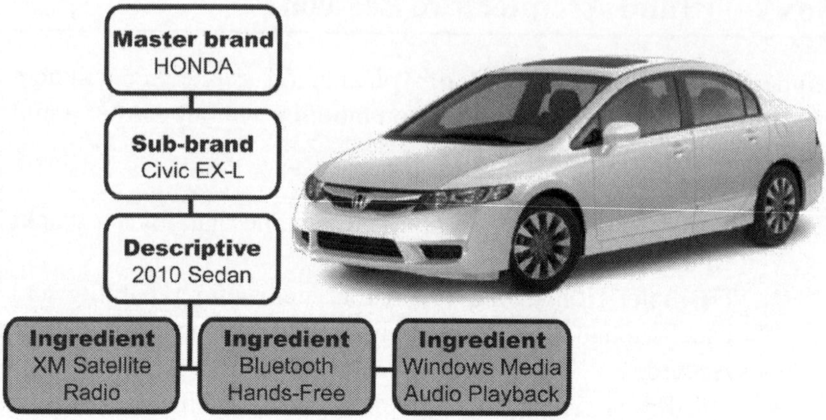

Brand Architecture Components (HONDA example).

Build Master Brand Value

Effective brand architecture typically has a master brand (usually the company name); sub-brands (product lines); and descriptive products, customer service, or program names (offerings within a product line).

While many companies use this system, they often overlook the step of understanding how each component of the architecture contributes to the customer brand experience. Everything we've said about defining your brand promise through brand tools should lead to customers associating clear value with your master and product brands. Master brand value clarity provides your employees and customers with preexisting value to support new sub-brand product introductions. They'll know that, if a product is a Zeiss, it is has unmatched image clarity; if it is a Bose, it has incredible acoustics.

Another aspect of effective architecture requires limiting evocative, nondescript names to two levels: the master brand and product sub-brands. People won't remember more than two levels of naming, be they employees or customers. Which products should be sub-brands? Sub-brands are those that contribute most to current and future revenues or have a strong, positive reputational impact on the master brand.

Nutritional supplements company, beveri™, uses a simple but effective architecture to keep its master brand and sub-brands on track. beveri's strategic role is "Making healthy choices easy" with products that are simple to use, of the highest quality, great tasting, and do what they say they're going to do. beveri uses a formula of parent brand, usage category, and descriptive product name for its brand architecture. This allows consumers to associate "easy" with all beveri products while immediately understanding how to use a product that they might not have seen before. The beveri golden flaxseed product packaging below illustrates this.

Product packaging used with permission from beveri.

Box 8—Examples of Strategic Roles

Company	Category	Strategic Role
Group Health	Health coverage and delivery	Innovation for better health
Bowker	Book discovery tools	Powers the ultimate book experience
Freestone Capital Management	Investment advisor	Investment boutique for alternative thinkers
beveri™	Nutritional supplements	Making healthy choices easy

University of Washington Foster School of Business	Undergraduate and graduate business school	Fostering leaders who think differently and make a difference
Renomics	Develops smart, connected, sustainable infrastructures for cities and developments	Delivering re-sourcing communities
Plexipixel	Interactive design	Creators of sticky brand play
Optimum Energy	Energy conservation that leads buildings to their best futures	Strategic HVAC applications

Brands can also be used to introduce new ideas that enhance the master brand's reputation. Ingredient brands emphasize aspects of a brand's value or a new trend that may not be well understood but may be important for the future of a market. A company that uses brand in this way is considered to be a thought leader, which deepens its reputation as an industry expert. A General Electric (GE) ingredient brand, ecomagination, speaks to GE's work in creating more sustainable products. According to a GE news release, "Introduced in May 2005, ecomagination is GE's commitment to conceive and construct pioneering technologies that help customers address their environmental and financial needs and help GE grow."[lxxxiv] Since then, GE has expanded the meaning of this ingredient brand to include investing in cleaner technologies to reducing greenhouse gases and improving water use.

Ecomagination is a great example of how a very complex and hard-to-define concept (sustainability) can be attached to an evocative symbol that acts as shorthand for many supporting ideas. This symbol then becomes something customers use to make product choices. Which would you rather choose, a sustainable product that you have good feelings about (strongly reinforced by ecomagination) or a product that doesn't have this pedigree? To support this cognitive and emotional response to ecomagination, GE has created a website[lxxxv] and an annual ecomagination report and is encouraging social networking discussions about sustainability. The social networking efforts include Facebook groups about ecomagination and an annual ecomagination challenge cosponsored by GE and mtvU that encourages college students to find innovative approaches to making their campuses greener with the winning team receiving a $25,000 grant. More than 100 teams took part in the first year of the challenge.[lxxxvi]

Case Study: Using a Master Brand to Do the Heavy Lifting [Group Health]

Award-winning, not-for-profit health care provider Group Health uses its brand architecture to define how to focus its business and marketing strategy around its promise of "Innovation for better health." Group Health is a Washington state–based cooperative medical system with more than 8,500 employees. It is a little unusual, because it offers both health insurance and health care, allowing it to act in a more comprehensive and coordinated fashion to help patients achieve better health.

Among the issues it wanted to solve with brand architecture was supporting a workforce that felt its work wasn't as valued by the public as it should be, even though the level of care Group Health provides is better than state and national peers by most measurements. While the United States was still having discussions about a future in which each person had an electronic health record, Group Health members had already had this in place for many years. This allowed their doctors to coordinate an individual's care and allowed patients to use their records to manage their health. Viewing current prescriptions and ordering refills, making appointments online, and even consulting with their physicians via e-mail are all parts of everyday health care for Group Health patients.

Because innovation is part of its brand DNA, Group Health continues to push new models for helping members achieve better health. It is leading an effort to use patient engagement to encourage behavior change and healthier living. As part of this, Group Health uses a medical home model, developed by its research arm, Group Health Research Institute. This advanced care model puts the patient at the center of a medical team and results in more patient/physician interaction.

While the integration of Group Health's health plans and health care is an asset for providing better healthcare, it was also part of their public perception challenge. Staff has had a difficult time describing Group Health's offering in a focused way, and prospective members have also had a difficult time comparing Group Health to other providers.

Simplified brand architecture contributed to message and organizational focus. Brand architecture is the design and use of brand names and entities to enhance ease of doing business, employee and customer clarity, and brand value. Group Health needed an architecture that focused its master brand (the primary holder of value, usually the company name) on better health and innovation, while the sub-brands (essential business components or areas of value) enhanced this value and added other qualities to it.

As part of this process, Group Health:

- aligned brand architecture with its brand promise of "Innovation for better health";
- placed the master brand name (Group Health) in front of all sub-brands to ensure that employees and customers understood everything it offered;
- simplified sub-brand names when possible so the master brand would carry more of the meaning;
- eliminated sub-brands that weren't either areas of growth or key aspects of better health care;
- eliminated most internally focused names (they had been using several for their medical practice that had no meaning to members or employers, for instance); and
- placed an emphasis on physicians, research, and community involvement, which senior leaders believed to be important for better health and health care (Group Health has an impressive record in groundbreaking research and helping uninsured children receive care).

While this is still a work in progress, the effect of focusing its master brand on health care and innovation is helping Group Health accrue awareness and value.

Box 9—Group Health Brand Architecture

GroupHealth

Group health's brand promise is *innovating for better health.*

Brand type	Name	Strategic function
Master brand	Group Health	Helps members live healthier lives through innovation and collaboration
Sub-brand	Group Health Physicians	Emphasizes physician quality and importance
Sub-brand	Group Health Medical Centers	Concretely defines places where health care is delivered
Sub-brand	Group Health Research Institute	Demonstrates innovation for better health
Sub-brand	Group Health Foundation	Demonstrates innovative community support for better health

Used with permission from Group Health Cooperative.

Group Health has been repeatedly cited in US media as a model for how to make health care more effective. It is also receiving greater recognition for its quality: it was cited as one of America's best health insurance plans for the third year in a row by *US News & World Report* and the National Committee for Quality Assurance; it is the highest ranked plan for both "health plan quality" and "prescription drug plan quality," earning 4 out of 5 stars and 4.5 out of 5 respectively for its Medicare plans; and it is the 2008 J.D. Power winner of "Highest Member Satisfaction Among Commercial Health Plans in the Northwest Region." Finally, its medical centers have been rated in the top category in 11 out of 15 measures; more than any of the other 45 Puget Sound medical groups that were rated on all 15 measures in a July 2009 report.[lxxxvii]

"We believe that our simplified brand architecture is making it easier for our staff to tell a compelling story," explained Jay Gusick, executive director, brand, communications, and public relations.

"Our consistent focus on the Group Health brand and equating the brand with excellent health care gives both staff and members an easier way to understand the value Group Health brings to the community."[lxxxviii]

---

lxxxiii "DHL Divisions," accessed January 31, 2010, http://dhl-sy.com/old/dhldivision.htm

lxxxiv "GE's 2008 Ecomagination Revenues to Rise 21%, Cross $17 Billion," General Electric press release, October 21, 2008, http://www.gereports.com/wp-content/uploads/2008/10/ecomagination_2008-revenues-forecast-october-21-_2_.pdf

lxxxv "Ecomagination," accessed October 3, 2009, http://www.ecomagination.com/

lxxxvi "About the Challenge," accessed October 5, 2009, http://ecocollegechallenge.com/aboutTheChallenge.html

lxxxvii "Group Health Medical Centers Rated in 2009 'Community Checkup,'" accessed January 6, 2010, http://www.ghc.org/about_gh/Quality/PSHA2009.jhtml

lxxxviii Jay Gusick (executive director, brand, communications, and public relations, Group Health), in discussion with the authors, January 2010.

CHAPTER 10

Creating Understandable and Compelling Brand Strategies

Operationalizing brand into company systems is one of several prerequisites to living your brand. The others include defining your brand tools, getting the CEO on board, integrating brand criteria in employee performance evaluations, and incorporating brand into the strategic and physical infrastructure of the company. Whether you are a for-profit, a not-for-profit, an NGO, or a government entity, you provide unique value that can be built from year to year.

Operationalizing happens by defining internal branding actions as strategies. Strategies make your brand promise real to employees and customers. They elevate your brand from being a marketing tool to being the basis for business planning.

The Importance of the Strategic Role

The organizational view of internal branding image titled *An Organizational View of Internal Branding* (chapter 4) illustrates how brand strategy drives business strategy and vice versa. In fact, your core brand strategy (your strategic role) is the one strategy that shouldn't change over the life of your brand. It is the über strategy to complement your über behavior.

The strategic role supplies the answer to why prospective customers must consider you. It defines the organization from a customer point of view, specifically speaking to the need the organization fills in the customer's professional or personal life. Operationally, strategic roles are used to set parameters for everything the organization does, including new and existing product development, customer service, R&D, marketing, sales, and communications. Without a strategic role, your brand effectiveness will lack a coordinated, distinct, big picture, customer-oriented business approach. In turn, employees will be most aligned to support the brand only when they clearly understand how brand makes your business strategy more successful. Finally, the strategic role sets boundaries for new directions. It will help you accurately determine what is on-brand or off-brand while keeping company management out of the minutia.

To understand how a strategic role works, it's helpful to see examples (see Box 8), since a strategic role is not a message. It may or may not be used in external communications; its primary use is to serve as a compass, setting the parameters for everything the organization does, including new and existing product development, customer service, R&D, marketing, and sales.

From Strategic Role to Brand Strategies

Senior management uses its strategic role in strategic planning and business plan creation.

We recommend that you convene special visioning sessions with senior management for an annual review of how you are currently demonstrating your strategic role and how you wish to use it in the future. Depending on your process, you may also want to involve middle managers and line employees to solicit more ideas for strategic role demonstration.

One practice that works well is to ask the following questions:

- What do we need to change to improve strategic role delivery?
- What do we wish to add to improve strategic role delivery?
- What do we need to eliminate to improve strategic role delivery?

Brand strategies are the action plans you develop to strengthen your brand based on your strategic role. When you start internal branding, there will be some strategies that you'll always want to consider. One of the most important is ensuring that employees understand how to use your brand tools to deliver your promise. No matter what job an employee has, *taking action* means using the guiding principle in their job every day to deliver your strategic role, demonstrate your personality and tell your story. Another foundational strategy is integrating the brand promise into employee hiring, orientation, and job performance.

Here's a partial list of strategic initiatives for Salal Credit Union. Its strategic role is "Your money management made easy." Salal also uses its guiding principle of connecting as a brand strategy driver.

1. "Create an updated and searchable knowledgebase housing all policies, processes, and procedures for employee use."
   Rationale: For current and future employees to consistently deliver our brand promise, it's critical that they have access to the information they need to make money management easy for members. This will reduce overhead by reducing training needs, mistakes, and employee turnover as well as contribute to increased member satisfaction by having questions answered correctly the first time.
2. "Improve overall technology to make member access and interactions easy."
   Rationale: Improving current banking technology makes banking with the credit union easier for members. Deliver on the brand principle of connecting by giving members more ways to connect with us and manage their money. Improved technology makes our core system easier to use for employees and members.
3. "Assess current products and develop plan for new products and relationship benefits that make money management easy and connect members to us, each other, and the community."
   Rationale: We need to make sure all products are making money management easy for members and connecting them to the products, people and resources they need. This will reduce expenses and increase fee incomes.

After you've created your first set of brand strategies, the next step is to prioritize based on urgency and budget. Once you've prioritized, you can then build out the work plan for each strategy to include milestones, benchmarks, project lead, and timeline.

The City of Olympia Public Works has closely tied its strategic plan to its brand promise. Its brand promise is "Supporting systems for an extraordinary Olympia through integrating sustainability into vital community services." The city's brand plan booklet puts the brand in the context of what needs to be done by tying it to specific strategies and benchmarks:

Chapter 1	Defining Our Promise
Chapter 2	Using Our Promise as a Filter
Chapter 3	Adapting to Change
Chapter 4	Honoring Our Commitments
Chapter 5	Making Balanced Decisions
Chapter 6	Living Our Promise
Chapter 7	Delivering on Our Promise

In the chapter "Delivering on Our Promise," the plan makes use of easy-to-understand visuals and tools to help employees act on its strategies.

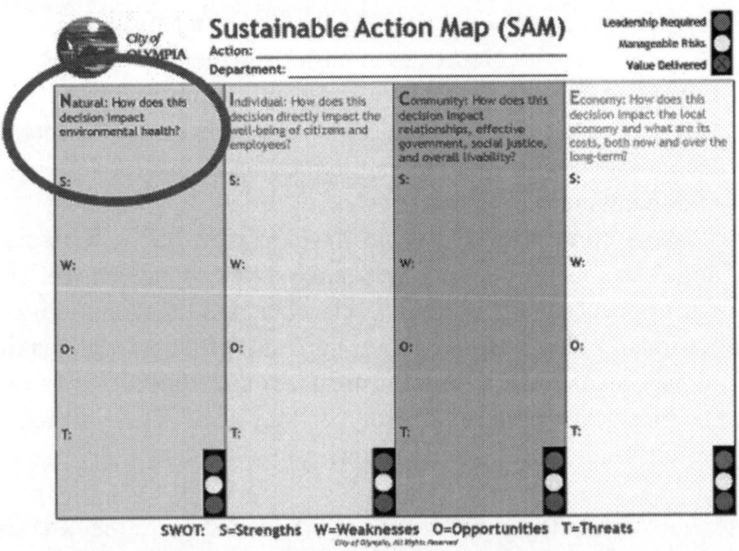

Simple and effective visuals from City of Olympia Public Works.[lxxxix]

Case Study: Staying True to Your Brand Strategy [Mayo Clinic]

Mayo Clinic stands out as having a brand promise that was easily understood by staff and demonstrated to patients from its inception. Its über strategy can be stated as "Collaboration among physicians to get to the right answer" and to always keep the staff acting on a guiding principle of "The patient comes first." Doing what was in the interest of the patients resulted in every employee asking themselves the question, "Is this best for the patient?" as they went about their daily work.

Mayo Clinic has grown to become the world's first and largest integrated, not-for-profit group medical practice. Its three-shield logo underpins its reputation as a pioneer and innovator in medicine/patient care, medical research, and academic education.

Strategic Role Established by First Leaders

The Mayo Clinic strategy was described in a 1910 address by William Mayo, who said:

> As we grow in learning, we more justly appreciate our dependence upon each other. The sum total of medical knowledge is now so great and wide-spreading that it would be futile for one man to attempt to acquire, or for any one man to assume that he has, even a good working knowledge of any large part of the whole. The very necessities of the case are driving practitioners into cooperation. The best interest of the patient is the only interest to be considered, and in order that the sick may have the benefit of advancing knowledge, union of forces is necessary.[xc]

Early demonstrations of collaborating to find answers included inventing a patient record system that assigned each patient a number that was always associated with their medical history and establishing a medical library to help physicians and others more easily get answers.[xci] One early demonstration of "The patient comes first" was the story of one Mayo Clinic brother mortgaging his house to buy a microscope.

As a result of its brand promise, Mayo Clinic produced many brand-based innovations in health care, including the tumor grading scale (1920), the identification of cortisone to treat rheumatoid arthritis (1950), and the first open-heart bypass machine (1955).[xcii] Mayo Clinic demonstrates its brand online with its web-based Care Pages service. Care Pages are free, personal and private web pages that easily allow Mayo Clinic patients and their loved ones to post messages, pictures, and updates as a means to keep in touch during a patient stay.

Mayo Clinic's strategy for communicating brand value relies heavily on the power of positive staff and patient word-of-mouth. The Mayo Clinic's brand management team believes this is the most powerful influence on patient preference, even ahead of doctors' recommendations and media coverage. In a study of post visit patient reviews, 95 percent of patients said good things about the Mayo Clinic to an average of 46 peers. With an average of 500,000 patients per year, word-of-mouth recommendations can deliver a reach of ten to 20 million consumers. Better still, when 20 people were advised by a patient to come to Mayo Clinic, an average of 7 would actually make the visit—a usage rate of nearly 30 percent.[xciii]

Integrated Internal Branding

Mayo Clinic's approach to internal branding echoes its approach to patient care in its dedication to consistency and integration. An outside consultant observed that the Mayo Clinic brand "is created every day by every employee in every interaction with every patient," though within the organization the word *brand* isn't used. The success of the word-of-mouth branding approach absolutely depends on the near perfection of care delivery; employees are the primary brand demonstration and communications channel. [xciv]

One of Mayo Clinic's brand strategies is to find people who are motivated by teamwork in the service of patients. It won't be a good place to work for a clinician who prefers working independently.[xcv] Once a clinician is on board, Mayo Clinic reinforces the team approach and the importance of delivering quality care through its compensation structure. Almost all employees are on salary, so there is no incentive to rush patient care or to be territorial about case management. According to one surgeon, "by not having our economics tied to our cases, we are free to do what comes naturally, and that is to help one another out . . . [and] to make all clinical decisions on the basis of what is best for the patient."[xcvi]

A strategy for getting staff to live the brand is its visual integration into daily life. The facilities are full of quotations from the Mayo brothers, most pertaining to the primacy of patient care.[xcvii] In one building at the Rochester campus, the lower floor walls are devoted to a photo history of the brothers and the early Mayo Clinic.[xcviii] The message even pervades speeches and daily meetings; one staff member claims that they couldn't "recall a speech or meeting . . . where the core values of the institution were not mentioned."[xcix]

Even senior leadership is designed to keep people connected to putting the patient first. For example, each of Mayo's three core areas—clinical practice, education, and research—has a physician leader. But this position is not a permanent or a full-time assignment; the leader continues to practice medicine and remains in the post for around 8 to 10 years, after which they return to full-time clinical practice, teaching, or research. This enables physicians to maintain strong connections to patients.

Measures of Success

The Mayo Clinic is not driven by making money. However, success at living its brand promise has led to financial success and significant growth opportunities; this in turn has allowed Mayo Clinic to better fulfill its mission. In 2007, Mayo Clinic had a staff of nearly 55,000 overseeing 520,000 thousand patients for total gross revenues of $5.6 billion.[c]

Another important measure of success for Mayo Clinic is its ability to keep the right people. Because so much of its external success depends on the quality of its internal branding efforts, hiring, training, and retaining those who can deliver on that brand promise are keys to success. Benchmarking Mayo Clinic against industry peers reflects its success; whereas the nurse turnover rate industry-wide is 20 percent, for Mayo Clinic in 2003, it was 3 percent at Rochester and 7 percent at Scottsdale.[ci] Physician turnover at Mayo Clinic in 2008 was lower than 6.9 percent, less than half the national average.[cii]

Brand strategy applied over time is a powerful lever for building a strong, compelling, and successful brand, but it takes discipline and a willingness to stay the course. Leaders must use it to develop products and processes while employees must live it. When this happens, you can turn a clinic situated in rural Minnesota into the most prestigious and well-known health care brand on earth.

---

lxxxix "Public Works Business Plan 2008," accessed October 2, 2009, http://olympiawa.gov/documents/PublicWorks/business_plan/2008_Business_Plan.pdf

xc William J. Mayo, "Mayo Clinic," accessed October 7, 2009, http://www.mayoclinic.org/needs-of-patient/mayo-quote.html

xci Berry, "The Collaborative Organization."

xcii Mayo Clinic home page, accessed October 7, 2009, http://www.mayoclinic.com

xciii Davis, *Bringing The Brand To Life,* Presentation at the American Advanced Learning Institute, Washington, D.C., April 26-28, 2006

xciv Ibid.

xcv Berry, "The Collaborative Organization."

xcvi Ibid.

xcvii Ibid.

xcviii Ibid.

xcix Ibid.

c "Our Shared Commitment," accessed October 7, 2009, http://www.mayoclinic.org/mcitems/mc0700-mc0799/mc0710-2007.pdf

ci Berry, "The Collaborative Organization."

cii "Mayo Clinic Connection," accessed October 7, 2009, http://www.mayoclinic.org/connection/

CHAPTER 11

Creating an Employee Culture That Builds Your Brand Community

In chapter 5, we talked about how employees are brand ambassadors and critical members in shaping your online brand. In this chapter, we'll take that one more step and talk about how to add social branding to your internal branding efforts, creating a culture that builds a shared brand community.

With the advent of social media, companies now must ponder how online social interactions impact brand perceptions. The online experience you provide on your website and that occurs in other social media allows customers to experience and impact your brand when, where, and how they want to.

The Shared Brand Community

Online brand communities represent something new in the brand world. While brand experiences were transactional (e.g., customer service interactions) in the past, social media has resulted in the development of meaningful virtual communities. Unlike digital transactions, social media allows individuals to have a continuous web presence with much the same experience they would have if they were walking through a village.

Your profile page on Facebook, for instance, allows you to interact with others in ways that grow friendships, foster personal expression, and even get work done. Your "friends" are other people in your virtual neighborhood, and together you are a community. Further, there is much less separation between your professional and personal self in this world. People are rapidly moving beyond the narcissistic look-at-me social media stage and finding online sharing to be supportive, educational, and self-esteem enhancing.

Online communities require shifting how you think about branding from exclusively company-based to a shared process. Becoming a social brand is all about opening up your internal culture to engage your customers in online communities that encourage sharing personal information, insights, and beliefs. Online brand communities take your brand outside the four walls of the company and allow it to be shaped by employees, customers, and other community members. New brand value, in the form of online experiences, then comes back to influence your company, products, and messaging. It's a mutually beneficial relationship that can occur in many places, including your website, any number of social media sites, and one-on-one forums.

What Is a Social Brand?

A social brand can be defined as all employee, customer, and influencer interactions that build brand value. It demands a different level of thinking that embraces listening, participation, and engagement. It's most powerful when based on a culture that is open, has clearly defined guidelines for employee engagement, and encourages employees to act as cultural ambassadors. It occurs in online brand communities—company-sponsored websites and social media—and as part of thousands of other communities, networks, and face-to-face experiences in which employees, customers, and other interested parties talk about you. For instance, I can take part in the Apple community directly on the Apple-sponsored Facebook site, or I can indulge my need for behind-the-scenes Apple news on the independent webzine *Apple Matters*.

From Telling to Talking

If traditional branding pushes opinions and information to customers, social branding, in contrast, is about encouraging information to flow between every combination—employees and customers, customers and customers, employees and employees, influencers and everyone. Social branding goes well beyond receiving information to engagement, networking, and community building.

By changing branding from a one-way experience to a series of conversations, social branding turns the company—collectively and its individual members—into participants finding ways to fuel meaningful conversations. While your company will experience this as losing some control over the brand, the upside is a much more powerful and meaningful brand experience. A strong social brand builds preference through peer endorsements, positive product, and company experiences. By having a lot of fans, you will also be building a defense and extended support team in times of crisis.

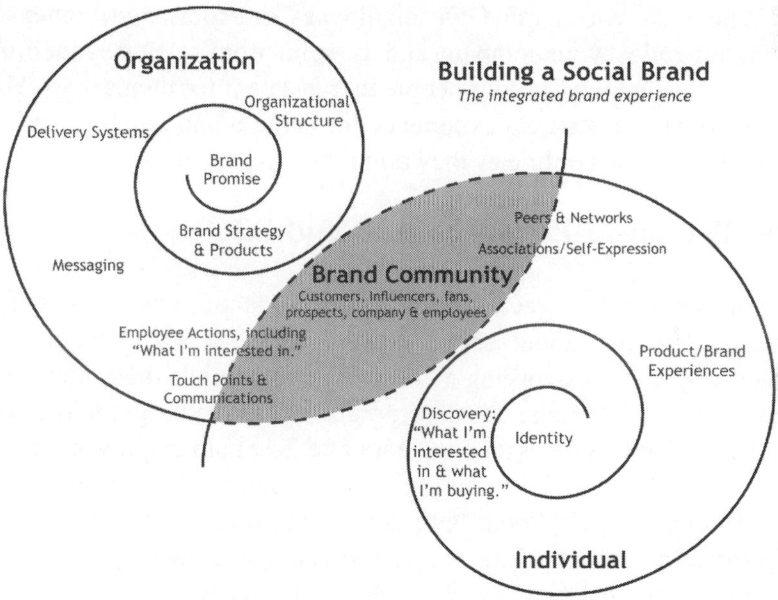

Brand Relationship Model. Brand communities make the employee's role in brand building even more essential.

Trust Your Employees: Make Guidelines Rather Than Rules

While corporate lawyers all over the world lie sleepless trying to rein in employee online expression, that genie is out of the bottle. You can't control everything employees do on the web. Brand communities are not a push marketing function, so even if you could rein employees in, you wouldn't want to. The best communities are those in which employees are so much a part of the brand that they naturally express it when they are online.

This means that customers and other online followers will have a voice in building your brand. Therefore, you'll want to encourage community members to learn as much as possible about your organization. This will result in more online recommendations for your products.

Where do you start? Give employees the tools and context to accurately reflect your company and its brand promise. State your brand in a way that empowers your people to translate it for themselves. Your goal is to have customers experience the same brand qualities and the same relationships online as they do in the physical world.

Add Person-to-Person to B2B and B2C

Person-to-person interactions are at the core of what people find valuable and fun about social networking. Can organizations use person-to-person networking in a way that both builds their brands and is still authentic? While most corporate social media guidelines pay close attention to legal issues and etiquette, few help employees tell the brand story. Your social branding needs to balance giving employees tools to express your brand with not forcing them to play the role of shill for your company. This was reinforced by Comodo's CEO, Melih Abdulhayoglu, in a *Practical Ecommerce* interview:

> It's great that you have a pretty website, but do I know who you are? I want to get to know you. Show me who you really are so that I will then talk about you. You don't have to employ a social media officer. You can get opinion leaders. You can get people to talk about you. The only way you can do that is by making sure that you give them visibility about who you are.[ciii]

IBM has been a pioneer in helping employees express themselves online. Early on, it had a chief blogger position and a blog policy that gave employees plenty of room to air their views while helping the company build its brand.

Box 10—IBM Blog Guidelines

1. Know and follow IBM's Business Conduct Guidelines.
2. Blogs, wikis, and other forms of online discourse are individual interactions, not corporate communications. IBMers are personally responsible for their posts. Be mindful that what you write will be public for a long time—protect your privacy.
3. Identify yourself—name and, when relevant, role at IBM—when you blog about IBM or IBM-related matters. And write in the first person. You must make it clear that you are speaking for yourself and not on behalf of IBM.
4. If you publish a blog or post to a blog and it has something to do with work you do or subjects associated with IBM, use a disclaimer such as this: "The postings on this site are my own and don't necessarily represent IBM's positions, strategies, or opinions."
5. Respect copyright and fair use laws.
6. Don't provide IBM's or another's confidential or other proprietary information.
7. Don't cite or reference clients without their approval.
8. Respect your audience. Don't use ethnic slurs, personal insults, obscenity, etc. Show proper consideration for others' privacy and for topics that may be considered objectionable or inflammatory, such as politics and religion.
9. Find out who else is blogging on a topic and cite them.
10. Don't pick fights; be the first to correct your own mistakes; don't alter previous posts without indicating you have done so.
11. Try to add value. Provide worthwhile information and perspective. [civ]

IBM has since created social media guidelines that help employees reflect its personality. One of IBM's core values is "Trust and personal responsibility in all relationships."[cv] As a company, IBM trusts—and expects—employees (IBMers) to exercise personal responsibility whenever they participate in social media. This includes not violating the trust of those with whom they are engaging. IBMers should not use these media for covert marketing or public relations. What does an IBMer's personal responsibility mean in online social media activities? Online social media enables individuals to share their insights, express their opinions and share information within the context of a globally distributed conversation.[cvi]

Intel is another organization that has helped its employees represent its brand promise online:

> *Create some excitement.* As a business and as a corporate citizen, Intel is making *important contributions to the world, to the future of technology,* and to public dialogue on a broad range of issues. Our business activities are increasingly focused on *high-value innovation* [emphasis added]. Let's share with the world the exciting things we're learning and doing—and open up the channels to learn from others.[cvii]

Building a Brand Community

Collaboration to Build Relationships

Best Buy's social media strategy is all about linking dispersed team members for collaboration and to promote individual contributions. Their strategies put employees in the driver's seat. Employees then feel empowered to help customers. "Social media is a great way to show off our culture," said Barry Judge, the company's chief marketing officer, a soft-spoken executive who joined Best Buy a decade ago. "That's really all we've got. We sell the same stuff, generally, as anyone. We're competing against the low-price leaders, the Internet, and everyone who's pushing a value proposition. But it's our people, our culture that differentiates us. Social media lets you show who you are—the good and the bad."[cviii]

Another community-building example, My Starbucks Idea, is not only breaking down traditional silos between customers and the company, but any idea picked up by Starbucks receives the attention of a cross-functional team that makes it happen. This encourages collaboration across departments and with the customer and is a great example of the company extending its "third place" brand promise on to the web.[cix]

At an even more personal level, Comcast monitors Twitter for customer concerns and uses that information to advance product development efforts and solve problems. They've also taken monitoring to another level by responding to customer problems when identified in Twitter. Comcast's brand promise is "Innovation and reliability." By monitoring Twitter, this allows them to be highly responsive to customer service issues like downtime, thereby improving reliability while demonstrating that they are tech savvy.[cx]

Focusing the Internal Culture

Software maker SAP has encouraged all employees to blog, tweet, and participate in other social media platforms, because this demonstrates the company's commitment to individual contributions. As a result they have 15,000 employee bloggers and 400 employees actively publishing content in other forms. By encouraging employees to publish their thoughts on such concepts as cloud computing and timeless software, they have demonstrated their prowess as a team of innovators. They have a culture that appreciates and values this support and creates thousands of internal champions.

Another online community experience is the intranet. When organizations reach a size at which people can't keep each other abreast of everything that is happening—somewhere upward of 20 people—the intranet becomes the employee living room. It performs two functions: disseminating new information about company guidelines and successes and serving as a social network for reinforcing positive brand actions. The intranet has moved beyond its initial role of repository for the company handbook and product education to where company leaders can compare notes and speak out on new company challenges, making it a key place for bonding as a team.

Using the intranet as a place for building community requires that you think about your company's online presence in a different way. How do you use your internal network to support your public brand community? What needs to be proprietary? An approach that recognizes the intranet as a part of your brand community will lead you into new ways of thinking.

According to Pam McCoy, director of marketing and brand strategy at Milliman Care Guidelines, former executive director of marketing communications at Foster School of Business of University of Washington, and previous head of marketing communications for Philips Healthcare North America Sales and Service:

> The role of an intranet is to give employees basic information and be the place for telling internal stories that reinforce and showcase the brand promise. In large organizations, everyone is in their own world. If I as a salesperson can better understand how customer service or supply chain managers live the brand, then I've broadened my ability to use the brand effectively. At Philips Healthcare, we'd ask, 'How does our brand of Sense and Simplicity manifest itself? Does the customer have the experience of Sense and Simplicity when he is trying to secure replacement parts?' That brand discussion should be 60 percent of the intranet content.
>
> Finally, an intranet is perfect for collaborating with other employees in a richer way than phone or e-mail allows. If I have a video camera and videotape myself giving a critique of a proposal to a team located around the world, I now have created a three-dimensional experience and a dialogue without getting someone real-time on the phone or through IM. Collaboration programs, such as Microsoft SharePoint, also allow the addition of a CEO blog to your intranet to extend the CEO's reach and brand, even though he may live in another place and rarely see you face-to-face.
>
> When Philips launched its Sense and Simplicity brand, they developed a whole intranet section featuring an interactive quiz asking about what the brand meant in terms of product design and employee action. They went on a road tour, which featured a Mack truck populated with products

from all divisions—medical, lighting, consumer electronics, health care, and semiconductors—explained how every product supported the Sense and Simplicity brand. If you won the quiz contest, you got to go to New York for an exclusive 'meet the press' rollout of Sense and Simplicity. This approach was not only educational but actively engaged the entire employee population in an internal brand dialogue, which made the brand real to all of us inside the walls of the organization.[cxi]

Box 11—Getting Started: Building an Online Brand Community

- Recognize that the online brand community is something you influence but don't control.
- Include strategies for building community around areas of interest, communicating your message, and getting feedback from customers.
- Develop a set of employee guidelines that include legal, etiquette, and on-brand actions.
- Train employees on the basics of being a company brand ambassador.
- Augment employee brand knowledge through your intranet, including ways for them to tell their own stories about the brand.
- Monitor existing and up-and-coming social media vehicles.
- Experiment and continuously improve.

Case Study: A Brand Two-Step: Zappos' Cultural Journey to Online Expression [Zappos.com]

Because shoe retailer Zappos.com provides an online experience, it just makes sense that it would figure out how to build an online employee community. The brand two-step for Zappos consists of hiring people who share the CEO's beliefs about valuing people and how together they can make a unique company—Zappos' brand culture—and then setting those people loose online. According to CEO Tony Hsieh, "In order for us to succeed as a service company, we need to create, maintain, and grow a culture where employees want to play a part in providing great service. I've been asked a number of times what the company's biggest asset is, and my answer is always the same: the culture."[cxii]

Zappos speaks about relinquishing the brand to employees[cxiii] and asks employees "what the Zappos' culture means to [them] specifically at this point in time, and we expect different responses from different people."[cxiv]

Human resources employee Cheryl Anne F. states it this way, "Zappos culture asks me to be aware of the present and to find my own unique value and meaning to what I am doing beyond its contribution to the company's bottom line . . . [it is] a place where unique personal relationships matter and every day brings a chance and a desire to do something great."[cxv] By encouraging employees to think of their online networking as a part of their job, Zappos deepens what would be a typically superficial customer experience (buying shoes) from many other retail brands.

Zappos also helps employees create the online brand experience through the Inside Zappos employee blogs and the twitter.zappos.com employee tweets. One of the things you'll notice right away about the Zappos online employee experience is that Tony Hsieh is right out there with the rest of employees—sometimes talking about philosophy and other times showing something funny, like his participation in their annual head-shaving day. Tony also reflects on how to use social media and how it has positively impacted his life.

Zappos demonstrates how leadership by example and employee empowerment are keys to building an online brand community.

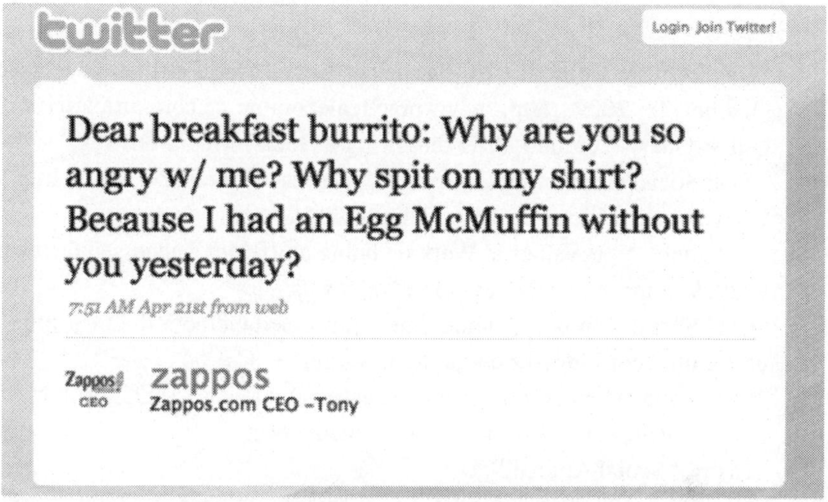

Photo of Zappos Twitter post on April 21, 2009 (accessed from www.twitter.com/zappos). Used with permission from Zappos.

Has this focus on culture and employee branding created results? Zappos has more than 8 million customers and more than 75 percent are returning customers. They grew by 20 percent in 2008[cxvi] and reportedly have more than 1 billion dollars in sales from selling more than 950,000 different products. Finally, in 2009, Amazon purchased Zappos for 928 million US dollars. Amazon CEO Jeff Bezos said that part of the reason for the purchase was Zappos' customer obsession and its totally unique culture, which he cited as a significant asset that was essential to the Zappos brand, its customers, and employees.[cxvii]

---

ciii "Quick Query: Comodo CEO on Hiring a Social Media Officer," accessed October 8, 2009, http://www.practicalecommerce.com/articles/1060-Quick-Query-Comodo-CEO-on-Hiring-a-Social-Media-Officer

civ "IBM Social Computing Guidelines," accessed October 8, 2009, http://www.ibm.com/blogs/zz/en/guidelines.html

cv Palmisano, "Our Values at Work on being an IBMer," accessed October 8, 2009, http://www.ibm.com/ibm/values/us/

cvi "IBM Social Computing Guidelines," accessed October 8, 2009, http://www.ibm.com/blogs/zz/en/guidelines.html

cvii "Intel Social Media Guidelines," accessed October 8, 2009, http://www.intel.com/sites/sitewide/en_us/social-media.htm

cviii Crosby, "Social Animal."

cix "My Starbucks Idea," Starbucks, accessed October 8, 2009, http://mystarbucksidea.force.com./

cx Parr, "HOW TO: Use Twitter for Customer Service," accessed October 8, 2009, http://mashable.com/2009/05/09/twitter-customer-service/

cxi Pam McCoy (director, marketing and brand strategy, Milliman Care Guidelines), in discussion with the authors, August 2009.

cxii Sybil F. Stershic, "Internal Marketing Spotlight: Zappos.com (Part 3)," *Quality Service Marking Blog*, November 18, 2008, http://qualityservicemarketing.blogs.com/quality_service_marketing/2008/11/internal-marketing-spotlight-zapposcom-part-3.html

cxiii Ellen Davis, "Building a Brand That Matters, One Employee at a Time: The Zappos Story," *Shop.org Blog*, February 3, 2009, http://blog.shop.org/2009/02/03/building-a-brand-that-matters-one-employee-at-a-time-the-zappos-story/

cxiv Hsieh, "Letter from the CEO," accessed October 8, 2009, http://culturebook.erinkjones.com/letter-ceo

cxv Ibid.

cxvi Ellen Davis, "Building a Brand That Matters, One Employee at a Time: The Zappos Story," *Shop.org Blog*, February 3, 2009, http://blog.shop.org/2009/02/03/building-a-brand-that-matters-one-employee-at-a-time-the-zappos-story/

cxvii "Video from Jeff Bezos about Amazon and Zappos," http://www.youtube.com/watch?v=-hxX_Q5CnaA

CHAPTER 12

Developing Employee Brand Ambassadors

The connection between a strong brand and employee aspirations is a win-win for the company and employee. A strong, integrated brand gives companies a competitive advantage in employee recruitment. If your organization is very clear about what it stands for, it will attract like-minded employees. According to a survey by Universum Communications, the best employees do not simply work where they can earn the most money but where they can make a difference and contribute to some greater goal.[cxviii] The way an employee chooses a company is very similar to the way a consumer chooses to use a product or service. People who become the best employees look at the market and ask: "At which company do I want to work?"

[cxix]

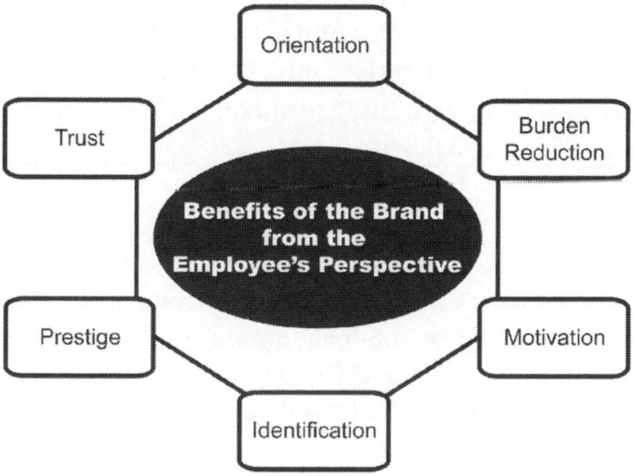

A strong brand benefits employees in a number of ways. It can help them orient around a focus, identify with a larger group, get motivated, build trust, and enhance their feelings of importance or prestige. The ability of brand to influence work choices starts early; high school graduates choose strong brands as their favorite employers.[cxx]

Box 12—Employee Brand Benefits Explained

Function	Description	Benefit
Orientation	Identification of the desired employer	Reduction of effort and cost of information gathering
Burden reduction	Acceleration of the decision-making process	Increase in efficiency and effectiveness of work
Trust	Proof of job security	Risk reduction
Prestige	Status	Self-differentiation and personal value proposition
Identification	Transfer of brand attributes to the employee	Social affiliation
Motivation	Alignment with the goals of the enterprise and supporting positive behavior	Increase in efficiency and effectiveness of work

Effective internal branding includes strategies for employee development and recognizes the importance of aligning employees emotionally with the brand and developing recruiting, orientation, and training processes based on the brand promise. This is only possible if the company offers employees an authentic experience and the company keeps its promises and lives its values.

The Role of Human Resources

Too few human resources departments take culture and the brand promise into consideration when hiring. That's because, although most companies claim that people are their greatest assets, human resources has often been viewed as a tactical rather than a strategic member of the management team.

A tactical human resources function won't work for companies seeking long-term brand success. If the customer experience is essential, then hiring and training employees to be brand ambassadors makes human resources one of the most important company assets. This goes beyond creating a highly engaged workforce. While that is necessary, it's a prerequisite rather than a result of a strong, branded culture. Employees must understand not only how to be engaged and do great work, but also how to do their jobs differently—in all the ways that contribute to their brand's success.

One of the more misguided trends that we've seen in the past few years is the idea of the *employee or employer brand*—terms that refer to something that is separate from the company's integrated brand. Creating a separate employee brand distances employees from their purpose and, therefore, their true value: serving customers. All employees need to understand and be able to act and interact in ways that create satisfied, committed customers. The lack of clarity about this connection dilutes purpose and morale. Worse still, in organizations that create a separate employee brand, employees are often engaged in activities that have no connection, even indirectly, to improving the customer experience.

Despite the strength of their brands, some organizations find it hard to recruit the right people, because their industry isn't perceived as exciting. This is DHL's and the logistics industry's challenge. The company's human resources marketing department approached this challenge by clearly spelling out brand appeal from an employee recruiting perspective.

Collaborating closely with the branding and advertising team in 2009, the human resources department developed an employer value proposition to attract those people whose values correspond with DHL brand values of personal commitment, proactive solutions, and local strength worldwide. In several cross-regional and cross-divisional workshops, DHL human resources managers defined three anchors for the employer value proposition—growth, impact and pride—and corresponding employee benefits. These are used in internal and external human resources communications throughout the entire employee life cycle, helping to design attractive employee programs and at the same time strengthening the brand.

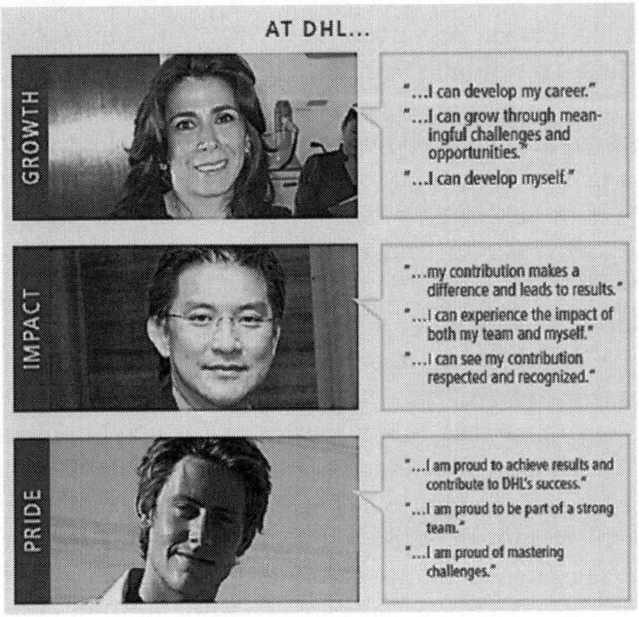

DHL Employer Value Proposition Anchors and Key Benefits.[cxxi]

Who Is an Ideal Employee?

To employ the right people, an organization first needs to describe its ideal employee. In some cases, such as McKinsey's exclusive focus on candidates from certain select schools, these characteristics are descriptive and immediately verifiable. In most cases, though, the components of the ideal are softer and can only be discovered through personal interaction with candidates. Personal interactions can take different forms.

Some organizations make extensive use of employee referrals. Southwest Airlines, Cisco Systems, and Four Seasons encourage employees to solicit qualified acquaintances. This emphasis on referrals has three benefits:

1. It puts recruiting power in the hands of those who best understand what it takes to support your brand promise and culture.
2. It gives employees a chance to contribute to the team.
3. It empowers employees to take responsibility for building the brand.

Organizations with strong brands frequently benefit from candidate self-selection. Strong brands enable prospective employees to say "the company's goals are the same as mine."

While brand clarity alone won't scare away all the wrong candidates and attract all the right ones, it helps. If you want to be a superstar doctor, you know you shouldn't work at Mayo Clinic because your ambition will be at odds with their team ethos. If you want to work in hospitality, you will need to be the type of person who values people relationships because strong hospitality brands celebrate and reward employees who enhance the guest experience.

Box 13—Brand-based Hiring Checklist

The more a prospective employee knows going into an interview the better. Prospects need to know about:

- ✓ your brand promise (strategic role, guiding principle, personality and story, values, and/or cultural norms),
- ✓ future product direction,
- ✓ knowledge leadership and important trends,
- ✓ market growth prospects, and
- ✓ competitor strengths and weaknesses.

What Are Best Practices for a Brand-Based Hiring Experience?

Even if you excel at hiring people with the right values and aspirations, it's still easy to go astray when filling senior positions. It's vital that senior employees are a good cultural fit and share the same passion for your brand as your current team. The challenge is to not equate past job excellence with a person's ability to live your brand. An effective candidate will be able to maintain the balancing act of living your brand while shaking things up and improving the brand with their own unique skills.

While it's impossible to boil a brand-based mind-set down to just a few concepts, we can offer some ideas that we believe any senior manager you are considering should be comfortable with:

- Brands are definable and manageable.
- Brand management results in significant bottom-line revenue and salary overhead savings.
- Employees need to deliver the brand as part of their jobs.
- A brand means what you do every day.
- How you deliver your brand promise is based on all of your brand tools.
- While your company culture and brand tools will evolve, they can't completely change without damaging brand value.

By thoroughly understanding these points yourself and discussing each point with candidates, you will find out if they can live in your brand-based world. This approach will also give them a deep grounding in your organization and a head start on getting up to speed as an employee. If they won't buy into these concepts, you'll find yourself working at cross-purposes once they've entered the company.

Case Study: Motivating Employee Associates [Health New England]

US health insurer, Health New England (HNE) makes certain that its brand promise "Personal and accountable" is applied by every associate (employee) in every interaction every day, and HNE has the results to prove it. In 2008, according to a report by the National Committee for Quality Assurance, HNE achieved the highest rating in customer service among 160 commercial health management organization/point of service health plans surveyed in the United States. In 2010, they placed among the top 10 health plans in the nation for the third year in a row—8th among the 239 plans reviewed—as rated by *US News & World Report*/National Committee for Quality Assurance America's Best Health Plans 2009-2010.

One of the secrets to HNE's success is its innovative way of ensuring that customers get what they need when they need it. The brand is created through every interaction between its associates, customers, and other stakeholders. HNE associates are committed to keeping their promise. To do this, associates apply the brand filter, "Am I acting like someone I would trust; listening; talking like a real person; preventing problems rather than just solving them; and committed to following through? If my customer calls again, will they ask for me?" If not, associates are required to make an adjustment in the moment so they act in line with the brand. Each associate wears a badge, and attached to each badge is a brand badge that lists these questions as a constant reminder of what it takes to keep the promise HNE makes.

A brand is what the customer experiences, even though it may not necessarily be what the company or organization intended when designing its products and service delivery. Therefore, what the customer experiences at each touchpoint determines their satisfaction and loyalty to the brand. Because every touchpoint is important, HNE understands that getting associates to use the brand is much more than a one-time or a top-down experience. Company leaders know they have limited face time with associates but believe that, as Lynn Ostrowski, director of brand and corporate relations, says, "If they can't get all associates to embrace the brand, regardless of level or role in the organization, then they don't consider themselves to be successful as leaders."[cxxii]

Vice President of Marketing Maura McCaffrey adds another viewpoint on how HNE has been successful at building its brand:

> It has been a top-down mentality. President and CEO Peter Straley truly believes in brand and what it can bring to an organization. Brand is one of the three tools he uses to manage organizational action along with profitability and growth. This focus helps keep all associates pulling in the same direction through ensuring that company initiatives are aligned with brand direction. No matter what initiatives we are working on, brand is always part of who we are, how we act, and the way we care for our members. At HNE, we have

> this great culture of associate engagement, which helps us drive that alignment. If a department was doing its own thing, one or more of our executive leadership team would call this out as a problem. That was also cultivated by the CEO; Peter has a mantra that "we are all in this together."[cxxiii]

In 2010, one brand focus was to inventory and catalog all the touchpoints people could experience with HNE as a member, a provider, an employer, a broker, or a member of the general public. Ostrowski explains:

> Our goal was to understand what all of these touchpoints were—good, bad, or indifferent. Then we took this defined touchpoint map around to different departments to work on improving opportunities for demonstrating our brand. The biggest problem with this is that we haven't figured out a way to share touchpoint mapping that is replicable across the organization.[cxxiv]

One way that HNE has improved the customer experience at each touchpoint is through focusing on associate brand training. The brand committee created the HNE Brand University, a year-long program in which associates can earn a bachelor degree, master's degree, or "HNED" in branding. This year-long program culminates with a graduation ceremony, and diplomas are awarded at the organization's all-associates meeting. "We can work all day to bring in new clients, but if I don't have everyone inside excited about, believing in, and acting on our promise, the brand just won't work," says Ostrowski.[cxxv]

While brand education is important, success of the HNE Brand University is really measured by how often associates take on-brand action. At HNE 70 percent of associates have participated in and achieved a degree level. In order to achieve the associate degree level, an associate would need to take conscious on-brand actions at least once per quarter. Many associates have received their doctorate, which means they take on-brand actions every day.

Administrative Assistant Laura Dellapenna achieved her doctorate and enjoyed the journey along the way:

> You would get e-mails with different branding kinds of questions that examined what you were loyal to and asked you to describe the characteristics of brands that work for you. These questions really delved into what makes HNE stand apart at a nitty-gritty level. They would give me a brand example of someone calling in with a customer complaint and ask how I would handle it. It was interesting to be able to read the observations of other associates who had tackled the same problem before me. It really helped me expand my base of knowledge about what other departments do while helping me really see all of the dimensions that acting "personally and accountably" could take on.[cxxvi]

Another doctoral-level associate, Maura McCaffrey adds:

> I don't know if I necessarily think differently after going through Brand University; it just reinforces my beliefs. The way it was presented—sometimes as "quick knowledge hits" and other times demanding some significant work—reminded me that our brand is "always on." "Personal and accountable" to me means that every voice mail or e-mail that comes to my computer is important; even if I can't respond, I get someone else to respond within 24 hours. I also ask people to e-mail me back if they didn't get what they needed. "Personal and accountable" means that, no matter whom you interact with, you receive the same level of accountability and care.[cxxvii]

One of the secrets to HNE's success is that it doesn't consider its brand work to be a program but an integral function of the organization. Ostrowski says:

> We might do a program around our brand work to help keep it fresh, but the day-to-day nuts and bolts—such as a new associates' breakfast at which employees learn about key opportunities for department-level improvement—really asks everyone to be a brand ambassador. At the core, associates really need to see that brand is about being genuine; for the brand to be effective, it can't be something we are told we

> need to say; it must be something that we feel passionate about living.[cxxviii]

Laura Dellapenna puts it this way:

> Being a brand champion has allowed me to use my creativity in a different way. They wanted my opinion on what I do that makes HNE unique. They helped me by comparing it to other things I value in my life—like why I've driven a Honda for 9 years. They got me to dig deep about why I value what I value and apply that knowledge to making HNE a better place for our customers.[cxxix]

Dellapenna continued:

> It's really apparent to me that one of HNE's strengths as a regional plan is that we can get to know our people and members in a very intimate way, a way that isn't possible for our larger competitors. I often think about the brand being recognized for personal customer service and going the extra mile. When I came here, I also applied the brand to my own life. A huge attraction to working here was the opportunity to be more accountable for my own life/work balance. It's been a transformative experience for me, and the HNE wellness team honored me with the Associate Wellness Champion Award in 2009. Our culture encourages me to take on new challenges—in 2010, I did 14 5K runs—and I think this commitment shows up in our customer service.[cxxx]

Even though there has never been a formal budget line item for internal branding at HNE, associates are encouraged to use company time and resources to participate in brand programs. HNE also has an internal advertising and graphic design department that supports internal communications. Their primary mode of communication is through leveraging simple methods like PDFs, e-mails, and blogs. The e-mail depicted in *Materials for Health New England Brand University* is an example of how associates learned about the HNE Brand University.

Materials for Health New England Brand University.
Used with permission from Health New England.

HNE has created a rich internal learning experience with blogging. Ostrowski explains:

> We lay out the member interaction and invite associates to talk about how they could improve our actual response by asking questions like "How would you apply the brand?" and "What would you do differently?" Associates went crazy; some wrote dissertations trying to help people think through and apply being "Personal and accountable" in the interaction and figuring out how to change or improve the experience. Over 150 associates responded to the blog and to each other. Living the brand is not rocket science; keeping your promise is simply getting the right people in the room, exercising our imaginations, and being persistent.[cxxxi]

HNE has more challenges reaching associates who work for production-based groups like member services, who have very little unscheduled time. Programs, like Brand University training, are offered on more than one occasion, and activities are tailored for department staff meetings to provide more learning opportunities.

> We try to be flexible in how we offer programs, and we also seek to recognize participants in a special way. These low-cost but genuine actions are very effective at getting people involved, because they both engage them and recognize achievement. Last year, we gave everyone a certificate and a "padfolio" from HNE Brand University. We also made a badge-sized "What it means to be a brand ambassador" so people could wear them with their ID badges.[cxxxii]

The HNE Brand Ambassador Card

Elevator Story

Our local, personal service helps you get the most out of your health care benefits. We'll reduce the hassles, and if there's a problem, whatever it is, we'll help solve it.

How Can I Help?

What If I Was the Customer?

Am I:

- acting like someone I would trust?
- talking like a real person?
- preventing problems not just solving them?
- committed to following through?

If my customer calls again, will they ask for me?

The HNE brand committee manages brand work at HNE; members carry information back from meetings and become the voice of the HNE brand for their peers. Ostrowski explains:

> Our brand committee includes someone from every department at every level of customer experience. We feel this gives us a true picture of all of the interactions where we need to make sure we keep our promise and allows staff members to focus on opportunities to enhance the brand. [cxxxiii]

The committee is tasked with designing HNE's programs, like Brand University. The brand committee took a month to design the Brand University and then spent the rest of the year instituting it. This year's "Mission Possible" focuses on helping associates learn more about and apply tools (coaching, engagement, brand, opportunity for improvement, quality, and wellness) to achieve a high-performance work environment. Part of this work is illustrating how all the tools are interrelated. The brand committee is working to integrate communications across the organization and is creating a year's worth of activities demonstrating the relationships between the various tools as well as benchmarks that will be used to determine the impact of this work. Ostrowski adds:

> Associates were getting bombarded by communications about everything from brand to wellness and engagement. So with Mission Possible, we'll have all communications under one umbrella. The wellness committee will still have their walks, and we will still participate in community events, but having one focused, brand-based communications program will be a big change.[cxxxiv]
>
> The brand committee also includes senior leaders such as Jim Kessler, vice president and general counsel, and Amy Trombley, vice president of human resources engagement. These leaders are committed to the goals of the group and enable HNE to better integrate brand communications. With two of human resources' current initiatives dealing with coaching and high performance, HNE is demonstrating to associates how each improvement is in the service of building the brand.

Another reason that integrated brand communications is part of this year's focus is the belief that associates have a lot on their plates. Ostrowski explains:

> We have added two lines of business in Medicare and Medicaid and associates are asking "What else do they want me to do? I no longer have time to do what they pay me to do!" Recognizing the problem at a senior management level made getting buy-in easy from all the committees that wanted associates to engage in what they are doing. Because the brand committee is comprised of people from all levels and all departments, we have the authority to make decisions. Our goal is to demonstrate that brand is how we do our existing jobs; it is not extra work.[cxxxv]

McCaffrey feels that the brand benefits HNE in many ways:

> We are in a smaller community, so if someone hasn't had a chance to experience us, chances are they know an employer who has. All of those positive experiences their friends or family have had with us make a big difference when it comes to recommendations. And when there is a problem, other people speak up for us in the community. We trade on our name, and it is based on our promise of "Personal and accountable." We can't sell a promise we are willing to break. Would you buy something that continually breaks? Our brand is the foundation for every success.[cxxxvi]

Adds Ostrowski:

> This year, HNE had one of the toughest challenges ever with Massachusetts capping rates and the recession hitting our small group business segment hard. In spite of that, we just had the largest growth in membership for any year. I am confident that some component of our success must be our brand.[cxxxvii]

[cxviii] Wienröder, "Hochschulabsolventen."

[cxix] Meffert, Burmann, and Koers, *Markenmanagement*, 9f [adapted and translated by the authors].

[cxx] Universität St. Gallen, "The Universum Graduate Survey 2006."

[cxxi] DHL, *DHL Employer Branding E-Handbook.*

[cxxii] Lynn Ostrowski (director of brand and corporate relations, Health New England), in discussion with the authors, June 2011.

[cxxiii] Maura McCaffrey (vice president of marketing, Health New England), in discussion with the authors, June 2011.

[cxxiv] Lynn Ostrowski (director of brand and corporate relations, Health New England), in discussion with the authors, June 2011.

[cxxv] Ibid.

[cxxvi] Laura Dellapenna (administrative assistant, Health New England), in discussion with the authors, June 2011.

[cxxvii] Maura McCaffrey (vice president of marketing, Health New England), in discussion with the authors, June 2011.

[cxxviii] Lynn Ostrowski (director of brand and corporate relations, Health New England), in discussion with the authors, June 2011.

[cxxix] Laura Dellapenna (administrative assistant, Health New England), in discussion with the authors, June 2011.

[cxxx] Ibid.

[cxxxi] Lynn Ostrowski (director of brand and corporate relations, Health New England), in discussion with the authors, June 2011.

[cxxxii] Ibid.

[cxxxiii] Ibid.

[cxxxiv] Ibid.

[cxxxv] Ibid.

[cxxxvi] Maura McCaffrey (vice president of marketing, Health New England), in discussion with the authors, June 2011.

[cxxxvii] Lynn Ostrowski (director of brand and corporate relations, Health New England), in discussion with the authors, June 2011.

CHAPTER 13

Rewarding the Moment of Truth

Even with the best recruiting process and the right hires, new recruits must still make the leap from understanding your brand to living it. Only certain hands-on learning experiences with your culture can turn potential into action.

First, employees have to want to live your brand. They need an emotional connection to why brand actions will help them and help the company. It has to be worth the time and effort. Being handed a mission or strategic role with the threat of being tested misses the mark. They may be able to recite the mission, but will that create change? Employees become brand believers when they see people they respect acting on-brand and when they are rewarded for on-brand actions. A moment of truth occurs every time an employee sees a manager applying the brand promise. This sets up the new employee's own moment of truth—when faced with the choice, will they do their job in a way that reflects your brand?

A best practice here is for managers to make flagging their new employees' moments of truth part of their jobs. Recognition of these moments can be very positive experiences for the new employee, solidifying their team identification and enthusiasm for living your brand. Effective managers look for multiple opportunities to review a new employee's actions to help align them with the brand.

The First-Day Experience

To the extent one can't "teach an old dog new tricks," the time to start training is hour one on day one. The challenge is that employees are hired for their skills and abilities. Any well-adjusted person will believe that they've learned a lot about how to do their job in past situations. The key to branding is to help each new employee distinguish between personal best practices and distinctive brand actions.

Most companies focus an employee's early experiences on learning company procedures for getting things done—such as reporting structures or reimbursement rules or expectations of the work itself. Relatively few companies demonstrate what on-brand action looks like when bringing employees on board.

The following are a few examples of how a CEO or manager might demonstrate on-brand actions to a new employee.

Cultural Norms

As we mentioned earlier, cultural norms are "the way we do things around here." If your organization has a cultural norm of "A team is more creative than any one individual," then you might invite a new employee into a brainstorm on their first day. Since you have defined your norms, you might also mention this norm as a preamble to the invitation, further cementing the relationship between job expectations and brand.

Strategic Role

While you are in the brainstorm, you might remind everyone that ideas need to align with the organization's strategic role—let's say it's "Championing the underserved"—thus demonstrating to the new employee and reinforcing for everyone else the unique approach your organization takes in neighborhood health care. You might also eliminate ideas that don't help the organization fulfill its role.

At the end of the session, you might ask the new employee and others how they would deliver on these new ideas in their jobs. This is especially important for new employees who play a behind-the-scenes role. We know of one information technology director who determined,

"Well, we don't directly deliver on our brand promise, but our job is to enable other departments to do just that." Based on this reasoning, he instituted a policy of having his staff ask each department requesting a new service from information technology, "How does this help us build our strategic role?"

Creating a first-day experience that demonstrates the organization's brand rather than just talking about it will result in much greater credibility.

Mayo Clinic takes a new employee directly into an in-depth employee orientation period that lasts a minimum of 2 days. They share their brand through stories, videos, and an employee brand handbook. They follow this up 12 weeks later with one-on-one discussions with senior leadership.

Likewise, the Ritz Carlton will place new employees (independent of their level) in a two-day orientation that includes training on "The Gold Standards." The class is then reunited again on day 21 and day 365. The Ritz Carlton reinforces this intensive training with special business cards to remind employees of the firm's brand promise.

Whether you conduct initial intensive brand instruction or you train as you go, periodic check-ins are important. Because living the brand is part of each employee's job, this should also be part of each employee's performance review.

By using these immersion approaches, you can build an emotional framework for on-brand action. At McKinsey, you learn one way to approach, break down, and analyze a strategic challenge. At Four Seasons, you are only introduced to processes and policies that deliver the highest levels of guest service. At Mayo Clinic, you quickly come to understand how the team approach can bring every patient the answers they need. In all of these examples, it's important to keep in mind that the brand tools don't dictate rules. They are about empowerment—this means it takes more effort to get new employees oriented at the start but pays off with much bigger dividends over the long-term.

Many companies also conduct formal mentoring programs to reinforce on-brand actions. Four Seasons also offers an interesting model. A mentor is assigned to a new employee at the beginning of the training process. At the end of the classroom training, the new employee is required to spend a night as a guest of the hotel. When coupled with other forms of training, this extended in-their-shoes approach provides valuable grounding in the guest's brand experience.

Who should be responsible for the first-day experience? We think that the best results come when the experience is handled by the new employee's immediate supervisor. This person will be most aware of the employee's job responsibilities and what on-brand action would look like in their job.

Brand-Based Incentives

The best incentives balance general performance bonuses with ones that promote brand-enhancing action. This is the concept behind McKinsey's rewarding of consultants based on how a project impacts the clients' bottom lines. This is also the motivation behind Four Seasons' rewarding of ad-hoc, outstanding customer service with gift certificates and free event tickets. At Southwest Airlines, valuable suggestions for improving operational efficiency (a key underpinning of their brand promise) are highlighted in an article in the company newsletter. At Four Seasons, ideas for improving the guest experience are disseminated organization-wide as best practices.

In addition to providing cash and other incentives, many successful organizations also have a robust framework for brand quality assurance. At McKinsey, the organizational structure itself acts as a quality assurance mechanism for its "One firm" brand promise. Geographic redeployments and leadership role limitations ensure that no one individual is able to consolidate power and authority to elevate their success above that of the firm.

Case Study: Transforming the Moment of Truth [Infosys]

Infosys was founded in 1981 by N. R. Narayana Murthy and six others in Pune, India. Murthy started the company out of a makeshift office in his home, using a loan from his wife, Sudha. In 1983, the company headquarters moved to Bangalore, and by 1987, Infosys had taken on its first foreign client, US-based Data Basics Corporation, and established its first global office in Boston. By 1999, Infosys had hit 100 million

US dollars in revenues on its way to an amazing 2 billion US dollars by 2006 and 4 billion US dollars by 2008.

At the heart of its success was the growth of information technology outsourcing. But rather than just position itself as a lower cost, offshore information technology provider, Infosys decided that its brand distinctiveness was about "Being a transformational partner" for the clients it served. The organization did this by shifting the discussion to how to become a flat world company—to effectively use global reach as a competitive advantage both for themselves and for their clients.

For Infosys, countries don't matter. Brand recognition becomes especially important because there are minimal barriers to entering the outsourcing marketplace. While countries aren't important, cultures are, because employees with diverse cultural backgrounds and experiences can bring new ideas and new ways of looking at and solving problems.

When asked about the company's rapid growth, Infosys cofounder Nandan Nilekani stated, "There aren't many companies growing like this. Companies haven't been investing enough in people. Rather than train them, they let them go. Our people are our capital. The more we invest in them, the more they can be effective.[cxxxviii] He adds, "At this point in time, building the global presence, building the brand as a global transformation partner, helping global corporations in their transformation—that's really our main strategic priority."[cxxxix]

Leveraging Word-of-Mouth Referrals

Infosys encourages employees to do exemplary work and talk about it. In the words of Srinivas Uppaluri, global head of Infosys marketing:

> Since we do little advertising, we believe we are quite dependent on word-of-mouth whether passed along in verbal or written form. We have had some clients grow from 1 million to 150 million a year. Some of the increase is with the original buyer, but a lot is because we are recommended to others in the same firm.[cxl]

Infosys uses positive incentives to create word-of-mouth via its workforce. According to Uppaluri:

> The business units that can show more "proof points" will get more money. Proof points are a variety of things: get a good rating or award, the customer will provide a written testimonial; customers will stand up and talk to [their] peers about their use of Infosys.[cxli]

Rather than trying to compete head-to-head with major advertisers like IBM, Infosys has chosen to route promotional expenditures into actions that will create exemplary employees. There is high demand for Infosys jobs; only 1 or 2 of hundreds applicants get to work there. According to *Fortune Magazine*'s Julie Schlosser, "gaining admission to Infosys is more competitive than gaining admission to Harvard": the company receives 1.3 million applicants for full-time positions and hires about 1 percent of the applicants versus Harvard's 9 percent acceptance rate.[cxlii] Infosys has hired as many as 25,000 engineers a year from an application pool of up to 250,000. The company's investment in training and lifestyle results in a better product and in more qualified candidates.

Bonding Through Extensive Early Training

Incoming employees are called "freshers" and are first trained in Mysore, India, at Infosys University for an intensive 14 weeks to learn the Infosys way.[cxliii] The $120 million facility features a gym, movie theaters, bowling allies, hair salons, and other amenities and might be considered a cross between Disney World, Club Med, and a modern American university.[cxliv] Infosys University was recently expanded to train 10,0000 employees at a time.[cxlv]

The experience of a fresher is similar to that of someone starting boot camp. The facilities may be pleasant, but new employees must be able to pass two 3-hour exams on programming and the dos and don'ts of global etiquette.[cxlvi] The etiquette classes also focus on how to be a brand ambassador using real-life, what-if scenarios.[cxlvii] In 2006, the cost of this intensive training was 5,000 US dollars per new employee.[cxlviii]

According to Aditya Nath Jha, head of Infosys' global branding, Infosys is perceived as the best company to work for in India.[cxlix] Infosys has taken the concept of the first-day experience to an extreme, and it has helped the organization achieve astounding revenue growth and profitability by differentiating Infosys from its global competitors.

[cxxxviii] Schlosser, "Harder Than Harvard."

[cxxxix] Roy, "Infosys Woos the World to Become Global Brand."

[cxl] Srinivas Uppaluri (global head of marketing, Infosys), in discussion with the authors, August 2007.

[cxli] Ibid.

[cxlii] Schlosser, "Harder Than Harvard."

[cxliii] Ibid.

[cxliv] Ibid.

[cxlv] Ibid., "Infosys U."

[cxlvi] Ibid., "Harder Than Harvard."

[cxlvii] Ibid.

[cxlviii] Ibid.

[cxlix] Aditya Nath Jha (head of global branding, Infosys), in discussion with the authors, August 2007.

CHAPTER 14

Translating Brand Tools into Operational Reality

Aligning every aspect of your organization with your brand promise is a big job. While initial employee training will get you started, aligning the company and its brand promise is a continuous process rather than a one-time project.

For human resources, every new employee is a brand opportunity; therefore, recruitment, selection, and orientation must be brand based. For facilities and information technology, this is about managers using brand tools as a central criterion in their planning processes. For sales, this is making sure that sales people are selling company brand value as well as product features.

Getting the right company processes and infrastructure in place can make it easier for employees to live your brand. Everything from new employee orientation to wayfinding signage at a corporate campus to your use of information technology needs to support the customer brand experience.

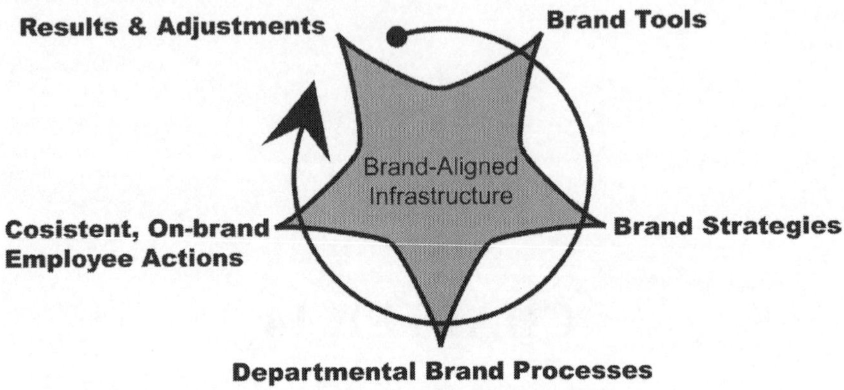

Effective internal branding aligns the organization around the brand.

The Principles behind Cascading Brand Knowledge

The most difficult part about internal branding isn't determining your brand promise and tools, strategies, or desired customer experience; the real challenge is getting the rest of the organization to come with you on the journey. Since an effective brand is based on what your organization is already doing well, you'd think it would be easy for people to align with it. That would be true if there wasn't change involved. The way any group accepts change looks like a bell curve—outlined by Geoffrey Moore in *Crossing the Chasm*[cl]—beginning with early adopters who will jump right in with you from the start to the majority of employees, extending all the way to laggards who will only come along kicking and screaming.

One way to think of brand alignment is to compare it to a cascade of water. A cascade is a series of steps the water traverses to reach its destination. Similar to the idea of training trainers who then teach everyone else, cascading relies on each new level to pass on brand knowledge.

Knowing a few cascade principles will help you get to brand alignment more quickly:

Principle 1: You Need a Brand to Be Successful Long-Term

Branding is not a nice window dressing that you only think about once the company is built. Your brand impacts how much the organization can charge and whether customers stay loyal as well as refer your products to others. It is a key determinant of whether you'll succeed over the long-term. For employees who want to prove their value, there's no better way to do it than by contributing to actions that build customer loyalty and commitment. Tying employees living the brand to customer success is a win-win.

Principle 2: High Quality Is Not a Substitute for Acting On-Brand

Many people have a difficult time understanding why simply creating a high-quality experience isn't enough. Even management systems such as Six Sigma and Lean manufacturing suggest that higher quality is the end all and be all. But high quality isn't the same as a point of difference. When you can choose from 5 super premium hotels that all can tout their fantastic beds and customer service, the reason that quality isn't enough becomes clearer. Your brand promise helps you establish a differentiated customer experience that employees can learn how to deliver.

Principle 3: To Understand a Brand You Need to Use It

How many times have you listened to an inspiring teacher and then tried to explain what you heard? That same issue exists in brand training. That's why employees need to experience hands-on workshops and multiple opportunities to apply brand tools in their jobs. Conduct brand tool usage training when you first introduce your brand tools. After that point, training employees to use the brand tools starts in the new employee orientation process. For all employees, create a brand thread through the supervisory process and all in-house trainings, using every opportunity to demonstrate how new and existing processes deliver on the company's brand promise.

Principle 4: Become a Culture of Brand-Telling

Cultures with the strongest brands never tire of telling their stories. *Brand-telling* isn't about preaching the brand; in fact, many organizations don't emphasize the *B-word* at all. Instead, it's about the many ways the company expresses itself every day. It's about how employees are empowered and what that has caused them to do differently. It's intensely personal and yet motivating all at once. It is like the idea of affirmative statements—the more I talk about my goals in a positive way, the more excited I am. Telling your brand stories can give others better ideas about how to use the brand in their jobs. By flagging examples and calling for stories at every company meeting, you'll build the muscle memory until living your brand really is second nature.

Principle 5: Celebrate Progress

Some say that "nothing gets truly done until it receives recognition." We find examples of this throughout history: the guy who is credited with inventing the radio may not have and we know there are many people who can lay claim to the first electric light. When you move to a new way of doing things, you create brand reality based on how and what you talk about it. Therefore it's important to understand how you want to define progress and then celebrate it when you see it.

This means acknowledging employees for on-brand actions. People are more motivated by short-term rewards than by delayed gratification according to a study by Kevin G. Volpp, director for health incentives at the University of Pennsylvania's Wharton School and the Philadelphia VA Medical Center, and colleagues. The study points out that immediate rewards are much more engaging than changes that might help sometime in the future.[cli]

This is one reason why it's so difficult for people to lose weight. But a cautionary note: this can't replace integrating brand tools at the job description and performance levels, but it does create the right cultural environment for change.

CEO Brand Management Infrastructure

One of the biggest problems in getting employees to live the brand is getting the right person to lead the project. Since internal branding crosses all company departments and divisions, there is no more natural sponsor than the CEO. Although marketing or human resources could own it, placing internal branding within either area may pigeonhole and limit the usefulness of the effort.

We've seen two CEO-related brand management solutions work well. The first is to establish a project manager position in the CEO's office to manage internal branding. This person would be less of a policy maker and more of a doer who would leverage thoughts and ideas from the CEO and CEO staff. The second solution is to create a higher-level position, an independent global brand manager, who still reports directly to the CEO. Either way, it's always better to have a single owner for internal branding. Many brands stagnate due to a lack of a buck-stops-here person whose job is ensuring that employees live the brand.

The background for either management model makes that person hard to find. The best candidate would be a creative thinker who also had a good sense of how to navigate the political waters and strong project management skills. Perhaps most importantly, this candidate will have experience in turning strategy into action. That requires the ability to collaborate on new service models, methodologies, and products that no one in the company has seen before—a tall order.

Turf Wars

Since brand work is highly visible, it's an easy target for employees who want to consolidate power rather than do what's in the organization's best interest. Because branding advocates for change, internal branding managers always fight an uphill battle against the status quo. The only way to avoid major turf wars is to ensure that the CEO is willing to spend political capital to ensure brand acceptance.

What if a company's CEO isn't up to this challenge? While we'd like to say that never happens, the reality is that most organizations muddle through somewhere between what's best and what's possible. Even when the attempt results in a company initiative that is less than the best, it will produce measurable, positive results. We believe that this is because effective internal branding is based on what the organization is already doing at some level. Therefore it is an alignment that can occur to some degree, even if every process isn't in place. That said, companies that choose to go wholeheartedly into brand management are standouts and their success becomes more obvious over time. Otherwise, how could Volvo, a company from a small, northern European country, become one of the top automotive brands in the world and keep that distinction for over 75 years?

Infrastructure That Supports Brand

As we mentioned at the start of this chapter, brand alignment doesn't end with employee orientation. Your brand should permeate each employee's experience every day. Infrastructure is a major tool for internal branding. Therefore, supporting brand-building infrastructure is not a "down the road" investment decision but should be an early strategy following brand promise and brand tool definition.

Something as simple as McKinsey's use of consistent report templates and standardized formats represents a similar commitment to brand-enabling infrastructure. McKinsey's adoption of the report template came early in the history of the firm under the direction and guidance of the internal brand visionary, Marvin Bower. Bower believed in the power of consistency and professionalism of appearance, and this belief manifested itself not only in the hats all male employees were required to wear for the first several decades of the firm's history but also in the creation and dissemination of these standardized formats for client reports, which have since become part of McKinsey's information technology.

A component of Mayo Clinic's drive for collaborative patient care is a patient record that is standardized, accessible, and understandable across specialties. The idea of having a complete medical record tied to each patient was an outgrowth of the organization's mission to deliver patient care through a team-based approach that leveraged the expertise of specialists. In fact, Mayo Clinic pioneered the patient record long before shareable, digitized information was conceived. This team-based approach could not have been possible without this infrastructure, which enables a neurologist in Mayo Clinic's Florida facility to discuss treatment options with a cardiologist in Minnesota using shared data.

While the technology platform for the patient record has evolved, the supporting infrastructure here was not the result of new hardware, software, or electronic gadgets but a concept born of a revolutionary brand promise. The lesson is that, if an organization is open to investing time and resources into translating brand tools into operational reality, the results can be transforming.

Branding Within Facilities: AAA Northern California, Nevada, and Utah

AAA Northern California, Nevada and Utah was looking for more ways to strengthen its 100-year-old brand, which stands for safety, security and responsible transportation. Research showed a strong connection between internal and external brand and loyalty. "Knowledge of what I can do to build the brand" had the second highest impact on employee engagement and members' perceptions of AAA employees and the AAA brand had the highest impact on members' intents to renew.[clii]

How could AAA build the brand further? One solution was to build the elements of their brand into their new company headquarters. Working with architects Gensler and Associates, AAA took advantage of the need for new facilities to surround employees with the brand.

"We felt this was a huge opportunity to engage employees with our brand, celebrate our heritage, and highlight the importance of our staff in delivering our brand experience. We made this a primary objective of our move," explains Virginia Vovchuk, director of brand strategy and design. Leaders from across business lines used the move to jump-start the culture. She adds:

> We are a customer-focused and caring organization, and we used those concepts as guiding principles to create a space that supported individual work as well as collaboration. From that, the architect designed service hubs, huddle rooms, hoteling solutions for working remotely, and wellness rooms. We developed quality touchpoints for employees that then worked hand-in-hand with the architect's designs.[cliii]

AAA Station Landing Design Team: James Lesko, Svetlana Royzen, Mary Hayano, Beth Brann, Peter Merridew, and Glen Archibald in partnership with Taras Design, Bedrock Brands, and Identity Services. Used with permission from AAA Northern California, Nevada, and Utah.

Another guiding principle was "Productive, efficient environments," which paid special attention to convenient technology, sensible floor plans, clear way finding, and ensuring that every employee would have a quality work experience with easy access to shared amenities and support systems.

Senior executive sponsors wanted to make sure that, as soon as you walked in the door, you recognized AAA as a contemporary, relevant, safety-focused and caring company. A series of inset niches on each of the floors of the building were designed to house 2-D and 3-D artifacts from AAA's history and to tell the story of brand relevance through the decades. The wall in the background was covered with a large image from Arches National Monument, an example of how the common areas in the building are linked to a series of conference rooms named after US national parks to celebrate AAA's legacy of enabling countless road trips for members' adventures.

Brand Relevance Niches. A series of inset "niches" on each of the floors of the building were designed to house 2-D and 3-D artifacts from AAA's history and to tell the story of brand relevance through the decades. Photography by Kevin Ng. Used with permission from AAA Northern California, Nevada, and Utah.

Vovchuck adds:

> People were getting on board with the idea that there's an opportunity to engage employees in a way that is unique to the company rather than simply adopting engagement best practices and off-the-shelf metrics. Revitalizing a brand requires a rigorous review of its heritage and customer viewpoints to make something real and lasting. That work then needs to be translated into actions, communications and infrastructure that get employees excited and aligned.[cliv]

A large component of the branding at the new headquarters is based on interactivity in the sense of walking up and looking closely to discover details about AAA's history and its people. Engagement and learning in visually appealing displays in physical space invites employees to create a deeper relationship with the AAA brand.

Discovering Values. The company's values (vinyl decals appear like etched glass surface) serve as a safety barrier across large glass walls on main conference rooms and elevator lobbies. Photography by Kevin Ng. Used with permission from AAA Northern California, Nevada, and Utah.

Vovchuck:

> One of the key elements is our heritage museum, which starts with our earliest green efforts and takes visitors to the present day. We have a challenge in that the AAA brand has so many benefits and facets that it's difficult to communicate as a whole to members. The same is true for employees who need to be knowledgeable about the brand and its offerings in order to better share who we are with customers.[clv]

The Lobby Experience.[clvi] *A central focus of the lobby experience, the Fast Forward exhibit traces AAA's history in leading safe and responsible transportation for over 100 years, including an actual super mileage race car created in collaboration with fuel innovators at the University of California Davis. Photography by Kevin Ng. Used with permission from AAA Northern California, Nevada, and Utah.*

Translating Brand Tools into Infrastructure

How do you start translating your brand into infrastructure? Once you have defined brand tools, infrastructure develops as part of performance expectations. Depending on your current infrastructure needs, it also can become part of your strategic business plan (discussed in detail in chapter 10).

HealthPoint, a community health center, provides health care for low-income populations. It has a strategic role of "A caring health community" and a guiding principle of "We go the extra step." Because health care is about in-person service, HealthPoint's brand tools and strategies had a big impact on infrastructure. HealthPoint's brand-based infrastructure includes:

- Solving the challenge of making its services as accessible as possible to all patients. This meant creating a welcoming environment for a diverse population that speaks dozens of languages, which had implications for signage and privacy needs in the waiting and examination rooms. They also developed a single brand name and identity, HealthPoint, for all external signage. Previously, they had more than seven different location names, which confused patients.

- Creating processes that provide care to low-income populations more effectively. They created a partnership with a local community hospital to shift people from using that hospital's emergency department for nonemergency health issues to HealthPoint. Infrastructure changes that made this possible included extending HealthPoint clinic hours to evenings and weekends, offering case management services, and screening uninsured patients for insurance eligibility.
- Expanding its caring health community to include services that don't traditionally fall under health care. For instance, the organization began linking patients to other services they needed, such as behavioral health care.
- A website that links people in their local communities to the notions of "Health care for all" and "A strong community."[clvii]

These and other infrastructure changes are helping HealthPoint serve the right people while building a caring community. "In 2008, 40 percent of the people we served had no form of health insurance coverage whatsoever," said Thomas Trompeter, CEO of HealthPoint. Last year, 49,000 people received treatment in the HealthPoint network of clinics. Of the total number served, 51 percent lived below the federal poverty level. An additional 27 percent only had household incomes between 100 percent and 200 percent of the poverty level.[clviii]

Hertz enhanced its premium brand image of "Fast, problem-free rental and personalized attention" in the early 1970s by becoming the first rental car company to establish a customer profile database—the Hertz #1 Club. Through tracking such data as driver's licenses, home addresses, and credit cards, this information technology system helped Hertz reinforce its premium brand by reducing the time customers had to spend making reservations and ultimately renting a car.[clix] In 1989, Hertz added a feature for its best customers that allowed them to skip the check-in counter and go directly to a preassigned car, where their keys were waiting for them.

The value of standardized supporting infrastructure, when established early, echoes through the internal branding success of Southwest Airlines as well. In Southwest's case, however, the supporting infrastructure is the airline's fleet of 737s, which had a powerful impact on Southwest's operational efficiency and internal branding.[clx] Using one type of plane means that Southwest needs fewer specialized maintenance personnel and spare parts. By freeing up head count and cash, Southwest can apply these savings to hiring and training the right people. In addition, the standardization of the fleet reduces potential distractions from delivering outrageous service.

These examples illustrate the important role of infrastructures for the internal branding process. Standardization, done correctly, makes the way employees live the brand that much more compelling and distinctive for customers.

Case Study: Paying Attention to the Details [Forrester Research]

Since Forrester Research's inception in 1983, its commitment to its brand promise of providing "Unique and fact-based advice on the future of information technology" has made it one of the most successful technology and market research firms. Forrester Research's CEO, George F. Colony, has exemplified this brand promise. One of Colony's early and very accurate predictions came in 1988 when he foretold that personal computers (PCs) connected by networks would replace big mainframes hooked to "dumb" terminals. Since then, he and his firm have predicted several major sea changes, including the growth of the Internet, the dot.com bust, and the rise of social networking.

After the company went public in 1996, it grew at a compounded rate of 52 percent through 1999.[clxi] It has garnered accolades from *Forbes* as one of the "200 best small companies in America,"[clxii] and in 2006, Forrester was included in the *Business 2.0* list of the "100 fastest-growing technology companies."[clxiii]

Brand Positioning and Communications Strategy

Forrester does little or no advertising, so it communicates its brand through its website, its published reports, its events, its employees, its offices, and its many media mentions during the course of a year. Its brand supports the concept of "We make leaders successful every day."

Internal Branding That's Baked In

Forrester culture focuses on developing qualified and confident analysts who provide compelling research and analysis. Colony sets the tone with his analysis and creative insight and the demands he places on his staff. Great care is given to the training and nurturing of staff in a way that encourages individual achievement as well as collaboration. This results in a company that feels driven and laid back, informal but highly focused, individualistic and collaborative.[clxiv]

Forrester designed its infrastructure to build confidence, collaboration, individual achievement, and insight.

Brand Orientation

Every business card has the company values on the back, written as "4C2Q1S," which is shorthand for the seven values of the company. The 4 *C*s are client, communications, creativity, and consistency; the 2 *Q*s are quality and quickness; the 1 *S* stands for service. These values pose tradeoffs that employees must learn to balance. For example, quickness in response to clients is important, but quality can't be compromised. Creativity and consistency can at first seem to be at odds with each other, but the two values urge employees to think creatively while acting in a consistent, high-quality manner. The company expects everyone to internalize these seven values and use them as talking points with outsiders.

Mentorship and Feedback

How do analysts live the Forrester brand? They learn how to write slide decks, analyze the research, and make speeches by watching seasoned analysts. Analysts are measured by client ratings on documents and on speeches. Additionally, Forrester has an estimated 20,000 inquiries a year from its clients, and they measure analysts on how quickly they respond. Every inquiry is supposed to be acknowledged by the analyst within 24 hours. Overall, 98 percent of inquiries meet this goal.

Knowledge Leadership

In the late 1990s, Forrester began fielding an annual survey of online households called "Technographics." Now it is the largest ongoing consumer survey specializing in computer and Internet use. The survey includes a panel of 10,000 US households, surveys of 250,000 consumers in the United States and Canada, and surveys of European and Asian consumers as well. Forrester has used this capability to help distinguish itself as having deep capability for understanding Internet usage trends.

Event Infrastructure

Client conferences are another piece of internal branding infrastructure. It starts with registration. While the analysts and outside keynote speaker are the main features of these events, Forrester staff has an important supporting role. Forrester assigns staff to specific attendees at registration so that all attendees are looked after throughout the conference. This ensures a high level of relationship building and reaffirms the 4C2Q1S brand tool.

Forrester puts a lot of emphasis on the quality of its analysts' speeches. "The rule of 20" is the number of times analysts practice speeches. The speech has to be memorized, or close to it, so the speaker can anticipate and easily comment on all the questions that arise. About 5 days before the event, speakers dress in a suit, go into a large meeting room, and present to Forrester peers. Analysts compete for the best peer ratings.

Office Design

Analysts work in pods of 8 to 10 people. They came up with this design when, in 1994, the company launched its first major Internet study. Previously, the company had had separate offices with a common room for computer tables—"the room where we always had the most fun," according to Colony. At the outset of the study, Colony suggested that a group of 8 to 10 core analysts tackle this study in a large room like the computer room and volunteered to be part of the group. As he describes it, "We shared our tears and our fears. And at the end of the year, we danced on our desks to celebrate our success." They have operated in pods ever since.[clxv]

All Forrester offices around the world have similar furniture and the same connection to Internet and internal information technology systems. Even the jacks on the wall are consistently color-coded so analysts can set up immediately in any office.

Infrastructure is an often overlooked aspect of internal branding. But these processes are critically important to employee alignment and building a unique brand experience. The additional upfront work and budget they require is offset by the consistency that good process brings to internal branding.

---

cl Moore, *Crossing the Chasm,* 12-54

cli Volpp, Troxel, Norton, et al, "Financial Incentive–Based Approaches for Weight Loss."

clii Vovchuk, "How to Identify Cost Efficient Ways."

cliii Virginia Vovchuk (director of brand strategy and design, AAA Northern California, Nevada, and Utah), in discussion with the authors, October 2009.

cliv Ibid.

clv Ibid.

clvi Ibid.

clvii "Services," accessed October 28, 2009, http://www.healthpointchc.org/Services

clviii "Community," accessed October 28, 2009, http://www.healthpointchc.org/Services/Community

clix PR Newswire, "Hertz Announces New, Elite Levels for #1 Club Gold Members in the US," http://www2.prnewswire.com/cgi-bin/stories.pl?ACCT=104&STORY=/www/story/07-11-2000/0001262390&EDATE

clx Srinivasan, "Southwest Airlines Operations."

clxi Schwartz, "Life/Work: Issue 41."

clxii "The 200 Best Small Companies, #160 Forrester Research," *Forbes Magazine.*

clxiii "*Business 2.0*: 100 Fastest-Growing Tech Companies."

clxiv Schwartz, Life/Work: Issue 41."

clxv Ibid.

SECTION III

Sustaining Your Brand

CHAPTER 15

Internal Branding Measurement

Effective internal branding creates value. Internal branding contributes to customer brand loyalty, product price premiums, lower overhead and employee related costs, and the ability to attract and retain the best employees. But without effective measurements, you won't be able to sustain internal branding. For senior management to take brand seriously and appropriately budget for it, they need an accurate picture of its contributions.

Financial types first began to measure the brand value of packaged goods companies to facilitate mergers in the 1970s and 1980s. Many of these companies had few hard assets yet received large sums for intangible brand value. The goodwill brand value represented the predictability of future sales and profits that a brand or set of brands offered, even when managed by a new owner.

These valuations gave credence to the idea that brands had value beyond a company's revenues and profits. Since then, many methods of measuring brand value have been put forth, but none have accurately predicted monetary value. In a 2004 study by German business magazine Absatzwirtschaft and Price Waterhouse Coopers that compared alternative brand valuation approaches, a fictitious brand was valued by 9 institutions. The resulting brand values ranged from 173 million euros to 958 million euros.[clxvi] This is why we don't recommend using brand valuation as your primary internal branding measurement. Nevertheless, it does make sense to measure brand actions that accrue to the bottom line.

The importance of intangible brand assets can't be overstated. Many of today's strongest brands—such as IBM, GE, Microsoft, and

McDonalds—all have substantial service components in their offerings. As a result, their values are tied to the approach every employee takes every day to do their job as well as to the products they deliver. It's a given in service companies that management teams must invest in their people to be competitive. From there, it's a small step to place value on and measure what you do well, what customers value, and what you can own (see chapter 14). The best brand valuation systems are those that measure employee, customer, and community understanding of a brand in all its forms and then provide clear direction for brand improvement.

The following internal branding measurement checkpoints show one model for effectively measuring the customer experience. You can use this to think about what to measure or compare it to your existing brand measurement system to look for gaps. Regardless, internal branding checkpoint measurement should be based on the brand promise with an emphasis on continuous improvement.

Box 14—Internal Branding Measurement Checkpoints

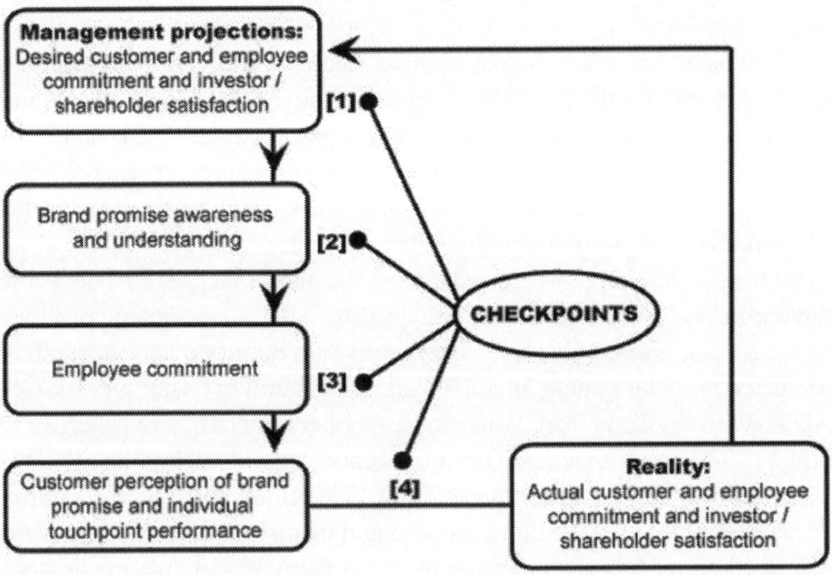

Checkpoint 1:

- Customer and employee brand goals
    - Satisfaction (customer and employee requirements, perceived quality in relation to competitors)
    - Loyalty (customer and employee engagement)
    - Advocacy (trust, readiness to recommend brand to others)
- Shareholder/Investor level
    - Brand equity

Checkpoint 2: Review brand promise and brand tools to get answers to the following questions:

- Is our brand promise understood?
- Do people emotionally identify with it?
- Do people believe it?
- Does it need clarifying or changing?
- Are there differences in views among different stakeholders?
- Is there awareness of brand tools?
- What is the perception of how they are put into practice?
- What are the views of different stakeholders on the brand promise?
- How can commitment to the brand promise be strengthened?
- What changes should be made in future strategies or plans?
- What changes should be made in our practices to support the brand?
- What changes are needed in brand management or measurement?
- Is any other action required?

Checkpoint 3: Employee level

- Knowledge/understanding of brand promise/brand tools
- Emotional identification with brand promise
- Understanding and effectiveness of performance and reward systems
- Individual and team performance (team members all pulling the same way, doing their jobs in ways that live the brand)

Checkpoint 4: Customer reality

- Awareness and commitment to brand and brand promise
- Perception of communications/marketing activities
- Perception of staff performance
- Willingness to pay price premiums
- Willingness to recommend
- Gap analysis
- Recommendations for improvement

What to Measure

We recommend measuring four areas to help organizations codify results and make improvements:

- Brand Equity
- Brand Tool Understanding and Application
- Value Versus Performance
- Brand Assets

Brand Equity

Brand equity measures emotional and cognitive indicators that are associated with employee commitment. Interactions that result in emotional bonding with customers and cognitive understanding of your vision reinforce loyalty. They result in an increased willingness to pay a price premium and to recommend your products to others. Therefore, measuring baseline brand equity and subsequent movement indicates what's working and what isn't.

Employee brand equity measurements typically include measuring whether employees are:

- ✓ talking about your brand online;
- ✓ willing to recommend your organization to others as a place to work or buy products;
- ✓ willing to work for less money than they would for a competitor;

- ✓ giving you high overall opinion and day-to-day experience ratings; and
- ✓ giving you high product quality and customer service ratings.

Brand Tool Understanding and Application

Effective every day use of brand tools by every employee is key to a strong and authentic brand. Asking a series of open-ended questions about brand tool understanding and use will help you gauge how well your brand is translated into action. Ask employees questions such as: What is our promise? What is our strategic role and guiding principle? How do you deliver it? What do you do differently based on these tools? What story do you tell when asked about the company? What are some of the ways we do things around here? These are all ways to measure understanding and use.

Value Versus Performance

Value versus performance is a more directed way to measure employee brand knowledge and morale. In this instance, you are asking employees to rate predetermined brand concepts in terms of their absolute value to customers and how well employees think customers will say the company performed on each concept. For example, you might ask them, "Please rate the importance of same-day customer service when choosing a company of this type." You would then ask, "Please rate how well you think our company performs on this criterion." The difference between the absolute value given and company performance is called the *gap*. Significant negative gaps (performance lower than absolute value) demonstrate areas where employees believe the company needs to improve. Sometimes this reflects a real customer brand experience gap, but for others it's an internal, self-image problem. Either finding is helpful in fine-tuning your internal branding.

Brand Assets

Brand tools are based on brand assets. Brand assets can be anything from a software system that allows people to easily track their packages anywhere in the world (DHL) to health care call center workers who represent hospital brands with a uniquely personal touch (Beryl). The value of internal branding is closely tied to the assets built by employees. If you understand what your assets are and further understand their value to customers, you can then include asset management in your internal branding. Identifying and measuring these assets will also ensure that you don't accidentally destroy a valuable company practice.

Case Study: Measuring a Global Brand Powerhouse [Henkel]

Henkel is a conglomerate with sales in approximately125 countries of 750 product brands. Headquartered in Düsseldorf, Germany, it has about 52,000 employees worldwide in three business areas: laundry and home care, cosmetics and toiletries, and adhesive technologies.[clxvii]

Image of Persil. Used with permission from Henkel AG and Co. KGaA.

The company advanced branding practice 100 years ago with the introduction of Persil. In 1907, Persil was branded as the first self-acting laundry detergent, which meant it eliminated the need for the toil of the washboard and the step of sun-bleaching.[clxviii] Henkel is now breaking new ground with a globally managed and measured brand. Its reason for doing this is to increase value: "If the company is now positioned and managed systematically as a brand, this will provide additional potentials for increasing corporate value."[clxix]

The company determined that its brand should stand for a series of values including economic, ecological and social responsibility; innovation; and quality. All of these are reflected in its vision of "Making people's lives easier, better, and more beautiful." This, in turn, is translated to employees and customers as a "global brand for quality of life."[clxx] Henkel believes that "trust in the Henkel brand, paired with trust in its individual product brands, plays an increasingly important role for sales success."[clxxi]

Henkel uses an eloquent tree metaphor to describe how this translates into employee behavior:

> The daily striving to fulfill our Vision and live our Values results in an identity, a very specific Henkel identity. The idea was not and is not that of creating uniform Henkel people but rather that of combining individuality and group identity in a way that permits us to function as a cohesive team. Just as no two leaves on a tree are identical and yet each leaf tells us what tree it comes from.[clxxii]

As a shorthand for this vision/value brand promise, Henkel has developed an ingredient brand that it has translated into 13 languages—"Quality and responsibility."

[clxxiii]

Henkel has been adding this mark to all laundry and home care packaging since 2008.

Finally, Henkel positions itself with a tagline that helps define the emotional state it wants to achieve with its customers: "A Brand Like a Friend." Helmut Sihler, former chairman of the Henkel management board, says it this way:

> The old statement was "Henkel—Specialist in Applied Chemistry." This was a description of capability but did not trigger any emotions . . . . An offer is always a commitment, too. Not only must the products satisfy this claim, but the employees [must] as well.[clxxiv]

One measure of Henkel's global branding initiative success has been how well it's been supported by senior management. This has been graphically displayed by Henkel to employee audiences in its internal newsletter.

[clxxv]

Henkel Internal Newsletter.

Another measurement that Henkel uses is based on being the global brand for quality of life to improving employee safety and global sustainability.

Henkel's Sustainability Performance clxxvi

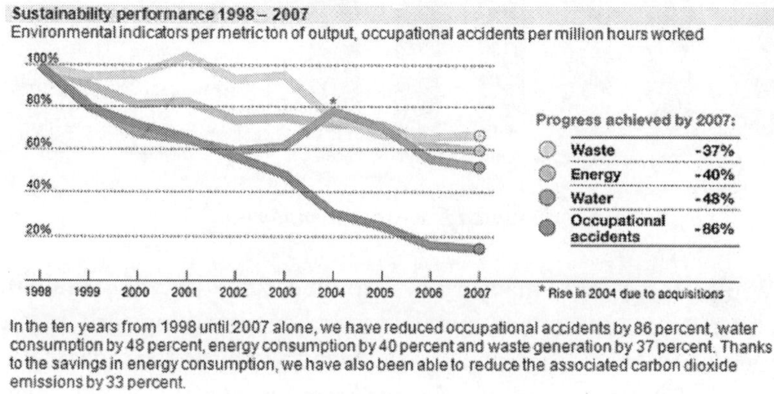

Henkel has also set 2012 targets based on its past track record.

Henkel's 2012 Targets clxxvii

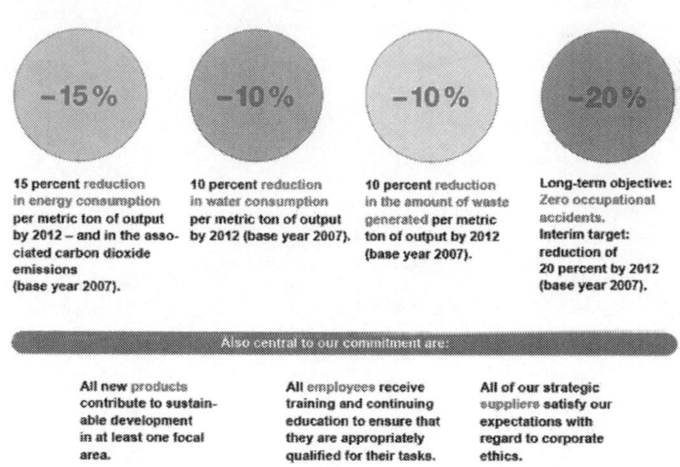

Henkel uses multiple brand valuation models coupled with "harder" figures such as sales increases to show brand value growth.

Brand Value of Henkel 2001 to 2006

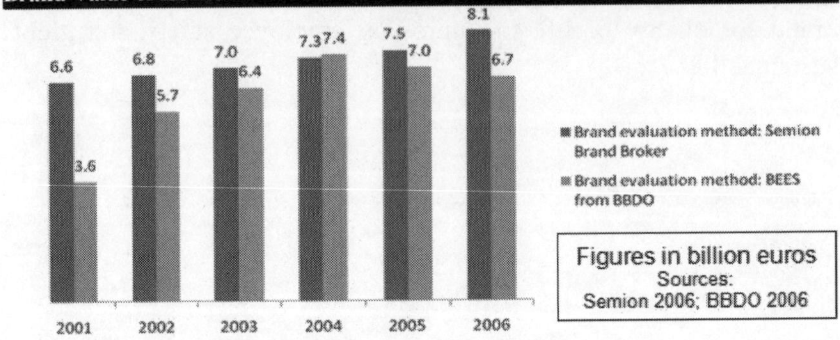

Image recreated from source material.[clxxviii]

While there are many ways to measure internal branding effectiveness, the important thing is to start benchmarking early in your program's life. Measurement keeps the brand's value to the organization at the top of the mind and justifies program investment. Measurement also allows you to see cumulative results and therefore reinforces the importance of living the brand to everyone.

[clxvi] Seiwert M., "Führende Markenbewertungsverfahren im Vergleich", 34-37

[clxvii] "About Henkel," accessed October 28, 2009, http://www.henkel.com/about-henkel-11779.htm

[clxviii] "Henkel Company History," accessed October 28, 2009, http://www.henkel.com/about-henkel/company-history-24908.htm

[clxix] Krug, Primosch, Schmidhuber, et al, "Henkel-Life," http://www.henkel.co.kr/krk/content_data/78132_HL5yoABlaF.pdf

[clxx] Ibid.

[clxxi] Ibid.

[clxxii] Ibid.

[clxxiii] "Modern Laundry and Home Care Detergents Offer More Performance While Saving on Resources," accessed October 28, 2009, http://www.henkel.com/laundry-and-home-care/news-11580-modern-laundry-and-home-care-detergents-offer-more-14719.htm

[clxxiv] Krug, Primosch, Schmidhuber, et al, "Henkel-Life," http://www.henkel.co.kr/krk/content_data/78132_HL5yoABlaF.pdf

[clxxv] Ibid.

[clxxvi] "Our Objectives,", http://www.henkelna.com/sustainability/objectives-9246.htm

[clxxvii] Ibid.

[clxxviii] Krug, Primosch, Schmidhuber, et al, "Henkel-Life," http://www.henkel.co.kr/krk/content_data/78132_HL5yoABlaF.pdf

CHAPTER 16

Surviving the Visionary

All great brands start somewhere. Most begin in the minds of a company founder, who then gets everyone else enthused. The visionary CEO keeps the company on track long enough for the followers to see results. But what happens to a strong brand when the visionary steps down and a new CEO steps in? While companies hire successors for their experience and unique abilities, new CEOs who don't understand branding frequently do great harm. When Michael Dell stepped down as CEO of Dell Computer, the company's exemplary service brand seemed to leave with him, damaging that core company asset.

When companies conduct CEO searches, they frequently give lip service to brand and culture fit, but these are rarely primary hiring criteria. If a primary CEO task is leadership, then new CEOs must explicitly understand the need for them to adopt the role of chief brand champion. According to Eric Kriss, a two-time *Inc 500* CEO, "The basic job of a CEO is a leadership job. By leadership, I mean the pursuit of a coherent strategy and the marshaling of all resources to be able to pursue that strategy."[clxxix]

How can CEO succession ensure brand continuity? By ensuring that CEO candidates fully buy into your brand, brand model, and brand practices before taking the job. One of the best investments an organization can make is to create a successor's survival guide while the current CEO is still in place. Think of this like a living will—when you need it, it will be there to direct you.

Guide Elements

A guide includes the accumulated wisdom of the current CEO and brand team with examples of on-brand strategy development. It covers everything the new CEO needs to lead, particularly regarding the aspects of strategy, alignment, and infrastructure.

Include your brand tools, metrics, strategies, and brand architecture with specific examples of each. Here's a quick review of what to include:

- ✓ Brand Tools: These are how you deliver your brand promise. They include your strategic role, guiding principle, personality, story, and cultural norms. They may also include your vision, mission, and values.
- ✓ Strategies: These are the actions that you will take in a given year as a result of the question, "What do we need to add, change, or eliminate to build a stronger brand?" They are part of your strategic business plan. The entire strategic plan is driven by your strategic role, which can be thought of as your über strategy.
- ✓ Architecture: This describes how the company's master brand and its product sub-brands relate to each other from a customer's point of view and typically includes value propositions for each sub-brand.
- ✓ Metrics: These benchmark and track progress in ways that allow you to make improvements. Metrics measure the level of brand strength of core audiences, including employees, customers, and communities.

The CEO's Personal Brand Perspective

There's always more to understand about a brand beyond its component pieces. One of the most important parts of the guide is a section in which the CEO talks about your brand in their own words. This can look like a letter, a blog, or a video—whatever is natural. It really helps if the CEO can cite examples of how they put the brand into action.

This succession approach isn't an industry norm. If there is even a letter from the former CEO, it's usually about what was accomplished during that CEO's reign. Rarely do CEOs codify the principles and strategies they used to build the company. This is a huge opportunity squandered. We believe this happens because this kind of knowledge has typically been considered 'soft'—not something that has an impact on the bottom line. Succession is like a merger, in which studies show that high failure rates are often connected to cultural problems.[clxxx]

The concept of passing on knowledge from one generation to the next is as old as human existence, but its value as a succession tool for company brands has yet to be fully plumbed.

The New CEO and the Old Brand

Since an effective brand promise sets boundaries rather than rules for brand actions, it follows that the new CEO will want and need to put their own stamp on the brand. A management transition is an opportunity for organizations to think in new ways. This opportunity, though, should mean interpreting the brand differently not throwing it out. The current CEO of Ben & Jerry's, Walt Freese, is one of the most successful purveyors of premium ice creams ever and a long way down the line from the founders of the company. Yet his actions reinforce the original brand while adding his unique take. If the brand was originally about being socially responsible, Walt's addition can be interpreted as "Making a good profit." The following is from an article about Freese's address to students at Georgetown University's McDonough School of Business in 2007:

> "Brand is what people say about you when you're not in the room," Ben & Jerry's CEO Walt Freese told a group of marketing students last week [. . .]. Characterizing the ice cream company's marketing strategy as "conscious capitalism," Freese assured students, "You can lead with your values and deliver shareholder value too." According to Freese, Ben & Jerry's aims to build a brand that reflects an image of the company as a responsible member of society and a progressive force for social and economic justice. "We want people to see us as a company that stands for something," Freese asserts, "and we try and keep our social

mission and marketing separate—consumers can see through the artifice."[clxxxi]

Leveraging Internal Visionaries

Once you introduce employees to and begin aligning them with your brand, groups of brand champions will emerge. You can use champions to help the succession team navigate the CEO transition. Champions can give the new CEO a lot of moral support, provided they work within the company's existing brand model. Strong brands also discourage CEO personality cults, because people focus on brand delivery rather than blindly follow a leader.

Training managers in brand building is the other piece of the succession puzzle. This organizational harmony only comes through discipline, consistency, and time. Much of the effort that produces brand-minded managers is described in the preceding chapters: hiring the right people, training them according to the internal branding vision using brand tools, and holding them to performance criteria that bolster the brand.

Internal branding resists a command-and-control structure. For example, almost from its founding, Mayo Clinic had decentralization of internal branding responsibility as a part of its DNA. The organization's collaborative, team-based medical care is in contrast with the model of care focused on a star physician. This collaborative approach, aimed at delivering a patient-centric experience, requires everyone in the organization to take individual and collective responsibility for putting the patient first. With the number of interactions with patients and other employees every day, it would be impossible to impose an authoritative, centralized control over every interaction. Every employee takes the patient first vision seriously, because that is what they have been hired and trained to do. The strength of the Mayo Clinic brand is a function of the strength of every employee's commitment to the brand.

A very similar story could be told for McKinsey, Four Seasons, Beryl, Group Health, and Southwest Airlines as well. While all of these organizations started with a brand promise, ongoing responsibility for brand delivery is in the hands of all employees. In order to build a sustainable brand, this decentralizing must take place.

Succession Done Well

When Marvin Bower stepped down as McKinsey CEO, he did several things that conveyed the importance of the McKinsey brand. Given the central role he played in building McKinsey, creating and nurturing its brand promise and guiding it through decades of growth and success, it would have been understandable for Bower to use the occasion of his departure to reap some of the bounty that his work had sowed. He could have cashed out by banking all of his shares in anticipation of an enormous future payday; he could have handpicked his successor; he could have even pushed through some kind of significant organizational or strategic change.

Instead, Bower sent a clear message to the organization by cashing in his shares of McKinsey stock at book value—in effect giving away significant amounts of money—so that the younger members of the firm could be given shares.[clxxxii] He also left the selection of his successor up to the vote of the partners. Through these actions, Bower articulated many of the core values of the organization including the "One firm" brand promise with its ethos of sublimating the personal to the organization; the sense of responsibility and contribution to peers and the firm.

Succession in high-level positions is both a threat and an opportunity for your brand. The key to internal branding success, especially when you change CEOs, is to create continuity between the past and the present. Making brand buy-in a job prerequisite for candidates and the creation of a succession guide are two ways to ensure continuity and future brand success.

Case Study: The Rise and Fall of a German Mail Order Giant [Quelle]

80-year-old German mail order firm, Quelle, is an example of a company that lost its innovative leadership after the passing of its founder Gustav Schickedanz in 1977 and his wife, Grete Schickedanz, in 1994.[clxxxiii]

In the 1920s, Gustav Schickedanz was a young merchant with a big idea. He had a vision of bringing affordable luxury to the general population. The concept of democratizing luxury by selling quality goods at lower prices made Quelle a predecessor to such current brands as H&M and IKEA. He was able to accomplish this by eliminating the intermediary and providing goods directly from the manufacturer. He combined this distribution model with innovative mail order marketing, which was only used for some specialty items at the time. This gave Quelle a specific advantage in rural areas, which uniformly lacked retail infrastructure.

After the Second World War, Quelle's revenues grew rapidly from 260 million Deutsche marks in 1954 to 6.4 billion Deutsche marks in 1974. By then, the company had more than 36,000 employees serving 25 million German customers with about 10 million catalogs per season. Although Gustav Schickedanz turned his mail order business into a group of synergistic business activities—for example, he owned Germany's national paper mill that produced not only the catalogs for the mail order business but also handkerchiefs for the German population—he never lost his focus on building customer trust.

By the time Gustav died, Quelle was a household name in almost every European country. Although growth slowed in the 1980s, his wife Grete was able to create a new era of prosperity for the brand by overwhelming East German households with catalogs as soon as the Wall fell in 1989.

When Grete Schickedanz died in 1994, the new CEO didn't provide the same innovative, entrepreneurial leadership; the management style became reactive. Partnerships, which had long been key to sales and distribution, became less of a focus. Management began to focus on short-term gains rather than on stable, long-term growth. This focus on the financials of the business was further exacerbated in 1998, when Quelle merged with Karstadt, the biggest warehouse retailer in Germany, in order to turn the former family-owned business into a publicly listed corporation. As a result of the merger, the company rebranded itself as Arcandor and reframed its promise from affordable luxury to strictly talking to investors about its financial goals.

According to brand experts Jack G. Kaikati and Andrew M. Kaikati:

> Following the global rebranding crowd blindly may be not only costly but counterproductive. Each company has to identify its rebranding motives and objectives concisely [. . .] While the rebranding responsibility may be delegated

> to the marketing department, top management must sponsor the initiative and model behavior that supports the rebranding initiative.[clxxxiv]

In the case of Arcandor, the CEO and management didn't reinforce or create a customer value–based successor to the Quelle promise about affordable luxury, thereby effectively leverage its nearly 100 percent German public awareness. Further, the focus on financial results instead of customer-based values may have contributed to Arcandor not seeing the implications of the web and therefore not following its customers into online shopping, which subsequently replaced much of the mail order business. The company was liquidated in October 2009 and sold to competitor Otto for 65 million euro—15 years after the death of its last visionary.

Retail analyst Marco Atzberger describes it this way, "Fundamentally, Quelle is a great German brand. It is a great name that awakens a lot of associations [. . .] It is a name with history that stands for a great past. Everyone remembers seeing the catalog on their table at home. It is a brand that radiates trust and security. That has, however, been somewhat shaken by what has happened, but it does not mean that this trust cannot be won back." Writing about the situation, Julie Gregson said, "In addition to the problems caused by Arcandor's failure, Atzberger said Quelle had also made mistakes in recent years. 'It did not manage to sufficiently expand its Internet business and remained too focused on the catalog.'"[clxxxv]

There are several lessons to learn from Quelle. First, a strong, integrated brand is a tremendously robust system. It not only takes a huge effort to build one; it also takes a huge effort to destroy one. Brand failure does not occur by happenstance. It is part of a chain of actions—often beginning with the loss of a CEO visionary and the lack of a process to hire and align the new CEO with the brand promise.

CEO understanding of the brand promise is the single most important predictor of sustained financial success. This can be observed with Apple and Starbucks; when the original visionaries left so did focus and profitability. When Apple's founder Steve Jobs returned, the company recaptured its former brand brilliance with products like the iPod and the iPhone. Starbucks, hurt by competition and a perceived decline in the taste of its coffee, recaptured its market leadership with the return of Howard Shultz, who immediately began to create new coffee drinks and better preparation methods.

Does this mean that brands can't survive the visionary? No. But it does mean that they are much more likely to survive and thrive when the company has a visionary succession plan that results in a new CEO who understands and bases their actions and vision on the brand promise. A brand-centered CEO and active internal branding ensure long-term market share and financial success because they build on enduring brand value.

[clxxix] Reingold, "The Most Dangerous Hire."

[clxxx] LePla, Davis, and Parker, *Brand Driven,* 291-314

[clxxxi] "Ben & Jerry's CEO Discusses 'The Power of the Brand' with McDonough Students," Georgetown University McDonough School of Business press release, April 25, 2007.

[clxxxii] "Marvin Bower," McKinsey, accessed October 27, 2009, http://www.mckinsey.com/en/About_us/History/Marvin_Bower.aspx

[clxxxiii] "Quelle Case Study," unpublished text and materials provided by Christiane Arnscheidt.

[clxxxiv] Kaikati, and Kaikati, "A Rose by Any Other Name."

[clxxxv] Gregson, "Otto Picks the Cherries from Quelle Wreckage."

CHAPTER 17

The Future Is for the Agile

One conclusion we've reached about branding is that it's more than skin deep. The most effective brands have been based on demonstrating consistent, unique value. With social branding, that value is created in a manner that has much more to do with sharing and participation. Employees, customers, and online community members all have a hand in building the brand. If led by employee ambassadors, companies that choose to live their brands will realize the potential of a truly integrated brand. The focus of internal branding will be culture, brand tools, and brand communities that differentiate brand experience.

Websites and social media have ensured that the shift from marketing campaigns to online social brands are here to stay. The organization's job now is to convince its CEO and senior management team that this is a sea change in order to realize "first mover" advantages. This transformation to brand communities, in turn, will make the CEO's job as chief brand champion even more important. Social branding will require CEOs to personally give voice to the company's culture and brand promise. CEOs will work side-by-side with employees and customers to build a shared understanding of the organization's value.

We've shown you examples of brands that get it, firms that understand that your brand is the promise you keep and the relationships you create. History shows shining examples of companies that understood promise alignment and used it to create something amazing. Henkel and Volvo are two companies that come to mind. Kellogg and Nordstrom are two more. Given that retail pioneered modern branding, it makes sense that a company like Zappos.com should be pointing the way to what's happening next.

Developments in any given industry might make change unavoidable. In the past, many brand re-launches were the result of mergers and acquisitions. The speed of technological change demands a new level of brand flexibility. This has led to the decline of many strong brands, such as German mail order retailer Quelle. Its decline was partly caused by not responding quickly enough to the new challenges posed by e-commerce.

Web connectedness has increased the need for internal branding and has accelerated the rate of change. This giant online experiment in competition, interdependence, and individual expression is creating new experiences that your brand must address if it is to stay fresh. Therefore, agility is a necessary cultural norm of any brand that wants to stay around. Becoming truly agile is difficult, because companies and employees want to keep doing what they've done to be successful in the past. The new organizational forms that social branding will spawn will revolutionize the way companies run.

Internal Branding Best Practices Revisited

We've talked about several concepts in this study that we believe are internal branding best practices.

Use Your Strategic Role for Business Planning

Competition is always getting more intense. Even worse, markets you depend on can quickly change or even disappear. These are compelling reasons for defining your brand promise through brand tools. A strategic role will help you stay focused on what's important and allow you to interpret trends and market changes with agility and effectiveness. Although brand tools are created by a management team, they are given substance by employees. Sustainable brand building is an endeavor that demands continuous top-down, bottom-up, and horizontal exchange at all company levels.

Restore the Strategic Vision . . . Often

Brand strategies describe what you want to make happen within the boundaries of your strategic role. An effective strategic plan requires a complete understanding of your brand environment. You need to monitor the moves of competitors and the observations of analysts while listening closely to your customers and communities. Because of these factors, strategies require frequent course corrections.

Share Brand Development

Imagine if, instead of just having your senior management team, you had 50 or 500 or 5,000 thousand people all thinking about the future of your business. In our connected world, it's the community that will do the listening, talking, expressing, and selling; it will build your brand.

Internalize Change Principles

Human resources can significantly improve brand delivery by applying brand tools to employee recruiting, training, and performance. To build agility, integrate change management principles directly into the organizational knowledge base. Employees and managers need to understand how change happens, what the barriers are to making it happen, and how to help employees embrace helpful changes.

Network, Network, Network

Five years ago, we would have said, "Communicate, communicate, communicate." Now, networking is the new face of communication. Help your employees continue to learn and adapt to new social networking vehicles. From here on out, effective internal branding will have a large social branding component.

What Are You Doing Right Now?

In chapter 1, we asked you to answer some questions to measure your current brand-building capabilities. Here they are again:

- Do you have a clear and actionable brand promise?
- Does the promise include actionable brand tools such as a strategic role, a guiding principle, culture norms, a story, and a personality?
- Do you use your brand to develop strategy?
- Have you hired employees who buy into your brand?
- Are employees brand ambassadors?
- Are brand goals integrated into employee performance expectations?
- Does human resources use change management principles?
- Do your employee social media guidelines integrate your brand approach?

After reading this, you may now feel that the answers to these questions are more important than you first thought. Together, these questions point to the need for clarity, authenticity, transparency, and accountability throughout an organization; they are the building blocks of a strong brand.

Effective internal branding builds successful brands that offer clear and sustainable value. Companies that share brand-building responsibilities with employees and customers are much less vulnerable to market, product, and social changes. They are much more likely to see the road ahead.

GLOSSARY

alignment. The process of making all company actions and communications consistent with brand tool direction.
associations. Shortcuts to brand value that immediately come to mind when you hear the organization's name. Examples include the Aflac duck, the Intel Inside four-tone jingle, and the Nike swoosh.
behaviors. Specific and repeatable actions often identified with a particular corporate culture.
brand. The sum total of customer experience; includes all of your company's actions, communications, and customer interactions; results from your brand promise, strategic role, tools, culture, brand assets, practices, and communications—in short, it is the promise that you keep as an organization.
brand ambassador. Any person who appears and acts as a representative of the brand and influences the brand experience; all employees of a company, on all levels, should be aware of their roles as brand ambassadors.
brand architecture. The naming of brands and the overall structuring of the brand portfolio of an organization to enhance ease of doing business, clarity, and brand value.
brand assets. The result of any company activity that benefits customers, such as unique customer experience, unique company approach, company reputation, industry leadership position, quality control systems, employee experience/training, company culture, employee compensation and rewards, or delivery systems.

brand category. Generic classification of a company or product brand; similar and competing products (or services) fall into the same brand category. The most effective business categories align with a particular organization's brand strengths or assets.

brand community. All brand stakeholders who contribute to building the brand.

brand equity. The value your brand has in the target customer's mind. High equity brands translate into bottom-line benefits, because their customers will pay more for their products, tend not to shop around, and are influential in getting others to buy products.

brand gap. The difference between the absolute value an employee or customer places on an activity and the company's or product's rated performance for that activity.

brand heritage. The roots and history of a brand that can create higher employee identification with and understanding of your brand and culture.

brand identity. The total of all characteristics (brand tools/positioning elements) that define and are associated with the brand; the brand identity implies a promise to the brand stakeholders. The visual and verbal communications elements of a brand.

brand plan. The brand strategy broken down into work items and deliverables.

brand promise. The promise you make to and keep with customers through your product or service, consistent employee actions, and communications; defined by brand tools, which include the strategic role, guiding principle, personality, story, and cultural norms.

brand strategy. The action plan for aligning and enhancing company actions with its brand to improve the customer experience over time; should be part of the corporate strategic planning process.

brand structure. The relationship between the company's umbrella brand and sub-brands and other unbranded services; differs from an organizational structure that defines how job functions are related to each other. A brand and its related products can be delivered from a variety of organizational structures.

brand tools. The set concepts that create the framework for effective on-brand action. These may include the mission, vision, strategic role, cultural norms, guiding principle, personality, and stories that collectively define the brand promise (see positioning elements).

business category. The term the marketplace uses to classify your organization. Reinventing the business category to align closely with an organization's strengths while demonstrating it through leadership is an effective branding strategy (see brand category).
corporate culture. Your company's shared behavioral norms, values, approaches to decisions, and personality traits.
cultural norms. A shared set of actionable values that can be described as "the way we do things around here."
customer. Your clients, funders, donors, constituents, dealers, partners, or even the general public; anyone the organization sells to, sells with, or services.
customer experience. The sum total of experiences your customer has with your company, including product use, communications, sales, service, and word-of-mouth information.
customer touchpoint mapping. The process of identifying all customer interactions with your brand, creating a consistent delivery plan for every touchpoint, measuring results, and making continuous improvements.
external branding. The process of becoming that enables customers and other external stakeholders to experience the organization's brand.
guiding principle. One of the brand tools, representing a company's unique approach to its business; a compass for employees to make decisions and communicate; serves as a differentiator that provides direction for on-brand activities.
ingredient brand. A named brand that provides supporting value to other brands, often expressed as an icon.
integrated branding. The process of aligning company structure, culture, business strategy, employee actions and expression, visual brand, marketing and communications to create compelling customer experiences.
interaction. An enhanced, synergistic effect that occurs between two or more people in contrast to a unidirectional, causal effect that occurs in a transaction.
internal branding. The process of becoming that enables employees to live the organization's brand.
living the brand. An entire company taking the appropriate actions to fulfill its brand promise.

marketing. The viewing of customers in terms of markets to be sold to; a focus on transactional sales relationships.
master brand. The primary name brand that holds a shared value across all products.
measurement. Monitoring of brand-relevant metrics to supervise the success of actions and to unearth gaps for the purpose of continuous improvement.
mission. One of the brand tools, describing what a company does and the business it is in.
off-brand. An action or message that is not consistent with (and perhaps conflicts with) a company's brand tools and strategic role.
on-brand. An action or message that is consistent with a company's brand tools and strategic role.
online brand community. The group of people interacting on a web-based platform to contribute to the brand experience.
owner. The person who is responsible for making sure the work gets done.
personality. One of the brand tools, representing your brand's public face; usually experienced through the tone and manner of your communications and marketing materials.
positioning. The unique characteristics or elements that result in the distinctiveness of a brand (see brand tools). The foundational story that describes the business, benefits, and what is better about a company or product.
practices. Group activities that are necessary to conduct business; can be Inter- or intradepartmental.
social brand. Opening up your internal culture to engage your customers in online communities that encourage sharing personal information, insights, and beliefs.
sponsors. The individuals who have the power to legitimize a work item or deliverable; those who demonstrate approval through communicating decisions, prioritization, allocation of resources, reward, and redirection.
story. One of the brand tools, organizing the compelling points of the brand, including a version of its strategic role and why it's unique; can also be referred to as positioning or "elevator statement."
strategic role. An organization's über business strategy; defines the organization in the context of its relationships with customers and

answers the question, "Why must customers consider you?" Keeps companies open to new trends in meeting customer needs by taking the long-term focus off of specific products.

strong brand. A brand with a clear promise, which the organization keeps and which resonates with stakeholders' needs; a brand that engages the whole community; a brand that motivates employees, creates trust and loyalty with customers and other stakeholders, and gives companies a sustainable competitive advantage.

sub-brand. A product brand that typically has an evocative name and always exists in relation to a master brand.

sustainable business. The ability to retain a healthy market share and margins over many years; also refers to the level to which a business uses "green" practices and acts in a socially responsible manner.

touchpoints. The places where a brand is experienced, including any interaction with an employee or other customers (as often occurs in an online brand community). A company can map its touchpoints and create a plan to more consistently manage its brand experiences. While employees are frequently the delivery mechanism for the brand at a touchpoint, they can be on the receiving end of a brand experience as well.

über behaviors. Defining behaviors for the organization that are necessary to deliver its brand.

über strategy. The company's top-level business strategy.

values. One of the brand tools, representing cherished beliefs (often unwritten) that influence how individuals work and are followed even in difficult situations and one input to the formation of corporate cultures.

vision. The long-term aim and ideal that the organization and its sub-brands are continuously striving to achieve.

visual branding. A corporate identity; typically consists of a logo and business paper design but may also include graphic templates and illustration and photographic style treatments.

BIBLIOGRAPHY

"The 200 Best Small Companies: #160 Forrester Research." *Forbes*, October 14, 2009. http://www.forbes.com/lists/2009/23/small-companies-09_Forrester-Research_77TB.html

Aaker, David A., and Erich Joachimsthaler. *Brand Leadership: The Next Level of the Brand Revolution*. New York: The Free Press, 2000.

Abboud, Leila. "France Telecom Talks with Unions on Suicide Spate." *Reuters*, October 7, 2009. http:/reuters.com/article/managementissues/idUSL711729320091007?pageNumber=1&virtualBrandChannel=11604

Accenture. "Our Core Values." Accessed January 5, 2010. http://www.accenture.com/us-en/company/overview/values/Pages/index.aspx

Appel, Frank. "Group Strategy 2015." Accessed January 12, 2010. http://www.dphl.com/content/dam/dpdhl/investoren/en/investoren/publikationen/archiv/2009/praesentationen/dpwn_presentation_strategy_2015_en.pdf

Ballard. "Careers." Accessed September 30, 2009. http://www.ballard.com/About_Ballard/Careers/

— "Business Focus." Accessed September 30, 2009. http://www.ballard.com/About_Ballard/Corporate_Direction/Business_Focus.

"Ben & Jerry's CEO Discusses 'The Power of the Brand' with McDonough Students." Georgetown University McDonough School of Business press release, April 25, 2007. http://msb.georgetown.edu/story/1242660543074.html

Berry, Leonard L. "The Collaborative Organization: Leadership Lessons from Mayo Clinic." *Organizational Dynamics* 33 (2004): 228-242.

Bridges, William. *Managing Transitions: Making the Most of Change*. Cambridge, MA: Da Capo Press, 2003.

"*Business 2.0:* 100 Fastest-Growing Tech Companies." *CNNMoney* June 2006. http://money.cnn.com/magazines/business2/b2fastest growing/snapshots/89.html

City of Olympia Public Works. "Public Works Business Plan 2008." Accessed October 2, 2009. http://olympiawa.gov/documents/PublicWorks/business_plan/2008_Business_Plan.pdf

Clark, Evelyn. *Around the Corporate Campfire: How Great Leaders Use Stories to Inspire Success*. Sevierville, TN: Insight Publishing Company, 2004.

Clifford, Stephanie. "A Video Prank at Domino's Taints Brand." *New York Times*, April 15, 2009. http://www.nytimes.com/2009/04/16/business/media/16dominos.html

Coppetti, C. "Young and Rubicam's Brand Asset Consulting." Unpublished raw data, last modified 2005, word

Crosby, Jackie. "Social Animal." *Star Tribune*, November 22, 2009. http://www.startribune.com/business/70972522.html

Davis, A. *Bringing the Brand to Life: How Mayo Clinic Encourages Employees at All Levels to Deliver the Brand Promise*. Washington, DC: Advanced Learning Institute, 2006.

Denning, Stephen. *The Leader's Guide to Storytelling: Mastering the Art and Discipline of the Business Narrative*. San Francisco, CA: Jossey-Bass, 2005.

DHL. "DHL Divisions." Accessed January 31, 2010. http://dhl-sy.com/old/dhldivision.htm

— *DHL Employer Branding E-Handbook*. Bonn, Germany: Deutsche Post AG, 2009.

— "DHL Material Based on DHL Research." Unpublished raw data, last modified 2005, word.

— "McKinsey & Company/MCM Marketing Centrum Münster." Unpublished raw data, last modified 2002, word

"DHL Company Story Contest." Unpublished DHL intranet site, last modified 2007.

Edelman. "Annual Edelman Trust Barometer." http://edelmaneditions.com/wp-content/uploads/2010/12/edelman-trust-barometer-2006.pdf

"Firmen profitieren von Familienförderung." *Financial Times Deutschland*, September 3, 2003.

"*Fortune* Global Most Admired Companies 2006." *CNNMoney*. http://money.cnn.com/magazines/fortune/globalmostadmired/top50/

Four Seasons. "About Us." Accessed July 7, 2009. http://www.fourseasons.com/about_us/

"GE's 2008 ecomagination Revenues to Rise 21%, Cross $17 Billion." General Electric press release, October 21, 2008. http://www.gereports.com/wp—http://www.gereports.com/wp-content/uploads/2008/10/ecomagination_2008-revenues-forecast-october-21-_2_.pdf

General Electric. "About the Challenge." Accessed October 5, 2009. http://ecocollegechallenge.com/aboutTheChallenge.html

— "Ecomagination." Accessed October 3, 2009. http://www.ecomagination.com/

Good, Catherine Bamber Crowden. "Führen durch Marken: Interdependenz von Marken, Markenführung und CEO-Rollen" PhD diss., Universität St. Gallen, 2008. http://www1.unisg.ch/www/edis.nsf/wwwDisplayIdentifier/3422/$FILE/dis3422.pdf

Great Place to Work. "2007 Best Small and Medium Companies to Work for in America." Accessed July 2, 2009. http://www.greatplacetowork.com/what_we_do/lists-us-sme-2007.htm

Gregson, Julie. "Otto Picks the Cherries from Quelle Wreckage." *Deutsche Welle,* June 11, 2009. http://www.dw-world.de/dw/article/0,4866328,00.html

Group Health. "Group Health Medical Centers Rated in 2009 'Community Checkup'." Accessed January 6, 2010. http://www.ghc.org/about_gh/Quality/PSHA2009.jhtml

HealthPoint. "Community." Accessed October 28, 2009. http://www.healthpointchc.org/Services/Community

— "Services." Accessed October 28, 2009. http://www.healthpointchc.org/Services

Henkel. "About Henkel." Accessed October 28, 2009. http://www.henkel.com/about-henkel-11779.htm

— "Henkel Company History." Accessed October 28, 2009. http://www.henkel.com/about-henkel/company-history-24908.htm

—"Modern Laundry and Home Care Detergents Offer More Performance While Saving on Resources." Accessed October 28, 2009. http://www.henkel.com/laundry-and-home-care/news-11580-modern-laundry-and-home-care-detergents-offer-more-14719.htm

— "Our Objectives." Accessed October 27, 2009 http://www.henkelna.com/sustainability/objectives-9246.htm

"Hertz Announces New, Elite Levels for #1 Club Gold Members in the US: Revamps Its #1 Club Membership with Free Upgrade to #1 Club Gold Service." *PR Newswire*, July 11, 2000. http://www2.prnewswire.com/cgi-bin/stories.pl?ACCT=104&STORY=/www/story/07-11-2000/0001262390&EDATE

Hewitt. "Best Employer Canada." Accessed July 2, 2009. http://was2.hewitt.com/bestemployers/canada/pages/index.htm

HSBC home page. Accessed October 3, 2009. http://www.hsbc.com/1/2/home

Hsieh, Tony. "Letter from the CEO." Accessed October 8, 2009. http://culturebook.erinkjones.com/letter-ceo

IBM. "IBM Social Computing Guidelines: Blogs, Wikis, Social Networks, Virtual Worlds and Social Media." Accessed October 8, 2009. http://www.ibm.com/blogs/zz/en/guidelines.html

ING home page. Accessed October 3, 2009. http://www.ing.be/private/index.jsp

Intel. "Intel Social Media Guidelines." Accessed October 8, 2009. http://www.intel.com/sites/sitewide/en_us/social-media.htm

InterBrand. "Best Global Brands 2008." Accessed September 26, 2009. http://www.interbrand.com/en/best-global-brands/best-global-brands-2008/best-global-brands-2008.aspx

Kaikati, Jack G., and Andrew M. Kaikati. "A Rose by Any Other Name: Rebranding Campaigns That Work." *Journal of Business Strategy* 24 (2003): 17-23, doi: 10.1108/02756660310509451

Koppel, Tom. *Powering the Future: The Ballard Fuel Cell and the Race to Change the World.* Hoboken, NJ: John Wiley & Sons, 1999.

Krug, V., E. Primosch, K. Schmidhuber, J. Sterzenbach, and B. Swoboda. "Henkel-Life: 5 years of 'A Brand like a Friend.'" http://www.henkel.co.kr/krk/content_data/78132_HL5yoABlaF.pdf

Labhart, Gaby. "Das Geheimnis des Schäumchens. Wie gelingt der perfekte Espresso?" *SonntagsZeitung*, May 7, 2007. http://www.rogalla.ch/upload/rogalla/files/Kopie_sonntagszeitung.ch___Trend.pdf

LePla, F. Joseph, Susan V. Davis, and Lynn M. Parker. *Brand Driven: The Route to Integrated Branding Through Great Leadership*. Bloomington, IN: AuthorHouse, 2003.

"Markenwelten—marken und ihre macher, Weltmarke DHL." *Europa Fachpresse-Verlag,* München: Germany, 2007.

Mayo Clinic home page. Accessed October 7, 2009. http://www.mayoclinic.com

Mayo Clinic. "Connection." Accessed October 7, 2009. http://www.mayoclinic.org/connection/

— "Our Shared Commitment." Accessed October 7, 2009. http://www.mayoclinic.org/mcitems/mc0700-mc0799/mc0710-2007.pdf

Mayo, William J. "Mayo Clinic" Accessed October 7, 2009. http://www.mayoclinic.org/about/missionvalues.html

McCarthy, Jim. *Entertainment Habits Survey Results.* Altadena, CA: Goldstar Events, 2007.

McKinsey. "Marvin Bower." Accessed October 27, 2009. http://www.mckinsey.com/en/About_us/History/Marvin_Bower.aspx

Medtronic. "Mission and Culture." Accessed October 2, 2009. http://www.medtronic.com/careers/mission-culture/index.htm

Meffert, Heribert, Cristoph Burmann, and Martin Koers. *Markenmanagement: Grundfragen der identitätsorientierten Markenführung*. Germany: Gabler Verlag, 1st edition, 2002.

Miles, Raymond E., and Charles C. Snow. *Organizational Strategy, Structure and Process*. Stanford, CA: Stanford University Press, 2003.

Miles, Sandra Jeanquart, and W. Glynn Mangold. "Positioning Southwest Airlines Through Employee Branding." *Harvard Business Review*, November 15, 2005. http://hbr.org/product/positioning-southwest-airlines-through-employee-br/an/BH180-PDF-ENG

Millward Brown. "BrandZ Ranking." Accessed October 2, 2009. http://www.millwardbrown.com/Sites/mbOptimor/BrandZ/default.aspx

Moore, Geoffrey A. *Crossing the Chasm: Marketing and Selling High-Tech Products to Mainstream Customers*. New York: Harper Collins, 1999.

Nespresso. "New Nespresso Flagship in Munich Debuts Personalized Service Concept to Further Enhance the Ultimate Coffee Experience Accessed October 3, 2006. http://www.nespresso.com/mediacenter/index.php?page=international-press-detail&id=3

Nestlé. "The Nestlé Creating Shared Value Report." Last modified March 2008. http://www.nestle.com/Common/NestléDocuments/Documents/Library/Documents/Corporate_Social_Responsibility/Nestlé-CSV-Report-Mar2008-EN.pdf

Palmisano, Samuel J. "Our Values at Work on Being an IBMer: Business Value, and a Company's Value." Accessed October 8, 2009. http://www.ibm.com/ibm/values/us/

Parker LePla. "Client Research 2004-2009." Unpublished raw data, last modified December 2009, word.

Parr, Ben. "HOW TO: Use Twitter for Customer Service." Accessed October 8, 2009. http://mashable.com/2009/05/09/twittercustomer-service/

Poss, J. "Wisdom in the Forrester Style." *The Boston Globe*, December 25, 1995.

"Quelle Case Study." Unpublished raw data, last modified 2009, word.

"Quick Query: Comodo CEO on Hiring a Social Media Officer." *Practical eCommerce*, April 16, 2009. http://www.practicalecommerce.com/articles/1060-Quick-Query-Comodo-CEO-on-Hiring-a-Social-Media-Officer

Reingold, Jennifer. "The Most Dangerous Hire." *Inc. Magazine*, June 1, 2002. http://www.inc.com/magazine/20020601/24257.html

Rogers, Everett M. *Diffusion of Innovations*. Glencoe, IL: Free Press, 1994.

Roy, Subir. "Infosys Woos the World to Become Global Brand." *Rediff India Abroad*, January 2, 2007. http://www.rediff.com/money/2007/jan/02infy.htm

Schlosser, Julie. "Harder Than Harvard: A Fast-Growing Indian Outsourcing Company Admits Only 1 Percent of Applicants—Here's How It Trains 15,000 Recruits a Year." *Fortune Magazine*, March 17, 2006. http://money.cnn.com/2006/03/15/magazines/fortune/infosys_fortune_032006/

— "Infosys U: At the Taj Mahal of Training Centers, a Fast-Growing Indian Outsourcing Company Lavishes Attention on Its Recruits."

Fortune, March 16, 2006. http://money.cnn.com/magazines/fortune/fortune_archive/2006/03/20/8371802/index.htm

Schwartz, Tony. "Life/Work: Issue 40." *Fast Company*, October 31, 2000. http://www.fastcompany.com/magazine/40/tschwartz.html

— "Life/Work: Issue 41." *FastCompany*, November 30, 2000. http://www.fastcompany.com/magazine/41/tschwartz.html

Seidel, Hagen. "Wenn Kunden Gern Teuer Trinken." *WELT ONLINE*, September 3, 2007. http://www.welt.de/wirtschaft/article752783/Wenn_Kunden_gern_teuer_trinken.html

Seiwert, M. "Führende Markenbewertungsverfahren im Vergleich", *Absatzwirtschaft*, 47, 2004

Southwest Airlines. "Benefits." Accessed October 2, 2009. http://www.southwest.com/html/about-southwest/careers/benefits.html

— "Southwest Airlines Safety Commitment." Accessed October 1, 2009. http://www.southwest.com/about_swa/safety_commitment.pdf

— "Southwest Cares: Doing the Right Thing." Accessed October 2, 2009. http://www.southwest.com/about_swa/southwest_cares/our_people.html

Srinivasan, Mukund. "Southwest Airlines Operations: A Strategic Perspective." *Ezine Articles*. http://ezinearticles.com/?Southwest-Airlines-Operations—A-Strategic-Perspective&id=111277

Starbucks. "My Starbucks Idea." Accessed October 8, 2009. http://mystarbucksidea.force.com./

Suzuki, David. *The David Suzuki Reader*. Berkley, CA: Greystone Books, 2004.

The Beryl Companies. "Beryl." Accessed July 2, 2009. http://www.beryl.net/

— "Our Culture." Accessed September 26, 2009. http://www.beryl.net/about-us/our-culture

Universität St.Gallen. "The Universum Graduate Survey 2006: Swiss Edition University Report." Stockholm: Universum Communications Sweden AB, 2006. http://www.csc.unisg.ch/org/es/csc.nsf/SysWebRessources/CSC-HSG_UniversumGraduateSurvey_2006_english/$FILE/CSC-HSG+-Universum+Graduate+Survey +2006+english.pdf

"Video from Jeff Bezos about Amazon and Zappos." YouTube video, 8:10. Posted by "07272009july," July 22, 2009. http://www.youtube.com/watch?v=-hxX_Q5CnaA

Volpp, Kevin G., Leslie K. John, Andrea B. Troxel, Laurie Norton, Jennifer Fassbender, and George Loewenstein. "Financial Incentive–Based Approaches for Weight Loss: A Randomized Trial. *Journal of the American Medical Association* 300 (2008): 2631-7. doi: 10.1001/jama.2008.804

Volvo. "About Volvo." (2009). Retrieved October 3, 2009 from http://www.volvocars.com/us/top/about/values/Pages/safety.aspx

Vovchuk, Virginia. "How to Identify Cost Efficient Ways to Align Internal and External Brand Truths to Build Brand Strength." Paper presented at the 26th National Forum on Internal Branding, Chicago, Illinois, August 3-6, 2009.

Wienröder, Helga. "Hochschulabsolventen: Topfit für den Sprung nach oben." *Handelszeitung*, December 13, 2006. http://www.handelszeitung.ch/unternehmen/hochschulabsolventen-topfit-fuer-den-sprung-nach-oben

ABOUT THE AUTHORS

Wolfgang Giehl is Betriebswirt (MBA) and senior vice president of corporate brand marketing for Deutsche Post DHL, the world's leading mail and logistics services group. He is responsible for the group's global brand architecture and brand management of DHL worldwide. Prior to joining Deutsche Post DHL in 1995, Giehl was in charge of the national and international budgets of several advertising agencies. He is coauthor of *Focus Internal Branding* and author of various articles and publications on brand management.

F. Joseph LePla received a bachelor of arts from Wayne State University with majors in English (writing emphasis) and secondary education. He is a principal at Parker LePla, a brand strategy consultancy in Seattle, Washington. Parker LePla helps its clients create brand defining experiences. LePla is the coauthor of two previous books on integrated branding: *Integrated Brand* and *Brand Driven*.

ABOUT THE BOOK

It takes strength to compete. Becoming a well-known and well-regarded brand enhances a company's strength. Internal branding—especially in service industries—is essential for longevity, great competitive strength, and high financial value. Driven by a shared, authentic corporate culture and guided by top management, employees will build brand value in all their actions and interactions every day.

Create A Brand That Inspires: How to Sell, Organize, and Sustain Internal Branding effectively addresses three core brand management challenges in readers' organizations: selling the brand to senior management, organizing the brand on all management levels, and living the brand within each of the company's internal communities.

The book includes 16 international case studies complete with pictures, interviews and examples from a wide range of industries. The long-term, hands-on experience of the co-authors and their unique perspectives on how to successfully develop and manage internal branding make this study a rewarding read for executives, managers and team leaders.

INDEX

2844442R00116

Printed in Great Britain
by Amazon.co.uk, Ltd.,
Marston Gate.

COUNSELLING FOR DEPRESSION

By

Paul Lockley

Free Association Books

FA^B

Published in the United Kingdom 2005
by Free Association Books
57 Warren Street W1T 5NR

British Library Cataloguing in Publication Data
A catalogue record for this book is available from the British Library

Produced by Bookchase (UK) Ltd
Printed and bound in the EU

ISBN 1 853437 79 4

Contents

Introduction

About 5% of the population is likely to be affected by severe depression. Put another way, three million people in Great Britain will become clinically depressed in their lifetime. Many more people, family and friends, will come into contact with depression. Work colleagues and, ultimately, national productivity will be affected. Tackling depression is more than a personal requirement; it is a potential benefit for the whole of society.

For anyone who has suffered from depression – and I include myself in this category – it brings a restriction in life and a diminution of the sense of control over life. Counselling is seen here as a way of opening up life again for the depressed, a method that requires the active participation of clients. The depressed have to work on their depression.

Counselling, within limits and if well done, can help those who are, or have been, depressed. Counselling for depression should not be separated from other forms of counselling, but be integrated into them. What is provided in this book is based on my own work. As everyone works slightly differently, readers will hopefully find much that is of use, while leaving room for their own thoughts and ways of working.

Counselling those affected by depression can be challenging but it can also be very worthwhile. Depression is part of a person's life, and is often embedded in other client difficulties, so counsellors must be informed on many different conditions, whether biological, psychological, or sociological. The learning should never stop. Indeed, the more we know, the more we need to know. It is worth considering some system whereby counsellors constantly review and expand their experiences and knowledge. They have to be responsible for their own learning.

Hopefully this book will alert readers to possible causes. There can never be total certainty, so our work is a matter of judgement, knowledge, and experience. There will always be human situations that are new to us, situations we cannot really comprehend, and experiences that are to a degree unknowable to us. Even having known depression, I could never say to a client, "I know how you feel". There will always be a gap in our understanding.

To help clients, we have to use our knowledge and admit our ignorance. We have to ensure the passing of power in the working relationship to clients.

It is essential that clients be given the power and the belief in themselves to be able to survive without counselling. If this is not done, the counsellors are counselling for their own benefit, and not that of the client.

There are aspects of depression-related work, which has not been included in this book. These include the role of advocacy of the depressed, the legal implications of the Mental Health Acts, and the use of depression support groups. These are not strictly counselling issues, but are issues that can be relevant. I apologise for their absence, but no book can contain everything that will be needed by counsellors.

I would like to express my appreciation, and thank all those who have helped me. That includes clients who have willingly and freely shared their experiences in this book.

I also thank Dr Charles Anderson for reading through the draft, fighting through my grammar, and making suggestions in his usual perceptive and thorough manner.

And, to the reader – thanks for buying the book.

Chapter 1

The Nature of Depression

Setting the scene

Josie came into my office, many years ago. She was 18, a heroin user, and suffered from depression. She was an hour late for her appointment, which, for her, was good going. Luckily, I had some spare time. We sat down and were discussing her relationships, a topic that always required considerable time. Then the office tannoy went, calling me to reception. I did not want to take a possibly confidential message in front of Josie, so told her to stay in my office, saying I would be back in half a minute – and I did return in that time. And Josie had disappeared. Now, working with drug users can make you suspicious, so I looked round to see if anything was missing. Nothing. Still unconvinced, I decided to phone reception and ask if Josie could be stopped at the door. It was then that I discovered that she had stolen my phone.

When counselling we expect clients to act in certain ways, but clients do not always play from the same script. So we have to be able to move to another script, get into the mind of clients, and see the world from their point of view. We need to be able to put clients in their social context, have an idea about their family and friends. Counsellors have to understand their clients.

And the phone? Asking around locally, it was not hard to discover it was about to be sold for £10 to a local dealer. A quick chat, the promise of no police interference, and the phone was returned. The dealer was suitably sympathetic; "Josie should have stolen from someone else, not you".

And what does this have to do with depression? Perhaps that is not the right question. As counsellors, we are dealing with people first, and clients second. We have to be aware of ourselves, attuned to the people we meet. What this book will try to do is to bring counsellors closer to clients and their lives, specifically those who happen to suffer from depression.

From the start

It is assumed that the reader will have a basic grasp of counselling, so there is no attempt in this book to describe how to counsel. This is not a textbook. Rather, it is assumed that its readers have knowledge and experience; what is intended in the following pages is to add to that knowledge and experience. Readers will hopefully benefit from working through the information and ideas set out here, take on board client experiences, and review different methods of counselling. It is not for me to tell counsellors what to do; it is for counsellors to further discover who they are, what feels right for them, and then put what they learn into their personal way of counselling. Whatever that way of counselling is, it should be appropriate for each client and thus should be varied according to the feelings and thinking of depressed clients, which may call for some modifications in working. So, readers are alerted in the following pages to those aspects of depression that might affect their counselling.

What is required for counselling?

The first requirement to counselling clients is a knowledge and understanding of depression. Not so easy a task. We could go back to basics and ask what is meant by the term "depression". The snag is that there are different views as to what exactly depression is, and we would then have to decide whose definition should be used. And this is an ongoing debate. Rather than entering into a debate, my solution is indirect. It is to try and examine some of the reasons for there being a debate. Readers will not get a direct answer as to what depression is, but they should not expect one. They have to work towards providing their own.

Depression in history

If we start at the beginning, we note that depression is not a new phenomenon, a recent discovery, a product of modern society. It has always been part of human existence. The illness was known to the Ancient Greeks. Hippocrates noted there were some people who suffered from aversion to food, despondency, sleeplessness, irritability and restlessness (Jones and Withington, 1923), all of which are depressive symptoms. He suggested a cause, an excess of black bile, which gave the condition the name of melancholia (Jackson, 1986). Melancholia continued to be a recognised condition, noted by Galen in the second century AD. Commentators also observed the existence of somatic signs, such as gastrointestinal symptoms and a psychological sign, that of being tired with life (Jackson, 1986). In the seventeenth centuries, as witnessed in Burton's Anatomy of Melancholy, the concept of guilt was added.

Before looking at recent views of depression, we might contrast this historical longevity of depression with some mental states which appear to have largely disappeared, states such as hysteria in late Victorian times, catatonia, and nowadays possibly multiple personalities (Ofshe and Watters, 1995). These alleged mental conditions are of debatable status. However, this does not seem to be the case with depression. As far as we know, it has always existed.

Depression and its image

Although depression or melancholia of past centuries was mentioned, we are accustomed to a modern medicalised perspective. There is a danger of thinking of melancholia in the same way we see depression today. Yet in Renaissance times, melancholia was associated with a degree of giftedness or genius. Mild depression in the nineteenth century was romanticised as ennui or weltschmerz, an encompassing sorrow for all people (Jackson, 1985). So when thinking about depression, we have to realise that there is more than one way of looking at depression, more than the purely medical and psychiatric formulations.

Depression and universality

We also find that different views of depression are to be found in different cultures. But perhaps the first point is to observe the near universality of depression, as it occurs in almost every country around the globe. Yet there seem to be occasional exceptions. There is no word for the condition among the Kaluli people (Schlieffelin, 1985). Indeed, the very concept appears to be unknown to them. However, neither fact excludes native inhabitants from having symptoms Westerners call depression (Marsella, 1979). It is a mistake to look for the Western picture of depression, as its symptoms are culturally mediated. For instance, extreme sadness or anxiety are both parts of depression, yet they have a strong social component (Rosenblatt, 1988), and how they are expressed may be culturally determined. Oriental cases of depression are harder to detect for Westerners (Bridges and Goldberg, 1985), since the symptoms tend to be more somatic or of the body, than psychological, and symptoms may be differently classified locally. The converse is also likely to be true. Western cases of depression may be more difficult for Easterners to detect as the symptoms are more psychologised. So in a few societies, depression may be hard to recognise, but there is no reason to believe depression has not always been a feature of every human society.

Reviewing depression

If depression is a universal phenomenon, then it should be relatively easy for trained persons to identify. And this is done in the West by doctors and psychiatrists, using the medical model. This starts with identifying the symptoms, moving to diagnosis of the condition, and finally to treatment. The medical model has proved outstandingly successful in medicine, so its extension to psychiatry seemed a natural progression. But there are problems. In the medical model, symptoms of a disease are taken together as they occur together, and most of the same symptoms are seen in the cases of a specific illness. Confirmation is then made by recourse to physical or laboratory findings, if necessary. The laboratory findings are the final basis for determining what may or may not be symptoms in specific cases.

What constitutes the symptoms of depression cannot be determined by physical means. It is not like an illness, where a bacterium or virus can be identified and the illness confirmed. There is no such process possible for depressive conditions. All the evidence consists of certain symptoms tending to occur together. For example, there is a debate whether or not anxiety is one of the principal symptoms of depression. The decision on whether it is part of depression, or is a separate condition is often a matter of choice.

What makes the problem more complicated is that symptoms can vary between cases of depression. Not only do they vary, but symptoms can be very different. There can be insomnia or oversleeping, decreased or increased appetite. Then there may, or may not be panic attacks, phobias, obsession or hallucinations (Casper et al., 1985). We may be unsure of the symptoms of depression, and this has consequences. For instance, we may be unsure of the prevalence of depression (Weissman et al., 1988).

The Diagnostic and Statistical Manual

There was one way of deciding which symptoms should be taken together, and this was to have them linked together, embedded in an underlying theory.

This was done in the 1950s, and the theory used was psychoanalysis. The outcome was the publishing, under the aegis of the internationally influential American Psychiatric Association, of a reference book called the Diagnostic and Statistical Manual (DSM). This manual contains a list of all psychiatric conditions, not just depression, with their symptoms, to aid psychiatric diagnosis. The first edition of the manual, DSM-I, was a mere 20 pages and made little impact. Neither did the second edition.

Nevertheless, the DSMs were important in the evolution of psychiatry, as its listing of symptoms was a way of reducing inconsistencies in diagnoses. In particular, it was seen that the rate of diagnosed schizophrenia in the USA was twice that of Great Britain, a result of the use of differing symptoms for the illness. The American psychiatrists, for example, tended to include symptoms which British psychiatrists diagnosed as belonging to manic depression. Clearly, if mental states were universal, there had to be a shared set of criteria for their identification. More importantly, if psychiatry was to be well regarded then there had to be consistency.

DSM and psychiatry

The use of psychoanalytical theory may have linked psychiatric symptoms, but this was only useful provided the theory was accepted. But, there were problems. There was a profusion of different and competing psychoanalytical theories, and no reason to choose one rather than another. Also, psychoanalysis in general was falling out of favour, especially in Europe. There were attacks on the approach as being unprovable and consequently irrelevant (Rie, 1966).

With regard to depression, there was a special problem. Psychoanalytic theory denied it could affect children. Indeed, there did not seem to be such a thing as childhood depression – until researchers began to look for it. The Isle of Wight study (Rutter et al., 1975), using adult depression criteria, did find cases. The rate was very low for 10-year olds, and increased for 14-year olds, an increase associated with the onset of puberty. Similar results came later from New Zealand (Anderson et al., 1987) and Canada (Fleming et al., 1989). All of this put the validity of psychoanalysis and even the DSM in doubt.

Solving the problem?

The solution was seen to be that of rejecting the idea of any symptom linkage by theory and, instead, relies on ongoing research to decide what the symptoms should be. This required the use of standardised clinical interviews and methods (Robins et al., 1981) first developed by the St Louis Group (Feighner et al., 1972), which were then refined into the Research Diagnostic Criteria (Spitzer et al., 1978), which became the basis for DSM-III, the third edition of the manual. One result was that the size of DSM increased to a couple of hundred pages, but it did seem comprehensive and scientifically based.

By now the manual was seen by many as the final reference in psychiatric diagnoses. Yet the process contained a fundamental weakness. The use of questionnaires rested on what questions were asked, and this was determined by what researchers thought were symptoms. But this depended on what psychiatrists thought were the symptoms – and that was determined by which psychiatrists were used to provide a list of symptoms. Questionnaires will show what symptoms make up a psychiatrist's diagnosis, but fail to determine which psychiatrist's diagnosis is correct. The outcome is that the questionnaires varied according to psychiatric symptoms used, and each researcher found that their views were confirmed.

For instance, questions on the Hamilton Rating Scale emphasised vegetative rather than psychological symptoms (Hamilton, 1968), whereas the Beck Inventory emphasises cognitive aspects of depression (Hammen, 1981). Anxiety is not included in the Zung Self-rating Scale or the Beck Depression Inventory, but included on the Hamilton Scale. The debatable nature of research means there is debate about DSM criteria, and this is not helped when DSM criteria do not correspond to clinical realities (Kirmayer et al., 1994).

DSM-IV

The fourth edition of the DSM appeared in 1987. This manual introduced yet another approach to diagnosis to circumvent the difficulties of the previous edition. This was to include every possible symptom in psychiatric diagnoses. Not surprisingly, DSM-IV ran for hundreds of pages. If we confine our attention to depression, we find that there are dozens of different types and a patient might not fall perfectly into any single category. The proposed solution was twofold. The patient did not have to have all the symptoms. For example, depression was taken as being present if three of the four or seven of the ten symptoms were present. If that did not work, then there was the alternative of "atypical" cases; a subcategory for hard-to-place cases.

This might be democratic, but it is not science (Kendell, 1988; Costello, 1993). In fact, contrary to popular opinion, psychiatry is not well supported by scientific method. This does not devalue psychiatry; it merely describes it as more of an art than a science. Nor do we have to go to the extremes of writers like Szasz (1974; 1987), and reject the idea of mental illness, thereby ignoring personal suffering. Rather, we realise that the concepts surrounding depression are debatable, and we should not simply accept the findings of research, as these may rest on uncertain concepts.

International diagnoses

A different manual, International Classification of Diseases, Tenth Revision (ICD-10), was brought out by the World Health Organisation in 1992. This differed from DSM-IV, in that attention was given to the degrees of severity of the conditions such as depression, and also single episodes as opposed to multiple episodes. There were also a smaller number of categories, different types of each psychiatric condition, including depression. Clearly, the existence of two manuals with rather different content is somewhat confusing. The ICD-10 manual appears more vague than DSM-IV, and relies more on the person using it.

Reprise

It might seem that the existence of psychiatric manuals would be of little importance; it is not as if psychiatrists carry them about when making a diagnosis. Yet they are important for two reasons. The first is that they underline psychiatric training, and form an essential reference. They also form a basis for research, which feeds back into training and future manuals. There is also another point that is less obvious. They give an impression of scientific rigour to an extent that is unwarranted. In fact, a lot of psychiatric ideas are open to question. That does not make them wrong, but it does mean that they are not authoritative. Counsellors should not take them at face value.

Gender and depression

Counsellors have to think outside the box, but also appreciate what is common knowledge. For example, depression rates differ according to gender. It has been long appreciated that the depression rate for women is higher, about twice that for men (Nolen-Hoeksema, 1987). Also relevant is how gender differences are expressed. The fact that the difference in depression rate disappears for women who are unemployed or unmarried (Aneshensel et al., 1981) suggests social factors apply. Working-class women are three times more likely to be diagnosed as depressed compared with middle-class women

(Brown and Harris, 1978). But class is not the sole factor. For instance, the main factor in rural areas is the degree to which the person is integrated into the local community.

Yet the idea of gender being an overall factor in depression is reinforced by the fact that the rate for prepubertal girls and boys is the same, whereas in adolescence, when gender becomes socially important, the rate for girls is greater (Garrison et al., 1991). This information is often overlooked as it leads to uncomfortable ideas such as the high rate for women's depression being a result of the stereotyping of women, products of the male definintion of women's experience (Ehrenrich and English, 1978) in the medico-psychiatric profession. This leads to an overuse of mood disorder labels (Klerman and Weissman, 1980), as symptoms tend to be those such as crying, increased dependency, difficulty in expressing anger, self-deprecation and indecisiveness; those of the common female stereotype (Loring and Powell, 1986). Not only is the attribution of depression more likely with women, but also at a greater severity (Zetin et al., 1984).

Depression and treatment

What a study of gender and depression suggests is that psychiatry has to be supplemented for a fuller understanding of depression. While psychiatry is confined to the areas of diagnosis and treatment it is clear that treatment is important, not just for its humanity but because results suggest that psychiatry, whatever the imprecisions and debates, is at least effective. Success with treating patients points to the accuracy of psychiatric ideas.

First of all, we should observe that psychiatry has a history of treatments of a somewhat dubious nature, including hydrotherapy, insulin treatment and lobotomy, which have proved ineffective. So there was a time when psychiatry could be seen as inadequate. However it is comforting to think that the advent of modern drugs has greatly changed the picture. They have supplanted the old institutions, the mental asylums and have ushered in an age of effective treatment. It should nevertheless be noted that anti-depressants are not always effective in treating depression, though sometimes this might be due to too small a dosage being prescribed (Brugha and Bebbington, 1992). Their effectiveness ranges from 50% to 70%, which is fairly impressive, until we remember that placebos can effectively "treat" over 30% of cases (Holister, 1994). Even worse, these drugs are quite poor in countering depression in children (Alessi, 1991). As we shall see later, there is surprisingly little evidence for how drug treatments work.

Researchers and psychiatrists

It is important to understand that there is a complex interaction between research and psychiatry. Psychiatrists cannot ignore the findings of research, even if they feel they should have the final say as regards diagnosis. But we also have to appreciate that researchers and psychiatrists have differing aims. Psychiatrists want to make a definite diagnosis – as is required by the medical model. For instance, a patient either has, or does not have, chickenpox and there is no room for the half pregnant patient. However, psychiatric conditions differ in that there are degrees of depression – as researchers have identified and ICD-10 noted. The upshot of such research was that psychiatry moved and began to recognise not merely categories of depression but subcategories. These include a separate category of lesser depression, known as dysthymia, characterised by low self-esteem, self-blaming and guilt, pessimism, and lethargy. Then, a lesser form of dysthymia, which was milder, short-term and occurs within 3 months of an identifiable source of stress called adjustment disorder, was promoted. However, we might note that these conditions – depression, dysthmia and adjustment disorder – are taken as separate states thus allowing the idea that subjects can have "double depression", a combination of major depression and dysthymia (Weissman and Myers, 1978; Depression Guideline Panel, 1993).

This formation of subcategories was extended to other forms of depression. Seasonally affective disorder, a depression associated with the winter months and a lack of sunlight, which affects 5% of the population, had a lesser form that affects about three times as many people (Lewy, 1994). Similarly, post-natal or post-partum depression, has a lesser form, known as post-partum blues (Thirkettle and Knight, 1985), characterised by depressed mood, tearfulness, emotion swings, anxiety and sleep disturbance for up to 10 days (Pitt, 1973; Cutrona, 1982). And this lesser form of depression is relatively common, one estimate putting the number of women sufferers between 20% and 30%. There have even been proposals that there are other forms of post-partum depression intermediate between post-partum blues and full post-partum depression (Landy et al., 1989).

Depression as a continuum

Although there is an interaction of researchers and psychiatrists, the two are not the same, as they have different remits and aims. As counsellors have different aims from both, their approach should differ too. My approach is to see depression not as a category, or as a series of categories and subcategories, but as a continuum.

It is worth considering the nature of a continuum, such as the spectrum. The colours of the spectrum gradually merge into each other. This does not prevent us from calling different degrees of the spectrum red, orange, green or blue. Sometimes we may be unsure which category applies, whether, say, it is green or blue, but usually there is little trouble. Similarly, categorising depression can be done by grading the degree or severity of the depression. Symptoms of depression are just one way of grading severity and enabling us to name the severity of the condition (see Klerman, 1989; Mirowsky and Ross, 1989).

What the continuum approach does is emphasise the importance of the person who makes the decision as to the nature of the depression: and for counsellors this is partly the role of the depressed person – unlike psychiatric diagnoses.

This becomes clearer if we return to the ICD-10 manual, and look up the symptoms of mild depression. We find that it is a state characterised by two of the following:

- Depressed mood to a degree that is definitely abnormal for the individual, present for most of the day and almost every day and unchanged by circumstances, and sustained for at least two weeks.
- Loss of interest or pleasure in activities that are normally pleasurable.
- Decreased energy and increased fatigability.

In addition, there must be two from the following three:

- A loss of confidence and self-esteem.
- Unreasonable feelings of self-reproach, or excessive and inappropriate guilt.
- Recurrent thoughts of death or suicide.

Reading this through, we recognise participation of the patient in the diagnosis. "Loss of self-esteem", "Loss of normal pleasurable activities", "Inappropriate guilt"; these are all terms that are meaningful only with client participation. Mild depression very much depends on the participation of patients. Only they know what is normal for them, whether they sense a loss of self-esteem, or feel guilty. Thus depressed clients take a part not just in their treatment but also in their diagnosis.

Implications of the depressive continuum

There are some consequences of taking this counselling perspective. Although the above applies only to mild depression, this is the form of depression most likely to be encountered by counsellors (Dunner and Schmaling, 1994). The idea of a continuum also helps to normalise the idea of depression. We all get down from time to time, so can be said to be open to some degree of depression (Blashfield and Livesley, 1991). Depression can be seen as a severe variant of this. It might be argued that severe depression is qualitatively different to mild depression, as this is true – just as we can say green is different from blue. But this does not mean the idea of the continuum is wrong.

The cycling of depression

Another aspect which points to depression not being a set category is the variation experienced during depressive episodes. It varies over 24 hours, usually being more severe in the morning. There is a further change in that the condition is remitting, so depression usually rights itself without any outside help within 9–24 months. Even this may not be the end, as there is a likelihood that there will be further episodes. Of those who have recovered, 45% can expect a second bout, and 33% a third bout (Lewinsohn et al., 1989), but even these estimates might be too low. Lee and Murray (1988) followed up admissions over a period of 18 years and found that less than 20% were surviving free from depression and at least 95% had experienced at least another further episode. Kiloh's 15-year study gave a figure of only 15% who remained well.

This cycling of depression, whether over days, months, or years is little regarded by psychiatric research, yet is highly significant. It shows that depression is not static, but a dynamic condition, which is self-righting, based on a mechanism that works on feedback. Usually, the mechanism is taken for granted, and people are not depressed. However, a failure in control leads to the condition we know as depression. Luckily, the control mechanism eventually takes over and the person's depression alleviates.

Depression as an extreme condition

If we return to the idea of a continuum of depression, then we might ask what this means in practice. We have degrees of depression and this might be seen, for example, in differing degrees of grief. However, a clear distinction has been drawn between ordinary grief and complicated grief, previously known as melancholia. We may be sure we can distinguish the two conditions, but this is only a result of cultural considerations. We have become accustomed to seeing things in certain ways. In Arab countries, a mother can be in deep mourning for her dead son for 7 years. We would probably judge such women to be depressed, rather than being in grief. This is not likely to be the case in Arab countries.

The point is that the reliance on symptoms is inadequate. We have to be aware of the total context. Human behaviour is variable, and we have to be careful of jumping to unwarranted conclusions. Take the following scenario:

> *Jill*: "How I feel is something I can't control. The moods change so quick. I can be crying one minute, laughing the next, violent the next. I feel physically sick, dizzy, have palpitations and am on the point of hyperventilating – sometimes to the point of almost passing out. I have nightmares and migraines, though not as bad as when I was young; flashing lights, pain, and vision is such that I can't see a hand in front of my hand, its outline seems to move so you can never see the whole of it. The migraines are not so bad now but can still be set off by stress or things like cheese or chocolate. I also pick things up wrongly and am suspicious. I get irritable for no reason at all, feel like screaming, and get agitated. My concentration gets worse. My thinking gets faster and I get impatient as everyone seems slow."

Such behaviour might seem fairly extreme, perhaps some sort of manic depression. In fact, the client was describing how premenstrual tension affects her. So we have to be careful of assessing people by symptoms alone, which, to be fair, no professional would do.

The continuum and manic depression

It should not be thought that counselling favours the continuum hypothesis merely because it is convenient and fits in with its requirements. On the other hand, we should not imagine that the continuum is so different from other professional views of depression. It is just a matter of different emphasis. However, the hypothesis does lead to some further insights.

One example of that is manic depression, now clinically called bipolar affective disorder which can be pictured as the opposite of depression, and is characterised by overactivity, manic enjoyment, thinking which runs at a furious pace and poor concentration. All of this appears to be the polar opposite of depression. Yet depression and manic depression are intimately linked. Manic depression is typified by periods of mania alternating with depressive episodes. But these depressive episodes are similar to those of ordinary or unipolar depression (Mitchell et al., 1992). Moreover bipolar affective disorder can take a lesser form, cyclothymia, as categorised by DSM-IV, just as depression has the lesser form of depression, dysthymia. The connection between depression and manic depression can be seen by the fact that both usually respond positively to treatment by lithium salts (Coppen et al., 1982). In fact, lithium is not widely used in cases of unipolar depression, reflecting the fact that depression and manic depression are seen as different, and so are believed to require different treatments.

The complete separation of the conditions of depression and manic depression is misleading. Yet it can be argued that they must be, as manic depression is a much less common condition. This view rests on information from patients, who underestimate their more manic episodes. They see good and bad days, as opposed to disordered days or days out of control (Goodwin, 1994). This can be a product of how they see the condition, based on how others view it. Similarly, depression is seen as always being about low mood and negativity. Depressed patients are seldom asked about when they might feel less negative or even happy.

So, how clients view their situation depends to some extent on the views of professionals, including counsellors, who have to acknowledge this fact and take responsibility. They simply cannot use accepted wisdom about depression because it is the accepted wisdom. They have to come to their own conclusions.

Role of counselling

Although we see the underlying unity of human behaviour, we are also aware of differences. We are aware of the different aspects of depression and mania. The counsellor is presented with different degrees of behaviour that must be received with an open mind. We see that there are similarities, such as that both are characterised by a degree of lack of control.

Carol: "I could not stop myself crying. People think it helps, but crying for hours just leaves you tired and exhausted. I wished I could stop, but I couldn't."

Robert: "When I'm up, I tend to get out of control, but it's funny as well. Once I paid a beggar a fiver to play 'Knocking on heaven's door'. Then I went into the restaurant and bought every member of staff a glass of wine.

But if it gets worse then I get irritable and become aggressive. No-one can do anything about it."

In both these instances, the role of counselling is to help clients increase their sense of control and exert as much control as they want. Such control comes from an understanding, not merely of depression, but of related conditions. This rests on clients wanting to change. Counsellors cannot make a person change. The client has to want to change. This does not mean people cannot be influenced, but in the end they have to do the changing.

Iain: "You have to do something about it, depression, or it will swallow you up."

From these preliminary quotes, we can see that clients are not merely affected by depression. They interact with it; they can reflect on it, they have their own views about it. These will all enter into the counselling.

The role of helpers, counsellors and psychiatrists

Working with depressed clients helps them regain greater control over their lives, partly through the use of prescribed drugs, partly through non-drug means. If we expect clients to take that self-control, then the same applies to the work of counsellors. They have to take more self-control and be responsible for their work. This includes knowing about depression and allied conditions, about medical treatments, and being able to usefully link in with the work of other professionals. This does not mean they have to take the work of others uncritically, nor does it mean that they know better than others. There is a lot unknown about psychiatric conditions. This is not to criticise the work of anyone involved helping those with psychiatric problems. It is to admit that there is a lot we do not know, and so it is even more important that we monitor our work, listen carefully to clients and try to understand what is going on.

And the first task is to listen to clients.

Chapter 2

Client Experiences

Introduction

In keeping with depression being largely a condition of long lasting uncontrolled negative moods, any understanding must come from being in touch with the experience of being depressed. The possible causes and categorisation can come later. To get this experience as precise as possible, I have investigated both my own experiences of depression and those of others.

What is given in this chapter is not a definitive description. The number of cases used is restricted in number. However this does provide the advantage of allowing a greater concentration on the quality of the experience. In particular, we can pick up on those qualities that may be difficult to put into words, yet may be of importance, making it easier to check out largely ignored aspects of depression. There can, indeed, be masked depression, detectable through demeanour and behaviour, even when persons deny experiencing any depressive mood (Barrett et al., 1988). The signs might be those such as posture, lack of eye contact, looking down and a comparative lack of hand movement (Waxer, 1976).

The progress of depression

The following description follows the chronological progress of a number of cases of depression. In order to ease understanding, such progress has been divided into discrete stages, but this is solely for the purpose of comprehension, and not meant to illustrate separate situations or conditions.

It should be said that the early stages of depression are not easy to detect, and are not always recognised or even recalled by depressives until long after an identified depressive episode. What seems to characterise this very early stage is a feeling of strangeness, a sense that things are not quite right. However this feeling is not clear at the time, and the strangeness only recognised later, sometimes after the depression has ended. What seems slightly unsettling in retrospect seemed quite normal at the time.

Alice: "I believe with hindsight that I was depressed for a good six or seven years before I was told by the doctor that I was depressed. I had never thought of myself as depressed, as I am one of those people who get on with things, pick myself up and go on. But I did feel apart from the human race, though not all the time. I always said I put confidence on with my clothes, so if I was going out then I would feel confident. But it was an act. It wasn't really me. Most people put on an air at times, but with me it was more than that."

Paul: "When you are young you don't know what is normal or abnormal. You don't even think that way. When thirteen, I would cry in my bedroom from some vague worry. But what about, I had no idea. Perhaps that is what teenagers do ... I remember when young having to cross a field on going to school. There was a difference in the level of that field, so you had to go down a small slope. Sometimes when walking down this slope I would feel as if I was walking into another universe, and had to convince myself I was still going to school as normal. It was really weird. Two years later I was suffering from depression, but whether that was in any way related to what had happened earlier I don't know."

And indeed, it is difficult to know whether earlier experiences and events are in any way tied in with later depression. It is tempting to select such experiences as causes of depression, rather than seeing them merely as examples of strangeness, or of inappropriate feelings, thoughts and perceptions.

The next stage of depression can also be imperceptible, a stage when there are the beginnings of what might be acknowledged as symptoms of depression. But the person is most unlikely to connect them with depression; instead, they seem to be variations in the normal range of behaviour.

Developing depression

In this next stage, there is no unreasonable personal sadness and no great anxiety, but there is a blunted enjoyment of pleasure. The person is less talkative and may be seen by others as being rather quiet. There might also be a degree of low anxiety, which is experienced as things not seeming quite right – but why this is so remains hidden. Concentration can start to diminish, and this can make the person fidgety, unable to settle. There can also be a desire to eat sweet foods, take in carbohydrates. Then lethargy can start to take over and a desire to sleep increases, so staying in bed may be increased (Wells et al.,

1988). These symptoms are in the context of possible stress or physical exertion; they are experienced but are likely to be rationalised or explained away.

> *Iain*: "I began to feel myself beginning to retreat from the company of others a bit. There was nothing negative about them. It was just that there was less good about being in a group or crowd. And at times I would begin to worry for no particular reason, but then I would buck myself up, get my head straight. Part of the trouble was beginning to think too much. Yet the curious thing was that those thoughts would not be about anything definite."

Listening to slightly depressed clients can be difficult, as the negative feelings they put across do not lead to good social communication (Hammen and Peters, 1978). This may not be obvious to the listener, who, nevertheless, begins to feel uncomfortable and sometimes rather irritated by the client (Coyne, 1976). There can be different feelings in the counselling session, including an indefinable sense that something is not right, or missing, or perhaps the counsellor is failing in some way but the cause is not obvious.

Gathering depression

As depression gains in severity, there follows a stage of diminished mental concentration; television merely stared at, newspapers left unread and tasks postponed. However this gradual lessening of mental abilities is not noticed by the depressed person. Another feature can be a feeling of depersonalisation, partly because subjects are unsure how they feel, and are unsure of themselves.

> *Jill*: "I have a feeling of disaster, but not specific; just that I'm prepared for something bad. You do not know why you have it, but you know it's there. There's a pit in your stomach; it's hard to describe. It's as if there is an extra brain in your stomach, and there is a fight between your stomach and your real brain."

> *Lenny*: "You can concentrate if you want to, but it is an effort. It is like your mind decides to take a wee wander, prefers to float rather than concentrate. You, I mean me, feel no real sadness, but my moods are jumpy – if that makes any sense. I'm not sure how I feel; sometimes this, sometimes that."

The difficulty of explaining such experiences is important, as it shows clients are increasingly feeling a loss of control and find it hard to make sense of what is happening.

Awareness of depression

The growing sense of unease in those depressed can develop into anxiety. This is definitely an unpleasant feeling. There can also be somatic sensations, such as a shortness of breath, slight tightness in the upper chest and a sensation of constriction along the sides of the lower chest. In addition, there can be a strange sensation around the area of the heart.

> *Carol*: "I would get these feelings in my stomach and above, around my heart. Then my reaction would be, 'Oh, oh!' I knew the depression was coming on – and it would. Those feelings, they were not really unpleasant, but they were not pleasant either. It was really strange. It's difficult to describe what they were like."

Incidentally, it can be quite useful to get clients to describe their early feelings and sensations of depression. This can help them if they get depressed again, as it is likely to happen at some time. Familiarity diminishes anxiety.

Moods and depression

A different aspect of growing depression is that of sadness with no discernible cause. However this sadness is not total, as there can also be flashes of anger and also moments of normality. Somatic sensations increase with a pit-of-the-stomach emptiness. Negative feelings such as sadness and somatic sensations combine to produce an increasingly unpleasant sensation. There can also be an awareness of different sensations and a conscious interaction with them. At this point, those depressed might benefit from taking remedial action and medication to prevent matters spiralling out of control.

> *Paul*: "I discovered that contracting the muscles of the abdomen could reduce the empty feeling in my stomach, though this action was not always successful and would not be effective for long."

> *Jill*: "It would start when I decided to have a lazy day and just read and sleep. By the third day I would become agitated and unable to do anything. I would feel down and weepy, but also angry. I get angry at myself

but also blame others. Then it gets deeper and I get angry with myself for having wasted my life."

Severe depression

The following stage has been taken as one, but varies in intensity and might indeed be comprised of different discernible sub-stages. However the more severe the condition, the harder it is to remember and describe. Various aspects have been highlighted but they still fail to give the entire picture. The greater complexity of the sensations reflects the fact that the condition is now growing from personal symptoms to an overwhelming personal state.

There is a change from the over-stimulated anxiety stage or the normal functioning rate to a progressive slowing down caused by a sense of lethargy. Part of this arises from the mental energy required to keep things together, to try and lead a normal life. This may mean having to suppress how one feels, having to act sociably when not feeling like it, or having to put a rein on increasingly negative and possibly destructive thoughts. This contest is continuous, so can either lead to sleeplessness as thoughts are marshalled at night, or it can result in prolonged sleep simply because the process is exhausting. There is also a reduction in sex drive or even interest; a lack of go, spontaneity and motivation, all of which have interpersonal and social consequences.

Jill: "When I feel depressed everything is such an effort. Even walking upstairs is painful. And everything seems to happen so fast that I cannot keep up and am no longer in control. The flat looks different, unlived in, grubby, and not like a home. Then nothing gets done; the washing and the dishes are such an effort. At times I could not even get it together to make a cup of coffee. Personal hygiene went down – I knew it but had not got the energy to do anything about it. I tried to cope but found I couldn't."

There is a narrowing of interest as the person is caught up in the depression and fighting against it. Not only are matters ignored or quickly passed by, but there is also a diminution in what makes us human. Communication is less, and is perfunctory and flat. There is no appreciation of paralinguistic features such as jokes and irony, and non-verbal signals can be dulled. Not surprisingly, this greatly weakens social interaction as the depressed person finds it increasingly hard to contribute fully, and others find the depressed person boring and uninteresting. The end result is social isolation, and this can happen even in the company of others.

Alice: "It's as if your whole world has been shut down. Things that would interest you, make you annoyed or make you laugh now do not touch you. You do not notice people or have any idea what is going on. The spark has gone. And then people would notice. If the depression was really bad then all of this passed you by, but if it was not that severe or you were getting better then you would know others had noticed your behaviour – but you could not do anything about it. Everything was there in your head but you could not move it. There would be a mile between brain and mouth; a million miles."

Further characteristics of severe depression

Another mood change is that the person's whole world becomes sombre, is seen in a way that demands words such as "without hope", "meaningless", "grey", but the precise picture is difficult to paint. There is a progression from "the world seems pointless" to "the world is pointless". At this stage, there is no way depressed persons can be argued out of their view of the world, as their world *is* the logical one. The more others argue, the more apparent it is that they do not understand the real nature of existence. The depressed person now has a total view of life and a logical one. To say that it is incorrect, that the depressed person has an unrealistic view of life, fails to understand that there is no answer one way or another to the question "Is life meaningful?" or "Is life worth living?" In fact, the answer largely depends on respondents' circumstances and how they feel. Of course, depressed persons may agree with outsiders that things are really not that bad, but always at the back of their mind lies the thought that life is meaningless.

Sharon: "It's like you've walked into a different and more restricted life. The walls are enclosed in and you become more preoccupied with yourself as it seems there is little else. The world is a bad place. By bad, I suppose I am saying it is meaningless. There are people and there are things out there, but you are not really connected to them, and don't really want to be. You have to do everything just to survive. Living from minute to minute is an effort, and not a pleasant one. All of this sounds pretty grim, but when you are depressed it is somehow different. It's like you live because you have to; that's your penance."

Moods are very changeable, though negative ones predominate. Those moods often do not link in with the person's external situation. For example, the depressed person may spontaneously burst into tears for no reason. Initially there may not even be any sadness to accompany this reaction. One result can be that the depressive feels out of control and his world becomes even more threatening.

> *Lenny*: "One of the most important signs of depression is when you cannot stop yourself from crying, however much you try. You just find yourself doing it, and you don't even know the cause. It's then that you realise that something is wrong, and I know I'm depressed. Other people latch onto it as well. If you seem miserable then you are a miserable old git. If you avoid others then you are anti-social, but if you cry continuously then something's up. Having said that, people imagine the depressed are miserable all the time, but there are brief moments of being OK, the flash of almost happiness, but mainly sadness, an unutterable miserable sadness; a sadness you can't escape."

As the depression worsens, all mental processes are liable to be affected. They slow down, as if the mind is wading through treacle.

> *Paul*: "You can have only one thought in your head at a time, and it becomes easy to lose the thread of an argument. When really bad, you can barely string a sentence together as mentally you lose your way. You just don't want to think. And by now you are losing confidence in your mental abilities anyway."

> *Carol*: "It is hard to describe. Your mind is there, it should be able to function, but it is like someone has put a tin box over it. It is still there but is a prisoner and cannot communicate with you or the world. You do not feel well, in fact you feel terrible, but there is nothing the mind can do."

As mentioned above, depression is often viewed as a state of chronic sadness, a view that overlooks the role of anger. There may be a lesser degree of anger compared with unhappiness, but it can be very intense. However it is unlikely to be exhibited.

> *Jill*: "I find myself very sad, breaking into tears, and then getting angry with myself – 'Stop crying, you idiot!' When depressed I often get angry, 'Don't you think I've been punished enough!' I would shout it out, but I don't think anyone was listening."

There can also be a preoccupation with the ongoing thoughts and feelings, and this affects the ability to concentrate, which is diminishing anyway.

This means that conversation becomes an effort, reading and watching television more difficult, so there is an even greater preoccupation with self. The lack of interaction only adds to a decreasing concentration.

> *Lenny*: "It's like the least feeling can topple the balance and will destroy me entirely. I don't want to be exposed to any feelings, as I can't deal with them, whether they are mine or anyone else's. This even applies to helpful or kind feelings. I just want to be left alone, left without experiencing any feeling at all."

Sleep disturbances occur, and they can seem contradictory. Some depressed people stay in bed and sleep, whereas others cannot get to sleep or have very interrupted sleep. The reason is that there are separate processes taking place. The sleep can be a result of trying to deal with the ongoing situation, which can be stressful and tiring (Casper et al., 1985) and staying in bed may even be an avoidance tactic. Interrupted sleep reflects anxiety and the thoughts that are going round and round in the subject's mind.

Mental aspects of depression

Depression can lead to what is usually described as thought-blocking, but the situation is actually more than one of simple blocking. Firstly, lethargy extends to mental operations, so the depressive does not care whether thoughts are completed or whether they are going anywhere and there is also a disinclination to mentally go in other directions. The temptation is to play safe when the world appears so threatening and allow thoughts to go along well-known paths. This can eventually lead to going round in circles. Thirdly, there can be blocking, when thoughts are consciously or unconsciously blocked by the depressed person. It should be said that extreme thought blocking brings the client's normal social functioning to a halt, so it is a very important feature of depression. There are important changes to the sense of self. As the depressed person is unable to function as normal, he has a restricted range and so feels inferior, an evaluation that is reinforced by the actions of others, even if well-meaning. In addition, the world appears meaningless and worthless, so the client, being part of this world, feels the same about himself or herself. This low self opinion can lead to thoughts of suicide, especially in countries as in the West where the individual, as opposed to the group, is thought to be of such value. Again, it should be stressed that such thoughts and any subsequent actions are a logical product of the depressive's ongoing state. Considering the number of times these self-destructive thoughts occur, there is rarely a follow-up in physical terms – though the possible finality of such resultant action makes it of interest, if not of importance.

Another aspect of the ongoing state is that the client has a sense of depersonalisation, a dangerous state incidentally when combined with self-destructive impulses. Such depersonalisation makes wild imaginings or even hallucinations more likely, and these are of concern when aligned with a lack of control.

Personal reactions to depression

By now the subject is aware that something is not right, but still may not realise the extent of the state of depression. The natural course is to get on with life, especially if there is a partner or family to consider. Already the depressed person has had to change behaviour merely to keep up, running faster and faster to stay in the same place. Longer hours at work, checking everything three times, and similar measures may be required as concentration and memory are blocked.

> *Paul*: "Work became an obsession, but it was also a way out. I hid myself in it. Up to fourteen hours a day, which meant I did not have to think of anything else. Some of this might be because I was now less efficient, some of it because it gave the impression of normality to me. I would convince myself the work had to be done, that only I could really do it, and there was a feeling that if it was not done then the world would somehow fall apart – which was true if that meant my world. Relationships with colleagues became more distant, and my feelings towards them would change this way and that. Sometimes they were great people, sometimes they were trying to interfere, stop me, or attempting to put one over me. Yet at the time my behaviour not only seemed normal but it seemed to me that everyone else was slightly out of step."

One common reaction is that of helping the situation by the use of alcohol or drugs, which may include prescribed medication. The first is of special importance as alcohol provides a socially acceptable means of self-medication. Even when it becomes excessive and needs treatment, or the person needs help, the emphasis is usually on the drug, and the idea of any underlying depression is not considered.

Gary: "Doctors will tell you that depression can lead to you drinking more alcohol than is good for you. They say alcohol is a depressant – which is true – and that it only aggravates the situation. So you get more depressed, drink more, and descend a downward spiral. If you persist in drinking, then that proves that you are either stupid and do not understand, or that you are just bloody-minded and are suffering from a personality disorder. What they fail to recognise is the fact that alcohol makes you feel better in the short-term and when you are really down you desperately want to feel better. It does not matter if this is merely for a short time. A few hours of relief or being out of your head is worth it. It is like being poor all your life, scrimping and saving, and then someone gives you a handful of money. Do you act sensibly and pay off your debts, or do you think, 'What the hell! For once in my life I'm going to enjoy myself!'? You know you will be back scrimping and saving but at least you have the memory of a good time, at least you have got something out of life. It is a bit like that with drink."

Crisis point

After a time there comes a crisis, either minor or major. What becomes plain is that the depressed person is not behaving normally. Sometimes the person is all too aware of this.

Jane: "I said I was going to have a nervous breakdown, and though it was said as a joke, it was also serious. But as a single parent, I hadn't got time to have one! Finally, it all fell apart and I knew I had to get help."

Doctors tend to be the first port of call, as the person feels not right, though this does not mean depression has been recognised. In fact, it is often someone in the family or a close friend who suggests that some form of help is needed (Zola, 1973).

Marisa: "The family realised that something was up, as I was acting so strangely. I was not just uptight but really uptight. My sister and brother were both worried about me as they had never seen me like that before, and kept saying, 'What's wrong? What's wrong?' My partner told me to go to the doctor. We had been together for nine years, so he knew something wasn't right. My partner was understanding and helpful. I've always been positive person and been able to work out solutions to problems, but I couldn't even begin to work things out. The depression lasted six months. I don't know how it would have worked out if it had been for longer."

However there is a difficulty in that the onset of depression can be slow and insidious, and not really noticed. The family makes allowances for depressive behaviour and adjusts its behaviour to accommodate it. Also, it depends how far from the norm the behaviour is seen to be (Mechanic, 1967). Nevertheless, the subject has to finally accept the diagnosis of the doctor or psychiatrist (Bloor and Horobin, 1975) when in extremes. Usually, by then, the patient is in such a state that anything is acceptable.

Gareth: "My life seemed to be falling apart, I was falling apart. There seemed no sense in anything. Then the doctor diagnosed me as being clinically depressed and I felt a little better. Even words like 'endogenous' and 'exogenous' seemed somehow reassuring; there's nothing like a scientific term to lend importance to the occasion. Depressive, that was what I was. It was something to cling on to. But then it was like the psychiatrist was dragging me into another world, the world of depression. I was now a case of depression, and my thoughts were of little consequence. I was treated and told what to do. On one hand that was great as I needed someone to make decisions, on the other it was annoying. I felt I was losing myself, just as I was losing myself when depressed, losing myself in a different way. Perhaps it is just something you have to go through."

Roy: "See, psychies, they get money for old rope. For a start, if you are depressed, then in time you recover, so they are onto a winner. Then, any improvement over that is 'cos they bung you some pills. Do you know psychiatrists prescribe you double what you need? That's what my GP says. He cut me down after I came out. Those tablets were like speed, stopped me sleeping and made me paranoid. Actually, the bloke wasn't a bad guy. Towards the end I found he had an interest in modern jazz and we would chat about that. At first I thought it was a bit of a waste of time, I thought he was going to analyse me, or something. Thinking about it now it seems as good as anything. At least we did chat and it was quite enjoyable, better than having your head fucked up – any more than it was already! Better Coltrane than Freud. It was towards the end he asked me if I knew anything about Freud. I said, 'You whistle it and I'll play the fucker'. That was at the end. I was feeling better and back on form."

The use of personal understanding

It would be a mistake to imagine that the accounts above describe depression in general. They are just some accounts, but they do give some examples of the signs of depression to which some readers might be able to relate. But everyone has to relate to their own form of depression. To help this process, it can be useful to write down the experience of one's depression. What strikes me is that people liable to depression can describe their condition well, and have their own insights into it.

Jill: "Rejection is another theme relevant to my depression. It is associated with humiliation, and can leave me weeping, as I wear my heart on my sleeve. I get anxious, feeling of panic, palpitations, feel as if I am about to hyperventilate and have flashes in my head. I get intrusive thoughts, which are horrible, such as my Mum being in a coffin dead or my dog being put to sleep. At times I have shouted, 'No!' to get them out of my mind. It is like an outside thing is putting the thoughts there. Also thoughts can come around and around again. I try and deal with this by switching off my phone and buzzer, as I don't want others to know I'm like this. My mind is floating and I find it difficult to finalise a thought. The thought I want is blocked and other thoughts pop into my head."

Reoccurring depression

My idea was that a description of the development of depression might help people connect with growing or reoccurring depression. While drafting this book, my own depression reappeared, so it gave me the chance to give another description.

"I had been feeling nervy for about three days, rather uptight, though there was little reason for this feeling. But this day I felt tired and concentration became harder. The muscles on my face tightened up, and my expression felt fixed. The anxiety, which was felt in my stomach, became stronger and nauseous. I also felt cold, despite the summer temperature. I was aware of what was happening to me, and the question was whether to let others know how I felt and what was happening. Being more self-aware meant I was more aware of my reactions, and spent energy trying to monitor and control my behaviour."

Review of depression as experienced

Descriptions of depression have been given here to help readers get a feel for the condition or compare how they felt with the examples provided. There are likely to be variations in the individual experiences of depression and also how different cultures experience it. Much of depression is hard to put into words, so we tend to fall back on stock phrases and ways of describing what is happening to us.

This means that counsellors have to keep an open mind, and this is not easy as depression has been psychiatrised, largely through the description of depression in the Diagnostic and Statistical Manual (DSM) and other manuals. However, we have to be aware of the process of the construction of depression as a psychiatric category. In particular, we have to be careful with cases of mild depression, as these cases are less commonly seen by psychiatrists, resulting in their description being open to wide interpretation (Brown, 1991). Furthermore, the tendency to diagnose not from symptoms but from a collection of symptoms, from syndromes, and in a fairly arbitrary manner, further confuses the picture (Costello, 1993). Counsellors have to be aware of psychiatric categories, but also need to be aware of clients and their context; they have to know the categories, yet remain open-minded.

Chapter 3

Causes and Treatment

Depression and biological cause

There are no definite known causes of depression, though there are several likely contributing factors. The factors may be divided into biological, neurological and psychological; separate but interacting. Exactly how they interact is not known, though there is research being done on possible underlying mechanisms. Firstly, we see a degree of inherited cause of depression, so there are biological origins (Blehar et al., 1988). When we consider depression as a condition where the control mechanism for feelings and associated thinking goes awry, it may be attributed to the person having inherited a potentially defective control mechanism. Evidence comes from the fact that if one identical twin has mood disorders, there is at least a 60% chance of the other being similar (Tsaung and Faraone, 1990). In ordinary non-identical twins, the rate is 14% (Wesner and Winokur, 1990).

The genetic component is not overwhelming, but cases of depression that occur before the age of thirty are more likely to have a strong genetic factor, whereas depression in later life may be associated more strongly with factors such as personal loss, chronic pain, sudden trauma, or stress. The genetic basis for depression may be of interest, but is of little use to the counsellor. There is nothing counselling can do to alter genetic causes. However, depression often has effects on the client as well as those around the client, and they can be helped.

Neurological hypotheses

The role of control in human activities such as feelings, thoughts and behaviour has already been mentioned. Such control is exercised through the central nervous system. Messages are sent along nerve fibres, most of which are in the brain. Models of the brain have likened it to a computer. However, the model is incomplete. It has been discovered that the nerves carrying messages in the brain do not actually connect with each other, so the question arose as to how messages are transmitted. The answer is that the messages, which consist of electrical impulses, are capable of causing the release of chemicals, known as neurotransmitters, from the end of one nerve across a small gap, or synapse, to another nerve. However, neurotransmitters use a lock-and-key device, whereby their molecular form has to fit the receptors on the second nerve. As this gate mechanism exists, messages can be directed to different parts of the brain along established pathways.

The first neurotransmitter to be discovered was norepinephrine as long ago as 1929. This chemical was known as a constituent of the fight-or-flight reaction in stress, and a deficiency of it was thought to be linked with depression (Schildkraut, 1965). As there was little evidence found through research for this idea, a second and currently the most popular idea was that depression was linked with a deficit in the neurotransmitter serotonin, which directs messages along the pathway in the brain associated with the sensation of pleasure. So, the lack of serotonin caused a lack of pleasure. In addition, serotonin is linked with sleep, appetite and libido regulation (Depue and Spoont, 1986): all of them are factors in depression. Serotonin is also involved in the regulation of goal-directed behaviour (Jacobs, 1991), which could further explain depressive lack of action. Furthermore, it is suggested that the basic level of serotonin is partly under genetic control (Higley et al., 1992) and chronic stress depletes the stores of serotonin (Depue and Spoont, 1986).

All of this provides strong pointers to serotonin depletion being a cause of depression; a conclusion that is reinforced by the effect of anti-depressants such as fluoxetine (Prozac) and paroxetine (Seroxat). These drugs, called Selective Serotonin Reuptake Inhibitors (SSRIs), work through stopping serotonin being reabsorbed at the synapse. Their success would appear to confirm the idea of serotonin deficit being a cause of depression.

Review of the serotonin hypothesis

In fact, the picture is lot more complicated. Firstly, other neurotransmitters might be involved. The pleasure pathway involves not merely serotonin but the neurotransmitter dopamine, a deficit of which is also associated with lethargy, difficulties in decision-making and a lack of pleasure (van Praag, 1980). This led to the suggestion that serotonin regulates other neurotransmitter systems in the brain, such as dopamine and norepinephrine systems (Cooper et al., 1991). In fact, the various pathways in the brain are likely to be interconnected to some extent (Dubovsky and Thomas, 1995), so the idea seems reasonable. However, there is little real evidence that there is depletion of serotonin in the depressed. The evidence for the use of anti-depressants being successful is, to an extent, debatable.

Firstly, depression does clear up spontaneously, so the test is not whether anti-depressants cure depression, but if they do so quickly. Moreover, they have to be compared with placebos (sugar pills), to ensure the cure does not come from clients *thinking* they are receiving effective treatment. We find that minor depression can be dealt with by non-drug methods as effectively as anti-depressants. With severe depression, anti-depressants are not always successful – the effectiveness rate is about 60% for severe depression (Nierenberg, 1995), though this does depend on what counts as a treatment success. Also, it takes 2 or 3 weeks for anti-depressants to work, and there is no known explanation for this delay. All in all, the fact that anti-depressants work only to a degree and there are other treatment methods which do not rely on theories of neurotransmission, such as the use of lithium, electro-convulsive therapy (ECT), and sunlight for Seasonally Affective Disorder, illustrate the gaps in our understanding.

Although a deficit of serotonin is the current favourite explanation for depression there are problems with it. Recently, depression in children has been suggested to be due to a surfeit, not a deficit, of serotonin. Certainly, SSRIs such as fluoxetine and paroxetine have been shown to be of little use in cases of childhood depression. In fact, there is no overwhelming evidence for a biological deficit of serotonin in depression.

Psychoanalytic approach

Freud linked depression with acute grief, seeing the latter as the reaction to the loss of a loved person, or abstractions such as liberty or fatherland (Freud, 1917). Severe depression, or melancholia, has the same traits as those of grief, such as painful dejection, lethargy and feelings of guilt. The only difference is that depression is associated with a loss of self-esteem, unlike grief.

As the loved person no longer exists, all libido, or sexual drive, is withdrawn from that person through a difficult process. Mourning is the redirection of libido away from the dead person. Melancholia or depression is the reaction to loss, not necessarily a death. In fact, the loss may not be identifiable, as it is an unconscious loss. On the other hand, persons might be conscious of the cause of their depression. They know whom they have lost, but not what they have lost.

The advantage of this and later similar theories, is that they move from a purely biological explanation to what actually happens to those who are depressed. It explains why the depressed are not depressed from birth, as might be expected from a purely biological explanation. Furthermore, the modified biological hypothesis that a depressed person has a "vulnerability" to depression actually explains nothing at all. However, the Freudian theory is unscientific in its nature, treating concepts such as libido and the unconscious as if they exist in reality.

Cognitive-behavioural perspective

Another approach, which bypasses the biological and neurological theories, rests on a cognitive-behavioural perspective. This view of depression is currently the most popular, especially with the medical profession. Indeed, counselling for depression is often assumed to be cognitive-behavioural based. As counsellors, we have a responsibility to examine the underlying theories and concepts of this perspective, and as we shall see, the perspective has both its strengths and weaknesses.

The cognitive perspective is based on the idea that depression comes through faulty thinking (Beck et al., 1979) that causes negative moods. An immediate objection is that depression is marked not just by impoverished thinking but also by extreme sadness. However, such moods are seen as the product of thinking. Specifically, emotion is a result of a cognitive appraisal (Lazarus, 1991). For example, we are afraid when we appraise our situation as one where we might be harmed. After seeing a danger, then we are afraid.

So, faulty thinking is the basis not just of the impaired thought processes in depression but in false or uncontrolled emotions as well. Faulty thinking can be seen as unduly negative, and research has shown that depressed people do have more negative thoughts compared to those not depressed (Kendall, 1987). Furthermore, negative thinking can become automatic (Beck, 1976). Beck saw such negativity as a triad: a negative view of oneself, of the world and one's interactions with it, and of the future (Haaga et al., 1991). This negative triad leads to a sense of hopelessness and a lack of effort to help oneself (Peterson and Seligman, 1984). Furthermore, there is a behavioural component, in that depressives, even if they are successful in what they do, are unable to enjoy their success; they do not see their successes as successes. This lack of positive reinforcement makes them even more depressed, and they get caught in a downward spiral.

Reason for depressive thinking

So far, the approach has described depression, but not explained it. Faulty thinking is assumed to arise through stressful events. Such events affect the very process of thinking, the basic patterns or schemata, which determine one's beliefs and assumptions about the world and how one is related to it. These in turn are based on experiences from the past, which determine a person's view of the present. Stressful occurrences can lead to distortions not merely in thoughts but the very process of thinking. Therefore, the depressed cannot easily be convinced they are being unrealistic, as their thought process is faulty.

Depression is a complex reaction, as faulty thinking can produce low moods, but low moods can affect thinking, cognitive processes such as how they judge satisfaction with life (Schwartz and Clore, 1983), their social skills (Forgas et al., 1984), and perception of risk (Johnson and Tversky, 1983). These then contribute to the extent to which people attribute failure to their own inadequacies.

Review of the cognitive-behavioural approach

The idea that faulty thinking causes low mood is not one in which many persons believe. Lazarus' belief that cognitive appraisal underlies emotion is only tautologously correct, as he includes cognitive appraisal in his definition of emotion. It appears much of the confusion about cognition and emotions arises from the definition of terms. While cognitive theorists and researchers are right in part, it is still possible that emotions can arise independently of cognitions (Davidson and Ekman, 1994). While some moods such as contentment or nostalgia call for thinking, and judgements to be made, other simpler moods such as happiness, sadness, anxiety and anger are not always dependent on thinking. We can just feel happy or sad, without having to be happy or sad about anything. This is important, as sadness is not merely such a simple emotion, but also an essential part of depression. Consider the following example, which happened to myself and so can be given in some detail.

> *Being off work and at home through depression, I was feeling neither up nor down. There was a knock on the front door, and I opened it. As I was opening it, I felt a wave of sadness wash over me. This was before I had seen who was at the door. This so startled me that I told the visitor to hold on a second, and shut the door. The sadness left me. I thought the wave of sadness when opening the door must have been a coincidence, so I did not expect what happened next. On opening the door again, the sadness again swept over me, only to disappear when I finally closed the door.*

Thus thinking does not have to determine mood. It is equally possible that mood affects thinking; negative and faulty thinking may be the product of depression rather than its cause. In fact, this is what most commentators believe. If faulty thinking caused depression, then we would expect such faulty patterns of thinking to be present before the onset of depression (Simons et al., 1984; Keller et al., 1987). Moreover, faulty thinking should persist after the depression is lifted, but there is no evidence for either (Teasdale, 1988). We should remember that one depressive episode may well be followed by others, and it might be assumed that faulty thinking would persist between such episodes, yet we find that adolescents make good social and academic progress (McCauley et al., 1988) between episodes.

It might seem that faulty thinking not being the basis for low mood takes away all justification for the cognitive-behavioural perspective. This is not the case, as thinking and mood are closely bound together. What is necessary is to appreciate the limitations of this approach.

Thinking and depression

One of the limitations of the cognitive approach consists of those cases of which are not due to stress. There is also a less obvious limitation, which rests on the questioning of the concept of faulty thinking, which is taken to mean thinking which does not align with reality. What is not considered is whether the thinking of the non-depressed aligns completely with reality. In fact, much of normal thinking may be open to fault, being biased and one-sided (Perkins et al., 1991), and having problems with both logical and probabilistic thinking (Tversky and Kahneman, 1982; Evans et al., 1983; Johnson-Laird and Byrne, 1991). So faulty thinking is characteristic not merely of depressed thinking; it happens to all of us. However, it is persistent with the depressed. Thus persistent faulty thinking characterises depression.

Another question is that while the depressed tend to be very negative, might the non-depressed take an unduly optimistic view of life (Parducci, 1968)? In fact, their information processing also tends to be slightly positive, so they remember more good things than bad (Matlin and Stang, 1978). This results in the Pollyanna effect, where most people take a slightly unrealistically positive view of life and themselves (Hampson and Dawson, 1985), and people see themselves as rather better than others (Taylor and Brown, 1988). This leads to the possibility that perhaps depressives were in fact not so unrealistic after all (Alloy and Abramson, 1988). Indeed it could be that those who are slightly depressed are more accurate in their self-perceptions (Coyne and Gotlib, 1983), but there is little evidence for this (Campbell and Fehr, 1990).

There is a danger of seeing depression as a fault, caused by faulty thinking, which causes low mood. However, it is equally possible to see mania as a fault, caused by faulty thinking, which causes elevated mood. The danger comes from concentrating solely on depression, and not being open to the wider context.

Counselling and the cognitive-behavioural approach

There is a further limitation to the cognitive-behavioural approach of which we should be aware. It is not possible to simply argue depressed clients into "seeing sense", unless the depression is very mild. They will tend to remember negative events (Blaney, 1986) and under-remember those events which are positive (Ingram et al., 1983). They will also under-estimate possible success when having control (Craighead et al., 1979) and even perceive failure being down to bad moods (Baumgardner et al., 1985). Using rational argument ignores the fact that it is negative moods that make people judge themselves and others negatively (Clark and Williams, 1989), and until such moods are lifted, the chance of cognitive improvement remains poor.

An argument for the use of cognitive-behavioural counselling is that it is effective. This has been supported by the research of Miller et al. (1989). Yet, a close review of their work shows weaknesses: small sample sizes, pre-treatment differences between samples, a lack of uniformity in administering medication, a high fall-out rate (30%) and no account being taken of the placebo effect. In another study, cognitive treatment was found to be no more effective than other forms of psychological treatment for depression (Williams, 1992). They were all equally effective or ineffective.

Implications for counselling

In fairness, it would be wrong to declare the cognitive-behavioural approach as ineffective. It might not work for moderate to severe depression, but is as effective as anything else in mild depression. Equally, this approach is as good as other forms of helping, such as behavioural methods (Imber et al., 1990). The danger would be to assume that the approach necessarily does work – and if this is not the case, then clients are being resistant or uncooperative.

In addition, the idea of faulty thinking can mark depressed clients out as in some way deficient or abnormal, whereas they are as capable as anyone else of rational thought. The problem is not their thinking as such, but how depression affects their thinking. The trouble is, there is little appreciation of the capabilities of those depressed. When severely depressed, clients can accomplish logical tasks, provided they do not require too much concentration and do not involve interacting with other people and their feelings. Even when severely depressed, I could do crosswords.

The idea of faulty thinking being typical of those depressed can result in counsellors taking a poor view of clients, seeing them as mistaken in their ideas, views and actions. They fail to grasp that the depressed, like everyone else, have their strengths and deserve to be heard as much as anyone else. For example, Beck says that statements such as "I believe what you say intellectually, but not emotionally" should not be taken at face value (Beck et al., 1979). He maintains that is merely a statement about their degree of belief. In fact, the statement reflects precisely the problems of those depressed; the difference between how they feel and what they think, between the affective and the cognitive.

Stress and depression

It seems that stress has a place in the development of depression, sometimes as a cause and sometimes as an aggravating factor. Part of the argument rests on the fact that pain, especially pain and distress in chronic conditions such as Parkinsonism, multiple sclerosis, Alzheimer's disease, and strokes, is linked with depression (Katon and Sullivan, 1990). Other depression-inducing conditions include thyroid disease and vitamin B12 deficiency, and cases of cancer, especially that of the pancreas. Furthermore, the severity of pain and illness may be associated with the severity of depression (Parmalee et al., 1991).

Stress is in part a product of perception. For instance, time-limited stress can be borne, but stress seen to be endless makes the person feel helpless. Temporary severe pain can be endured, in the expectation of it ending, but this is not the case with chronic pain.

Stress factors

There are various factors that might turn stress into depression. The concept of helplessness is one where control will never be gained, and clients, rather than combating it, can see themselves as the victims of stress. Even when they try to change their situation and avoid stress, they are likely to fail – partly because of their belief of not being able to change things. This reinforces their sense of helplessness (Abramson et al., 1978). So, there are more than just beliefs that support helplessness; there are tested beliefs. This means that those depressed cannot be argued out of their sense of helplessness.

There is also a view that hopelessness can also be a factor in depression (Abramson et al., 1989). However, it would appear hopelessness is more closely related to anxiety and suicide than depression (Alloy et al., 1990).

Role of stress in counselling

Stress can trigger depression, worsen it, or delay recovery from it. It is not the cause of all cases of depression, so dealing with stress is not necessarily the whole treatment for it. The other aspect is that it is not possible to live in a completely stress-free environment or have a stress-free life. So stress has to be managed rather than eliminated. This in turn means it is difficult to eliminate all causes of depression.

MEDICAL TREATMENT OF DEPRESSION

Introduction

Our understanding of clients and their treatment is extended by knowing their possible causes of depression. And the causes of depression are better understood on knowing what treatments are successful. And all of this is relevant to our counselling. For example, counsellors might say, "Have you been taking your medication regularly?" If counsellors are not aware of what is implied in this question, then not only is the question pointless, but clients soon see it as pointless. This does little for the building of a good working relationship.

Understanding psychiatric treatment is essential. We are required not just to know about treatments, but have an understanding of how they work, their drawbacks, and the role of psychiatrists and doctors who are advocating different treatment regimes. Counsellors have to know what other professionals do, though this does not give them licence to overstep their remit.

Drug treatments

The most commonly-used treatment for depression today is that of anti-depressants. The first anti-depressants were monoamine oxidase inhibitors (MAOIs), which stopped the loss of the neurotransmission chemicals, serotonin and noradrenalin. The first MAOI, iproniazid, was tested in the United States as a treatment for tuberculosis, and proved to be not very successful. By chance, it was noticed that some patients were unnaturally euphoric on this drug, and so it was tried out to treat depression. It is worth noting that the unexpected effect of the drug rules out the possibility that it merely had a placebo effect, as there was no expectation that the drug would work with depressed patients. These MAOIs, such as phenelzine and isocarboxazid, are now rarely used. A trial run in 1965 by the Medical Research Council found that tricyclics and electro-convulsive treatment (ECT) were effective, but the MAOI, phenelzine, was no more effective than a placebo. It was subsequently found that the dosage given for phenelzine had been too low, but MAOIs never did regain popularity. This was partly because they interact with a variety of foods that contain the chemical tyramine, such as cheese, red wine, pickled herrings, meat or yeast extracts and game. Oh yes, and caviar! They also interact dangerously with other classes of anti-depressants.

In the late 1950s, another drug, imipramine was used to treat cases of schizophrenia. Although it was not successful in treating schizophrenia, it was found to work in cases of depression. This brought in the class of tricyclic anti-depressants, such as amitriptyline and dothiepin. It should be said that there are marked side-effects with tricyclics. Amitriptyline has caused heart dysrhythmias, and has occasionally had fatal results in patients with cardiac disease. All tricyclic anti-depressants tend to cause drowsiness, dry mouth, blurred vision, constipation, urine retention and sweating. These effects lessen over 2 or 3 weeks of taking the drugs. Care needs to be taken when giving the drugs to the elderly, as fainting can occur. The amount should be very gradually increased to the correct dosage. Tricyclic anti-depressants have a sedative effect, and so may be prescribed when sleeping is a problem. They also cause weight gain, which can be a problem with some clients, especially if they already feel bad about themselves. Sexual dysfunction is another possible side -effect, though sexual activity in the depressed is likely to be low.

Although doctors are likely to reassure patients and say that anti-depressants are not addictive, suddenly stopping their use is not recommended. This can result in a degree of nausea, possible vomiting, insomnia, occasional panic attacks and restlessness.

The world of Prozac

In the 1980s, a new class of drug, known as SSRIs were introduced. These blocked the uptake of serotonin and the result was an elimination of depression and increased pleasure. They had fewer side-effects than the tricyclics and MAOIs, and were much less toxic – an important factor if there was a risk of suicide. There was also little risk to the heart. The commonly used SSRIs are fluoxetine (Prozac), paroxetine (Seroxat) and sertraline (Lustral). Indeed, fluoxetine has become a best seller. However, there have been problems stopping the use of such drugs, and a few patients have become suicidal on them. They can cause over-activity and agitation, and in some patients cause nausea, and difficulties related to sexual activity are common.

Long-term drug use

Anti-depressants are used not just to lift depression but as continuation therapy, using the drugs for another 6 months to ensure the patient stays on an even keel. There can also be long-term therapy where patients are kept on these drugs for years to prevent reoccurrence of further depressive episodes. There has been little research done into such long-term therapies (Fava and Kaji, 1994), though there are some indications that drugs may have some preventative use (Kupfer et al., 1992).

In fact, it may be that clients become tolerant to some of the effects of the drugs;

> *Lenny*: "The first time I had amitriptyline it was great, as I got a good night's sleep, the first for ages. But now it does little for me. I sleep only three or four hours at night. And if I take more than one tablet, the side -effects get really bad."

We should also remember that some side-effects are effects which clients do not like, and not just medical side-effects;

> *Eloise*: "I would prefer to be skinny than fat. These tablets make you put on weight. And I'm still depressed; fat and depressed."

There are further possible disadvantages, such as that of patients becoming reliant on drugs, and so failing to make necessary changes in their lifestyle and social networks. Clients want to return to "normality", and having to attend doctors or psychiatrists is not normality; it is a reminder that they are depressed.

Anti-depressant drugs review

Anti-depressants do appear to lessen the length of depression, and are used for moderate to severe depression. Although these drugs are promoted as having full scientific backing, their actual mechanism of working is not fully understood. Many alleged mechanisms are little more than hypotheses. There is no definite proof that there is a lack of serotonin or other neurotransmitters in depressed persons. While SSRIs appear to point to the importance of serotonin depletion in depression, we should not forget that other treatments such as tricyclics are thought to affect norepinephrine, ECT is thought to affect dopamine, and lithium affects depression directly, not through a neurotransmitter. It is best to say that anti-depressant drugs may work, but we do not really know why, at present. Even when considering neurotransmitters such as serotonin, we do not know for sure whether depression is a product of neurotransmitter irregularities or whether those irregularities are a product of depression, which is caused by more fundamental processes. We do not know when there are natural changes in neurotransmission, say with age (Alexopoulos, 1991). Nor has there been any agreed demonstration that recovery from depression is directly related to changes in neurotransmitters in adults (Greenberg and Fisher, 1989). None of the above is reason enough to doubt that anti-depressants can be effective, but it does show we should be realistic, and not accept at face value simplistic explanations of depression.

The marketing of psychiatric disorders

Depression was not a widely recognised condition, at least by the general public, until the 1980s and the emergence of the newer anti-depressants such as fluoxetine (Prozac). The financial interests of the pharmaceutical companies played a part in publicising the concept of depression being a relatively common condition (Healy, 1991). In fact, pharmaceutical companies sell not merely drugs, but reasons to take them, and this includes popularising psychiatric categories. The idea of widespread obsessive–compulsion disorders was used by Geigy to sell the tricyclic cloripramine (Beaumont, 1996), and social phobia was used to sell the drug moclobemide.

Clinical trials

Trials, comparing new drugs with placebos, were brought in to get away from the overblown claims of drug manufacturers. However, such trials merely prove the drugs tested have an effect, not that they result in patients' recovery. Moreover, the tests are usually done on small recruited samples of the population, usually young and fit persons, so side-effects may not be found. Nor does the Medicines Control Agency ensure drug effectiveness, as its role is to prevent mislabelling and ensure the drug has been tested.

Clinical trials that do not show a positive result from the manufacturer's viewpoint, are often not reported. In fact, the greatest determinant of whether research is published is sponsorship (Gilbody and Song, 2000). All of the above warns us about the acceptance of the claims of drug manufacturers, even when they are said to be backed by the company's research.

Electro-convulsive treatment

Ignorance about the mechanisms of treatment is echoed when we turn to electro-convulsive treatment, ECT. This treatment method, whereby a current is sent through electrodes on the temples and through the brain to promote a seizure, is one way of treating severe depression immediately (Rodger et al., 1994), as opposed to drug therapy which can take 2 or 3 weeks. This is helpful where there is a high risk of suicide. There are likely to be side -effects from ECT, such as disorientation and short-term memory loss, so treatment is recommended for a maximum of three times a week otherwise side-effects become too great (Sackheim et al., 1987).

Electro-convulsive treatment is said to lead to an increase in the neuro-transmitter dopamine, but it is fair to say the mechanism of such treatment is far from understood. It is a method to be used only after drug therapy has failed. Rather worryingly, it has been recommended for those with learning disabilities or psychosis (Buchan et al., 1992), categories of patients with little power to protest against its use on them. There are different views of the effectiveness and the ethics of this treatment (Sackheim, 1989).

Other treatments

In cases of Seasonally Affective Disorder, depressive bouts during winter months, it has been found that exposure to light, containing as little ultra-violet light as possible, is beneficial (Rosenthal, 1989). There are possible side-effects from the bright light, such as eyestrain, headaches, irritability and insomnia. This treatment has not been proved to be of use in other forms of depression and the mechanism of its working is unknown. Another drug that is used in combination with anti-depressants is lithium (Ontiveros et al., 1991). This is relatively effective, but its use needs to be closely monitored, as it can be toxic.

Reprise

The fact that there are very different forms of treatment for depression, that treatment does have its limitations, and patients do not always respond positively, underlines the fact that our understanding of treatment and depression still leaves much to be desired. The current popularity of SSRIs, such as fluoxetine (Prozac), appears to point to the depletion of serotonin being a factor in depression. Yet, the fact that they can be augmented by the use of lithium, tricyclics (Salzman, 1993), thyroid medication (Joffe et al., 1993), and stimulants such as Ritalin and amphetamine (Nierenberg, 1995), shows that neither treatment nor depression itself is fully understood.

Chapter 4

Counselling Preliminaries

Introduction

It is assumed that the reader has some familiarity with counselling, so the emphasis is not on counselling in general, but on work with depressed clients.

There is no reason why counsellors cannot counsel depressed clients, and they probably have done so. What follows may be fairly obvious to some, but it never harms having to rethink how one is counselling before maybe taking on new perspectives. We will use some of the previous information, and also be sensitive to the fact that depression is still not a totally familiar country and there are limits to our knowledge, understanding and ability to help.

Before counselling begins, counsellors may have some questions to consider. They have to come to grips with some practical considerations.

Choice of helping

Clients generally choose to come for counselling; it is something they want. However, depressed clients are more likely to come because they have been referred by professionals or persuaded to come by spouses, close friends, or colleagues at work. When asked, referrers will say that the client agreed to the referral. And that is the first potential difficulty, as those depressed tend to go along with what others say, and may even feel compelled to do as a professional worker suggests. This is not necessarily unwelcome, as it avoids having to make a decision, and satisfies the professional.

So, rather than pressurising clients, the counsellor introduces client choice; options such as self-help, befriending, group support, individual, couple or family counselling. However, depressed clients are liable to experience difficulties in making a choice, and the list of options is intimidating. So counsellors may have to take a lead, making suggestions as to what may be in the best interests of the client. Unfortunately, counsellors often suggest what is familiar, what seems comfortable to them. Unknowingly, they make the decision for their own benefit rather than that of clients.

Thus before diving in, counsellors should take their time. Some clients might not want counselling as much as non-counselling help. For instance, some elderly clients might benefit more from social support or pain management. Severely depressed persons might first benefit from taking anti-depressants. Counsellors have to be aware of their agendas at this point. They usually want to work with clients; they have a financial interest in counselling them; they do not want to appear unable to help clients. Counsellors have to be conscious of the ethics of counselling, and work towards the benefit of their clients, and not of themselves.

If clients want and would benefit from counselling, then what further help they require remains to be discovered. Counsellors should be patient, as the usual counselling tasks may take longer with depressed clients.

Depth of counselling

Counselling is an interactional communication process. The question that arises with depressed clients is the extent to which they are able to enter into it. When reading about the counselling of depressed clients, I read what they have to say and am struck by how verbal the clients are. This might reflect they are often American and very forthcoming; or is that just a stereotype? It does make me wonder as to the degree of depression they are experiencing. Are they only very mildly depressed? If so, are the more depressed clients being missed? The apparent ease of counselling depressed clients is misleading. It can be hard going at times. The amount of interactional feedback is reduced, clients are lethargic and unmotivated, and they are liable to misunderstand the counsellor. But this may reflect an inappropriate depth of counselling; reduce it, and clients may well benefit. The counselling must vary according to the degree of depression.

Problem ownership and treatment displacement

One of the tasks to be decided by client and counsellor is whose problem or problems the client is carrying. In practice clients live in a social context so their difficulties affect and are affected by several persons.

For instance, we might find that stress is an important part of a client's depression, and this can arise through work. But to what degree is the depression originating from the client, and how much from colleagues, managers, or systems in the work? Again, there is an ethical question, as to the legitimacy of working with an individual client rather than all those involved in the problem.

Clients might be affected, but so might others, such as family members, who are in regular contact with the depressed person. They might not be depressed, but they might want help for themselves.

Apart from the interactional nature of depression, we also have to be aware of the politics of problem ownership. Parents will declare their children are having problems, and so distance themselves from the family difficulties. In cases of physical abuse, women can be depressed, but the cause lies primarily with the abuser. Counselling the abused can go towards rationalising or excusing the abuser's behaviour.

Client difficulties

Sometimes clients may experience difficulties in life, but find it far from easy to put them into words. It is worth counsellors taking their time if this is the case, and not judging the client as being unable to describe how he or she feels. If there are problems for clients, it may help to consider the following possibilities:

- The client is at the stage of incipient depression, when description is difficult.
- The client has many problems and does not know where to start. Alternatively one problem can drift into others, so it is difficult to say what the difficulties are.
- The client sees the world as pointless, so it is equally pointless to describe one's own problems.
- For some clients the signs or symptoms of depression are strange and difficult to describe. In addition, it is difficult to know whether everything experienced needs to be told to the counsellor.
- Sometimes clients are depressed, but have an image of what depression is, and what they experience is different – at least to some extent. They may be reluctant to describe how they feel, and they feel they have got it wrong. They may also worry how the counsellor will react to the account of their experiences.
- It can happen that a client's problems are inextricably linked with those of others, often those of a partner. The association can be so close that it is difficult to begin to separate them or even see them as separate.

So if there are difficulties for clients in formulating their difficulties, they should be given plenty of time. Sometimes, the initial work with depressed clients can take twice as long as with non-depressed clients. However, pressurising them in any way merely exacerbates the problem.

Occasionally clients seem unable to get going. Their depression can come on and they simply blank out. If this happens, waiting will not produce any answers. It requires the counsellor to take the lead and make some suggestions, and ask the client if any of the following apply.

- Difficulty in talking to people
- Thinking processes seem to shut down
- Not knowing how to react
- Cannot be bothered with anything
- Too tired to continue.

Such suggestions, bedded in the here-and-now, usually produce a response. The point is not to look for overall problems, but to deal with the immediate difficulties. Once the client can talk about that, then it becomes easier to move on to the real reasons for coming for counselling.

It might seem that the difficulty of clients framing their precise problems is a problem for counsellors. In fact, it can be turned to counselling use, as it opens the way to discussing topics such as:

- Lack of belief in the client to take on his or her difficulties
- Inability to communicate fully
- Seeing counselling as ultimately pointless
- Client lacking self-confidence.

Counselling at times is a matter of turning apparent weaknesses into strengths, so clients have the belief that something can be done. This increases the belief that they can help themselves.

Sometimes the signs of depression are hard to describe and clients flounder around trying to explain how they feel. It can help if the counsellor gets the client to stick to describing bodily signs of depression, and also highlight the fact that description is difficult and there is a consequent gap between client experience and counsellor understanding. This gap can be used, so counsellors feed back how their clients' accounts seem to them. This in turn helps clients become more aware of themselves and their behaviour (Greenberg and Safran, 1989), which helps to connect them to their feelings.

Difficulties in counselling – rumination

In counselling, emphasis is placed on clients helping themselves, and this involves reflecting, thinking of what they are doing. And that is a problem. With depressed clients, reflection often descends into rumination, thinking about oneself (Baumeister, 1990), which aggravates depression (Gibbons et al., 1985). It may seem strange, as dealing with worries is usually seen as being preferable to avoiding them or pretending they do not exist (MacLeod et al., 1991). However, the presence of depression can affect the whole counselling process (Atkinson et al., 1991). People who are depressed say that they spend time thinking, but often they are prisoners of their own thought processes. What they do is think superficially, often returning to the same thought time and again. Such goalless thinking is not helpful.

> *Larry*: "Thinking about what has happened, what I've done and what could have happened. Thinking that way, I can put myself into a poor mood."

When caught up in one's own thinking processes, clients can't help themselves. Distractive ploys may prove useful (Wenzlaff et al., 1987). People cannot get rid of negative thoughts by thinking about them. A new thought is needed (Wegner et al., 1987).

> *Sharon*: "It is useful to stop dwelling on yourself, take a walk or concentrate on something easy. Write down what you are feeling, though the difficulty is that sometimes you cannot be bothered."

Difficulties in counselling – listening

Another difficulty for counsellors is that clients' communication can be poor; the act of listening is too much for them. This becomes more of a problem, the deeper the depression.

> *Carol*: "In times of high anxiety the last thing you want is someone speaking to you. The strain of having to listen is too much. But over that, it increases anxiety greatly and makes you feel so much worse. Yet I can listen to the soaps on television with little difficulty. I suppose it's a world that does not affect me. You know it's not real."

What can make the situation more problematic is that the degree of depression can vary. Indeed, sometimes it can change greatly or even come to an end.

> *Jill*: "I get out of the depressive mood quite suddenly. Just going out of the house can change things. It's like the black mood is on a switch, turning off and on."

So counsellors have to stay alert to the possibility that their clients might feel better and respond to deeper counselling. Clients have to be seen as people with differing degrees of depression. However, this does not mean they are depressive cases. They are people.

Client strengths

It is easy to get caught up in the limitations of clients due to their depression. This can reinforce how such clients feel about themselves. So we have to look at the client's achievements, which in the eyes of the non-depressed may appear to be very modest. Managing to get out of the house to come for counselling can be a considerable achievement for very depressed clients, as can the taking of medication (Rush et al., 1986). This positive perception of clients is not so easy when they are sending out negative messages.

> *Jill*: "I get depressed as everyone seems to use me and then leave me. There seems to be no point in life. Since as long as I can remember it has been like that. I think the world has it in for me, that I am always going to be a victim. People say I'm daft, exaggerating, and I should look on the bright side of things. I agree with them, but deep down I know I'm the one who's right. Whatever anyone says, life showed me that things were against me. It wasn't imagination. Nothing went right. Even when I tried to do right ... it would turn out wrong."

Our counselling has to reflect realistically where the client is at, and be appropriate for the client – rather than the client being appropriate for the counselling (Dimond and Havens, 1975). But being realistic means counsellor and client both being aware of strengths as well as weaknesses.

> *Roger*: "I have a history of depression, to let you know."
> *Me*: "It sounds as if you have been fighting it for a long time. How did you try to manage it? How did you cope?"
> *Roger*: "To be honest, I used to take amphetamine sulphate, speed every day at one time."
> *Me*: "Wasn't there a comedown after the effects wore off?"

Roger: "You're right. That's why I used to use constantly. But then I stopped. I wasn't really working for me. So I smoked hash. And that didn't really work either. Finally, I went to the doctor, and was on Prozac for two years."
Me: "But you are not on anything now."
Roger: "The doctor said I was OK. But I need to resolve some issues. It all goes back to my childhood."
Me: "And how are you managing now?"
Roger: "I go to work, am able to function there, but cannot get to sleep easily. Need to get half pissed to get a sleep. And I still get depressed."
Me: "So, can I ask you, what made you decide to come for counselling?"
Roger: "Well, I met this girl, and I like her, but keep shutting her out. It's like emotional shutters come down. There are unresolved issues."

If clients are moderately severely depressed, they might require support and direction, and a lack of counselling structure will be unhelpful. And if the depression is severe, counselling is not recommended (Depression Guideline Panel, 1993).

Overall approach: development and control

When working with clients, counsellors must have some basic aim, and this aim is carried out through numerous different methods. For me, this aim is to restore the person to good health. This does not mean clients will return to the same position they had before their depression; nobody can turn back time. It does mean clients will develop and reach a place where they are content. In this journey there are three main stages:

- The stage where clients are merely existing, hanging on in the face of an illness against which they feel virtually helpless.
- The stage where clients see themselves as survivors, able to cope with their daily situation, but largely unable to deal with the future.
- The stage where clients feel they are themselves, they are in control of their life, and have come to terms with their depression.

The length of time taken to reach the third stage depends in part on the severity of the depression, the support clients receive and the efforts they make.

The effect of depression is to limit, temporarily, the abilities of clients, cognitively, emotionally and behaviourally. So helpers will often try to remedy this by working on what are seen as those deficits. This may not be the best approach. It reinforces the fact that the client is incapable, abilities have been lost and the person is not managing. But the chief weakness of this approach is that it fails to take account of what is happening to the person. We are who we are because of our abilities, memories and relationships. When those are diminished, we are diminished; we feel we are no longer ourselves. Our very identity and being is threatened.

One of the themes in this book is that of clients regaining control. This is a multi-layered concept. Nobody can control everything that happens in life. So control is a balance. We can have too little control, and we can have too much. Those depressed almost always have too little control. Yet there is the danger of aiming for total control, ignoring others and imagining that control for itself is a good thing. We might take the example of relationships; what relationships should offer is a balance, such as a balance between oneself and the other person, between the couple and the individual.

To achieve balance, clients require a sense of control. Clients have to feel they have control, in order to exert it. For instance, a person in a sick role may indirectly control the rest of the family, yet not feel in control. The paradox is that if there was a sense of control, then, the client probably would not want to control the family.

Beyond control

This brings me to a further point. A sense of control occurs when people are aware of themselves as persons in their own right, and this means they say "This is me", and "I am becoming me". They realise they are themselves – not always so easy a task for depressed clients. Yet finally they also have to be aware of themselves as moving on, as developing. Clients are told, "You will be treated as a person, not as a depressive. You might have depression, but the first task is for you to recognise that you are you. We start with you, not your depression. And we move on. It is not just a matter of you recovering from depression. It is also a matter of your development as a person."

The client has to be content with that sense of control, and in the end, content with life as a whole. This might seem a rather imprecise objective, yet it reflects the nature of depression. By merely wanting a sense of control, we are aiming for purely cognitive objectives. Depression is not just about our thinking, intentions and beliefs. It is about our feelings and mood. By ignoring these, we are ignoring the very essence of depression. So aiming for contentment is not an idealistic hope. It is part of the overall plan.

In this book little will be said about contentment. While it might seem the topic has been raised and then forgotten, this is not the case. It reflects the fact that feelings, such as contentment, cannot be rationally injected into a person. We cannot make a person content. Contentment is something the client has to find. It comes from being at ease with oneself and the world, aided by others being the same, including counsellors, who see clients for themselves and not just their problems. Clients are taken as having potential, and this is increased through positivity. It does not help to concentrate on the negative, at least not until the client has the strength not merely to resist the negative but also to use it positively.

REFERRALS

Coming for help

The decision of a depressed person to go for help, whether taken by that person alone or with the support or the urging of others, is a defining moment. It defines the person as being not well. It is not a neutral act, but one that carries implications. It is not an act in isolation; it is the culmination of what has been going on for weeks, possibly even months or years.

When depressed clients come for help, it is usually not because they have suddenly become depressed. Rather, it is because they have been fighting depression and the fight has become too much for them. This is not always appreciated. Counsellors might ask what started the depression and how it has progressed; they seldom ask how clients fought their depression and how they feel at being overcome by it. How often are clients' past efforts acknowledged and integrated into future work countering depression? But even this may be assuming too much. Clients or patients may not realise what is wrong with them. They may have been fighting depression but using drugs or alcohol to manage the effects, and their drug or alcohol use is seen as the problem. Alternatively, even when clients do realise there is something amiss, they put it down to being the product of adverse circumstances, the product of stress, or the failure or actions of those around them.

The decision to go for help may be made with the help of another person, such as a spouse or parent. This sets up its own dynamic, as there can be feelings around such helping, possibly aggravated by the spouse or parent not being given the option of being included in what happens as regards further professional help. Much responsibility is suddenly taken away from the spouse or parent, leaving him or her with a very indeterminate role. This is unfortunate, as the depressed person is in a very vulnerable and suggestible state. There can be a need for someone at home who is able to offer clear support.

Paul: "The psychiatrist said I should come into hospital. The last thing I felt able to deal with was a ward full of mentally ill people. That does not make me any different or better than them. It's just that I wanted to hold onto a sense of normality, and that is to be found at home, not in a mental ward."

This does assume the spouse and family will be supportive, which may not be the case. Depression can affect the whole family, causing intense feelings such as anger, guilt, despair and grief in family members (Lefley, 1989). The effects of depression can vary according to the length a couple have been together, the ages of the children and the history of the family (Marsh, 1992). Plainly, a lot of counselling work is needed to help the client put what has happened into context.

Counselling around referral

The outcome is that counselling should include the process of referral. There can be strong feelings around it, and for the client, it is not a simple or automatic process.

Chloe: "After my husband died, I suppose a few months after, I became quite depressed. Both of my sons said I should get to a doctor."
Me: "How did you feel about them saying that?"
Chloe: "Well, they were concerned about me."
Me: "Um. But how did you really feel about it, being told to get to a doctor?"
Chloe: "Awkward. Awkward because they were awkward, didn't know what to say or do. It made me feel guilty. When my daughter Debbie visited from London, she said, 'Mum, you should know the boys couldn't support a paper bridge. Don't worry about them. Look after yourself. Go and see a doctor, and do it for yourself, not for them'."
Me: "Debbie sounds straightforward."
Chloe: "Yes, I miss her. Mind, she has a good job in public relations. So I did take her advice ... I wasn't sure what to say to the doctor."
Me: "Sometimes people going to the doctor rehearse what they are going to say."
Chloe: "Yes. Before going in I had worked it all out, but never really got a chance. I started off by saying I was not sleeping well, and he said he did not believe in giving out a lot of sleeping tablets. So I mentioned my husband had died abroad at his work. The doctor went on about the pills, saying he might consider prescribing anti-depressants. I don't know what I wanted, but that wasn't it. Finally, he said counselling might help."

As we can see, the process of referral is not just important for its own sake, giving an indication of client feelings even before coming for counselling: it also provides interesting hints and suggestions about the situation, about relationships in the family and about other problems. All of these can affect the subsequent course of the help given.

Summary of referral and counselling

Being helped is not a neutral act. Receiving help can lower clients' self-esteem (Fisher et al., 1982), and make them feel even more helpless and worthless. This can be aggravated by interaction with counsellors. Fortunately, there are ways of counteracting negative effects:

- Ensure the initial provision of help is done as quickly and informally as possible. Any referral should be replied to within 24 working hours, and an appointment made within a week. Though some counsellors have said this is not possible, what they are actually saying is it is not possible under their working system.
- Some clients may not be at the point of being able to deal with being helped by someone. Do not assume they should be counselled. However they can benefit from depression home packs, relevant literature and tapes about depression (Karabenick and Knapp, 1988).
- Coming for help may be eased by the thought that they might be able to help others in the future, directly or indirectly (Nadler et al., 1985). Advocacy by the agency for the better treatment of those depressed is built on the experiences of those who come for help. Mentioning this when explaining confidentiality can help even up the power imbalance between counsellor and client.

Doctors, psychiatrists and counsellors

Referrals usually come as part of a referral system. Accordingly, it is important that the presence and role of the counsellor is known to other professionals, and the different remits and limits are drawn. For instance, giving advice about a client's medication is not within the remit of counselling, though giving information about drugs (which may include what the client is taking) is admissible. If a client has difficulties with medication, then counsellors have the role of boosting the client's confidence so they feel able to speak to their doctor or psychiatrist. We also have to understand that medication not only helps clients with regard to their depression, but can improve cognitive abilities and so enhance counselling (DiMascio et al., 1987). We have to be careful not to separate drug treatment completely from counselling, but appreciate the fact that they can be interconnected.

INFORMAL COUNSELLING RULES

Introduction

To get the most from counselling, the sessions have to be between people; it has to be a human encounter. This means both counsellor and client have to have a good working relationship, and have contact on a personal level. Being in roles is restrictive, leaving both parties behaving as they think they should behave, as opposed to being themselves. Trainees learn the role of being a counsellor, but this has to be integrated into being themselves, so that the counsellor presents more than a counsellor in role. This all takes some time, and new counsellors are inclined to present a counselling face, act as they think counsellors *should* act rather than being themselves as counsellors. Clients are sensitive to being presented with a counsellor-in-role, and sometimes will remark that the counsellor seemed to be playing a game with them – which is not so far from the truth. We should not think clients do not see what is happening; some are well able to observe and even imitate counsellors, doctors and psychiatrists in role – sometimes alarmingly well.

Yet simply being oneself in counselling is not enough. There are objectives to be attained, work to be done together and a relationship to be established. The groundwork is done before both parties meet. The onus falls on the counsellor, who initially has to set the scene and oversee what is happening. Clients usually do not know what to expect; they do not know what to do. They are powerless, and this can reinforce feelings of depression. Such notions of powerlessness can be alleviated in part by the setting up of counselling rules. These help to give a sense of what the counselling is about, and, like all rules, give a sense of security.

Setting out rules

Rules themselves are of little help unless they are properly managed. This means they are not to be imposed on the client. They have to be explained, discussed and then accepted. This sets the tone of counselling being a joint enterprise. When to introduce rules and how much time to spend discussing them is a matter of judgement. Depressed clients will often not want to bother with much of a discussion. However it is still important to get the client's agreement to them. The rules might consist of:

- The counsellor will help the client to help himself or herself.
- The client will work to help himself or herself.
- All major decisions as regards counselling will be agreed and made jointly.
- The counselling sessions may be tape-recorded. Such tapes shall be confidential, and copies of them may be requested by the client. The client can also request to see any notes made by the counsellor after the counselling has terminated.

One possibility is to discuss these issues in the first session. Being the first, it is usually longer than the norm, so it can be broken up by a tea break. During the break, the issues can be discussed. Talking during a break can take away any sense of being counselled, and makes discussion easier.

The number of rules should be kept to a minimum. More than four increases the likelihood they will not be remembered and are consequently ineffective.

NO SHOWS

When clients fail to appear for counselling

What happens if the client does not turn up? The answer may vary from simply thinking that the client has changed their mind and will not be coming, to sending them a card saying they missed an appointment and suggesting another date and time, or even paying them an official home visit to see how they are. Clearly, procedures vary according to counsellor and agency. What I would say is that the following have to be borne in mind:

- Clients may be forgetful as a result of depression or associated anxiety. They may fail appointments, especially if they are not given or sent out an appointment card.
- Many things may occur in a client's life: falling physically ill, having a sudden appointment with the Incapacity Benefit Office, relatives turning up for a visit, or the client ends up in police cells. There is more to a client's life than counselling.
- Quite often if depression increases, then the client cannot face meeting people, including the counsellor.

It should be remembered that lack of adequate follow-up by the counsellor might be interpreted as rejection. Clients may not want to see a counsellor or cannot be bothered to see one, yet might still appreciate occasionally being contacted. This can make the decision to come for counselling at a later date easier.

PRIVACY

Introduction

It is commonly assumed that clients should come for counselling and pour their hearts out; that will help. To get rid of secrets, to get things off their chest, helps clients. This may be broadly right, but there are exceptions. Firstly, there are times when clients simply do not want to talk or listen.

> *Jill*: "It is hard to communicate when you are depressed. You can't be bothered with people. On the phone I cannot cope with conversation. I never know whether to answer the phone or not when it rings. It's not just the speaking; I am not sure how I come across."

But depression may not be the only problem. When giving intimate details, clients can make themselves vulnerable (Kelvin, 1977). This means that communication has to be controlled, and some things are held back (Burgoon et al., 1989). Clients do not tell us everything, and we have to appreciate that fact. If the working relationship is poor, they will never reveal very much at all. The length of counselling rests on the time taken to establish a good relationship, and that depends on both client and counsellor. Clients may be reluctant to communicate for reasons other than depression. They may be vulnerable as a result of their life experiences and be aware of their vulnerability, and disclose according to their perceived tolerance (Rawlins, 1983), and how they think the counsellor will react.

Sometimes it can help to discuss with clients why they find it difficult to talk – provided by this time a good working relationship has been established. One of the things to bear in mind is the Polar Bear Effect. Tell a person to think of anything – as long as it is not polar bears, then that person cannot get the thought of polar bears out of mind (Wegner et al., 1987). Similarly, those who do not talk about their spouse's suicide or their child's accidental death have more difficulty getting thoughts of death from their mind. This can result in an increase in health problems (Pennebaker and O'Heeron, 1984).

The other aspect is that non-disclosure can amount to concealment, and this can increase guilt, as the very act of concealment becomes equated with hiding something that is bad (Fishbein and Laird, 1979).

Nevertheless, there is no justification for making clients speak about what they would prefer not to speak about. Everyone is entitled to retain privacy; his or her personal defences. This is not being uncooperative or refusing to face reality. It is being sensible, especially if there is insufficient support, help and self-help.

PREVIOUS HELPING

Counselling in the past

As counselling progresses, it is likely that the counsellor will, at some point, ask clients whether they have previously been to counselling. If the answer is "yes", then the follow-up might be to say, "So you have some idea of what it is like . . ?", possibly returning to the topic at a later date. At that time, the client is asked what the previous counselling was like, as there can be anxieties or other feelings left over from the experience. Sometimes the counsellor has to be careful, as clients can say things like, "The last counsellor was rubbish!" This might be a client ploy to diminish the last counsellor, in order to boost the present counsellor and get him or her on side. Alternatively, clients sometimes say, "The last counsellor was brilliant!" This can be an indirect put-down, as the client is feeling threatened or rather powerless in the ongoing counselling. It is best to delay acceptance of such comments, but still bear them in mind. Counsellors would also be advised to look to their counselling in the light of such comments.

It is worth finding out about previous counselling, as it could have left feelings with the client, it could have felt unfinished, or sometimes clients may want to talk about subjects they failed to talk about previously.

Medical diagnosis

The diagnosis of depression, whether by doctor or psychiatrist, may seem a purely medical matter. Yet it has effects with which counsellors should be familiar. In particular, what does it mean to clients to be diagnosed as depressed? There are both good and bad aspects. The first time depression comes, clients and their families do not know what the trouble is, so everyone guesses, tries to make sense of what is happening. These guesses are often not shared, so the imagination can run riot. For example the client's partner notices a lack of interest and wonders if the client has fallen out of love or is having an affair with someone else. Or is the lack of communication because the client is angry about something? Has the partner done something wrong? What the diagnosis does is to put a meaning to what is taking place and thus end the imaginings and anxiety in the family.

The depressed client feels better because he or she is now able to look back and begin to understand what was really going on. This gives a sense of control, and that control can be used to make the decision to hand matters over to the doctor or psychiatrist. Clients take up the sick role, and this has the advantage of allowing clients to change from their routine, stop work, avoid making important decisions, and avoid facing many of life's problems. Their role in the family is reduced, and expectations are lowered. Stress is reduced, and they are in a role where they are ready to be treated.

> *Carrie*: "I had been looking forward to Ruth's birth, as had the whole family. She was to be my first child. Yet when she was born, I did not bond with her. The rest of the family came to the hospital and were making goo-goo noises at her, but I felt like saying, 'For God's sake, take her away!' I was uptight all the time and everyone knew something was up, as usually I had quite laid back. It was some time before I went to the doctor and he told me it was post-natal depression. I was relieved, as it was not my fault; it wasn't really me acting like that. It was the result of the birth and my body was not back to normal. I was put on medication and within 2 or 3 days I was beginning to feel better, and the depression went after 3 weeks. It was 2 years, however, before I bonded with Ruth."

The disadvantage of diagnosis is that clients enter into the sick role and may think they can be passive and not be responsible for themselves. This is reasonable when they are severely depressed, but not reasonable as they begin to recover. Moreover, leaving the sick role requires more than not being ill. They have to prove to themselves and others that they are well. And the fact of sickness does not leave entirely, as it is put on record. Depression is still a stigma; it still causes a loss of self-esteem. The person is never quite the same again. Only later do clients realise the diagnosis can bring its drawbacks.

Seeing the doctor

Apart from diagnosis, clients will see members of the medical profession. Generally, this is quite positive, and this can be reinforced in counselling. Yet we should not be blind to the fact that consultations do not always go well. Part of this simply arises through there being too little time, actual or perceived, for adequate consultations. But, in addition, doctors do not always understand what patients want.

> *Jill*: "He did not tell me what was really wrong, what was the matter. That was what I felt. He did not reassure me or tell me what to do. He was either writing or staring at his computer screen. He hardly looked at me. He didn't look at the rash on my face, and I wanted to ask him whether this was a side-effect of dothiepin. He said it was probably just stress. Later on I discovered from another doctor it was eczema."

On one level, there is a need for information on the possible side-effects of anti-depressants. Symptoms such as sweating, blurred vision, rashes, palpitations, dizziness and difficulties in passing urine may seem to patients almost as alarming as the depression itself. Often depression is diagnosed and treated, but the drug side-effects are not explained and nothing is done about them. From the medical perspective, these drug effects tend to diminish over time and are relatively unimportant. For patients, it is not the drug effects but how they see themselves being treated that may be the problem, especially as they are likely to have lowered self-esteem and feel vulnerable. Their trust in the medical profession might be partly destroyed, making clients more likely to ignore what doctors tell them, such as how and when the drugs should be taken.

Yet giving information is just one part. Consultation is an encounter that can be useful and also ensure that patients will take care of themselves. It can also, if poorly done, feed into other patient problems.

> *Jill*: "I could not say anything to the doctor, as I felt guilty, as if I had done something wrong. I've carried guilt all my life. It's because I feel so much for other people. I'm only logical when I'm angry, but after the anger has gone, then I'm liable change my mind."

In this case, the client wanted to ask about the possibility of being prescribed fluoxetine (Prozac). She felt unable to do so. So the counsellor has a variety of options, such as building up clients' self-esteem, encouraging them to go back to their doctor and talk about any difficulties or worries they were experiencing, or discuss the reason for clients wanting to change the drug prescribed.

ASSESSMENTS

Introduction

Assessing depressed clients is often done by counsellors, though the rationale for so doing is not always clear. The assessments follow the medical model of gathering symptoms in order to confirm a diagnosis of depression. But this is not the prime aim in counselling. Furthermore, assessments can diminish client power in the counselling relationship, resulting in less control. So, when thinking about assessments in counselling, it is helpful to ask the following questions:

- What am I trying to achieve?
- How will it help the client?
- What is the theoretical basis that underlies the assessment?
- How best should I do the assessment?
- How valid will the assessment be?
- Do I have a baseline for comparison?
- Will the information obtained change over time?
- Will I need to repeat the assessment?
- How can I integrate the assessment into my counselling?
- What will be the status of the assessment as regards confidentiality?

Another aspect to consider comes from the nature of depression. In order to ensure assessments are not overlong and drawn out, there is a tendency to go for Yes/No replies. However we have seen depression is an experience that is a continuum, and varies by degrees. So it can also help to look to subsidiary qualitative questions to back up the assessment. These might be:

- How long …?
- When …?
- How often …?
- Where …?
- How strong …?

The third aspect that might be taken on board is the nature of the information. Often clients are unsure, find it difficult to describe things, or will change their mind. Much of this can be picked up when the client is answering. If the assessment is given to the client to take away to fill in, then it is worth having a short section that asks about what questions were difficult to answer, where the client was unsure, and what was difficult to understand.

General assessment

Depression may not be the only problem a client presents. Usually it is associated with other problems. Depression may be overt or it may be hidden. It may be seen as the main problem, or seem less important than others the client is experiencing. In fact, depression may be completely missed, because the counsellor does not look for it. If the client presents with the following problems, it is worth considering the possibility of depression:

- Addictive states
- Problems with relationships
- Trauma
- Personal loss
- Chronic stress
- Large personal change, such as coming out, immigration
- Past history of depression
- Past problems such as physical or sexual abuse.

It might be thought that depression, even if not spoken of by clients, should be observable in their non-verbal language. This is not always the case, as some clients can put on a good face for others – including counsellors. Others will consciously compensate for depression, and present a façade so they appear anything but depressed. Counsellors have to be alert for what might be the case, without reading depression into every client's behaviour.

Content of assessments

Although a list of statements will be provided below, counsellors will probably prefer not present them en bloc. In a session, I try to remember half a dozen, and cover these in some depth. It is best to think of the following as topics, as themes for discussion. Of course, it may not be necessary to introduce them as they will already have been raised by the client. However as the subjects are discussed by the client, the counsellor gets a more complete picture.

- I have difficulty getting up in the morning
- I find I forget recent events easily
- I cook meals and do housework
- I am still at work
- I find myself getting angry for no reason
- I sleep poorly

- I do not laugh at jokes any more
- I am liable to cry for no reason
- I find talking in company difficult
- I find life pointless
- I feel better later in the day
- I think about doing things rather than actually doing them
- I find exercise helps
- I am on edge all the time
- I feel a failure in life
- I do not feel in control of things
- I have not had sex for some time
- I have a constant ache or feeling in my stomach
- I cannot concentrate for any length of time
- I feel as if all my feelings have been switched off
- I get up in the morning
- I watch TV during the day
- I get dressed every day
- I wash, have a shower, or take a bath every day.

It is important to include some positive questions in any assessment, rather than merely those which make the client describe failures, limitations, or problems, thereby reinforcing negativity.

The statements made by the client benefit from elaboration. For instance, take the first statement, "I am still at work". Further discussion might include how the client feels about it, whether working is easy, whether others at work know the client's situation, how work is going, how others are at work, whether the client intends to continue at work.

Or we might ask about the client's memory. Does the client often lose his keys; forget the names of those close to him from time to time; forget meetings with people; have to rely on writing down everything important? Or, if discussing a later statement such as "I cannot concentrate for any length of time", the talk might be about the client's ability when it comes to reading short articles in the papers, whether television programmes are watched through to the end, whether the client is happy driving his car, and whether listening to people is tiring.

Elaboration requires positive input by the counsellor, without being over-positive; otherwise client self-esteem might be further lowered.

> *Me*: "You say you do not drive the car any more. Is that a decision you have made? You decided it was better if you didn't drive?"

Eloise: "My concentration is not good."
Me: "You certainly need to be able to concentrate driving a car nowadays. So you made that decision, the decision not to drive."
Eloise: "I suppose so."
Me: "That sounds a good decision. Driving can be stressful, and taking time out from the car might help. Do you feel a bit more relaxed not having to deal with traffic?"
Eloise: "I used to like driving, but, yes, it's a relief not having to go across town."

As might be seen, the assessment melds into ordinary counselling. This is how it should be. It is impossible to arrive at an equitable working relationship if assessment is an activity separate from counselling.

Backing up client statements

In the counselling situation, the counsellor deals with more than what the client is saying. There are judgements to be made about the situation at the time. For instance, the counsellor may look to:

- The difficulty the client has in what is being said. Whether this is down to poor concentration or content of what is said. Whether the client follows what is being said, or seems to switch off. Whether the client listens, or just wants to forward personal issues or agendas.
- The client's tone of voice: whether it is animated or lifeless, slow or normal speed, monotone or normal in tone (Gotlib and Robinson, 1982): whether replies are immediate, hesitant, or slow. And how often the client smiles (Gotlib, 1982).
- The posture of the client, whether the back is bent, shoulders are slumped, hands hold each other or the seat, legs are crossed or not and whether the client is facing the counsellor, or at a slight or wide angle.
- The degree of eye contact, whether the client's eyes are fixed to the floor, at the counsellor, or elsewhere. Whether the client is engaging the counsellor by eye contact or is looking through the counsellor, whether the eye contact seems fleeting, over-long, or normal, and whether it is maintained when the counsellor returns the look.
- The form of client responses can be indicative. Sometimes they may be very short, or they can be normal; they can be off the point, over-long, or rambling; they can sound normal, angry, helpless, or uncertain.

- The counsellor might also pay attention to the level of client animation, such as the lack of movement of hands and legs, facial expressions and movement of body as a whole. Also, there is the degree of spontaneity shown by the client in asking questions, adding to statements, or interrupting.
- Further insight can be obtained by concentrating on the content, and noting whether the client's talk is centred on himself or herself (Blumberg and Hokansin, 1982).
- The degree of negativity that comes over from the client in the responses given, the reactions to counsellor statements and the ability to choose between options or make a decision.
- Questions that are not answered, unexpected replies and a sense of how the counselling is proceeding all give the counsellor an indication of the client's feelings.

All of the above help the counsellor gauge whether and to what extent the client is depressed, but this is in the context of the counselling. Anxiety can be a sign of depression, of feeling compelled to answer, or the working relationship being little developed.

Detailed questions

We have already seen that detailed questions can be discussed, but this is an ongoing process. The point is that counsellors need to know not just facts, but the meanings that those facts carry for clients. This entails bringing in their thoughts and feelings; of entering into their world. Feelings affect how depressed clients think, and counsellors have to get a feeling of how their thinking is affected. This has to be done through actual examples.

Suppose we take the instance of a client who finds it difficult to get up in the morning. This might seem a small detail, but it can be important. One feature of depression is that of the subject staying in bed. We may frame questions about this:

- Does the client think about getting up; perhaps think too much about it?
- Does the client normally feel very lethargic, and does the client feel more lethargic early in the morning?
- Does it seem pointless getting up in the morning?
- Does the client keep putting off getting up?
- Does the client feel very sleepy, have difficulty opening his eyes?
- Does the client feel guilty for staying in bed?

- Has the client always had difficulty getting up in the morning?
- Does the client not get up and then fall asleep again?

Only when the counsellor has such details and the client aware of them, is it possible to go further. Once the counsellor has an idea of the client's world and gives notice of this fact to the client, then it is time to begin to build up the picture rather than dissect or analyse it. In the above example, this might lead to discussions with the client as to whether the client is making excuses to himself, feels annoyed about having to get up, wants to hide from the world under the blankets, or is simply drifting through life at this time.

Again, as can be seen, there is no obvious dividing line between assessment and the main part of the counselling. Slowly, the counsellor is building a picture of the client's life. And the client is also both facing that reality and letting another person know of it. A good assessment can be helpful in itself.

Medication

Most clients who are depressed are likely to be on medication when they come for counselling. This needs to be thoroughly explored, as medication can affect the client as much as the depression – though, hopefully, in a more positive way. Counsellors need to discuss medication, as almost all clients have feelings around the subject.

- What medication does the client take? (All forms of medication)
- How long has the client been on medication? Has it is been changed?
- When and how is medication taken?
- Has the client ever forgotten to take medication?
- Is the medication unpleasant to take?
- Does the client drink alcohol? Is alcohol taken on top of medication, or vice-versa?
- Is the amount the client says he drinks realistic, or an under-estimate?
- Does the client take any drugs – smoke hash, smoke cigarettes, take street drugs, or are they prescribed any other medication?
- How much coffee, tea, or cola does the client drink?
- How much food does the client eat daily? Has the client's diet changed of late?

The idea is not to try and be a medical worker. Rather, it is to discover things which are extra-medical, to get an insight into the client's life.

A somewhat different aspect is that of how clients cope with their depression. This can include drug self-help, which includes alcohol, but can also include herbal remedies such as St John's Wort. It might be noted that many clients do not think of herbal alternatives as drugs, so counsellors should ask if any alternative medicines are taken. Sometimes clients are reluctant to reveal what they take, so the counsellor must explain that the inquiry is to see if there is any possibility of drug interactions.

Treatment

Counsellors may want to follow up the questions about medication; try to put medication in the context of a person's life. What does it mean to feel reliant on a drug, have to go to see a doctor, to discover that the drug might not be very effective, to hide from others the fact of being on medication, or to know that other depressed patients get different drugs prescribed?

> *Larry*: "I don't know why they prescribe amitriptyline, as all they do is make you go to sleep. They never did anything for my depression."

Clients can feel negatively about medication, but do not express their dissatisfaction, or feel themselves unable to, or morally bound not to do so. On the other hand, medication can be seen very positively by clients, and it helps if this also is expressed. Every client has his or her own story.

> *Claire*: "I was prescribed anti-depressants, and that's the only reason why I am here today. I could not have got through things without them. I owe my life to them."

It is important that the counsellor does not stray into a medical remit and pass judgement on the use, or not, of anti-depressants. However I do encourage clients to ask about the drugs prescribed and let the doctor know if there are side-effects.

The difficult area is that of clients who are on anti-depressants for years. The question might be raised as to how effective they are and whether they really are needed. The point is that to continue to use the drugs means that clients are reminded that they are depressed and not "normal" in their eyes. It can become a barrier to clients leaving the sick role.

> *Eloise*: "The doctor says I should not come off the tablets, but they don't really solve anything; they just keep you at a level, keep you numb. Your

brain feels it is packed with cotton wool and you live in an unreal world. That's fine, until you have to deal with reality."

The other point that I have come across is that coming off anti-depressants can be unpleasant, with definite physical effects. Despite assurances that anti-depressants are not addictive, in the long-term some clients do find difficulty in stopping their medication. The upside is that those who have stopped their long-term medication have felt much better for it. They have found much greater energy.

Claire: "I never realised, but I was always on the same level, neither up nor down. I regret those years when there was no real pleasure. With the energy I've got now, I feel more confident as I can do more."

This might not be a typical case, but it is worth counsellors discussing with clients when they will be off medication and how they feel about it. This should be approached gently, otherwise clients might think the counsellor is trying to make them stop taking their medication or tell their doctor to cut down their anti-depressants.

Other areas

Some assessments cover social areas, family details and personal history. These can make an assessment extremely lengthy and subject to the law of diminishing returns. The problem is that it becomes difficult to know what questions should be asked, other than mere factual ones. More importantly, the information should come from the client rather than being asked by the counsellor. We should remember that asking questions for the sake of asking them is little more than an abuse of privacy.

Assessments in counselling

Assessment is usually seen as important, and emphasis is laid on the content of what should be asked. What receives much less attention is how and when questions should be asked. Counsellors might also like to think whether they would appreciate the same or similar questions being asked of them. To say that they are doing their job as a counsellor is a reply worth reconsidering, both for themselves as counsellors and as persons in their own right.

Chapter 5

Attitudes and Relationships

THEORY AND INFORMATION

Information

Why do counsellors need to know about depression? There is sometimes the idea that counsellors should be able to deal with whatever the client presents, whatever the human condition and behaviour of clients. This is a grievous mistake. Counsellors have to know about their clients. This is a matter not merely of having information, but having knowledge. The information has to be fashioned into patterns of knowing, to be able to give a picture of a person's world.

Information is only useful if it is shared. Furthermore, the retention of information by the counsellor is a means of exerting power over clients and producing a very one-sided working relationship. Counsellors sometimes imagine they do share with their clients, whereas what they are doing is dribbling information to clients, thinking that is sufficient. It is not. That is merely a device to ensure clients are kept powerless; to ensure clients know their place; a device to help counsellors rather than clients.

So what counsellors have to do is to consider carefully the process of not just giving clients information, but bringing them into the counselling process. Participation by clients is important, not merely ethically, but because they will not improve unless they are part of the helping process. And that task rests with counsellors.

The form and assimilation of information

There are two aspects of information-giving to be considered. The first is that of giving facts, letting clients know what is happening. This may be simple enough, provided the following are managed:

- Clients have to be engaged from the outset. For depressed clients, this may be only partially possible, so giving them back-up literature is usually necessary. Some clients may not really take in information for a few months, then they'll suddenly decide to read the information provided.

- Clients should be encouraged to say what they know about being depressed and depression. Sometimes clients are asked, "What do you know about depression?" This is not really asking at all. It is a signal for the client to say a few words, then the counsellor explains "what depression is". In other words, someone who may never have experienced depression explains what it is to a person suffering from it. Clients have their information; they also have their misinformation. Checking out both is important.
- The content of what is said or written should be user-friendly. There is a tendency to use jargon, and this does not mean merely unfamiliar words. Phrases such as "the child within", "in search of oneself", or "in our unconscious" are liable to have little meaning to clients, and it may be wondered how much they have to counsellors as well. Sometimes counsellors will use technical terms and then explain them. What this strange action actually involves is the exclusion of the client – which is the effect of jargon – and then inclusion of the client through explanation, but as a person who needs things explaining. Similarly, literature can be given to clients, but needs to be made user-friendly.
- Counsellors can increase client participation by giving illustrative examples (Saper and Forest, 1992). This makes it easier for clients to grasp the information, and react to the information given; to distinguish the shades of grey by using the differences between examples.

Information turned to knowledge

If clients are just given facts, then they are being given nothing. They have to have knowledge. Everyone is knowledgeable; has ideas, patterns of information that amount to sets of beliefs. If such beliefs are widely accepted, then those beliefs are termed "knowledge". So the assimilation of information is not simply absorption. It is necessary to fit that information into existing beliefs (Strike and Posner, 1992). If such information does not fit, then it is likely to be forgotten, if not rejected (Fong et al., 1986). However, it can happen that new information can change existing beliefs. This means that clients who know little about depression may be more receptive than those with existing knowledge (Kuhara-Kojima and Hatano, 1991). Counsellors have to give clients time to be able to assimilate information or reject it (Boud and Pascoe, 1978).

Clients can accept information, but experience difficulty in retaining it. This is very common with depressed clients. Getting clients to speak about the information and to repeat it out loud helps integration with existing beliefs (Ross et al., 1976). This requires more than mere repetition of the information. It involves elaboration, discussing it (Elmes and Bjork, 1975), and allowing clients to ask questions.

Information and cooperation

As an example, clients might be told what anti-depressant it is that they are taking. This is scarcely meaningful, unless they are told the basis for its action, possible side-effects and the reasons for them, and what the expected benefits from taking such medication are. It might seem unnecessary; clients can function quite well without all the superfluous information, much of which they may not want anyway. Indeed, if clients do not want to take in information, that is their choice. However, if counsellors are going to work with their clients, then this is only really possible if the two are on a comparable power level. This means clients have no problems in raising issues, asking for information or disagreeing with their counsellor.

The medical model has the doctor eliciting symptoms, diagnosing, and arranging treatment by writing out a prescription. The patient is a passive part of the process. Yet a moment's reflection tells us this is not the case. The patient has to decide to come to the doctor, make the appointment to come, to go to the surgery or health centre, give answers to the doctor's questions and volunteer information, take the prescription to the chemist, and then take the tablets as directed. Without such cooperation, the medical profession would be in a parlous state. Such cooperation is required especially with depressed patients, who might be unmotivated to bother about taking tablets, or stop taking them because they taste somewhat nauseous or produce side-effects. The degree of non-compliance may be quite high for those on anti-depressants (Zoega et al., 1991), and this can be the case even when patients tell their doctor they are taking them (Kroll et al., 1990).

Knowledge, theory and counsellors

The assimilation of information is seen as relating very much to clients, but the problem is equally applicable to counsellors. Information-giving is a two-way process, and as counsellors are likely to have a great deal of beliefs about depression, as noted earlier, they will find the assimilation of new information harder compared with a person who knows nothing about the topic. This means counsellors have to retain a measure of flexibility in their beliefs, and to avoid dogmatism (Carlozzi et al., 1982). Such flexibility is not so simple to maintain. Clients often want precise answers, as these are reassuring. At times, we have to separate information and reassurance. Ultimately, clients have to learn to live with a degree of uncertainty, and accept that few things in life are certain.

ATTITUDES TO DEPRESSION

What view to take of depression

Experts have a variety of different views as to the nature of depression. Such views can affect client beliefs about depression, which in turn affect the depression itself (Teasdale, 1983) and treatment as well (Atkinson et al., 1991). Equally, counsellor beliefs can affect clients, so counsellors have to decide their own attitudes and beliefs about depression.

Counsellors' attitudes

Counsellor training generally covers the question of attitudes to categories of clients, but this is usually restricted to the stereotypical views of the general public. What are not taken on board are the attitudes contained in counselling itself. For example, those who are depressed are seen as lacking social skills and so require social skills training (Lewinsohn, 1986). Such training would raise skills to their former level, so increasing likely social interaction, elevation in mood, and a sense of competence. That sounds very reasonable, except it presumes the depressed are lacking in social skills, whereas that deficiency is the result of depression. It might be argued that this is irrelevant, as teaching skills to those lacking them, even temporarily, must help. However to be able to enter into social skills training requires the ability to self-monitor and make judgements, both of which are low in those depressed (Jones and Baumeister, 1976; Furnham and Capon, 1983). In fact, such training may be useful, but this will be unrelated to depression as such.

Another aspect of counsellors' attitudes with regard to those depressed is that they tend to emphasise faults, failings, inabilities, and weaknesses. Yet clients have their strengths, their abilities, and may know better than the counsellor how they feel and what they want.

Sharon: "One counsellor would tell me what to do, but I knew what was best for me. Worst of all, he did not understand that I was at the stage of

> knowing what to do, but not being able to get myself round to it. He did not ask me whether I thought I could do it. 'What you want are relaxation exercises!' Finally, I did try them, but they only made me feel worse. Physical exercise did me more use."

This points to the importance of some kind of assessment process, so counsellors have a good idea of how the client is placed and the extent of possible client participation. If clients are not part of the counselling, then they have to accept what is given to them. If nothing else, this can be confusing for those who have been to more than one counsellor.

> *John*: "Each counsellor is different, which means each has something to offer. But the differences make you wonder. One counsellor went on about my father falling ill years ago and kept coming back to it, whereas the second counsellor never bothered about my father at all. Then there was the gestalt counsellor, who kept asking me to visualise my depression and tell her how big it was, how long and how high. I thought she was playing games. OK, I would give her answers, but I didn't believe a word of them. I thought it was all a bit patronising."

COUNSELLING RELATIONSHIP

Counselling relationship

The counselling relationship is important, not merely a means of channelling help, but as a help in itself. Clients want to feel at ease, to be listened to, and have someone with whom to interact. This is done with another person, and not a role. We have to remember that roles link behaviour, but it is people who relate to each other.

For instance, I can go into a department store, make a purchase, and leave. The whole interaction has been one between customer and shop assistant. We did not relate, and I am no different after the experience, not a changed person. This can apply to helping, where clients can come away with information but still be unchanged. There is no reason for them to be changed – any more than I expect a trip to a store to change me. But clients coming for counselling do want to change. They want to be able to live their own lives as much as possible, and not have to depend on counselling. So the first point to remember is to be oneself when counselling – and this includes being a counsellor. Be a counsellor first, and you will be linking, but not relating.

Acceptance of the person

If we look to the Rogerian values which go to make a good relationship, then acceptance of the person is required. No matter what they have done or how they behave, they should be accepted as a person. The difficulty is that of knowing what is being accepted. Counsellors do not know the client; indeed, sometimes the client does not even know himself or herself. So what does acceptance mean? Does the depressed person want to accept himself as a depressed person? Does the counsellor want to accept the client as a depressed person? Clearly, it is for counsellors to find their own solutions, but it seems to me that we have to accept our ignorance of the client, and we have to accept our resultant uncertainty.

Acceptance of the person and positive regard for that person are often quoted, and quoted too easily. Too easily, as the client is not really known. When first working with drug users years ago, I did street work and visited families at home, apart from counselling. What was apparent was that simply counselling left me without a real idea of the person 'behind' the client. It is easy to accept people when you do not have to live with them; really know them. We can never get to know clients very well, but we can think about them from different perspectives: from those of a depressed person, a spouse, a parent, a work colleague, and so get a more rounded view of the person in the counselling room.

A second aspect of quick acceptance is that if we do know something bad about the client, then we tend to put it to the back of our mind. We suppress it. Acceptance is not then a positive process but a negative act. Take the example of a client who attempted suicide 4 years ago. We might say we accept the person, but not the deed. We disengage a person from his actions or behaviour. But this is nonsense! People have to take responsibility for their actions, unless they are so ill as to be incapable of doing so. The client is a person who has attempted suicide, who has that in his history. If it had been very recent, then we would probably mention it. After 4 years, should it be alluded to?

This information should be used, as it will have its effect. If it does not, then the act of attempted suicide really was pointless. My approach is to bring such matters up. In this case I say that clients as persons are important to me, but I do not like it when they attempt suicide. One client even admitted she stopped herself from taking an overdose because of what I had said. However the main point is that we have to be prepared to accept people unconditionally. And this means being able to work with what we find difficult about them.

Empathy

Being able to see the world from the client's perspective, to feel how the client feels, allows us to keep the counselling personalised to the client and realistic. The difficulty is that of knowing the extent to which empathy is possible. It is reasonable to assume that there are limitations on the degree to which the counsellor can be truly empathic. The more extreme the thinking, feeling, and subsequent behaviour of a client is, the less we can empathise. Of course, it is easier if we have been there ourselves; we have had similar thoughts and feelings. When we apply this to depression, then there are limitations. I might understand how a person can feel completely worthless, but that is purely intellectual. I am not feeling that feeling at the time. Furthermore I can think about anything, think negatively about something, but I cannot change the way I think. This means I cannot think negatively and believe what I am thinking – unlike a depressed client. This is also the case with traumatised clients, when it is almost impossible to understand the quality of their feelings and thoughts, as they are so extreme.

It is no use not having the slightest idea of how a client might be thinking or feeling. We have to be on some comparable wavelength. But there are places we cannot go. Again, we have to accept and be content with the fact we do not know and cannot have the same feelings. To some extent we are always dealing with a stranger.

Genuineness

Another factor that goes towards making a good counselling relationship is genuineness; counsellors being themselves. This means more than being honest to oneself; it is knowing oneself. It is tempting to bring in the concept of self, but this is not always a clear concept and we need to put it into operational terms. To know oneself is knowing where one fits into life and the social context. Everyone works that out for himself or herself. This rests on basic life beliefs. For instance, one might be that we come into the world not of our asking, we have no control initially, but gain control through life. Ultimately we die. So we live our life with a view to living and an end in death. Thus we might start with the basics of our existence – we are born and we die. It might seem simplistic, but until we accept that and its implications, we are not being genuine.

Counsellor feelings about clients

The working relationship is not something we achieve; it is an ideal to which we constantly strive. We have to be realistic and admit we are going to fall short for much of the time. This is because there never is any final objective; there is always a further mountaintop beyond. We go higher and higher because we come across more and more new and different experiences, which have to be included in the working relationship. And counselling clients with depression can be hard work at times, affecting how counsellors feel. This has a knock-on effect on their counselling. The difficulty can be that counsellors think they have to be nice, have to be professional, and consequently cannot say how they really feel.

Counsellors have to be honest about how clients affect them. My experience is that counsellors often say they are honest about how they feel, and they may even believe what they say. But they hide their true feelings behind their role. If we come out from behind the counselling role, then some of the things we notice and remark about might be:

- *"She gets me down."*
  It is easy to be overcome by the negativity of depressed clients. Even when we are aware of the dangers and are determined not to be affected, we can still feel ourselves sinking, feeling low. The problem comes not with this outcome, but failing to admit what is happening. It is only after such an admission that something can be done by the counsellor.

- *"I feel angry when I listen to her."*
  Feeling angry may be seen as even less admissible than being depressed when working with clients. Yet, frustration with depressed clients can arise because they seem so negative, seemingly needlessly so. Anger can arise through listening to the content of what the client says and taking sides, even if the counsellor is silent. Counsellors should keep a distance, but this is difficult when the client's account is very moving.

- *"He causes me to feel anxious."*
  It is acceptable to say that we are anxious about a client as long as our concern is specified. We may be anxious about the possibility he will commit suicide. However sometimes we pick up client anxiety, and worry, but are not certain what we are worrying about. We then have to put the cause in the counselling situation, and see whether we are contributing towards it.

- *"I do not really like the client."*
  The professional answer is that counsellors should work with any client, and put aside their dislike, but this does not tackle the problem. There is no reason why counsellors should like all their clients, any more than we like everyone socially. We have our preferences, and will not overcome this until we admit the fact. And those who are depressed are often not good company. However, when we analyse the situation more closely, we find that it is not the client we dislike; rather it is the thought of having to work with that client.

- *"I am bored with this client."*
  This can happen with any client, but is more likely with depressed clients as a result of their poor interacting, when counselled. It is also the result of counsellors not being sufficiently empathic and really being at one with the client. It might also represent counsellors distancing themselves – for whatever reason.

Negative remarks

Clients who are feeling low will make remarks such as "I can't do X", "I am to blame for Y", or "People always Z". These statements reflect how the client is feeling. However, if clients continue to make such statements, it can reinforce the way they feel. It makes them feel worse. Such statements can become a habit, and an unhelpful habit, and counsellors can help by highlighting and working on it.

Me: Hi, John. How are things?
John: Not very good. I had the feeling it was going to be a bad week.
Me: Mmmm. A bad week.
John: Yes, well, not so good.
Me: Not so bad, but not so good.
John: I suppose so.
Me: Not so good when you're feeling down.
John: No, not so good.

To avoid reinforcement, there is no point in denying how the client feels. What can be done is to reframe the expressed feelings – "bad" becomes "not good", a small change but one that lessens negative reinforcement. Too much positive reinforcement is likely to be unacceptable to anyone depressed.

Some difficulties counselling through depression

Counsellors have to be realistic and know what depressed clients are like. Once they know how clients are, then they can accept them. Counsellors have to be able to analyse what it is about the interaction with a depressed client that prevents better counselling. Often it is the quality of communication. We note this and feed it back, if appropriate, as it can be part of the client's ongoing difficulties.

> *Shelley*: "I can't form relationships as I cannot just talk to people. I have to think of a sentence to say, work it out in my mind, and still cannot get it out. And even if that sentence does come out then it is only one. I have nothing more I can say, though there's enough in my head."

However, it can happen in quite the contrary way. Clients can have problems in speaking to people who do not want to listen to a depressed person. One upshot can be that such clients can do a lot of talking with the counsellor, sometimes being demanding, or putting out unrealistic demands. This is not just a matter of being demanding; it is one of reacting to what is seen as rejection. This can in turn feed into existing feelings around rejection.

> *Jill*: "Rejection is another theme relevant to my depression. It is associated with humiliation and can leave me weeping, as I wear my heart on my sleeve."

Many people find the behaviour of depressives off-putting and unsocial (Coyne, 1976), partly due to the depressive's reduced social competence. This judgement is backed by looking at the content of the communication of the depressed (Hammen and Peters, 1978). There is an inability of depressives to give positive responses or positive reinforcement to the statements of others (Lewinsohn et al., 1980), an important aspect of any long-term communication. In fact, listeners can themselves become slightly depressed in conversation with depressives (Boswell and Murray, 1981), precisely because there is a lack of positive input.

Chapter 6

Counselling Methods

Prior concepts

Clients who come for counselling are likely to be in crisis. They are vulnerable and suggestible and will go along with what counsellors say. This means counsellors have to be very careful of the power that they wield. Unfortunately, counselling reflects its medical and Freudian roots, with clients seen as helpless and uncooperative if they do not react as expected. Concepts such as resistance and transference, which place clients in the wrong, are sometimes employed. But counselling is an interactional encounter. Counsellors have to take as much responsibility as clients if difficulties arise. In fact, clients come for counselling because they are experiencing difficulties, so most of the difficulties in counselling must be attributed to the actions of counsellors, not clients. We do not blame patients for being in pain when their leg is broken; equally, we should not blame clients for their pain.

Positive messages

Depression sheds negativity all around, so counsellors have to not only retain positivity, but send positive messages in counselling. This can help clients and, indirectly, help counsellors, who can themselves be affected by client negativity. This process of maintaining positivity has to be carried out carefully. When depressed, hearing something positive can be irritating, sound patronising, or simply demonstrate that the counsellor has no idea what he is talking about or is not being genuine. So counsellors have to be careful, and fashion what they say according to the degree of depression engulfing the client.

Positivity can be transmitted by encouraging clients to speak and for counsellors to actively listen to them. This is harder than it sounds. Clients can find themselves with little to say, and then they become conscious of the fact: that makes them feel worse. Sometimes they do speak but are very negative;

they hear their own negativity, and this reinforces a downward spiral in their behaviour. Counsellors may have to be prepared to intervene and put the discussion on a less negative track.

One way of altering the counselling in a positive manner is for counsellors to listen closely to what is being said and then react gently. This may be done by the use of phrases such as:

- "Right! I'm trying to get my head round ..."
- "I did not realise ..."
- "It has never struck me till now ..."

By intervening, the counsellor underlines the importance of what the client has said. Also, the self-deprecatory comments of the counsellor give more power to the client. This is positive as the client is being further drawn into the counselling situation. Finally, the degree of positivity is slight, and this avoids what clients feel is unrealistic.

These are not stock phrases to be used automatically, but are used as they show exactly where the counsellor is in the counselling at the time. Listening to the accounts of clients, it is hard to fully understand or grasp what it is like to be in their world. And this is the indirect message counsellors are giving. The sub-message is that the counsellor is not so smart, and the client has something to tell, even teach, him. All of this seems fine, except as a result clients might think their counsellor to be of little use. A useless counsellor who has let them down again; given them a bad deal. Certainly, if the phrases above are used frequently, then the image of counsellor ineffectiveness will be confirmed. Sometimes I merely stop in the counselling and ask if the client can hold on a moment and give me time to think about it. This is not acting. There are moments when I need to have such time.

The other part of the process is for counsellors not to expect a positive reaction. Depressed persons cannot suddenly make themselves positive or become positive. The reactions are very muted and counsellors should not be put off by what can seem at times rather one-sided interactions.

Helping clients move on

Counsellors will probably find counselling the depressed difficult at first and frustrating in the long-term. The first action is to admit to oneself that this is the case. Only then can counsellors do anything about the situation. They have to think of different ways of working. One difficulty arises from those affected by depression not being able to do anything to help themselves. This happens because clients do not have the belief in themselves to be able to do anything. Simply arguing that they can in fact do simple tasks is not likely to convince them. Motivating the depressed client is a process, and one that can take some time, and is comprised of several different steps.

The client's baseline must be established. This includes discussing how much the client can do. This might include getting up in the morning, washing, dressing, making breakfast, eating breakfast, putting the crockery into the sink, doing the washing-up, getting the children ready for school, going for a walk, watching television and many other seemingly insignificant actions. Even the fact that they were able to attend counselling points to a moderately high level of achievement. Clients might need to be reminded that are achieving much, and some in severe depression may not feel able to do any of the above.

The next step might be getting clients to think of modest objectives, where there is a good possibility of achieving them (Strube and Roemmele, 1985). Positivity is built upon achieving small successes and the acknowledgement by clients of such successes. Choosing what to do might require the help of the counsellor. There is always the danger that clients choose greater aims, saying it is not worth achieving insignificant objectives. They have to be persuaded against over-ambition and likely failure. We also have to watch for clients who do not want to move on, and so set themselves up to fail. This is not a fault in the client. It merely indicates a person not ready to move on, or that the counsellor is pushing too hard.

Counsellors have to be aware of clients' excuses such as self-handicapping, giving reasons for failure, whether in advance or given as an excuse afterwards for past failures. Reasons for these handicapping excuses can be given as low effort (Smith et al., 1982), bad mood (Baumgardner et al., 1985), distraction (Leary, 1986) or depression itself (Rhodewalt and Agustsdottir, 1986; Schouten and Handelsman, 1987). But the important factor is the reason why clients act in this way. It can be to reaffirm their identity, to reaffirm themselves in the sick role, to redeem themselves in their own eyes or the eyes of others (Arkin and Baumgardner, 1985). They may see themselves as failing, and want to lessen the impact, or to keep their self-image intact. If a client says a task is "too difficult", then counsellors might want to discuss it with the client.

Small task achievement

Helping clients to be positive and actually achieve small planned tasks is not helped by the counsellor being pushy or even confrontational. On the other hand, clients usually appreciate being encouraged to do a little bit more. So the counsellor has to get the right balance, and this requires sensitive negotiation.

Me: "OK, so you cannot go out of the house. I accept that. However it does strike me that you might like at some time to be able to go out and go down to the shops. Is that right?"
Gail: "Yes, kind of ... I have to get June to go to Tesco's. I would go if I could, as she doesn't always get the right things. She does her best ..."
Me: "Right. I'm not going to say you should go out. But I want you to go through your front door with me..."
Gail: "I couldn't do that!"
Me: "Well, we won't do it. What you can do is relax, sit back, and now just imagine the two of us walking through the door. Just relax. Take it seriously. I want you to imagine us going through that door. OK?"
Gail: "OK. Through the door.... Even that is ... scary."
Me: "And how far did you get."
Gail: "One foot on the front step, and then I ran back in ... Funny, I'm talking as if I actually did it. I suppose some day I might really to able to do it."

When talking of sensitive negotiation, this means having a good working relationship and knowing the client well. When mildly depressed, clients may require counsellors to be firm to break through negativity, and yet clients can use what is said against themselves. For this reason, indirect approaches, like the use of imagination, can initially be useful. When clients imagine themselves completing the task, it becomes more likely that they will complete it (Carroll, 1978). It might not work at the first attempt. This does not invalidate the method, as sometimes the process may need to be carried out more than once (Gregory et al., 1982).

Even so, some clients will say they cannot even imagine walking through their front door, or whatever the agreed task is. Their negativity swamps the counselling session, and it is easy for the counsellor to back off and not proceed any further. However, what can be useful is to cut through this negativity and ask the client to specify exactly what prevents him or her from being effective. Often what blocks clients is not actual fact, the idea of imagination, but their beliefs. For example, they think it is a waste of time, and it will not be effective. Now we can ask clients to go into secondary imagination, and to imagine that it was successful. Thinking of a different, successful outcome, taking up a contra-belief, can change ingrained beliefs (Anderson, 1982).

COGNITIVE METHODS

Thinking process difficulties

Counsellors have their own personal approach to carrying out counselling, so the following contains just some ideas on working with depressed clients. One topic that may be of interest is that of client thinking processes and how these affect their actions and behaviour. And with depressed clients we notice there are likely to be examples of less familiar thinking modes.

- *Blocked thinking*
  Often clients say that they simply cannot think at all. All thinking processes are blocked. This can arise through anxiety, through having several opposing thoughts in mind, or purely through the effects of depression. If thought blocking occurs, then clients are best advised to do something else. Trying to think will merely reinforce the blocking. Alternatively, it can help to partially bypass purely mental processes, and think using drawings or diagrams. Seeing pictures is easier than dealing with mental concepts.

- *Flitting thinking*
  Flitting thinking typifies a person with poor concentration, and often with poor short-term memory. Clients are quite aware of these difficulties, but are unable to manage them. Such thinking can be improved by slowing down it down. For example, blank cards can be used to write down different thoughts. Then the cards can be put in logical order. The whole action of doing something physical relaxes the client and aids thinking.

- *Obsessional thinking*
  Such thinking is of two main types. There is that when clients cannot get one fixed thought out of their mind. The more the client tries not to think of that particular thought, the more it comes to mind. The other form of thinking is that characterised by cycling. Thoughts go from one to another, but soon return to the original thought. The answer to both is to get out of the behavioural loop. One well-known method is to put a rubber band around the wrist and when such thinking takes place, to pull the band back and ping it. The sharp snap breaks the thinking loop. It is then important to follow this with another line of thought or action.

- *All-or-nothing thinking*
  This polarised thinking is one where the depressed person clings to one idea: it is that idea or nothing. This thinking does not even allow the consideration of options or degrees of grey. The whole process of thinking is too much for the client, and this total thinking is quick and prevents matters having to be thought through. Rather than disagreeing with the client, the counsellor might be better to agree and then work on the specific thinking. For instance, if a client says, "I will never ever go to the town of X", then, the counsellor can introduce the idea of degrees. Ask whether the client would go half way there, or a quarter, or one mile in the direction of X.

All these forms of thinking are not faulty thinking, but the person's way of dealing with the situation. Blocked thinking is when the person cannot think the situation at all; flitting thinking is also a way of not thinking, while obsessive thinking is a way of constantly reviewing a thought that cannot be fully taken on board. All-or-nothing thinking is yet another way of not really thinking, but clinging to one "answer". The problem is that we can all think in such ways occasionally, but depressed clients are much more likely to think in these ways, and such thinking may continue when it is not really necessary. It becomes a habit. In addition, poor thinking can be a barrier to progress.

It is insufficient to merely label such thinking. Clients may be only too aware that their thinking is blocked, obsessive or lacking in some manner. To help such clients, counsellors might:

- Let clients know that such thinking is quite usual in depression. This can diminish anxiety that clients have about their thinking, and thoughts that they are abnormal or that their "brains are rotting away", as one client remarked.
- Let clients know such styles of thinking are to a purpose. The brain does not want to deal with things at the moment as so much is going on internally. So the mind prevents conscious thought from entering as much as possible. The person is subconsciously defending or preserving himself or herself.
- Agree with the client that this process can get out of control. So action is necessary – not thought. The client should get up and go for a walk or some equivalent. This might seem a naïve solution, but we should remember that mind and body are closely interlinked, as are behavioural and cognitive remedies.
- Explain to clients that externalising their thinking is helpful; writing things down, using diagrams or pictures is to be recommended.

Content of thinking

Apart from the process of thinking, the content of thinking can prove unhelpful for clients if it is unrealistic. Such thinking tends to happen with less depressed clients, and they are able to think more widely than more severely depressed clients. So, paradoxically, being unrealistic has a positive side; it indicates that clients are not so badly depressed. Once again, we have to try and understand why clients think as they do. Why do they take up this pattern of negative thinking? It is the product of depression, the product of moods negatively affecting thinking, but this does not answer the question completely.

- *Catastrophic thinking*
  This thinking is typified by the notion that any possible action or failure to act will lead to disaster. Arguments are given as to why disaster will happen, and counsellors can spend much time arguing against the reasons given. But this does not alter how the client feels, and so thinks.

- *Over-generalisation*
  A less extreme version of catastrophic thinking is over-generalisation, which comes in two main varieties. There is that which is influenced by total thinking, and usually recognisable by words such as, "every", "none", "whenever", "never", "nothing" and "all". Examples might be, "Whenever I try to ..." or "There is nothing that can be done ..."

  The second type of over-generalisation is that of taking one instance and making it into a general rule, such as "It's no use doing that. I've tried it. It never works".

With both catastrophic thinking and over-generalisation, we have to analyse what the client is trying to communicate. Let us take the example of catastrophic thinking:

> "*It is no use, me trying to talk to him. It will end in a disaster. It always does.*"

When analysed, we find that the meaning can vary according to the depth of the depression. This will in turn vary the counselling response.

- The statement is not really meant seriously, and the client is merely waiting for the counsellor to reassure her that everything will be all right.

- The client is rather anxious, and talks about a potential disaster as a reason for not talking to him. The main emphasis is not on the disaster as such, which is only a vague cloud, but the client's anxiety.
- The client is both anxious and negative, so the emphasis is more on the idea of personal failure. If this is how the situation is viewed, then it is sensible not to risk further decreasing low self-esteem.
- The client sees everything negatively, and the risk of disaster is almost incidental. The idea of doing anything is pointless.

In practice, the situation is more complicated. Active listening is a requirement for counsellors, and this refers to communication as a whole. This covers not just non-verbal communication, but para-linguistic characteristics, such as jokes, intended exaggeration, irony and a variety of linguistic games that people might play. Working out what is meant can, paradoxically, be more difficult initially with depressed clients as there is an absence of para-linguistics. We expect shades of meaning, play with language, and these are mainly absent in the language of those depressed. For example, the expression, "I wish I were dead", usually is not taken seriously; it is a mock-serious joking expression. We can tell from the person making it that it should not be taken at face value. But with a depressed client, it is not so simple to know how it should be taken.

Apart from the rational part of what is communicated, we also have to be aware of the feelings that accompany it. "It's no use me trying to talk to him ..." has its rational part, but it also conveys that the client feels negative down, depressed. When listing possible options to depressed clients, I do not expect them to reply, "By George, that's a jolly good idea!" We have to be with the client, and appreciate where they are in their world. But there is more to this scenario. The client is also communicating to the counsellor, "I feel down, can't be bothered, don't really want to discuss this." Yet there may also be another quite dissimilar message being sent, "I can't do this. I am helpless. So help me."

We can go further. We can ask clients to examine exactly what they might have meant, directly and indirectly. They have to begin to analyse exactly what they are saying and communicating. They will often be able to say what exactly they mean. For the slightly depressed, this is simple, as they will admit to feeling low and perhaps not really meaning what they said. However, for those more depressed, it becomes more complicated. If is seems that the client meant what they said, and then the counsellor has to judge the situation. Is it worth pressing the point? For example, I might ask the client to imagine the situation as not working out, as being "a disaster". It may help to get the client to draw the situation with a felt-tip pen. Then the client is asked to add to the picture, making the disaster even worse. The idea is to pile more and more disasters into the scenario so that it becomes so improbable that it is unbelievable – even for the client. The client appreciates the fact that the original situation could be a lot worse (Dunning and Parpil, 1989). Like many such methods, the difficulty is that of knowing when to use them, as with more severely depressed clients depression may actually be aggravated.

Style of client thinking

Client thinking is generally diminished in content, and counsellors should be aware of not merely this fact, but also its implications.

- *Egocentric thinking*
  As depression grows, the person's world begins to contract and so the person becomes more and more the centre of that world. Equally, other people do not feature so highly in it. Clients personalise situations, so that whatever happens is related to them, and they are to blame for whatever goes wrong. This feeds into their sense of failure and negativity.

Depression can sneak up on a person, so the client is unaware of changes in behaviour, including communication. Clients are not fully aware, which makes them little different from everyone else. Discussion between client and counsellor can make the former more aware of what is being communicated, and the degree of egocentricity that characterises his or her world. The mildly depressed are well able to see this, though not always able to entirely control it.

The egocentricity of client thought can become a bit tiring after a time, and this is reinforced by another characteristic, the client's unbending and dogmatic thoughts and statements.

- *Rigidity of thought*
  The client's rigid thinking may be characterised by an unwillingness to discuss topics, and is often typified by the use of words such as "cannot", "need", or "must".

The rigidity of thought comes from fear of change, from anxiety about taking a risk. This is an unconscious means of defence of the self, a way to try to maintain things as they are, and thus uphold the self and prevent its diminution. To describe this as incorrect thinking rather misses the point.

Such thinking is a way whereby depressed clients can preserve their sense of their selves.

Another aspect of depressive thinking is that of poor reasoning; of coming to the wrong conclusions.

- *Arbitrary inference*
  Wrong conclusions can be arrived at or conclusions drawn without supporting evidence.

This also represents a disinclination to think things through. It is not so much the fact that the conclusion is wrong, but that once it has been made there is no inclination to change it that is important. Indeed, it is a feature of depressive thinking that there is no changing; ideas, statements and conclusions formed are not altered. We find that client conclusions may be supported by unwarranted abstraction, when ideas are taken out of context to support arguments, or events or persons are given unwarranted significance or importance.

Working on cognitive issues

An irritating aspect for some clients is the assumption that the counsellor knows what is happening – unlike the client. So it is the counsellor who explains things to the client and is in charge. This temporary role might be required, but should not be assumed. Those depressed can be aware of what is happening, if not at the time then later.

> *Claire*: "You get things out of proportion. My sister did not phone for a week and I said, 'What kind of sister are you!' I was rude to her, but apologised later."

If the counsellor is helping, then it is essential to avoid seeing the client's thinking as faulty and the clients as being in some way inferior, thereby reinforcing their negativity. If is far preferable to bring out client strengths with questions such as:

- Did you have strong feelings at the time? Were you very angry, sad, anxious?
- Did you feel a bit better after saying what you did?
- Did you think about what you had said immediately afterwards?

- Did you think about what you said some time afterwards?
- Did you follow up what you had said in any way?

Counsellors should be careful how these questions might be taken by the client. Sometimes it helps to take the heat off with observations such as, "I don't know, but I might have felt...." rather than asking a question. What the questions do is to place what was said in the context of the client's feelings. It is then a matter of trying to discover what were the feelings that gave rise to what was said; whether they came from a generalised feeling and were not directed at the specific individual. When clients themselves are aware of what they are doing, how they are seen by others, and why they might be behaving as they do, then they are more in control.

Thoughts about depressed thinking

Counsellors following Beck's approach label depressed thinking as faulty, whereas a better description is that it is different. Faulty thinking requires correction, but different thinking requires interpretation and an understanding of why clients think as they do. Thinking and behaving in a way that does not correlate with reality may seem to be faulty thinking, but we also have to appreciate what reality is for our depressed clients.

CLIENT SELF-ESTEEM

Self-esteem and assertiveness

One characteristic of being depressed is feeling oneself to be worthless, and having very low self-esteem. Self-esteem can remain low after the depression has lifted, since clients still see themselves as depressives, as having had depression, and liable to depression. Others might also judge them similarly. With this in mind, some commentators have suggested that clients should break through their low self-esteem and learn to act assertively.

As might be imagined, there are several difficulties with this approach. It shows a lack of understanding of the world of the depressed client, in that low self-esteem is a product of depression, and will persist as long as the depression lasts. However, we should note that there are degrees of depression, and very mild depression can be affected by rational means. So it is worth considering what can be done.

Social skills

Because depressed clients appear to lack social skills and tend to interact poorly, teaching social skills is seen as one way of not merely improving the situation for clients but also lessening depression. Such skills are best taught in groups and there is a need for assessment as to whether clients will benefit from the training (Wilkinson and Canter, 1983). However, the rewards with depressed clients are likely to be small. Firstly, assessment done on depressed clients is misleading, as it gives the skill level of a depressed client, not the other normal or non-depressed person. Depressed clients may have more than adequate social skills; it is the depression that causes the fall in skills, and those skills will be raised gradually after the depressions begins to lift. Personally, I have doubts about the idea that clients lack social skills. They may have different ones from the counsellor, but they still have skills.

A more specific approach is that of helping clients to become more assertive. But this fails to deal with their whole situation; their social context. Assertiveness includes knowing when to be assertive. The problem is not that of not knowing how to be assertive; it is a lack of belief in oneself, which stops the person from being assertive. Then as depression increases, the client simply cannot be bothered to be assertive. Finally, depression can increase to the point that clients are not assertive because there is nothing to be assertive about. However damning the things said about them, clients see them as right. They feed into and confirm the negative view such depressed clients have of themselves.

Low self-esteem

All of the above does not help clients who lack self-esteem and are conscious of lacking it. Rather than teaching social skills, it is preferable to include social skills in counselling. With respect to assertion, its integration in counselling can be started by helping clients consider the following statements and whether they apply to them:

- I do not put myself forward
- I am not confident of my own views
- I do not have the confidence to stick to my views
- I am easily swayed by others
- I go along with the decisions of others
- I am aware that I give in easily to others
- I do not feel able to act against the decisions of others

- I feel a failure because I do not say what I think
- I let others do the talking for me
- I know what I want to say, but do not say it
- I do not think other people listen to me
- I argue myself out of action.

This exercise is not a matter of the counsellor going through the list with the client. Rather, a couple of the statements can be discussed with the client and this can be expanded by:

- Finding out whether the client has always felt that way
- Whether it typifies dealing with everyone, or just specific people
- Asking the client to give a couple of examples

The counsellor can then work towards the client talking in general about self-esteem.

Building basic self-esteem

Only when the ground has been laid is it worth the client trying to work on self-esteem. The counsellor can help by being positive, and identifying every small client achievement.

> *Jill*: "I'm quite useless. I can't talk to my doctor. The tablets he gave me cause me to be jumpy, and I can't stop my legs from jiggling up and down. It just happens. My left leg gets it worse. I don't notice it till I look down and see it going up and down ... My Mum said she would ring the doctor and tell him, but I didn't want that either. I didn't want any fuss. Now my Mum is annoyed with me ... I can't do anything right."
> *Me*: "OK, Jill. Let's look at things in detail. But before I do that, there is something a bit strange about what is going on."
> *Jill*: "How do you mean?"
> *Me*: "You say you are useless, you cannot get anything right. You cannot say how the tablets your doctor prescribed affect you. And then, damn me, you give me a very good description of the effect they have on you. So in what way are you useless?"
> *Jill*: "I can tell you, but not the doctor. It's him I should tell."
> *Me*: "So the problem is between you and the doctor. You were able to tell me. You were able to tell your mother. Is it just the doctor or doctors in general you have these difficulties with?"

Jill: "It's not the doctor. I know what I want to say, but the moment I walk through his office door my mind goes blank. Then I see the doctor and all strength goes out of me."

We often speak of assertion as if it is one simple action. As we can see, it is not simple. Being assertive is a process, which can be stopped at any stage along the way; if this is the case, the result is a lack of assertion. If that happens, the perceived failure reinforces the client's low self-esteem. This means if a client intends to be assertive, we have to try and ensure the client is successful. Not all attempts will be successful, and apparent failures can be retrieved, but it requires a lot of work. So it is best if considerable preparatory work is put in at this stage. Clients might want, as their confidence is increased in the counselling session, to go and be assertive. The trouble is this confidence may well evaporate after leaving the session. Should the client attempt to be assertive, the result will be failure. So it can be helpful to explicitly state that the client is to leave any assertion until the time is right.

Confrontation

Another aspect of low esteem–esteem is given by the above example. Jill found it difficult to be assertive with her doctor, but not with everyone. Counsellors should not assume that low self-esteem will always be exhibited; it depends on the situation and the persons involved. Equally, just because a client does not exhibit low self-esteem, counsellors should not think it is not a factor in that client's behaviour. In fact, some clients can appear quite confrontational, and the conclusion is drawn that their self-esteem cannot be low. This can be a mistake, as those clients can easily feel attacked or put down, and will react as a result. Sometimes this is obvious, as clients seem to be confrontational for no reason or over-react to situations. Clients might also want to hide their feeling of worthlessness, more from themselves than counsellors.

Assertion and control

A lack of assertiveness is a lack of control, but there are times when clients will not have control of situations, but they can still have a sense of control. This comes from having options and knowing they can choose what they want to do. Clients can choose whether or not to be assertive, and that gives a sense of personal control. Sometimes failure to confront a situation is seen as bad, and clients are pressurised into confronting them. Yet walking away from a situation can be assertive in the right context. I sometimes remind clients of the stress reaction. When threatened our body goes into flight-or-fight mode, automatically the body prepares itself – but not just to fight; flight is an alternative.

If we return to the case of Jill, then changing to another doctor is an option. What we discover, though, is that this apparent easy way out of the situation, it did not seem easy to her.

Jill: "It would be no good going to someone else as they would know what had happened. And doctors stick together. It would just make things worse. And the new doctor could be even worse."
Me: "I get the feeling that you are panicking a bit at the very idea of changing your doctor, or telling someone that you want to change. Now I'm not saying that you should. It was just a possibility, and it does not suit you. Is that right?"
Jill: "Yes, I suppose so. I don't know what I want. It's impossible ..."
Me: "OK, just relax for a minute or so. It can be a bit scary at times thinking about telling doctors things. They are just human, but sometimes they come over all professional and seem unapproachable."
Jill: "I just can't speak to them, say how I really feel."

With a lifetime of low self-esteem, Jill is not going to suddenly become assertive. Assertion is something that is gained gradually over time for those depressed.

Feedback

Initially, clients can be self-absorbed, so they are unaware of the effect that they are having on others. However, at the start of counselling they do not need to have this fact pointed out. But as the working relationship grows, feedback by the counsellor can be of use.

Such feedback starts by being positive – how the client looks a bit better this session, has started to do some counselling homework, is trying a relaxation method to get to sleep.

The next step with feedback is that of telling clients how they seem to the counsellor. "You seem a bit more decisive, a bit more sure of yourself today. Am I right?" or "It strikes me you are taking your time, thinking about things. Is that true?" This is not just being slightly positive; it is also letting the client know how he or she seems to another person. Often clients are unsure of themselves. When their feelings no longer marry up with their external situation for example, they cry and there is no obvious triggering cause, then they can begin to lose faith in their judgement of themselves and consequently of others and the world in general. Having someone validate their feelings and thinking is useful. It gives them confidence in themselves.

After further counselling, counsellors can feedback how they and clients are interacting better. "You seem more interested now and we have more eye contact. I remember at first it seemed that you were hardly interested in what I had to say." Again, the message is positive, but there is an almost hidden message about the importance of maintaining eye contact and appearing interested. Also feedback can become integrated into the counselling, so it can be used not just as feedback but, as in this example, a way of entering into a discussion about social interactions and relationships.

CLIENT FEELINGS

Introduction

Depression is characterised by a lack of control of feelings and mood. Clients will be unable to stop themselves from crying. This is only part of the story. Feelings in general are largely outside our conscious control. What makes mood and feelings in depression unusual is that they may not be in line with the person's external reality. Clients can cry for no apparent reason. Their feelings can become extreme and they can get out of control. As a result, the feelings of those depressed can give rise to unanswered questions for the affected individuals.

The first question is what feelings represent if they do not reflect reality. In what way are they meaningful? It is arguable that in most cases there are reasons to be depressed. A loved one has died or the person has been subjected to chronic stress at work. These are reasons to be upset about thinking about the person or about work; they are not reasons why the person should be permanently sad and depressed. Sometimes clients will feel low for no reason apparent to them.

> *Eloise*: "For the last two or three days I have felt really sad. Nothing has happened, but I feel really, really sad, and it is unpleasant. I don't feel like speaking to people. I just feel sad."

Depression can be put down to some kind of chemical imbalance in the brain. This causes the whole process of evaluating feelings to be incorrect and thus not aligned with reality. The difficulty is that the depressed person is experiencing feelings, and these are not explained away by brain chemistry. Explanations do not change the feelings or totally encompass the experience. You can explain the greenness of grass as being due to the presence of chlorophyll, but that still does not explain the sensation of green. As it is when explaining things to children, there comes a point when you just have to say, "Well, that's the way things are."

Depression and feelings

The importance of the previous paragraph is that it illustrates the difficulty that depressed persons can have when they talk about feelings. "How do you feel?" might be a simple question, but to the depressed it can be a flummoxer. Do clients not feel anything, or is it that they do not know how they feel? Do clients not know how to interpret the sensations they do feel, or do they not know how to explain how they feel? Do clients not know how they are expected to feel, or do they not know how best to reply in the counselling situation? If we can rely on our feelings then being questioned about them is not a great problem, but if this is not the case, then people encounter difficulties. The difficulty may be put down to depression. This may be the case, but we also have to appreciate that when talking about feelings, counsellors are making assumptions about how clients interpret their feelings, assuming that it is the same for them as it is for counsellors.

There is more. If persons are not sure of their feelings, then they are unsure of themselves and unsure of others. This reinforces the uncertainty they have about themselves. That makes them unsure of what they are experiencing. When clients describe how they feel, it is often in stereotypical terms, "a pit in my stomach", "a black cloud hanging over me", as this is the safest way for them to describe the sensations they experience. They give a description but it may be a way of answering the question and covering up their uncertainty.

Counselling and client feelings

This introduction to feelings is necessary, as counsellors have to be aware that while feelings may be central to their work and to the understanding of the experience of being depressed, feelings can mean different things to counsellors and depressed clients. It is not just a matter of the two not experiencing the same thing; it is that clients may be aware of this difference, and have great difficulty in trying to bridge it.

Let me give you an illustration. It is hard for me to explain the colour green to anyone, but this does not stop me from talking about green to other people, and they will understand. However, suppose I am red-green colour blind (not much supposition there, unfortunately!), then I will be reluctant to talk about green things, as I know I could be talking about something different from what my listener sees. This not merely makes me lose faith in naming colours, but puts me in a difficult position when someone says, "In that case, what colour do you see?" The nature of the question shows that person does not understand, as there is not simple replacement of colours, seeing red for green. With strong shades, there is little confusion, whereas pastel colours, say, pale lime-green and pale pink are indistinguishable. So it is difficult to know what colours are seen.

The same applies to feelings in depression. When we talk about feelings in depression, counsellors have to remember that there is a difference between counsellors talking to other counsellors, and counsellors talking to depressed clients. It may be that clients give what appear to be reasonable answers about feelings in counselling. But to assume that the answers are as the counsellors understand them may be misleading.

Guilt

Bearing the possible problems of the subject of feelings in mind, we might note that a sense of guilt may often be experienced by depressed clients. Guilt can be specific and non-specific. In the former case, it can be that there are causes for the feeling of guilt, and clients can be helped by working on those causes. However, guilt might be exaggerated or misplaced. This takes us back to working with depressed thinking, and whether the depression is inducing untoward feelings.

We might also note that guilt can be destructive, or at least non-constructive, if nothing is done about it. Guilt can prevent progress, and clients moving on. This does not mean clients will always want to leave behind their sense of guilt concerning specific past actions or events. They may prefer to stay with it, even to the extent that it becomes a self-indulgence. This means that if the client talks about feeling guilty, feelings are being offloaded onto the counsellor. My reaction is simply to ask the "guilty" client, "And what have you done about it?" Unless that is done, the counsellor risks colluding with the client's guilt.

So, in brief, guilt can be reduced by:

- Getting clients to say exactly how they feel
- Getting clients to say what exactly they feel guilty about

- Getting clients to identify the cause of their guilt
- Getting clients to say how it is affecting their life at present
- Getting clients to say how others close to them react to their guilt
- Getting clients to say what they have done to lessen their guilt
- Getting clients to say what they intend to do about their guilt
- Getting clients to report back what they have done.

The other form of guilt is where there is no specified cause. This can occur in depression, when clients' sense of self is so diminished, and their world has collapsed into a bubble around them. Anything they see as going wrong, or anything that others see as wrong, is likely to be transformed into a sense of guilt.

> *Jill*: "I felt guilty. I felt if I was a really nice person, all of this would not have happened to me."

This can become a real problem if the client has experienced similar feelings in the past. Then depression and associated guilt are just what might be expected by clients, what they deserve.

> *Jill*: "I never really had any confidence. From my earliest years, before going to school, I had a tic in my face, and tried to avoid meeting people. I did not fit in locally, as my accent was different. Later I was bullied at school. I felt bad things happened to me. And as they kept happening to me, then I must deserve it."

As before, specification is helpful. Clients are encouraged to say precisely when they feel guilty. In particular, it helps if clients are aware of whether guilt is a long-standing factor in their life, or whether it has come about since they became depressed. If it is the former, then the whole lifetime of guilt has to be examined. If it is the latter, then the counsellor can explain about the effect that depression can have on thinking and feelings, and the two combined. In practice, this is not so simple, as even if guilt has come with the depression, clients might well see it as something that has always existed – this being another distortion of the thinking process through depression. So it is easier to ask whether the sense of guilt has increased during the depressive episode.

If the sense of guilt is depression related, then it is not likely to lift until the depression lifts. So the task is not guilt elimination but its management. This comes from seeing the sense of guilt as being in the context of depression. Clients have to be active, despite feelings of guilt. Rather than saying there is no need to feel guilty, and so expect clients to deny how they are feeling, it may be better to let them feel guilty and explain that they have to act to get past their guilt.

Anger

Anger, like other feelings, may have to be expressed before counselling work can be done. Whether clients can do this depends in part on counsellors, and whether they can accept highly charged emotions. I am aware that pure anger is not an emotion likely to be met in counselling training. In fact, most trainee counsellors are nice people, and so not always prepared for what clients can throw at them.

> *Eloise*: "See, fucking men! If I had my way, I'd stick dynamite up their arse and be first in the queue to light it. Twenty-five-year old, and all they want is their fucking mother to trail after them. If they sat down and had to think, their fucking head would explode. I swear to God, if one of them tries to be nice to me, I'll wrap his fucking balls round his neck!"

And that only gives the language, and not the intensity of feeling expressed.

The first point is to what extent clients can actually express their feelings? Counsellors, by non-verbal signals, can prevent clients from saying how they feel – even when we think we are quite agreeable to them saying whatever they want. We have to be able to get past the sheer violence of the way things may be said. This also means getting beyond our rationalisation of their violence in anger. In the example above, we have to get past thoughts of this client being a man-hater, an angry client, a person in distress or someone ventilating. This is simply someone who is very angry. She is able to say what she wants to say, but that is just the first step.

When dealing with anger, it is seen as necessary to ask why the client is so angry. The counsellor then gets caught up in the personal feelings of the client and tries to be reasonable, calming the person down. But this does not help the process of dealing with anger. This merely suppresses it. What we need to do is to see whether the anger is significant or not. To determine this, we need to know whether it affects the person or not. This might be likened to contrasting the statements, "You acted stupidly" to "You are stupid". The first is exterior to the person, merely describing behaviour, and does not criticise the person. The second statement, however, is a direct attack on self, on the person, and is not acceptable. The important criterion is whether or not the client feels under attack. So when there is real anger, it is worth asking clients whether they not merely feel under attack, but whether they feel:

- Limited
- Minimised
- Pressurised
- Used
- Ignored
- Rejected
- Blamed
- Denied
- Unacknowledged
- Over-ridden
- Attacked
- Ridiculed.

This helps clients to begin to specify what exactly their anger is about. But this is not the end of the process. For the attack on self to be meaningful, it has to hit home. This means, from the client's perspective:

- It is an accurate picture of myself, which I have tried to keep hidden.
- It is yet another attack made by another person about the same personal issue.
- It attacks the image of myself that I want the public to accept.
- It reinforces the attack made by someone dear to me or important to me.

When discussing anger with clients, some objective should be kept in mind. There can be several, according to the preference of the client. These might include:

- Sitting on one's anger, letting it seethe below the surface, in order to ensure some form of action, whatever it might be.
- Directing one's anger to some purpose, not to some person.
- Holding one's anger, mentally placing it away from oneself, so it can be used at some point in time.
- Dissolving one's anger through forgiveness or some other action.

What might be noted is that anger is neutral. It is a basic feeling, like sadness or love. Its presence is neither good nor bad. The question is what we do with it and how we manage it. Clients should be aware that there is likely to be outside pressure put on them as to how they should behave. This is often to deny feelings or to try and dissolve anger.

One action that is popular nowadays is the act of forgiveness. Clients may be pressurised to forgive those who have abused them, or to forgive themselves for how they feel. These courses may be useful for some clients; they are not necessarily best for all. It can avoid really coming to terms with one's anger, which can make others feel uncomfortable – including counsellors. There is no one way of dealing with feelings, but participation by clients is important, as they are the only ones who are in touch with their feelings.

Anxiety

Anxiety is a noticeable aspect of depression in many cases, and is usually taken as worry about what will happen in the future. It can take two forms. There can be worry about specific situations in the future. It helps to ask clients, "What exactly are you worried about?" Often the worry is put in general or even vague terms, and by being specific, clients can identify what precisely is their concern. This immediately reduces worry.

Adrian: "I suppose I'm worried about work."
Me: "You return next week. Is it the work you worry about or returning?"
Adrian: "Returning to work. I'm not really looking forward to it. No, that's not true. I'm worried how things will go."
Me: "Whether you can do the work or how others at work will be?"
Adrian: "The work does not bother me. No, how my section leader will be. He can be a bit of a you-know-what with some of the workers."
Me: "And has that included you in the past."
Adrian: "Yes. I don't mind being bawled out for a mistake, but not when I've done nothing."

The second form of anxiety is a more general feeling, where there seems to be no reason or identifiable source for the anxiety. As depression increases, this form of anxiety can become a sizeable part of the person's condition. There is no simple way of dispelling such anxiety, and it subsides as depression decreases, but can remain even after the depression has disappeared. This anxiety can be managed to a degree. Clients can be helped through relaxation exercises, through self-talk about their anxiety, through exercise, and through ongoing journal work. The main task is that of clients mentally separating general anxiety from action to be taken, to try and stop such anxiety interfering with their life.

One point to remember is that anxiety can gather a momentum, and this can engender further anxiety. One thing that clients can do is to slow down and thus decrease the momentum. This can be done by clients writing down specific examples of anxiety, and how they are experienced – linked to times, triggers and situations.

Anxiety and reactions

Anxiety may be taken as a problem, with little understanding of how it is felt by clients. Let us take the example of the ringing of a telephone. This can have no effect on the counsellor, or perhaps be a mild irritant. To the depressed client it can induce a state of near paralysis. The sound seems so insistent and the noise goes on and on. The client now has a dread of the telephone ringing. This is allied to the thought that the call may be important and should be answered. And the longer the phone rings, the more anxious the person becomes. Even when the phone has stopped, there can be anger that it rang and guilt because it was not answered.

Taking the ringing telephone as an example, we can work through the work of specific and general anxiety.

Dealing with telephone calls

Unfortunately, anyone who has been ill and had to stay at home will be aware that salespersons will ring up. If depressed, this is the last thing you want. People when depressed will say virtually anything just to end a phone conversation – not always a good idea with sales people. So the first thing is to have a plan about phones.

At one extreme is that of disconnecting the landline and switching off the mobile. This isolates the person, which may be fine, or may be unhelpful – depending on the client and the degree of depression. Another option is to disconnect the landline but keep the mobile switched on, as only people who know the number will then be able to contact. Unfortunately, many companies and agencies expect their workers to be contactable at any time and have their mobile numbers. This means work colleagues will have to be told not to contact. For those who have only a landline, relatives may be asked to phone, stop, and then phone again after 30 seconds or so. This code lets the client know it is a family member. Finally, some clients find that texting is more acceptable, as they do not actually have to talk to anybody. In fact, it is not the talking itself but having to deal with feelings that depressed clients can find so difficult.

Such practical measures are likely to prove more useful than all the talking about anxiety. Counsellors have to be prepared to be flexible, and get past the idea that talking and listening will be enough.

Panic attacks

Anxiety in extreme form may be exhibited in action; in panic attacks. Such attacks may build anxiety, as clients worry about the possibility of future attacks. The result can affect clients, who worry about going out because they might have a panic attack. As a result their social life can become very restricted.

It is worth discussing what is likely to happen, and reassuring clients that panic attacks will spontaneously stop, usually after 10–20 minutes. This is a very long time when a person is having an attack, but it helps if clients know they will eventually get through the experience all right. Clients may experience physical symptoms and think they are about to have a heart attack. This is not the case, unless they have a very weak heart.

Panic attacks are accompanied by hyperventilation, and clients sometimes imagine that, as they are gasping for breath, they are short of breath. In fact, they are taking in too much oxygen and need to calm their breathing. One well-known method is that of breathing into a paper bag. The exhaled air contains a greater amount of carbon dioxide, and this reduces the rate of breathing. In practice, it is better if clients do this by cupping their hands and breathing into them. This means they do not have to carry a paper bag and the action of self-help is not so visible – which can be a bonus.

Sometimes clients will begin to panic before actually doing what they want, as the anxiety gets to them. They need to learn to relax. Doing breathing exercises daily for 20 minutes or so, putting a hand under their chest so they breath slowly and regularly, and they can feel themselves doing so, can help. This is preferable to breathing quickly and shallowly from the upper chest, throat and mouth. The exercise reduces the chance of attacks. It also helps if clients subject to such attacks have a partner or friend with whom they feel safe, as this lessens the likelihood of panic incidents (Rachman, 1984). Depressed clients can benefit from a discussion about panic attacks, especially if it is supplemented by exercises during the counselling session.

BEHAVIOURAL METHODS

Introduction

As noted, there are problems with the cognitive approach, as mood is not necessarily mediated through thought. We can be sad, happy, or anxious, without thinking about how we feel. Yet it would be equally false to ignore the fact that feelings and thought affect cognition and can influence each other (Lewinsohn et al., 1981). This is especially the case in mild depression. Counselling can be of use in such situations as rational thought, if not able to change our mood directly, can help us manage our moods. So dealing with low mood and accompanying negativity is possible.

Inaction

In mild depression, clients can be negative and lacking in positive action, leaving things undone. This can lead to a downward spiral, as they are conscious of not doing things they fully intended to do. Clients get annoyed with themselves; see themselves as ineffective, even as failures. This further inhibits them from positive action.

There can be reasons given for not acting, and they are worth examining. Often these reasons are termed excuses, and clients are seen as weak or failing, rather than simply being mildly depressed. If the client is very mildly depressed, then pointing out these excuses can be helpful. However, when more depressed, there is nothing more irritating. It simply fails to be sensitive to clients and their attempts to manage their depression. What is required is to discuss that management, and how it might be bettered. And this starts with looking at reasons behind inaction.

Reasons for doing nothing

Counsellors should help clients see that their inaction is not a matter of not doing what they intended; it is a pattern of not doing, becoming conscious of not doing, and becoming negative about oneself for not doing. There can also be consequences of not doing. Failure to pay a bill early in the morning as intended may be insignificant, but continued failure to pay all bills will result in problems.

One of the reasons for inaction is simply lethargy. Life for the depressed can be like walking through treacle. Everything is an effort. The opposite side of this is that lethargy can be unrelated to depression, and may be a ploy by clients to stay in their sick role – but this is not common. Sometimes this lethargy can be partly caused by lack of sleep. This can come from anxiety, too much coffee, or unpleasant dreams.

Me: "So, you didn't do much to-day."
Adrian: "No. I was going to go out, but I was too tired."
Me: "Did you find it difficult to get ready?"

Adrian: "No. I decided I was too tired."
Me: "You decided you were too tired."
Adrian: "I was kind of tired."
Me: "Could it be that you thought about going out, and then you thought, 'Nah, I can't really be bothered. I'll do things to-morrow' ".
Adrian: "Yea, I bit like that; a lot, really."
Me: "So, let's be honest about it, can you get that paperwork done if you really wanted."
Adrian: "Yes, I can do it. I've just to give myself a kick up the arse. OK, I'll do it."

On the other hand, lethargy can be a real problem, arising from a lack of sleep, anxiety and poor diet. It might also be a product of some medication that is being taken.

Sleep problems

Many clients say that they cannot sleep, and this is a recognised feature of depression (Thase and Kupfer, 1987). This can be very debilitating, and contribute to attention and concentration difficulties (Horne, 1993). It can also cause a downward spiral, as anxiety about not sleeping aggravates the difficulties in getting to sleep. However, there are things that can be done:

- A distinction has to be made to clients between difficulties in sleeping, and being tired and not getting sleep. If a person does not sleep then they are lucky, in that they have extra hours in their day; and years on their life. If clients are tired as well, then they do have problems.
- We should realise that elderly clients require less sleep, and even being tired and unable to get to sleep for a couple of days will do no harm. Furthermore, the complaint by some clients that they have not slept for days or even weeks is not likely to be correct. This is not a matter of deception. They will merely have been resting and sleeping for short periods, a minute or two at a time, and not realising this fact.
- It is useful to know what clients have done or failed to do during the preceding days. For instance, if clients have done little physical that day, then they will not be physically tired. So taking exercise is useful, apart from its effect of lessening the severity of depression. Counsellors might also check out the amount of stimulants, usually caffeine, clients have taken. Caffeine is contained in coffee, tea, colas and chocolate. Some

clients can take in a surprisingly large amount of the drug, and this can account for sleeping problems.

- The clients have to allow themselves to sleep. They can expect to have a sleepless night, get anxious, and, as mentioned earlier, discover they have difficulties in getting to sleep. In addition, they might give themselves only a matter of a minute or so to get to sleep. If this fails, they then get anxious. It is best if clients give themselves time and try not to worry about sleeping.

Sleep and thoughts

Many clients will lie in bed at night, with thoughts swirling about. The result is that they get locked into thinking, and this interferes with their sleep. There are two main forms of thinking that are relevant. There can be obsessive thinking, where clients cannot get certain thoughts out of their mind. The more they try, the worse the situation seems to get. The answer is to break the sequence by getting out of bed and making a mug of soup, or doing something similar. Another form of unhelpful thinking is that of circular thought, where the client thinks of one thing, then another, and another, but eventually returns to the original thought. Again, distraction is required to break the cycle.

Getting a relationship with your thoughts

Another method that some clients find effective is to form a relationship with their thinking, so that there is a positive response to familiar returning thoughts. This relationship with their thoughts can be strengthened by clients talking out loud such thoughts. For instance, with cycling thoughts, a client might say, "So, you are back again. Look, that is enough for tonight; I know you are there, but please step back, further back, and disappear. Now I am going to sleep." This method can also be used for intrusive thoughts and disturbing dreams and nightmares. "That was a bad dream! I am just going to take a few seconds to recover, a few seconds, and now I feel a bit better. There was no need for you to be like that, to be quite so frightening. Next time will you please behave, and make it a pleasant dream." This might sound a bit odd, but the fact is that people often talk to themselves when alone, and it can be surprisingly effective.

An alternative is for clients to speak to someone about their bad dreams, preferably a partner or intimate friend, and offload as soon as possible.

Talking can help to defuse attendant anxiety, and the other person merely has to listen. This helps where there have been interrupted dreams, which can be frightening to some clients. The dream ends and the client wakes up, but then falls asleep and the dream continues. This is not unusual, though it can seem frightening, as clients see themselves as unable to escape the world of dreams.

Dreams and nightmares

Clients sometimes get upset about dreams and think they contain special significance and can be interpreted. I see this as mistaken. Dreams are the product of thoughts when we are asleep, and have as much or as little significance as our waking thoughts. Of far more importance are those dreams associated with trauma, where what happened, or what the client imagined, comes to haunt the client. Getting a relationship with the scene can be difficult, and may require visiting that scene in the imagination a step at a time. This should never be forced, otherwise clients may re-traumatise themselves.

Sleep and medication

In a very few extreme cases, a lack of sleep can be so debilitating and distressing that medication is required in the short term. The usual sleeping tablets, tranquillisers (benzodiazepines), are now prescribed less as their addictive potential has been recognised. What is not so widely recognised is the fact that they are effective only for a few weeks, and then stopping them can cause rebound symptoms, so clients can find getting to sleep even more difficult than before. There are still clients being prescribed long-life benzodiazepines such as diazepam (Valium), which continue to work when the client wakes – hence the feelings of having a hangover or being very tired on waking in the morning.

An alternative that is presently being increasingly used is the tricyclic antidepressants, as these have a sedative action. However, they do have side -effects, and may not be so highly regarded by clients as the well-advertised drugs and more recent drugs such as fluoxetine (Prozac). Clients also become tolerant to the sedative effect fairly quickly. My preference is for clients to make their own efforts as regards inducing or easing sleep.

Non-drug methods of sleep induction

Apart from taking exercise and working on problems which cause worry, clients can be offered a whole range of possibilities. Sometimes the placebo effect is more important that what is done or taken, but if clients do sleep better, there seems little point in arguing with positive results. Some stratagems to be used are:

- Taking a milk drink at night, a remedy that has been found effective by several clients.
- Eating protein such as chicken, fish, eggs or tofu for supper. This counteracts clients waking up at night because of a drop in the blood's sugar level, which in turn causes the production of adrenalin, a stimulant, which keeps the person awake.
- Eating foods such as beans or nuts may prove useful, as they contain magnesium, a relaxant.
- Eating bananas, as they provide a source of tryptophan, a precursor of serotonin, which is associated with possible depression and poor sleep.
- Eating lettuce, as this contains the very mild opiate lactucarium, which induces sleep.
- Drinking camomile tea.
- Using valerian, obtainable from health food shops – but be aware of possible drug interactions.
- Having a warm bath with pine salts for relaxation.
- Using relaxation tapes in bed.
- Putting a drop of lavender oil on the pillow or a handkerchief kept by the pillow.

One of the positive aspects of such methods is that it is clients who decide what to do and are in control. They feel they are helping themselves, with a resultant increase in self-esteem and confidence.

It might be noted in passing that sometimes we find that those depressed are sleeping very long hours. This is not a biological imperative, and there are no signs of daytime sleepiness (Nofzinger et al., 1991). This tiredness may be supplemented by a desire to cope by hiding from the world and looking for escape through sleep.

Exercise and exercises

For those with mild depression, any method of lessening stress is helpful. Exercise is particularly good, and even appears to counteract the depression itself (Griest et al., 1978). This has certainly been my experience.

Shelley: "Exercise helps – but you don't often feel like it."

The problem is that as depression comes on, there is a disinclination to take exercise, even when clients know it will do them good (Bosscher, 1993; Byrne and Byrne, 1993).

Paul: "I realised that depression was returning when I stopped exercising."

Those depressed have to try and force themselves to keep active, even when they do not feel like it. The involvement of family or friends increases motivation to continue to take moderate exercise and the mutual relationships make it more difficult to renege on the agreement (O'Brien et al., 1992). It can also help if there is someone to take feedback about the effects. An alternative is for clients to keep a record of their exercising. They might also consider taking a dog for a walk (Lago et al., 1983), even a neighbour's dog. The unconditional affection of animals such as dogs boosts the depressive's self-esteem and the physical contact can also be helpful (Cochrane, 1990).

Whatever methods are used, it is worth taking time to work on persuading clients to exercise, as it can also help in decreasing poor sleep patterns (Lacks, 1987) and increasing poor appetite (Patton, 1993). Research also suggests it is more effective than psychotherapy (Griest et al., 1978), as it affects mood-related biases in memory and judgement (Clark et al., 1983), and maintains the advances made through counselling (Matinsen and Medhus, 1989).

Further exercises

There are various exercises that can be used to help relax, and the best are those which clients can learn to do. These include simple breathing exercises. Clients are taught to relax in a chair, close their eyes and put their hands on their uncrossed legs. They then have to concentrate on their breathing. Sometimes an appropriate relaxation tape may be of use. However, some clients find a tape a distraction, as it interferes with the concentration on their breathing. It has to be stressed that such concentration may have to be learned, and a regular schedule of 20 minutes a day is required. In the Benson variation, clients say the number "one" each time they exhale. If external thoughts interfere, they say "one", and carry on breathing (Benson, 1976).

Another method is autogenic training (Kermani, 1992), which is a form of mild self-hypnosis. Sitting in a chair, the client, with closed eyes, repeats, "My right arm is heavy", then concentrates on breathing for three breathes, then repeats, "My breathing is steady", and then concentrates on breathing, before repeating, "My left arm is heavy", then concentrates on breathing, and then "My breathing is heavy". This sequence, which lasts for about a minute, is repeated. I find that it is easier to think the phrases rather than speaking them, as speaking aloud can disrupt the rhythm of breathing.

Counsellors should be aware that relaxation methods do not always work. For instance progressive relaxation, as developed by Jacobson and refined later (Wolpe and Lazarus, 1966) is a method of progressively tensing muscles, noting their tension and then releasing the tension. My interest in this is that it is often a method taught at medical schools and used by doctors. It is also a method that causes me acute stress. So we should not imagine that relaxation exercises suit everyone, or even that they are necessarily effective.

Role-play

Clients who make themselves act as if they were happy, are likely to actually feel happier (Laird, 1984). From personal experience, even trying to smile can be enough to bring about an elevation of mood. This is likely to last only a short time, so role-playing a happy situation can bring about a more prolonged effect. Attempting such an action when moderately depressed or worse can be counterproductive. It only works with very mildly depressed clients.

Food and drink

At a time when health warnings and exhortations as to what we should and should not eat and drink, it is easy to become cynical, especially when we remember how health messages change over the years. Nevertheless, it is advisable to stick to a healthy diet. Those depressed are more liable to eat quick meals and take in large amounts of carbohydrates.

Much of what we drink contains drugs. Alcohol is itself a depressant drug, while tea, coffee and colas all contain caffeine, which is a stimulant. Both stimulants and depressants affect as person's mood, making control of depression that much harder. Clients have to be aware of what they may be eating and drinking, and the possible effects.

Low blood sugar

When clients are nervous and agitated, as often happens in depression, their pancreas can be over-stimulated and thus produces too much insulin – the enzyme that breaks down sugar, in the form of glucose, in the blood. But if all the glucose is broken down quicker than it can be manufactured in the body, it causes a lack of blood sugar. This leads to a craving for sweet foods to replace the glucose, and the person feels faint, irritable and has headaches. Low sugar levels are also linked with panic attacks, as the lack of glucose results in adrenalin being produced. This acts as a stimulant, which can bring on panic attacks.

To counteract the sudden changes in blood sugar levels, which are caused by an overproduction of insulin, clients are advised to avoid sugar and sugary foods, some processed foods, and foodstuffs such as baked beans, and fizzy drinks, which both contain added sugar. In fact, clients should avoid carbohydrates which can quickly be converted into sugar. This includes white bread, polished rice, and many processed foods. By changing to wholemeal bread, brown rice and non-processed foods, the carbohydrates eaten take longer to be converted into glucose. This will reduce sudden surges in sugar level.

Reinforcement of action

The above behavioural resources and accompanying client actions are not seen as very important as they are not seen as part of counselling. In fact, they are as important as counselling, and should be integrated into it. Counselling is not just about talking, but also about action, and many clients feel better being able to do something.

Chapter 7

Depression and the Past

Clients and their past

Depression is more likely and more severe if clients have unfinished business from their past, if there are unsettling events which still affect their present thinking, feelings and behaviour. Not addressing such events can make depression more likely to continue. It should be noted that traumatic or highly distressing events do not have to cause depression. In fact, depressed clients can appear to be good at coping with difficulties until there is an event that is simply one difficulty too many. And sometimes just having to actually face the event can be enough. One example is that of a client who was suddenly devastated by recalling the death of his father, a death which had occurred over 20 years previously.

Some clients will have received help for past difficulties, but this might not have been sufficient. For example, past sexual abuse can have effects later in life (Bagley and Young, 1989), but it is often thought that one course of treatment will settle matters. And, at the time, matters did appear to have been successfully concluded. But further help may be required years later, as the thoughts and feelings of the client have changed. Or sometimes the help given dealt with the event but not secondary outcomes, such as stigma (Lindberg and Dinstad, 1985) and shame (Beitchman et al., 1992), which grow over the years and become the problems in later life (Lewis, 1992).

When examining with clients their past, it is easy to concentrate on important or traumatic times, and this is often seen as something that happens to clients. What is more difficult is seeing those times in the context of a client's total life, in the context of family and friends, and in the context of present and future.

Looking at the past

Reviewing the past is not a simple task. Clients, like all of us, fashion the past to assist their passage through life. This is usually not a conscious act.

We see things differently over time, perhaps more clearly, perhaps less. We have to live in the present, so we mould the past to help us do so. The past may have been a bad time for clients, yet they can be ambivalent about it.

> *Gerry*: "I am dragged back by my memories. I often think of those days. I even went back to my primary school, as they were about to knock it down. I took the camcorder with me ... I find myself going back in my life. You shouldn't think too much of your past. It's gone. But the past catches up with you."

The past can be a bad place, but it can also be a refuge, a time when things were simpler and easier – or so it seems in retrospect. This ambivalence means that clients will give differing versions of events, reflecting how they would like matters to be seen or have worked out. So the past is not clients listing off what occurred; it is more complex, a construction of a world in the past.

The forgotten past

Reviewing the past may be applied to depression itself, as it can slowly develop and last over months, if not years. In fact, this is not always appreciated.

> *Jill*: "The doctor kept asking me if anything had happened that triggered off the depression. I said there was nothing. So he seemed to lose interest. He said he would write me out a prescription."

At this point, the client was made to feel that her depression did not amount to much, as nothing had happened to cause her to feel as she did. Perhaps it would have been more accurate if she had said the whole of her life could be a cause. In fact, Jill had been a worrier from the age of eight, when her parents separated. Later her father had to sell their house when his business went bankrupt. His difficult behaviour was diagnosed as being a result of paranoid schizophrenia. Jill's only pregnancy had been terminated at the age of fourteen. All of this suggests the role of accumulated loss, which may well have contributed to the client's present depression. The client had not thought her past could be of importance, as the idea had not been mentioned.

Beginning to deal with the past

The immediate task is that of knowing what constitutes unfinished business for the client. And this poses a problem. The client has to open up and divulge intimate information, thus becoming vulnerable. Furthermore, there may be subjects which clients do not want to think about, and certainly do not want to talk about. So what should the counsellor do? Each of us has our own methods, so I can merely describe my approach.

Firstly, people like to talk. If they do not do so, then at least part of the reason lies with the counsellor. We give out non-verbal signals, we make ourselves approachable; and people speak. Clients are people, and people will talk. If they fail to do so, then it may be:

- The set-up in the counselling session is not conducive to talking. So take the client outside, have a stroll. Some clients will prefer to talk on the move or when active. Or stop counselling. Have a tea or coffee break. Other clients will talk more "when they are not being counselled".
- Do not be too keen or anxious to talk about important times for clients. Let them take their time. Clients can be sensitive to what counsellors are doing, and react accordingly.
- Do not over-emphasise confidentiality at the start of counselling. I tend to leave it to the end of the first session. Clients expect confidentiality, and to be told about it in detail at the start seems more for the counsellor's benefit than that of the client.
- Have a general interest, especially in the media. Clients will often watch television programmes about depression, or get information in the papers. This can provide a safe entry for clients into what they might see as difficult explanations.
- Be relaxed, appropriately self-disclosing, and prepared to go off track, talk about irrelevancies – at least for a time. Clients do not want sessions to be constantly intense. And do not concentrate merely on the client. Ask about others in the client's life.

Clients will speak to counsellors, but often only to the extent they see themselves as being clients. Consequently they give information that they think the counsellor wants or expects. Counsellors should be themselves, and get past the counselling role. This does not mean they should not monitor the counselling as to tone, intensity, pace and content.

Depression, loss and disclosure

One way of encouraging clients to discuss important past events is to get them to give a short resume of their past, in a matter of a minute or so. What comes to mind is usually what is most relevant to them.

Max: "I never knew my mother, as she died when I was a year old. My father could not deal with us, as he was a miner and had his job. I was the youngest in the family, and was put into a Children's Home. My brothers and sister were put to other homes. I got little education as I was moved around a lot."

But some clients will be careful of talking about their past. It is not that they do not want to speak about it. They want some signal from the counsellor to allow them to do so, some sign that allows them to continue. The signals might relate to:

- Competence: This might cover the fact that as a counsellor I have dealt with depressed clients previously – and I still find it difficult. I might assure the client I can do something for them – is that all right?
- Self-disclosure: I have experienced similar situations or feelings as the client – though probably not as bad. Even though I have experienced similar conditions as the client, I still find it difficult to know how they must feel.
- Sharing: Sharing can take a weight off the client's shoulders. – Does the client feel they have been carrying a weight around for a long time? And the past affects us all – so sometimes it is useful to look at it in detail.
- Feelings: The counsellor says what he is experiencing about the client in general. The counsellor also specifies what he feels here-and-now between him and the client. And the counsellor says how he feels.
- Positive feedback: Thanking the client for what they have said and picking out one item of particular interest. Or the counsellor can ask the client how they feels about saying a bit more, as he can probably help the counsellor to help him.

What is apparent is that the counsellor has to be careful, and avoid the client thinking the counsellor knows it all, the counsellor is downgrading the client's problems, the counsellor is reading from a script, the counsellor knows how the client feels, and the counsellor is jollying the client along. The other point is that the counsellor, at this point, does not know if there is anything very significant in the client's past. However it is safe to say clients, like all of us, do have a varied past and may want to allude to it. The counsellor assumes there is something the client wants to talk about and this almost always turns out to be true.

In fairness, it should be said that the counsellor often picks up a sense both of there being a hidden past, and that feeling may rest on the client's account to date, in that:

- Areas have been omitted. One client did not talk about her father. When this was pointed out, she began to admit she resented him for ignoring her, whilst paying attention to her younger sister.
- The account given is a bit strange. One example is that of a client who said she could not remember any of her childhood.
- Major changes in life are not elaborated on. For instance, moving to another town or city may be significant.
- The client gives few details of how the family gets on together, or another family member had difficulties.

It should be appreciated that clients can be very ambivalent about disclosing their past in full, but usually want to do so – provided it seems safe to do so. And counsellors have to provide that safety through the relationship and the counselling.

If we return to the client Max, when he gave an account of his past life, it was necessary to slow him down. It was almost as if he was talking about another person.

> *Max*: "I was living with this girl. I was 23 and she was 17 at the time. We were together for a year and then we fell out. I took it bad, and ended up taking an overdose."

Clients should not give their past as history; they should interact with it, they should allow their feelings to enter into it. They should become more aware of how they reacted at the time and how they feel now. There is also a matter of how other relevant persons reacted.

> *Max*: "Later I saw the doctor. He told me it was in my genes. It was me. Nothing could be done. That upset me, and I went into a depression."

The behaviour of the client in the counselling session gives the counsellor a good idea of, not just the client's past, but what that past meant to him or her.

Grief and the past

Attention is given here to the topic of loss, as loss underlies so many aspects of important events in a client's past. Any major life-change can be seen as involving loss. Change is both taking on the new and losing the old, whether this includes old behaviour, circumstances, beliefs or expectations. Dealing with change involves dealing with the loss of old behaviour, situations or beliefs, so a form of grieving might be required for all major changes. If this does not happen, depression is more likely.

However grief, or simply talking about loss, is not always seen as permissible. For instance, a heavy drinker turned teetotal may not be allowed to talk freely about his loss, the good times he had when drunk, as this is seen as preparing to go back on the drink. Similarly, a man about to get married may not be viewed kindly if he talks about the good times when he was single. Yet this is a way of preparing himself for married life.

There are other reasons for not grieving. The loss may be seen as a good thing, so grieving is considered unnecessary. Grief is not seen as applicable, as often happens in the case of young children. Grief is submerged with other priorities in life. Those in grief were expected to finish their grief in a short time. A person going on about their grief is simply viewed as embarrassing.

Loss, death and grief

The subject of death will be discussed, as it is the most familiar event that carries grief. This requires clients see grief and its role in change as normal. We also have to be aware of hidden grief, not just that which is not spoken about, but which can arise from hidden loss. Sometimes losses are overlooked, even by professionals. One example is that of loss by miscarriage, which may be largely overlooked as regards psychological effects, both as regards grieving (Hall et al., 1987) and associated trauma (Herz, 1983), by the medical profession.

Death, change and depression

There is much confusion around intimate loss and grief, partly because loss may be associated with death, still almost a taboo subject. So we have to be careful and not treat death and grief as unusual. Death is the one certainty in life, and grief a useful way of coping with it. Severe depression is not an inevitable result of death of a loved one, even if the death was traumatic.

Knowing when and what help to offer in grief requires thought. It may be that no help is required, that support alone is most appropriate. Or it may be that difficulties are experienced and counselling is required. For some people who are isolated, help may be required for grief itself, as a form of low-grade depression.

Depression in grief

More severe depression can happen and is much more probable if there has been difficult grief. Such grief is characterised by:

- The client's relationship with the deceased was ambivalent, and variable, going up and down. The reason for the difficulty is that the client does not know how to feel about the dead person.

  Marie: "Things had not been going well for some time. Then ten months ago we split up, but kept in touch. Just recently we had talked about possibly getting back together, but nothing had been decided. Now he is dead. I'm left wondering whether we had a life together."

- The relationship with the deceased is marked by dependence. The difficulty is the degree to which the client is himself or herself, and can exist as a person without the partner.
- If clients have had many losses in their lives, this can impede the grief process.

  Eloise: "I had a miscarriage; then James died when he was a year old, and Peter was eighteen when he was knocked down by a car and killed. I wonder what I've done in a past life to deserve this. I wonder who will be next to go."

- Violence in death is also a cause of difficult grief, even when it is a known risk; for example when the person was a member of the Armed Forces. For civilians, the sources of violent death are suicide, murder and road death.
- When there is "no body", the bereaved are likely to experience problems. "No body" can mean exactly that: the body is lost at sea or in heavy armed conflict. But there can also be occasions when there is a body, but the person never saw it as it was in a coffin, for example, when a person dies abroad and the body is brought back. There can be other examples:

  Sandy: "He killed himself in the woods, but his body was not found for several weeks. By then the body had been eaten by animals and partly decomposed. I wanted to see it, but the undertakers refused me. I was never sure whether it was him in that coffin. I even measured it to see if it was big enough to hold him."

Bryony: "I was surprised. We had been divorced for ten years and had not seen each other for years. Then I heard he was dead. I suddenly felt very upset and could not get him out of my mind, even though I had had a life without him."

Work with difficult grief

Initially, the counsellor encourages the client to talk about the dead person, their relationship and what happened. There are likely to be many repetitions, as the client has to incorporate the idea of the person's death into his or her understanding, to accept the reality of what has occurred. This entails fitting the fact into a matrix of beliefs and expectations, none of which are likely to include the possibility of the person dying. So there has to be almost a reprogramming of the client's brain, and this is helped by constantly going through what has taken place.

Another aspect is talking about the life or contact together of the deceased and the client. This might cover the good times together, and the daft or surprising things couples might do, as well as the normal or even humdrum activities that were shared.

What is not said

The above might apply to ordinary grief, but is still useful in difficult grief. However the latter requires the counsellor to be a bit more directive at times, and this means helping the client investigate and possibly discuss more sensitive areas. One way of introducing this is to say that many of those in grief have difficulty in talking about some aspects of the deceased. The following is a list of such topics, which might help guide the client. The list might be of the following feelings:

- Anger at being left alone
- Fear of being on one's own
- Guilt about what was not done
- Sadness at loss of companionship and intimacy
- Anxiety about others leaving you or your own death
- Irritation at the way others talk about the death, or the fact that they do.

Anger might result from being left with financial debts or having to do domestic duties. And after being with someone for several years, there can be fear of being on one's own – even if the relationship with the deceased had not been good. Returning to an empty house and having no-one to talk to can be very demoralising. Guilt can arise from thinking of what was not said and what needed to be said. There may have been promises made that cannot be kept now. Sadness may come from a realisation that life may be shared to a greater extent than was realised. Decisions may have been joint, even if purely nominal. And a loss of intimacy, and accompaniments such as personal touch, sound and smell – as well as sight, are often unspoken losses. Anxiety about the loss of an intimate, which lessens the client's social network, reminds people of their mortality and that nothing is permanent. Finally, irritation can arise as others often have not experienced and do not understand the nature of grief. What others say reflects this, and can be extremely annoying, especially when some inappropriate things are said.

Ambivalence and grief

The first point to notice is that ambivalence about the relationship to the deceased may be denied. If a person has died, there can be a difficulty in admitting any relationship problems, as there is a social rule of not speaking ill of the dead. Even if difficulties are admitted, it may not be easy to talk about them neutrally in the light of the person having died. From the counselling perspective, it is preferable that any discussion is not about personalities but primarily about the relationship with the deceased.

Any discussion about the relationship is likely to be coloured by feelings, and so there can be exaggeration and undervaluation, an unrealistic view of the past. This means the counsellor has to be prepared to ask factual questions, such as "Exactly how many times ...?" or "Where precisely did that happen?" Clearly, this should not come over as a cross-examination, and much rests on the style of counselling.

The first step is that of getting the client to describe the relationship with the deceased. This starts off with how the two met and any surrounding circumstances. Then questions might be around time spent together, activities that were shared, work and domestic roles, and visits or time spent with family and in-laws. The emphasis initially is on observable behaviour, as opposed to shared or differing beliefs and expectations, which are difficult to confirm. Only later is it worth returning to topics such as the first meeting and asking about hopes and expectations.

The role of the past

It can be that past relationships affect other relationships later in life. For this reason it can be useful if the client talks about relationships with parents, brothers and sisters, relationships at school and at work. The client is the best person to say whether such relationships may have indirectly affected the quality of the relationship with the deceased. We should see the ability to form relationships as being progressive, so when the relationship with the deceased began and how that relationship changed over time is important.

Looking at the relationship with the deceased

By discussing less intimate and controversial matters, the grounds are laid for examining the relationship with the deceased. Using the information already supplied, the counsellor can help the client look at difficulties in the relationship. Sometimes this can be like touching a button, and the client brings up old arguments, resentments and pain. There is a need for ventilation, for the expression of feelings. However there is also the need to talk about the relationship difficulties in as neutral a way as possible. This includes how differences might have arisen, and this might involve differing beliefs, attitudes and expectations.

Finally, it is important to ascertain how the client saw the relationship at the end. The act of bringing closure has both rational and emotional aspects. The rational aspect is covered by helping the client to see the relationship from a variety of possible perspectives. There is no attempt to see the relationship as it really was, as this will differ according to who views it. But what can be done is to offer differing views, so the client can get a composite perspective. This will not be precise, but building in flexibility of how the client sees the relationship is useful. This means clients can vary their views, which means that coping with loss is easier. They can believe, within certain limits, what they want to believe. This might seem unsatisfactory, but it is realistic. The client's view of the relationship is likely to change to some extent over the years.

Past losses

Past losses make depression more probable, but clients are not always consciously aware of their losses. When counsellors ask about past losses, even when examples are given, clients and even counsellors may not be aware of the different forms of personal losses that might be operating.

George: "No, I've never had any important losses in my life."
Me: "Except your father. I thought he died while fighting abroad."

George: "Yes, I forgot. That sounds terrible. Yes, there was my father's death."
Me: "And you moved around a bit, when he was alive. The family had to move house a few times."
George: "I see what you're getting at. Yes, that meant that I made friends and then had to leave them behind."
Me: "And didn't you mention some time ago that you were adopted?"
George: "Ah, yes. I wasn't sure whether I had told you or not. I have thought about finding out about my parents, even meeting them. Then things might go wrong. I think about it."
Me: "Would you say that is a loss in your life, or perhaps it is not important."
George: "I'm not sure. I suppose it is there, at the back of my head."

We all have losses in our life, so past losses are those personal losses which we see as important to us. In short, it depends whether they have affected us as persons, whether they have resulted in a permanent lowering of self-esteem, feeding into the feeling of personal helplessness, and leaving the individual more open to depression.

Dealing with past losses

Depression around past losses arises when those past losses affect the client's present; when the losses are unfinished business. They may have to be dealt with first if there is to be progress on the present situation.

Eloise: "I can't begin to deal with Jay's death when I haven't even begun to come to terms with Cindy's cot death ten years ago."

Dealing with old losses starts with revisiting the reality of that loss. This can be upsetting, such as looking at old photos, schoolbooks, and visiting the grave or memorial. A further step can be to say goodbye to the deceased, say by writing a letter. Sometimes a further "funeral service" may prove helpful. It might be said that there was one long ago, so why have another? Sometimes those at the funeral are in shock and in no condition to benefit from the service. And there is no reason why there should not be another ceremony, albeit an informal one, if it is needed. And all the time the client should be encouraged to talk about the early loss.

TRAUMA AND OTHER TOPICS

Introduction

A good number of clients who come for counselling will have experienced trauma in their lives. Clients dealt with by myself have ranged from those given an HIV diagnosis, to those who have been subjected to physical or sexual abuse, and to those who have been affected by traumatic loss, through suicide, murder or road death. It is this last category which will be highlighted here. However, trauma has similarities whatever its cause and nature.

Depression can result from trauma, but it can take some time for it to develop. It should be said that depression associated with trauma often responds poorly to the usual methods. Even anti-depressants can have little effect. So counsellors have to be careful of assuming they know how such clients are best helped.

The effects of trauma

When considering the effects of trauma, one characteristic stands out – their extreme nature. They can be so extreme that they become literally virtually indescribable. So there is likely to be a gap between the experiences of traumatised clients and the experiences of counsellors.

After the traumatic event, the affected person enters a period of shock, likely to last many months. It takes a long time before the total reality of the death is accepted. This is not denial. Clients will know rationally that the person is dead, but emotionally the loss is not accepted. This is rather different from normal deaths, where shock lasts a relatively short time. This point is often not understood by friends and relatives, who expect traumatised persons to react like those normally bereaved and soon recover.

Another difference is the amount of anger that is bound up with the grief. We should not see this as abnormal. Anyone who has dealt with bereaved children will be aware of how anger can follow a death. Perhaps the overall impression is that of a person in a state of personal chaos, with so much going on.

> *Joyce*: "I find I sleep a lot, with no dreams or nightmares. But I am jumpy, my concentration is poor, and I keep forgetting things."
> *Me*: "And how is your appetite?"
> *Joyce*: "I'm just not eating, hardly at all. I've lost a stone over the last two months."
> *Me*: "Umm. You seem a little distracted right now."

Joyce: "Yes... Sometimes I feel dead inside. I feel like I'm away on another planet. Other times I'm really down. Sometimes I feel angry. I get irritated with other people when they're speaking."
Me: "Lots of quite different feelings."
Joyce: "Yes. I don't know where I am."

The difficulty is initially that of making a list of effects of the trauma, and then making some sense of it.

Symptoms of trauma

There are signs of past trauma that are not normally associated with grief. These have been placed in the psychiatric category of post-traumatic stress disorder. We might remember that constructing a category gives us a name, but not any insight or explanation.

If we review the effects, some of the characteristics of traumatic loss include:

- Shock, when clients can take in little information. Counselling soon after the trauma is likely to be ineffective, and even harmful, as it interferes with the client's coping. This period is much longer than in non-traumatic death, though this is not generally appreciated. In one case, an employer expected a client back at work seven weeks after the loss of his son following a road death.
- Extreme lethargy, such that even getting out of bed can be an overwhelming task. This lethargy can be a combination of lack of sleep and mental exhaustion, continually thinking through what has happened or avoiding thinking about it. In general, the more the person thinks about getting up, the harder it becomes, so having a routine and always getting up at a given hour without thinking is best.
- Avoidance is often an almost unconscious reaction to painful associations, such as the place where the trauma took place. This can have practical implications if that place used to be one often visited, such as by the local supermarket or Benefits Office. Avoidance can extend to talking about what took place, which can affect counselling.
- Dreams and nightmares can disturb sleep, apart from often being frightening or upsetting. Dreams can continue after the client wakes and then goes back to sleep. Nightmares can be repeated every night. Even large amounts of tranquillisers will fail to ensure a good night's rest.

- Flashbacks often develop a few weeks after the trauma, giving clients the impression that things are getting worse rather than better. As these occur during daytime, they can be even more upsetting than nightmares.
- Startle reactions cause those affected by trauma to be very jumpy. The normal fight-or-flight reaction is never turned off, so sudden movements or noises can severely startle clients. One client used to jump a mile when her mobile phone rang.
- Dissociation, depersonalisation and derealisation, are reactions when clients feel outside their body, do not feel their real self, and feel the world is not real. These are defence mechanisms; ways whereby the mind protects the person from what has happened.

There are also variable effects on memory. Short-term memory becomes very poor in some cases, yet recollection of the traumatic event or incident can be vivid and persistent. Sometimes it is difficult to distinguish between the memory and imagining what took place. In one case, a client whose husband had been murdered gave a description of the murder and how he was chased from room to room to escape his pursuer. She said she could remember exactly – but admitted she was not present.

Action around trauma

The first point is for counsellors to emphasise normality – stressing that clients are acting normally in a totally abnormal situation. This is necessary, as the psychiatrising of trauma tends to reinforce abnormality and client helplessness.

Then basic information should be given, such as the fact that shock lasts a long time and recovery can be very slow indeed.

Clients can be told that the effects are those of the client's self taking care of the person, of protecting the self from the full horror and distress of what has happened.

The totally unexpected nature of the event overturns all expectations, the natural way of life, "the way life should be". We do not expect to be speaking to someone, and then discover a few hours later that person is dead. We do not expect children to die before their parents. These events are not easily taken in. Dreams, nightmares, flashbacks and constantly talking about the event are the mind's way of trying to review the situation; incorporate the totally improbable into a personal reality. This process can be carried on through counselling.

Clients have to be prepared to take their time – and this applies equally to counsellors. Clients are coping from the very start with their condition, and forcing this process is unhelpful. Techniques such as psychological debriefing rest on seeing clients as abnormal and needing treatment, rather than as coping persons who need support. Such debriefing, if done against clients' wishes, amounts to little more than client abuse.

Further counselling action

There are further measures that can be taken, usually after a time when clients are more able to deal consciously with the symptoms of trauma:

- The client is helped to see what advances have been made. As clients slowly come out of shock they have to deal with the reality of their loss. As a result, they feel worse not better. The reassuring "Time is a great healer" is unhelpful, especially as this is not how clients experience their life. For the first 6 months or more, life gets progressively more distressing and painful. This has to be seen positively as coming through shock. In addition, clients often fail to notice the advances they make, having a depressed view of themselves and the world. Keeping a journal so they can look back and see how they were weeks or months ago can go towards clients having a more realistic view.
- Clients can be helped to get a relationship with their problems, such as startle response, dreams, lethargy and avoidance. Rather than seeing them as the enemy, as harmful, clients can begin to talk to them; "Hello, it's you again! Come to shake me up. Well, you have done it, so now you can leave." Externalising, by drawing the different symptoms can also help clients achieve a degree of familiarity with their symptoms of trauma.
- Clients can start to deprogram their symptoms. For example, if there is a problem with avoidance, then the place can be approached, but in the imagination at first. Clients are helped to approach closer with each attempt, the help being no more than support. Once the client feels able, he can then approach the place in reality – again, a bit at a time. It is important that clients do not feel under pressure, as this increases a sense of helplessness and feeds into depression.

Retraumatisation

Once a client has been traumatised, then he or she is left very vulnerable. As a result, being retraumatised by apparently insignificant events is quite possible. This can occur through legal action, such as the judicial process in cases of murder or in cases of Fatal Accident Inquiries. We also have to be aware that insensitive counselling can be equally retraumatic.

The ripple effect

Trauma is like a stone cast into a pond; its effects, like ripples in the water, spread outwards and affect many people. The whole family is likely to be affected.

> *Me*: "It has obviously been very difficult for you. You mentioned earlier about having to think about your daughter. Perhaps I can ask her about it, OK? So, how have you been, Julie?"
> *Julie*: "I've been OK."
> *May*: "You've been depressed – tell the man!"
> *Julie*: "Well, I do feel sad ... I can't stop myself from crying. See, I don't want my Mum to get upset. She has been so upset she has been physically sick."
> *May*: "I get this really unpleasant hole in my stomach."
> *Me*: "You affect each other, then?"
> *Julie*: "Sometimes I look at my Mum and I know she's crying inside. That sets me off."

As we can see, the effects in the family are interactive. Everyone can be involved, and each person reacts to others, and others react in turn to that person. Sometimes the danger is that the counsellor's interest focuses on the identified client, and others in the family may be overlooked.

Trauma and the past

Trauma may be a problem in itself, but it can also resurrect old problems. Firstly, trauma breaks down client defences, so that the past returns.

> *Eloise*: "You think you have dealt with the past, you have stuck it all behind you. Then it suddenly comes back. All the defences I built up are of no use. All that hiding things away."

Then the past and the present can be intermingled and inter-react. Counsellors are presented with a whole raft of client difficulties.

Jill: "I was depressed, tearful, crying at times for no reason. And I was edgy, whirling round at people behind me as if they were going to jump me. I was not sleeping well, and was having dreams about my ex-(husband), and he was telling me how crap I was. Another time, guys were going to kill me, and yet another time, the room was full of snakes, their jaws open, and I had to walk over them. And the fear would be with me when I woke up. And all the time there was this anger building up inside me, building up over three months. During this time I drew into myself, making myself almost a prisoner in the flat, creeping around and avoiding people. I would sit in a chair and feel myself disappearing into it. And energy was lacking, and my self-esteem drained away.

It really all started from the rape. My anger started coming out, me shouting at people. Every morning I would wake up to the thought that I had been raped, contaminated, degraded, used and abused. All my goodness has been taken away... All bad memories came flooding back. I wanted to forget about it, but I couldn't."

The difficulty with counselling which is over-planned and does not give sufficient time to establishing a good working relationship is that clients do not have the opportunity to disclose fully about themselves, or prefer not to do so. We should not underestimate the potential difficulties that can arise when dealing with trauma-related depression.

Reprise

Depression may be associated with loss, and that loss may not be apparent to clients. Counsellors accordingly may have to help clients with the role of past losses in their life. Losses do not necessarily cause depression, but they do make it more likely and also aggravate it.

Chapter 8

Other Depressions

MANIC DEPRESSION

Introduction

Manic depression, or bipolar affective disorder, as it is now officially named, may be seen as the opposite to depression. Far from clients being affected by lethargy and reduced thinking, there is physical over-activity, accompanied by a flood of ideas – sometimes coming so fast they cannot all be voiced. There may be fits of laughter, but the mood can quickly change, and crying replaces the laughter. Concentration for clients is difficult, so they may be poor listeners.

> *Roddy*: I get swept up, talking and joking. I'm the man, and thoughts seem to come from God knows where. Nothing is too difficult and you feel everyone is your friend. But it doesn't always last.
> *Mother*: You can't tell him anything when he's in full flow. His mind jumps about and he believes he's right all the time. And if you try to stop him, Roddy can get angry and aggressive.

There are degrees of manic depression, as there are of depression, so the idea of a continuum still holds (Gershon et al., 1982; Fieve et al., 1984). However, mild manic depression is not always easy to identify, as variable mood is within the range of normal behaviour, whereas constant low mood is seen as somehow unacceptable.

Medical help

Because manic depression was seen as quite separate from depression, medical remedies were seen to be separate. Lithium salts were used for manic depression, and anti-depressants for unipolar depression. In fact, both states react to lithium, which is not as effective for mania as initially thought (Goodwin, 1994). As lithium medication requires careful monitoring, other drugs such as carbamazepine (Freeman et al., 1992) and valproic acid (Gerner, 1993) are increasingly used. Care has to be taken, as clients can be seen as merely depressed and are prescribed anti-depressants, which may bring on manic episodes for those suffering from manic depression (Goodwin, 1994).

Counselling

There are different emphases placed on counselling those subject to manic depression. It has been said that such clients react poorly to counselling, but those who come or are referred for help tend to be clients with major symptoms. Those with minor mania tend to stay away, partly because they are seen as little different from anyone else. Working with clients with non-minor mania is equivalent to working with clients affected by a considerable degree of depression. However, the following might be borne in mind:

- The constant variation in mood can make relationships, including the counselling relationship, subject to strain. The counsellor is not always sure of the client's mood and how to react. Checking out how the client is feeling is often a necessity.
- There appears to be a greater genetic component and less influence from the past in the production of manic depression compared with unipolar depression. This means less work may have to be done around the client's past history.
- There is likely to be less anxiety but more somatic symptoms with manic depression (Perris, 1992), so stress as a counselling topic may be less important.

However, there are two aspects that can be usefully covered when counselling:

- Counsellors should check out whether clients are self-medicating. They may be depressed and then use a stimulant, such as cocaine or amphetamine to give themselves a lift. This can give the misleading impression of mania.
- Counsellors should also check out whether clients have been taking their medication. The reason for this is that somewhat manic clients do not appreciate how disordered their behaviour is and how they affect others. The chaotic times are simply seen as good times (Goodwin, 1994). How they feel gives clients a rosy view of reality, which can make decision-making

risky, especially if money is involved. Counsellors cannot change the mania, but can help clients take time to look and think before acting.

Suicide is a definite risk with manic depression (Depression Guideline Panel, 1993). It may be imagined that the risk would be less, as the episodes of mania would bring a lift and some measure of relief. This is not the case.

Harry: "I've had this thing for years, manic depression. The hard bit is that you go up and down, up and down. After a while you get tired of it. You just want it to stop. You want some normality in your life. You never feel in control of anything. I just want everything to stop. I want to get off."

The variable uncontrollable moods are not merely tiring in the long-term; they result in clients not really knowing who they are. They can no longer trust how they feel about the world, including themselves. And this can be reinforced by how others react.

Harry: "When I'm up, then I like to be at the centre of things. Chatting and generally taking the party along. And people like that. They like someone to be the life and soul. So I carry on. But I don't know whether that is me or me acting. Sometimes I think I am nobody, a nobody acting to be me."

Form of counselling

Counselling benefits from clients being slowed down, not merely to aid concentration but also to get them to think about achieving reasonable goals. Clients, when slightly manic, can be over-ambitious, imagine they can do many different things. However, they are not likely to complete them. Another matter that is of concern is the practical lifestyle of clients – in particular, whether they have been sleeping and eating properly. Some clients can get by on little sleep and food, but only for so long.

As with unipolar depression, early detection of the condition is helpful (Joyce, 1985). This enables clients to take greater control and have a greater chance of avoiding hospitalisation.

Finally, manic clients tend to be very much orientated to the future and not to the past. While it is useful to have future hopes and expectations, it can also help on occasions to bear the past in mind, so clients can learn from the past. Manic clients may have to have past situations brought to their attention.

OTHER TYPES OF DEPRESSION

Identifying depression in the elderly

When thinking about depression, the elderly are an often overlooked source of adding to our understanding. Depression is relatively common (Barrett et al., 1988), and there are many depressed elderly who show loss of appetite, hopelessness and thoughts of death (Newman et al., 1991). But is this so strange for those nearing the end of their lives? In fact, there is no evidence that ageing itself is associated with a lesser satisfaction with life (Palmore and Kivett, 1977). Severe depression seems to be at no greater rate in the elderly than that in younger age bands (Blazer et al., 1987). However, the rate of mild depression may be underestimated, partly because anxiety of the elderly is often part of a depressive syndrome, but not always seen as such.

The difficulty is that of knowing what the symptoms of depression in the elderly are. They seem to be somatic rather than mood-linked, associated mostly with physical pain. But this raises the problem of whether the somatic pain of depression can be differentiated from physical pain (Rapp et al., 1988). As medical problems are much more likely among the elderly, the question also remains, whether the depression is an expected accompaniment or even part of physical illness and associated pain (Katon and Sullivan, 1990). Certainly there is an association between depression and medical symptoms (Williamson and Schultz, 1992), and it has been suggested that the severity of the depression may be linked with the number of medical symptoms (Parmalee et al., 1991).

So, the usual picture of depression as uncontrollable low moods is not that common with the elderly. The symptoms are mainly physical, such as lethargy, sleep difficulties and poor concentration – often associated with physical illness: cardiac, pulmonary and renal difficulties. It would seem that much of depression is a result of prolonged stress induced by physical pain. It should also be noted that severe depression for the first time in the over 50s is uncommon (Depression Guideline Panel, 1993). This would indicate that severe depression in the elderly is another depressive episode, and related to external pressures.

Further thoughts about depression and the elderly

The outcome is that depression in the elderly might be best relieved in many cases by pain management as opposed to anti-depressants. Severe depression occurs, but may be mistaken for as dementia. Even medication given for physical conditions can cause depressive states, and further medication might be given to counteract them. Also the role of doctors becomes more important:

> *Vivien*: "I'm so lethargic; my concentration is poor as is my memory. I stay longer in bed, as I'm exhausted most of the time. I don't cry; I wish I could. My anti-depressants leave me tired, so I used St John's Wort, but it didn't do much good. I'm not meant to use it because of my blood pressure, which has been creeping up these last three years. But I think doctors use people like me as guinea pigs. I've lost faith in them. They don't really listen. They are nice, but too quick to give you a drug."

Ultimately for most of the elderly, depression can be diminished by ending their isolation and helping them to be more active. One client was depressed following the death of his wife, and this was worsened by his severe deafness. He was isolated and did not know how to get a social life again. A society for the deaf was finally able to help him. Part of the problem of depression can lie, not in the elderly themselves, but how they are treated socially and politically.

What we have to do is revisit our ideas of depression, especially those of mood. Mild depression may be signalled by a lack of pleasure, but is this a suitable criterion for the elderly? Is contentment more appropriate? And is it useful to differentiate between the physical and the mental, to talk of "somatising the symptoms of depression", when the physical and mental are so closely bound? When working with those depressed, we concentrate on the nature of depression. What we learn from the elderly is that we all need to understand what it is to be old, and this means leaving a few stereotypes and preconceptions behind. The difficulties for the elderly are usually quite practical, such as isolation, finance, transport, sleep, hearing and sight. Attention to these will lift mild depression. Severe depression is usually recurrence of depression, and in extremes may be treated with drugs – though over-prescribing is sometimes a risk, as is interaction with other drugs taken for physical problems.

Finally, I have found that older adults tend to use prayer to help overcome depression, and access to a place of worship and clerics may be helpful (Koenig et al., 1988). Some elderly clients may appreciate a short prayer at the end of counselling or support, though some clients may be irreligious, and the mention of religion may well prove to be counterproductive.

Children and depression

It should be noted that the symptoms of depression in children are less psychological. It is interesting that a search for depression among a hospitalised paediatric sample showed most of those discovered had been admitted for gastrointestinal complaints (Kashani et al., 1981). Also, separation anxiety is more common (Ryan et al., 1987). This reflects the fact that children have had less social experience than adults and are likely to react more directly, and less according to social rules or etiquette. In addition, they react as might be expected from their social situation, an observation equally applicable to adolescents who exhibit more hopelessness, helplessness, and lack of pleasure in life (Carlson and Kashani, 1988).

Community studies have shown young children suffer from a low rate of diagnosed depression (Rutter et al., 1975; Fleming et al., 1989). What is also remarkable is that co-morbid psychiatric conditions are very common, whether conduct disorders, anxiety, phobias, and somatic complaints. In the Dunedin Study, 80% of children of those diagnosed with major depression had another possible diagnostic category (Anderson et al., 1987). When there is no organic disease or failing, it is not so easy to know what should be the main symptoms. Childhood depression can reappear later (Kovacs et al., 1984; Garrison et al., 1991) and appears to be related to the severity of the initial episode (McCauley et al., 1988).

OTHER FACTORS IN DEPRESSION

Self-management and alcohol use

We have seen clients affected by depression, and clients trying to manage their depression. Clients often resort to alcohol, but are told that they should not drink, as alcohol is a depressant. This does not stop them drinking, and so they are seen as uncooperative. The result can be confrontation, which is not helpful for counsellor or client. So, instead of rushing in, it may be better to listen to what the client has to say.

> *Peter*: "I have a drink or two, as it makes me feel better. At least, I get to feel happy even if it is for a few hours. Afterwards I feel really depressed, and I know it is doing me no good in the long run. I'll stop the drinking some time. I'll have to, or I'll never get away from this depression."

Here is a man who has been labelled as an alcoholic. He made appointments with the local clinic, turned up after drinking and was then termed uncooperative and having a personality problem. Yet, he was always reasonable and never drunk when I saw him. He used alcohol as a form of short-term self-medication, and was quite aware of the fact.

Now, we have to realise that most people can stand being depressed for a short time. The trouble comes when there is no escape, when depression seems never ending. Getting drunk brings some change, some sense of relief – if not enjoyment – into the client's life. This has to be set against the drawbacks.

> *Peter*: "Yes, I do drink more when depressed. It gives me energy, so I get out of bed, get myself something to eat, and clear the place up. But if I stop drinking then I go down, so I keep on drinking. Two or three days of heavy drinking is as long as I can keep it up, so then I sleep and afterwards feel OK."

If we tell clients simply to stop drinking, we are offering them nothing, and denying them some relief from their depression. What is needed is to have some alternative to the alcohol. This might be no more than someone to talk to, a volunteer to chat to, especially in the late evenings when people can feel very alone. The counsellor or helper works with the client, accepting the drinking until an alternative is taken up. Most clients are well aware of the problems and difficulties that come with alcohol use. They do not need to be told but they do need to discuss their alcohol use with a view to long-term coping with depression. Counsellors have to be very aware that they are working for the client primarily, and not for persons with other agendas. The task is to help, and not carry moral messages.

Religious belief

For some clients, religion is one way of helping them through life, supporting their management of life's difficulties. I should state that I am non-religious, so it is as an outside observer that these remarks are made.

The first point is to distinguish religion from spirituality. The latter can include ideas about creation, the meaning of life, the rules of social behaviour, and goodness and evil. The client's spiritual beliefs may have little to do with conventional religion. They may even be viewed as religion without the institutions. My experience is that most people do have similar beliefs, despite nominally coming from different religions. So counsellors should not assume what clients believe. My experience has been their beliefs have often been far more unorthodox than the stated religion. So, although the word "religion" will be used, we should remember this is a far more inclusive term than might seem.

Looking at religious belief in general, we find that any major life-event can have an effect on personal beliefs about life. In particular, it can affect religious belief; either turning a person to religion or causing a loss of faith.

> *Jill*: "The last time it happened, getting depressed, then I said a prayer that I should not meet certain people. I didn't want to meet them, but I found I was bumping into them all the time! And I felt I had had enough. 'Haven't I been punished enough?' So I thought religion was a waste of time. But this time I'm going into religion, saying a prayer and talking to my spirit guide. That makes me feel safer when I go out. Prayer gives me a nice warm feeling, acts like an invisible strength."

One of the strengths of religion is the use of ritual, which many people find reassuring and positive. If ritual is linked with times in the day, such as after waking up, at mealtimes, and at night, it can help give structure to the client's day. This in turn gives a sense of control, which can lead to greater control over life.

Chapter 9

Stress

Introduction

Stress can be a cause of depression. It can also be a trigger or an aggravating factor for depression. But before going any further, it might help to first come to grips with the basic nature of stress.

Stress is a part of everyday life. When under pressure, when we perceive a threat to ourselves, we react unconsciously and automatically go into fight-or-flight mode. This means our bodies react by producing the hormones, adrenalin and noradrenalin, both stimulants. These cause an increase in heart rate and breathing, sweating, dryness of the mouth. Blood moves from the skin and stomach to muscles in order to be ready for immediate action and causing pallor of the skin and "butterflies" in the stomach. The increased heart rate and breathing requires additional energy, and this is produced by the release of the sugar, glucose, in the body.

Clearly, what is a threat is whatever is perceived as a threat. And when that threat goes away, the person's body returns to normal. There is no problem, provided the threat goes away. If this does not happen, the person will be permanently tensed for action. So, stress is reflected in muscles tension and headaches. In the long-term, there will not be enough energy obtainable from glucose in the liver, so corticosteroids are produced to breakdown fats and make additional energy. But the presence of fats in the blood stream increases the chance of arteries clogging and subsequent heart conditions. In addition, there is an increased risk of diabetes, ulcers as a result of increased stomach acid, and skin conditions.

The effects of stress are well known. What is less mapped is the link between stress and depression. Certainly, there are links between stressors, stress-inducing factors, and depression (Lewinsohn et al., 1988). Newly depressed persons have had a significantly greater number of negative events in the previous year compared to non-depressed persons (Dohrenwend et al., 1986). But once a person becomes depressed, he is then more vulnerable to hostile events, so enters into a downward spiral (Folkman and Lazarus, 1986). Furthermore, though stress can generate depression, the reverse can also be true. Stress is generated by the fact of having to deal with one's depression (Hammen, 1991).

In fact, it can prove difficult to decide whether stress is an antecedent, concomitant, or consequence of depressive symptoms (Barnett and Gotlib, 1988). Depression-inducing stress can arise from life events (Hammen, 1992), those happenings in life which demand a substantial change in personal circumstances. These can include death of someone close, separation of partners, unemployment and failing health (Moos, 1992; Murphy, 1982). These events may bring out unexpectedness, sadness, lack of personal control and future changes which act against personal well-being. Severity of stress problems is also increased if there is more than one such life event or if such events are added to unresolved, past life events (Thoits, 1983). Another source of stress can arise through difficult circumstances from which the person sees no escape. These circumstances can cover chronic illness, financial problems, marital difficulties or having to care for infirm relatives (Pearlin, 1983; Moos, 1992). Finally, most attention has been given to large changes, but sometimes the constant small irritations in life, such as regular traffic congestion or annoying personal habits, can cause stress (Lazarus and Folkman, 1984).

Stress and perceived events

Stress is not merely caused by the occurrence of events, but of distressing events (Thoits, 1983). Distress is a result of how people individually perceive their situation and the meaning they give to it, whether they interpret the ongoing stimuli as good or bad. This means stress can proceed from too little as well as too much stimuli (Weiman, 1977). Thus the question moves to why events or circumstances should be seen in a negative light. There are a number of factors, often interconnected.

- *The subject's personality.* If this happens to be Type A, characterised by aggressiveness, impatience, perfectionism and inflexibility, then the person is more liable to stress and its effects such as heart conditions (Rosenman et al., 1964). Unfortunately, this has almost become a stereotype of someone liable to stress, and is not always the case (Burke, 1984).
- *Unfulfilled expectations.* This might easily be put down to contrary circumstances, but also to the subject being unrealistic, either unduly optimistic or pessimistic (Heckhausen, 1977). These may in turn be bound up with uncertainty about personal competence.

- *Lack of control.* This can either be when the subject sees control of the personal situation being in the hands of others (Krause and Stryker, 1984) or where there are high demands and low control (Karasek, 1979). The degree of possible control may depend on the environment and how the subject relates to it. So stress might be a product of the subject's family, environment or work organisation. To decrease stress, these have to be changed as well as the changing the subject's perceptions of them (Herrick and Maccoby, 1975).

Picking up the last point, it is important that counselling is not used as an instrument to assist in changing clients, whilst not changing the accompanying stressful environment. We might note that many employment programmes for the reduction of workers' stress do this; try to change workers but fail to alter the organisation's structure or dynamics.

Ideas about excessive stress

There are many methods and programmes for the relief of stress. Firstly, there needs to be some general understanding of stress, including:

- Stress is usually a temporary phenomenon, and we deal with it automatically. Lack of stimulation, like over-stimulation, can be stressful. This means that it is false to expect or search for a stress-free life. We do not avoid stress; we deal with it.
- Stress is bound up with perceptions, which in turn results in very different ideas as to what is stressful. One person's stress is another's challenge. So we have to look to both the individual client and the client's social context.
- As the forms of stress vary from person to person, there is no one way that is successful in dealing with stress. As the ability to deal with it is, to some extent, genetically based, this reinforces the fact that ways of stress management will differ.
- To help others cope, we need to help clients analyse the context that makes them stressed.

Analysis of stress

Stress is painful; long-term stress can cause medical and psychological problems. It is intimately bound up with depression, so we should not accept it or ignore it. Stress comes with not being able to deal with stimuli or stressors, which arise from the interaction of the person with the environment. So, there are two factors that may need to be changed – the person and the environment. Some of the questions to be determined are:

- What are the signs of stress in the client?
- How long has the client felt stressed?
- What things seem to bring on feelings of stress?
- Has the client felt like this before?
- Are others in the client's family suffering or have suffered from stress?
- Are there others who might also be stressed from the same cause – others in the family or colleagues at work?
- What aggravates the feelings of stress?
- What alleviates the feelings of stress?
- What does the client do to alleviate feelings of stress?
- Does the client drink alcohol or take non-prescribed substances?
- Does the client eat more under stress, or eat less?
- Has the client developed any medical symptoms as a result of stress?
- Has the client's weight changed due to stress?
- What things in the client's life have changed as a result of this stress?

As usual, these questions are not asked together but gradually covered in discussion. However, some clients do like to fill in lists, so some might like to take the list away to answer.

Stress symptoms

Once some of the basic facts have been established, the counsellor can move to more general items. Clients are sometimes happier sticking to concrete examples, so the counsellor will have to suggest the generalities and patterns in the client's behaviour. For example, clients might:

- Have a pre-occupation with certain anxiety-provoking thoughts, and a difficulty in being able to "switch them off".
- Have a feeling of being trapped, of having to behave in an undesired way, to stay in an unsatisfying job, being caught in an undesired relationship.
- Wonder what they are doing in life, or if their existence has any point.
- Think they are indispensable, and no-one else can replace them.
- Feel threatened by the idea of change.
- Think they know best and the views of others are inferior.

- Feel threatened or irritated when others talk about support and everyone needing it.
- Feel they cannot be bothered to finish tasks.
- Feel they are undervalued.
- Feel they are helpless.
- Feel others have a down on them.
- Feel beaten before they have started.

These thoughts and feelings may help to specify sources of stress, if the subjects think them through and try to determine what particular topics might apply to them.

Dealing with too much stress

There are many publications which purport to deal with the methods to reduce stress. For this reason I do not intend to give a list of recommended techniques. However, the following points may be worth considering:

- Many stress reduction programmes tend to be little more than awareness-raising, looking at general stressors but not at specific ones encountered in the course of the individual's life (McLeroy et al., 1984).
- Stress is seen as an individual characteristic, ignoring the fact that it may affect whole groups and organisations (Colligan and Murphy, 1979). Stress can originate from the group, from its structure and dynamics.
- Stress is not simply pressure on the individual, but the result of stress lessens the support. Those who are unsupported, shy or lonely are likely to suffer to a greater extent (Joiner, 1997). Equally important is the quality of this support, so that those who are part of a family under pressure are likely to receive less benefit.

The point is that the usual individual stress reduction methods, though useful, depend on a change in cognitions, such as reducing the need for perfectionism, timekeeping, and purely personal responsibility. There are two main problems. Firstly, these are characteristics that tend to be required in work and even, to an extent, in home situations. The requirement is that of knowing when to be perfectionist, not simply denying the trait. In practice, this aspect is seldom addressed. The second point is that we are asking clients who are depressed and having cognitive problems to make further cognitive changes. But those depressed are less able to help themselves, so helping must be attuned to their needs and ongoing capabilities.

Stress reduction

Stress can be reduced in three main ways. There is personal stress reduction, the increase in family support and the increase of work support. The three areas cover the main potential areas of client lives.

- *Personal stress reduction*
  (a) Clients having a sense of control.
  (b) Clients discussing what they would prefer and what they see as reasonable to achieve.
  (c) Planning for the future.

There is a danger here of being over-optimistic. Depressed clients are not likely to be able to change very much and plans have to be realistic and reflect this fact. We also have to appreciate that many de-stressing methods such as relaxation techniques are very transient in their effects, and often of little help to those depressed.

- *Family increased support*
  (a) Clients are helped if there are persons to whom they can talk intimately, someone beyond the counsellor.
  (b) Clients are helped if the family is able to discuss its problems.
  (c) Clients are helped if the family can temporarily reduce present current demands (Brown and Harris, 1978).

All of this means family members, or at least the client's partner or closest person, need information and support, so counsellors need to talk to them.

- *Work situation*
  (a) Helping clients become familiar with the idea of stress in organisations (Carroll, 1979).
  (b) Identifying individual stress signs at work, such as conflicts with colleagues, arguments over work remits, a decrease in the quality of work, and arguments with authority.
  (c) Identifying organisational stress features such as a high level of absenteeism and staff turnover, poor communication, decision elitism and increasingly formal as opposed to informal interactions and more energy being directed into fights within the organisation.

It is important to realise that if the main problem lies with the organisation then change has to begin there (DeFrank and Cooper, 1987). If this is not possible, then a further review is required.

Review of stress

Clients have to understand that they should be aware of their stress, and know how to avoid it. This requires clients take on board:

- The acceptance of excessive stress is equivalent to accepting continual physical injury.
- Client beliefs enter into stress, including the belief that he/she is responsible for everyone, not deserving of an individual life, and has no rights of expression.
- The client is not an island, but part of a social network, and should both give and receive from that network.

Some counsellors will help clients to compose a list of individual rights, which they should exercise in their life. These rights cover items such as the right to be heard, the right to choice, the right to self-development, and others. While these lists are useful for many clients, they are of debatable use with depressed clients, who are not able to see themselves exercising such rights. The effect can then be to increase personal stress. We have to remember that stress is very much a matter of perceptions, and the perceptions of depressed clients may differ from those of counsellors.

Chapter 10

Homework and Termination

HOMEWORK

Introduction

It is not enough to expect clients to benefit just from the counselling sessions. They have to be able to carry what they have learned into their ordinary lives. This transferral of learning is termed homework. It is not a reminder of school; it is literally work that clients can do and build upon at home. In privacy and safety, they can try out various techniques and reinforce advances they have already made. It has to be emphasised that control is an important aspect of recovery from depression, and clients have to be encouraged to practise regaining control. This is not done simply through counselling; that merely lays the ground for possible control. It is done through practice.

Homework rests on the idea of client self-help, yet is not always employed in cases of depression. The idea of self-help in depression sounds somewhat counter-intuitive. The outcome is that counsellors deny clients the opportunity to help themselves. This denial may even be supported by counsellor concerns, such as the fear that self-help requires clients to think, and such thinking may set off or aggravate depression (Greenberg and Pyszczynski, 1986; Carver and Scheier, 1990). However, this is not likely to happen provided clients avoid negative thinking; thinking which reinforces their depressive views of themselves and the world.

Just as we expect clients to take positive views and options, so the same applies to counsellors. This includes taking on board the fact that depressed clients might be able to help themselves.

Taking the first step

The first step may be the hardest. It is for depressives to believe they can help themselves. They have to consider why they think this is not the case. They are told they have restricted capabilities; they are treated as if they do.

But they are capable, and research shows this to be the case (Mayo and Tanaka-Matsumi, 1996). The problem is that depression can reinforce the negative beliefs and so anyone suffering from low mood does not really think they can be positive. It is pointless to try and logically argue for positivity, as mood-dependent beliefs tend to be inaccessible to logic.

One solution is to ask depressed clients to take on board that they can help themselves, that this is a possibility, and no more than a possibility. They suspend their disbelief and wait and see how things turn out, even if it takes some time to see any improvements. Clients are usually realistic enough to appreciate that if they have been depressed for a long time, they are not going to recover overnight.

Self-help

Despite the arguments given above, depressed clients may still tell themselves that they can do nothing; that they cannot help themselves. They have given themselves into the care of the psychiatrist, doctor and counsellor. They have done so because it is a relief not to have to fight depression all the time. In addition, this self-surrender is what they imagine is required. And it helps. The relief of not constantly having to worry about and fight one's depression is enormous. So why bother about self-help?

The fact is those liable to depression need to be able to detect the onset of a future depressive episode, so they can then take steps to prevent or minimise its effects. Reliance on medical help may not be effective. For example, if patients attend doctors with reports of bodily problems but fail to mention depression, then there is only a 10% chance that their depression will be diagnosed (Katon et al., 1982). People should be able to recognise possible illness to be able to get help but also to be able to do things for themselves. And if depression does take over, clients need to know what best to do and when possible to act to reinforce recovery. Even after the depression has lifted, there is work to be done, as worries about it are likely to continue (Nolan et al., 1998).

Self-distancing

What is required for self-help is for depressives to practise self-distancing, to mentally distance themselves from their feelings, thoughts and behaviour in order to examine them better. Distancing is a general process, thus the distance can be varied. Clients can see their behaviour in close-up, in the family, or in the local community. Seeing themselves in different contexts is important and helps them to escape self-absorption.

When it comes to the mechanics of distancing then it helps if clients are helped to prepare themselves:

- The client does not think what he is but what he is not; he does not think he is sad but that he is not happy. This is combined then with thinking what is required to be happy and what he wants to be.
- The client imagines himself being able to do what he wants, and then being able to actually do it. It is the lack of belief in themselves that prevents clients from trying (Seligman, 1975).
- The client should imagine he has achieved what he wanted and the task is completed. Then he should think how he would deal with it. How will he react to being successful?
- The client thinks through not merely achieving what he wanted, but what will be the next step. In fact, to think through a chain of things to be done.

This preliminary work is best started as part of counselling; further work is done on it by the client at home. This requires the client to be provided with printed matter, but the minimum; too much, and it will not be read.

Self-talk

If a client has had low self-esteem for a long time, perhaps many years, then there is no way that this is going to be quickly changed; nor is there any one way that is definitely going to be successful. Counsellors just have to be prepared to try a variety of procedures. One of these is self-talk, where clients talk themselves through what they are going to do, how they are feeling and reassuring themselves. The subject both talks and listens to himself (Meichenbaum,1977). This can be used to self-support, to review what is happening, to prompt oneself into action, and to question information and beliefs. Subjects can also give themselves instructions such as "Calm down", or deal with their anxiety such as "That's a worry but I can deal with that". Self-talk can be made into a short programme:

- Sensing how I feel right now.
- Giving myself permission to feel this way.
- Thinking how I would like to feel.
- Giving myself permission to feel like that.

- Starting to do what I want.
- Reassuring myself it is all right to feel this way.

The procedure needs to be practised. Often it helps if the various stages are spoken out loud or under the person's breath.

Work with suspended negativity

Yet another aspect of self-help for clients is for them to work on their negativity. It is not a matter of arguing against it but getting into a relationship with it, and so being able to handle it. So the client first has to examine the nature of personal negativity.

> *George*: "Everything is black. There are a hundred exits but you cannot leave. The answers to your difficulties are simple, easy, but you can't see them. You don't do anything, because you spend all your time convincing yourself you can't. I would be OK if I could swap this head."

Once the client feels familiar with such negativity, then the next task is to externalise it, for the client to get it out of his head. To do this, the client takes a large piece of paper and draws his negativity. Perhaps draw it as a black blob, as a large blob. He then has to draw it as a smaller blob, then one smaller still. He draws so many that the blobs decrease in size until they are virtually invisible. The client has made his negativity disappear. He has also shown he has the power to do that. Clients have sometimes commented, "But that's only a drawing! That is not my negativity." My reply is that it is as real as negativity. After all, what is it? You cannot see negativity; it is not a thing. It is action or behaviour, just like drawing is. But negativity represents something, just as a drawing of it does.

We have to turn the situation around. I might ask how people feel after drawing their negativity. And the surprising thing is; they almost always feel a little bit better. But the negativity does not go away, and questions may be asked as to what is the point of drawing. How is that going to change anything? Clients should ignore the question and return to the present. Do they feel any better? If they do, then they have to say so. In fact, it helps if they say this several times.

Looking at change in feelings

These kinds of exercises appeal to some clients, and are anathema to others. From my perspective, it is a matter of adding to counselling resources, in the hope that at least one client will find them appealing and useful. Exercises should never be forced on clients, but the counsellor can impress on clients that homework is part of the overall help offered, and it is recommended that some are attempted. The opposite scenario is that some clients are too keen on them. I have to explain that they are merely aids to the overall counselling, but are important in that they are done away from the counsellor. This prepares clients for helping themselves outside counselling. Such exercises bring about a change in thinking, and possibly feelings. They will not bring enlightenment, a greater sense of self or harmony with the universe.

There are other methods of depressed persons nudging themselves into change. This requires getting engaged in experiences that are slightly strange or unusual. Music or chanting can be used. Poetry can prove useful – I favour the reading of Japanese haiku. What is strange, but not too strange, is likely to be most effective. Remember that the objective is merely to produce a shift away from negative patterns of thought.

Embedded patterns of negative thought are not easily shifted. The brain automatically seeks out patterns and returns to those already existing. To escape this sequence, one idea is to use randomness, such as by getting a collection of matches, dropping them onto the floor and looking for patterns in them. Another method is to allow a few drops of ink to fall into a glass of water and stare at the shape and small turbidities. Yet another is that of simply staring at the flame of a candle. These are ways of clients bringing change to their way of looking at life.

Further exercises

Another approach is that of meditation. The following exercise is accompanied by rhythmic breathing, so it helps to sit down and listen at first merely to one's breathing, getting one's mind attuned to every inhalation and exhalation. Although the exercise is meditation, it can be easier to noiselessly talk through the following rather than merely think it. Alternatively, talking out loud might seem preferable.

Breathing in ... I calm my body
Breathing out ... I smile
Breathing in ... I am here
Breathing out ... I am now
Breathing in ... I grasp the moment
Breathing out ... A wonderful moment

(After Hanh, 1993)

This can be repeated slowly and constantly.

I should say that sometimes clients will ask for explanations or even give their own, talking about the unconscious, chakras, vidya or similar ideas. My reply is to say that they are not entering into the exercises properly. They are being cognitive, changing an experience into a rational explanation. There should be no explanation or rationale. There is just the experience and what flows from it. So repeat the exercise until it is accepted for itself and not for being part of some belief system. The point is that it is used to clear the mind, not fill it up other ideas and beliefs.

Another approach is that of using guided imagination. Once again, we can use deep breathing to begin with, and then imagine a favourite scene. Mine is that of lying in a rowing boat, drifting down a river as the sun beats down. Clients should try to choose their own scene, and not simply be given one. What might be peaceful for me – being in the rowing boat – might be highly unsettling to anyone who is frightened of water or who lost a relative in a boating accident. However, some depressed clients might find it difficult simply to think of a favourite and positive scene, so the counsellor offering possible ideas can be useful.

Guided imagination is a trip or event that has no point beyond itself. It is floating in a boat downstream. It is experiencing everything that accompanies that trip. But it is more than that. It is being at one with the whole trip, so I become the boat as it travels down the river. It is arriving not at a place, but moving in a state free of emotions.

These procedures can be effective, but to increase their effectiveness, bear in mind:

- Clients have to be prepared to really give the exercises a try. This means they give themselves permission to do something that might seem a bit stupid or something they think probably will not work. They have to take the risk of the first exercise not working. This is quite likely. But you will have lost nothing. What is on offer is merely a change of thought patterns, not treatment.
- It may be necessary to repeat the exercises several times before they do work. It requires hard work and real concentration. My recommendation is that they try and form an intimate relationship with the contents of the exercise. I say to clients, "If you stare at the flame of the candle, then allow your mind to metaphorically move from your head to the flame. Be part of that flame. And try not to finish abruptly, but slowly withdraw from the flame at the end".

Depression is about overwhelming negative mood, but logical thought cannot alter moods. You might think this is not the case. After all, telling a joke can make a person laugh, make them feel happy. But in depression that ability is lost. Jokes simply are not funny. What has to be emphasised that the above exercises are not intended to affect mood. They are intended to produce temporary chaos. But there is more. Out of chaos can come order and control, depending on the person and his or her perceptions. An analogy can be found in looking at pictures in a gallery. My favourite picture for this is Monet's "Water-lilies". To see this canvas properly, the observer has to stand 3 metres away. Stand close, and all that is visible is a chaotic collection of colour splodges. Chaos becomes resolved when we stand some way away. So we aim for chaos, the lack of reason and emotions. Only later can that chaos be resolved, by taking another more distant view of life.

Even more exercises

Sometimes clients feel too blocked to be able to use their imagination, so more visual exercises might serve instead. One form of help can be obtained from a large mirror. Simply staring at oneself minutely for several minutes can bring about a sense of depersonalisation and a change from one's usual emotional state. Alternatively, the person can stand in front of the mirror and put his hands palms towards the hand and held chest high. Then slowly move the hands back and forwards in circular motions, and watch them carefully. Controlling the mirror images rather than one's actual hands can also be a strange and slightly depersonalising experience. This slight depersonalisation is not avoided; on the contrary, it is embraced. It is used as a stepping-stone to a different world, to the world of personal imagination.

As clients can feel depersonalised, this might seem positively unhelpful. However, the client can overcome this by grasping something – say, the side of a chair, an orange or even clasping hands. This moves the action from virtual reality to sensed reality. What is important is that clients can become familiar with such changes, and can get accustomed to a degree of depersonalisation and being able to move back to reality.

Self-help – conclusion

It helps if clients can jot down a few notes or comments on their homework – how it felt and what the outcome was. These notes can be discussed in counselling. Whether the exercises were not attempted, were attempted but found to have been no use, or the client did find them helpful; all of these provide material that can be discussed. These mental exercises can be varied with physical exercises, such as walking, aerobics or massage.

The use of a journal

The beneficial effects of homework can be supplemented by keeping a diary or journal. This should be more than a record of the day's events – which for the depressed can be limited and routine. Instead, it should be a chronicle of what client is feeling, thinking, saying and doing. It should also include hopes and expectations. Comments can be positive or negative (Pennebaker and Francis, 1996). The positive aspect is difficult for most clients, as they tend to remember or see only the negative and minimise their successes (Craighead et al., 1979).

A variation is to ask clients to write their autobiographies. It should be understood that negative mood influences not merely how the present is viewed but the past as well (Bower, 1981). Asking for good times to be remembered may merely produce thought-blocking, so I sometimes ask clients to try and remember not just the bad times but also the less bad times. What journals can do is start to reinforce pleasant events (MacPhillamy and Lewinsohn, 1982).

There is another useful approach that can be employed. This is trying to work out how others in the family might view what is happening, how they might react to the depression. Another variation is to have two pages for each day. The writing about the day is done on one page, and on the other is written comments about the previous day's write-up. This helps the process of reflection and distancing oneself from the day's events – even if it is only by 24 hours. The final point is that the question may be asked as to what should then be done with the diary. The answer is people do what they want with their diaries, but there is nothing further they have to do. The usefulness of the exercise comes chiefly from doing it.

To help clients, I provide them with a pen and book for the purpose, and write on the inside cover what things they might like to include. Sometimes clients start writing and will move into areas of their past they want to deal with themselves, areas they may feel they have to work on alone initially (Brady, 1979). Reminiscing has been seen as useful for the elderly (Millar and Wilcox, 1984), but in my experience this is not a process confined to them. Many people like to talk over what has happened to them or record it in some way. However, for some clients, writing anything down does not come naturally and can be difficult. In such cases, the use of a small tape recorder is useful (Snider et al., 1984). Use of a journal or tape does not always bring immediate benefits, so it may be a few months before there are any observable results (Pennebaker and Beall, 1986).

TERMINATION OF COUNSELLING

Introduction

It is surprising that comparatively little thought is given to the process of ending counselling. When the process is considered, it is often done by limiting counselling to an arbitrary number of sessions. This certainly avoids counsellors working with clients indeterminately, where there is no recognisable ending, but it fails to make an ending in line with clients' needs. Often, if there is no termination planning, counselling simply fades away and the client fails to appear. This failure is rationalised into client choice, counsellor success or intervening circumstances; it is rarely seen as the fault of the counsellor.

If termination of counselling is planned, then the question arises as to when the end should come. One option is to end it when the symptoms of depression have disappeared. Apart from the fact that it is difficult to know exactly when this is likely to happen, counsellors do not suddenly stop counselling. The termination is a process lasting several sessions. Waiting for clients to indicate when they feel counselling should be stopped is also not completely satisfactory, as they may experience separation anxiety at the thought of the counselling ending and worry about being without support.

The counsellor has to take the lead and decide when the ending should start. This is very much a matter of judgement, but there are some indications:

- The degree to which the client is able to cope with his or her situation outside the counselling arena.
- The degree to which there have been improvements in client functioning.
- The degree to which counselling is useful, as indicated by the counselling itself, the homework done and how the client has responded.

There is also a sense counsellors can pick up about the working relationship. If it becomes too easy and comfortable, then it might be time for the client to begin to move on. I can only liken this to being in hospital: the patient is too ill to enjoy it, and when it does become enjoyable then it is time to leave.

The termination process

Ending counselling should be a positive process, and for this reason it can be helpful to have mini-endings, where there are breaks in the counselling for short periods. I favour 6–8 weeks. This allows clients to fully take in and integrate what has been said and what has occurred during counselling. The only drawback is that depressed clients can forget the return date, so it is worth sending out a reminder of when sessions are to be resumed. Another aspect of short breaks is that it gives the counsellor and client the opportunity to do some of the termination process. Often this is easier than one complete termination process, done all at once. It also ensures that some degree of ending has taken place, as clients can fail to come for counselling due to ill health or other events in their life. There is always the danger that leaving any form of ending too long, risking the client leaving prematurely.

The process itself can be divided into:

- Indicating to the client that the ending process is being entered into, and explaining what this means.
- Reassuring the client that the client can always return for counselling after the process has ended. This can seem a rather mixed message, so it can help to speak of returning for counselling Stage Two, post-counselling, or some other term that draws an arbitrary line between stages.
- Reviewing the advances that the counsellor has seen since the client first came for counselling. Even slightly depressed clients can have problems seeing progress they have made, so another person identifying them is useful. This covers the client's appearance, non-verbal signals and participation in the counselling process, what contributions the client has been able to make and what decisions the client made. Also the efforts the client made towards completing the homework.
- Client and counsellor discuss the progress made in the former's life outside the counselling sessions. The counsellor can help clients to identify the small steps forward, and those times when even coping and making no advances is an achievement. It can help if the counsellor asks how others in the family or friends have reacted and whether they have noticed any improvements. It can be useful to identify what advances are still required to be made – and whether they require counsellor help or can be accomplished by the client. The latter may need the help of others, so it is helpful to know if such help is likely to be forthcoming.

Identifying progress made is merely part of the review. The next step is to identify what the client has learned from such progress.

- Clients will often talk about what they have learned about themselves. I like them to objectify what they are saying. To say, "I feel a stronger person", is not very meaningful as it stands. My reaction is to ask what they would be able to do in future. If they had another depressive episode, how might they react and what might they do differently.
- Clients can go on about things they got wrong, failed to do, or things that went against them at the time. It is important that clients see "mistakes" as steps to success and their self-improvement. Talking about mistakes is purely negative; learning from them is positive. The client is not the person who makes mistakes but the person who is not afraid to take risks, even risking mistakes.
- Counsellors can help clients review ways they can maintain good health to help others. This places clients in a social context and not in isolation, and also eases any guilt they have about the effects of their depression. What is required are detailed plans, and how they are to be carried out. Good intentions are not enough.

Next stage

Termination of counselling is merely preparation for clients' next stage, that of doing without counselling and moving to a better life. Counsellors can help clients see depression, like any other major event in life, as the opportunity to enrich their life, provided they are willing to sit back and think what they want from life. What has happened may seem negative, but this is merely a perspective. We might also see the positive:

- It gives clients the opportunity to make a major change in their life.
- It can help clients look closely at their quality of life.
- It can help clients appreciate those who are close, like their family.
- It can help clients be realistic about themselves and their life.

Depression can change a person's life. It can also change how a person sees life. Whether depression becomes a liability, a disability or part of life depends in part on how clients manage it – and this is usually done on their own.

MONITORING AND SUPERVISION

Counsellor self-work

Just as clients have homework, counsellors are no different. They have to work on themselves and their work. They may have regular supervision, but counsellors have to take responsibility for their work. What can happen is the client's helplessness is mirrored in the counselling. So counsellors should not merely be supervised but should self-monitor and be positive and pro-active – as they would want their depressed clients to be. They have to initially investigate matters for themselves:

- How a client has been feeling in the session.
- How the counsellor felt in the session.
- How the counsellor feels about the client.
- Strong feelings of the client felt, not just detected, by the counsellor.
- Anything about the counselling that was surprising or unexpected.
- Any problems encountered in counselling.
- The degree of success that the counselling appears to be having.
- The degree of client cooperation.
- The strength of the working relationship.
- When counselling should be terminated.

This self-monitoring can be extended if there are cases of "stuck clients"; those for whom counselling does not seem very effective. Then the counsellor might want to review counselling for the possible presence of:

- Unrealistic expectations by the counsellor.
- Unrealistic expectations by the client.
- Client's past bad experiences of counselling.
- Poor working relationship due to past client relationships.
- Poor working relationship due to unresolved counsellor attitudes or beliefs.
- The long-standing nature of client difficulties.
- External restraints on the client, such as partner, officials or medical.
- The "forced" nature of counselling has not been addressed.
- The advances made are not visible in behaviour, as they are reflected only in changed attitudes or beliefs.
- The client has many problems, some of which are still hidden.
- There are limits to how much a counsellor can help.
- The restricted methods used in counselling.
- Poor counsellor empathy and understanding.
- Unhelpful counsellor beliefs.

I would also stress that the medical model of counselling favours one-to-one work, but it is worth considering whether this is appropriate. Sometimes the answer is not apparent until after a couple of sessions. So it is worth counsellors thinking about the client's choice or preference, and whether any of the statements below are relevant.

- Clients want others excluded, as they then can give just their view of what happened or is happening.
- Clients can get the counsellor onside, usually against others in the family.
- Clients want the fact of going to counselling to be used as a reason for subsequent actions or excusing past actions.
- Clients use counselling as a way of spreading blame onto others.
- Clients can use counselling around one issue as a way of diverting attention from other areas.

Counsellor supervision

Supervision is much more effective if the counsellor has a good idea of what to take to the supervisor. Hence the prior need for self-work. How supervisors work is beyond the compass of this book, but I would suggest that it would be worth being clear about and prioritising the role of supervision, covering major objectives such as:

- Management and administration of counselling and cases.
- Support for the counsellor.
- Learning and improving counselling.
- Dealing with counselling stress.

In addition, it helps if management is linked in with supervision and is aware of, and acts accordingly on:

- Even experienced counsellors require supervision.
- Experienced counsellors should not have excessive work offloaded on them.
- Difficulties in the agency can affect supervision.
- Working with depressives often lacks positive reinforcement and this needs to be addressed.
- The role of possible external difficulties which impinge on the counsellor must be clarified as to action.
- Account should be taken of any misalignment of agency and counsellor/ supervisor ideology.

Counselling depressed clients can be taxing, and before starting, the necessary learning and support mechanisms should be in place.

Chapter 11

Suicide

Introduction

At some time, when counselling depressed clients, counsellors will encounter clients who are suicidal or who talk about suicide. This is a concern not peculiar to counsellors. Other professionals who work with the depressed are faced with similar worries. They can occur even when suicide has not been spoken about by the client.

> *Eloise*: "The psychiatrist had said I wasn't to come off the tablets, as I would probably kill myself."

And, to be fair, this is not a misplaced fear. About half of all psychiatrists are likely to lose a patient by suicide (Bongar et al., 1992). This means there can be considerable concern about the possible death of a patient. And that anxiety can be passed on to counsellors. As such, we also have to face the fact that suicide is a possibility in cases of depression.

If a client does commit suicide, that does not mean our helping has been a failure, though to those helping it often feels like this is the case. We have to be realistic. It is difficult to prevent cases of suicide (Murphy, 1984). It is difficult to predict suicide, even when clients have indicated they are feeling suicidal. So suicide should not be a cause for counsellor guilt.

It has been maintained that suicide attempters are reluctant to make use of counselling or therapy (Morgan et al., 1976). This has not been my experience. However it might reflect the manner of referral and the emphasis placed on the attempted suicide rather than the person. Counsellors should remember that only a very small number of those who attempt suicide, go on to commit suicide (Cullberg et al., 1988). Of over 20 attempted suicide cases I've dealth with, none went on to commit suicide.

Nature of suicide

Depression is often linked with suicide, but we should realise that most cases of depression do not end in suicide, and there are cases of suicide unconnected to depression. For example, those with a chronic illness and in a deteriorating condition may commit suicide but not be depressed. However the situation is often complicated by the fact that such chronic conditions are often connected with depression. So there are grey areas when we come to try and explain reasons for suicide. This is especially the case with young people, where it is difficult to distinguish between mild depression, high risk behaviour, impulsive reactions and adolescent thinking.

Counsellors have to be aware that the chief criterion for suicide comes from what clients say and from their behaviour. It should not be thought that the more severe the depression, the greater the likelihood of suicide. In very severe acute depression, clients are almost in a vegetative state and unable to do anything. However, before they get to that state or as they recover from it, the chance of suicide is greater as they are able to act.

Access for the suicidal

I would suggest there are measures that can be taken to minimise the risk of suicide in attempted suicide cases. The first is that there must be easy and quick access to help. Having someone to talk to lessens the client's inclination to constantly think of suicide and get caught up in a negative cycle of thought. It also has to be recognised that people do not feel suicidal just between 9 and 5 o'clock, so there must be some mechanism for communication out of hours. This can be with Samaritans, volunteers, self-help group members or with counsellors. Clients usually do not contact counsellors unless they are feeling desperate, and this is not likely to be often. Doubtless there will be worries that counsellors working out of hours are crossing boundaries, but to me this is part of the job. You merely balance it with less daytime work in official hours.

In practice, I find that the mobile phone is a useful aid, as almost everyone has one, or can learn to use one if given a phone. The point is that often it is easier to phone people as opposed to talking face to face. For some clients, texting is even better as it cuts out the personal aspect of communicating.

But what if a client overuses the phone and keeps constantly contacting you after hours? This has not happened to me, but I would suggest that this behaviour shows constant anxiety rather than suicidal intent, and that anxiety has to be tackled. Alternatively, it shows that the working relationship has not been clarified for both the client and counsellor, and needs to be.

Self-preparation

Before doing any work, counsellors have to look at their feelings about and attitudes to those who attempt suicide. I have come across professionals who see such clients as self-centred, emotionally juvenile, manipulative, exhibitionist, weak or having a personality disorder. Alternatively, but infrequently, they may be seen as brave or heroic. These can be judgements passed on patients or clients who have not even been seen. They are the reactions of helpers in almost as much distress as the clients.

So it is important to be non-judgemental. This applies not merely to the counsellor but to all support services and the agency as a whole. It is pointless if counsellors can deal with the situation, but agency management gets highly worried. We have to be realistic. Some clients are likely to threaten suicide, especially those who have been troubled with depression.

Realism forces us to admit that threatened suicide can create high anxiety in the mind of the counsellor, and this can lead to misplaced actions. So the counsellor has to see the problem as how the client feels and not how the counsellor feels. This does not mean I take suicidal threats casually. My heart sinks and I do feel anxious. So my reaction is to say nothing, but take time to collect myself, and to think to myself, "OK, this person is threatening suicide. The person is very upset. I am upset. But that is all right. I can be upset. And now my anxiety is over. That anxiety I have put to the back of my head. I am ready."

Counsellors have to appear and sound calm. This in turn makes the client feel calmer and feel reassured that someone is going to listen. It is important to lessen client anxiety (Fawcett et al., 1990), so what is said can be taken in.

Further self-work by counsellors

Counsellors also have to investigate for themselves common beliefs about suicide and attempted suicide. These might be:

- The client has or had some form of death wish. This is simply lazy thinking, as it explains nothing. In particular, it fails to see suicide, attempted or actual, as the result of a process, a process containing many decisions and actions. That process is not determined and inevitable, but can be altered at any stage along the way.
- The client is out of control, with a disturbed state of mind. This misses the point that the client may well be in control, and that control is directed towards a set objective. Saying that a person lacks control is to

take away all responsibility and almost imply that suicides "simply happen". In fact, they happen because someone makes them happen.

- The opposite to the above is that all suicides are clearly intended. This is also too inadequate a description. Clients' view of their situation can be unrealistic, being influenced by a depressive outlook. Yet this does not take away responsibility. Decisions are made and these are not randomly made. Clients act in specific ways, but do not feel they necessarily have full control. Counsellors, in turn, cannot disapprove of actions where there is this lack of full control.
- The idea that the suicidal do not seek help is also often incorrect. The problem is that they are unable to communicate directly how they are feeling and thinking. So they might go to their doctor, but complain of vague pains or illness. They give indirect clues, but do not say what they might do.
- Another belief is that those who say they will commit suicide will not in fact carry it out. The danger here is that some people when they are not believed decide to carry out the action in part to show that they were speaking the truth. However manipulative counsellors think a client might be, to ignore the threats is dangerous. This does not mean counsellors should do what clients want, as this is also unsatisfactory as far as clients are concerned. Instead, the client should be encouraged to take responsibility and explain what exactly is going on.

(see McIntosh et al., 1985)

It might seem that the above is rather confusing, and that is exactly the case with clients. They are often confused, then apparently sure of what they want; have a set view of the situation, but then liable to change that view; claiming they are in full control, then blaming someone for making them behave in such a way. The client may have lots of conflicting thoughts and urges; the counsellor can help clients make sense of them.

Being positive

Once the initial counsellor anxiety is controlled, then it becomes possible to see the positive aspects of the situation. This is important, as it helps to guide the counsellor through the encounter. The positive aspects include:

- The client contacted you. The client could have simply committed suicide. This is not the case.
- The client chose to contact you. So you were seen as worth contacting.
- You have been given the opportunity to help.

Counsellors have to appreciate the positive aspects not merely in what has happened but for the future as well. The client might be at a crisis, but this gives both counsellor and client the opportunity to work on unresolved matters. The counsellor has to help the client see the situation not as a crisis, but as a chance for personal progress.

We should bear in mind that clients may feel suicidal, but this does not mean they are not coping with their situation.

> *Jill*: "When I am down then I feel suicidal. The thing that holds me back is my dog. She feels to sense how I am feeling and cuddles up to me. That's the thing about animals; they look at you and love you whatever."

Ventilation

Part of the process of dealing with depression is that of attending to feelings, especially their expression. The repression of feelings is not harmful in the short-term. Indeed, social interaction often demands we suppress feelings that arise in order to maintain relationships. It seems that the immediate danger is not the repression of feelings but the total unrestricted expression of them, which results in unwanted physical symptoms, such as those of the cardiovascular system (Siegman, 1993). However long-term repression can lead to emotional draining and injurious physical effects (Bruhn et al., 1968).

Though unrestrained emotional expression might not be physically good for clients, they often do feel better after it. The drawback is such improvement is short-term, and when this is realised by the subject, then the final result may be to feel even worse than before. To obtain benefit, ventilation has to be made a process. This comprises:

- Discussing how the client used to express feelings. This might include what might set him off, under what circumstances, how the presence of others affected him, how his parents expressed their feelings, and past occasions which have been very emotional. It helps to know whether there are specific triggers to feelings being expressed, such as certain smells, photographs, music, and whether drinking or taking substances increases the expression.
- For the client to describe the body sensations and changes when a client is under strong emotion and when expressing such emotion. This is accompanied by validation by the counsellor: people do feel like that, and it is all right to feel that way. Furthermore, feelings can be expressed in a variety of ways, and the counsellor can add to the list given by the client,

and then it is a matter of deciding which is the best method of expression for the client.

Sometimes clients find they cannot express their feelings. This might be due to upbringing.

> *Aimee*: "Both my parents were very strict, used to read the Bible on Sundays, and we had to keep quiet. We weren't supposed to get emotional, or show it. I've never been able to let go, let my feelings show."

Such a background is not all-powerful, so we should not simply accept such statements as closing the matter. Clients can get into ways of behaving, and then feel uncomfortable if they do not carry out such behaviour – even if they think they would like to change. Counsellors have the task of trying to persuade clients to give themselves permission to change. To this end, it helps to inquire more closely into clients and how they do let go of their feelings.

- Does the client show feelings often or seldom, mildly or explosively, easily or with difficulty?
- Are feelings expressed to the world in general, or directed to those near-by or towards specific people?
- How does the client feel when ventilating?
- How does the client feel afterwards?

Part of the work done is to slowly let clients become more familiar with the feelings and the expression of those feelings, allowing clients to express their feelings more freely.

Self-work and choosing to counsel

Counsellors have to self-assess and decide whether they want to work with the suicidal, as it can be demanding work. Clearly, no one is likely to be working just with suicidal clients, but the work is not to every counsellor's taste. The point is that counsellors have to feel confident in their work and not be anxious. On the contrary, they should radiate a quiet confidence, as clients can be very anxious, and this can be a trigger for suicide (Fawcett et al., 1990). Such client anxiety is usually diminished by a quiet manner and the counsellor's ability transfer calm.

Action with the suicidal

The work exampled here is that done over the telephone, when clients say they are feeling suicidal or are going to commit suicide. There are often other circumstances, such as alcohol or drug use, and secondary effects, such as clients feeling angry, sorry for themselves, apart from feeling depressed. Over the phone, the whole scenario will not be known at first, and might not even be known at the end.

So the initial task is to get the client to talk. Counsellors in turn have to be relaxed and give a sense of competency – even when they have no idea what the outcome will be. Part of this competency comes from not forcing the pace, as this merely reveals counsellor anxiety. The counsellor lets the client speak – I favour the counselling grunt or "Um" to signify listening. It is helpful to encourage the client to speak as long as possible, and after a while this means asking open questions. These can include not merely what led up to the present situation, but what feelings were experienced – anger, sadness, anxiety, helplessness or hopelessness.

All of this should relax the client, which makes it then easier to ask whether the client has anything with him, such as pills, razor or a gun. If the answer is "Yes", then the client can more easily be persuaded to put the offending article down or away from him.

Further work

The next stage is to ask what the client thinks would be helpful. This gives a signal that the counsellor is not seeing the situation as a crisis or the client as being helpless. Then the client might be asked if a certain course would be helpful, is there any specific reason why that course of action has not been taken, and what would be needed to make it come about. The point here is not to outline a plan for the client, but merely to show there are possibilities and to get his mind focused on the future.

The client is then asked to detail exactly what he is going to do for the next 24 hours. Clients usually give the minimum, so it helps to ask questions such as whether he will have something to eat in the morning, what he will eat and when. The reason for all of this is to reinforce the client thinking about the future, to shift his attention away from the past. Now it becomes easy to ask the client whether he would agree to further contact within the next day.

Follow-up meeting

Helping the client prevent an attempted suicide may seem enough from the counsellor's perspective, but the job is quite unfinished. As important is the follow-up interview, when the client is seen for himself rather than for the threatened suicide. Some of the things the counsellor can do are:

- Normalise the fact that people have thoughts of death
- Speak about the ambivalence that those with suicidal thoughts may have
- Ask if the client has felt suicidal previously.

This sets the atmosphere for doing an informal discussion of risk with the client. This can pick up issues, such as:

- Whether thoughts of suicide were passive or active; whether of the form "I wish I were dead" or "I want to kill myself", where the latter is plainly more risky. However we have to be realistic about assessing risk, as there is little that the counsellor can do to stop a client attempting or committing suicide. It is clients who have the option of stopping themselves. This is facilitated if all aspects of their situation – including suicide – are discussed.
- Following the last paragraph, we have to help clients to see that it is not so much death they want as an end to their pain and distress, whether physical or emotional. They are not indifferent to death, usually preferring what they see as a peaceful death (Feifel and Nagy, 1980), and a death in isolation. So concentrating on ending their emotional pain and ending them with a peaceful life rather than peaceful death can be another useful approach.
- It is important that the counsellor distinguishes between a client not seeing himself as helpless and matters being beyond his control, and the client at the same time seeing his situation as beyond all control. The client has to see matters as seeming beyond *his* control (Garber and Hollon, 1980).
- We have to touch on other points, such as previous suicide attempts, as this is an increased risk factor for suicide (Keitman and Casey, 1988). Furthermore, there can be special problems when suicidal thoughts include others (Robins, 1981). For instance, one young client threatened not merely to kill herself but her two small children as well, which gave me considerable concern – but did not change my approach.

Suicide is not always accompanied by depression, nor depression by suicide. But talking about what happened is vital in either case. Talking about suicide is not likely to make clients feel suicidal, or more suicidal (Linehan, 1981).

Depressed thinking

As noted earlier, depression does affect thinking, and this can be experienced by the suicidal. The result is sometimes described as being aggression turned against oneself, but this fails to take account of the role of the person who has a conscious role in what is happening. In fact, there may be no pressing reason for attempting suicide, but clients might feel there is no real reason for living. They see themselves as being of no importance in the whole scheme of things. They may see no point to their life and no-one would bother if they died. It would be as if they slipped away, like leaving a party.

> *Gina*: "I am perfectly all right normally, and don't think of suicide. But when depressed, then I feel that everyone would be better off without me. So I decide to kill myself, and that is the only time I'm happy, when I've made that decision. Then I'm at peace with myself."

Everyone else would carry on. This low importance attached to oneself can be reinforced by guilt, when clients believe that they deserve to die.

Medication

As clients try to deal with their situation, they will talk about feeling suicidal, and they should not be dissuaded from so doing. Clients feel how they feel, and denying their reality will not help. Yet counsellors can expand that reality so they realise they are feeling bad, and they are dealing with it – complaining is an acceptable way of management. Not only are they managing, but they are on the way up. This may be helped by the use of antidepressive medication (Isaacson et al., 1996). It has even been seen as a preventative measure.

Commitment and suicide

Before working with those who have attempted suicide, the counsellor commits himself to working with such clients, and helping them to uncover other options to that of suicide. In return, it is useful if clients commit both to working towards such options and trying to avoid suicide. This can be part of a written contract or simply a verbal agreement with handshake. This is done to ensure clients have a clear view of the counsellor's approach to attempted suicide, and do not expect counsellors to give them permission to attempt or even commit suicide (Quinnett, 1987). Such minimal commitment and associated action do appear to make contrary actions less likely (Pallak et al., 1972).

Suicidal thinking

One area that can be usefully covered in counselling is that of suicidal thinking. It can help clients to ask about suicidal thoughts and the reason why they did not put those thoughts into action.

> *May*: "I actually thought of hanging myself, but then thought 'What happens if Julie comes home and finds me hanging there'. But I was really going to do it."

Counselling might concentrate on the positive, and the fact that the client thought not just about herself, but about her daughter and how she would feel. But this should not be made explicit. Just talking about the client's daughter would be sufficient. Counsellors might think they have to positively steer clients away from suicide. This is for their benefit – not their clients. Such a procedure may well result in clients feeling guilty, being a bad mother, and so intensifying depression and making suicide more likely. We should also realise that mothers do not want to attempt or commit suicide because of their children.

> *Carol*: "I thought of taking an overdose and was on the point of doing it, when my daughter looked up at me and I knew I couldn't. I think it is her that keeps me sane."

We can discuss this situation with the client. The mother is caught having to care for a child, but also needing the child to live and carry on. Counselling is about broadening the whole subject, and not just concentrating on the suicide. Attempted suicide is a form of communication. It tells us something. It might not be clear what is said, so we should try and find out and listen to what clients say. We have to have faith in counselling as a process, in the encounter between people, and get away from the need for a recognisable cure or treatment. Being part of counselling is itself one solution.

Hopelessness

The trouble is that what is being said can be very negative. Suicide is strongly associated with hopelessness, with clients seeing their situation as being without hope. Because hopelessness is linked with suicidal thinking (Beck et al., 1993), with suicidal intent (Dyer and Kreitman, 1984) and with actual suicide (Beck et al., 1990), counsellors have to think how it might be tackled. This became an issue for myself when AIDS first became a problem locally, and clients had been tested for HIV. Many of those found antibody positive saw their situation as hopeless, as it was assumed in those early days that they would probably die within 2 years. Many attempted suicide, so the task was to dispel their feeling of hopelessness.

The first thing I discovered was that clients wanted to talk about themselves, AIDS, and their life. They were full of anxiety, and the very word "AIDS" was enough to send them into mental panic. Yet their anxiety was always diminished by allowing them to talk through their concerns. The degree to which that anxiety was reduced varied. Sometimes it was necessary to work on it, by getting clients to say specifically what worried them. They might say that they were afraid of death. I would ask what it was about death that troubled them most. Answers varied. It could be they were angry that they could not achieve what they wanted in life, that they had HIV infection and others not had, that being infected was unfair as they did not know they could be infected, that the authorities did not care if they died. There were a lot of feelings that needed to be identified, and then more direct concerns were expressed. They were afraid death would be painful, that they would end up disabled in a wheelchair, that they would not be around to look after the children, and that their partner would forget them and live with someone else. Once their real concerns were expressed, they were able to deal better with them. It was even possible to make tentative plans, such as thinking about providing memories for the children or talking things through with their partner.

Extreme anxiety

There were a couple of clients who could not easily be separated from their anxiety. They could not say what was worrying them and seemed stuck in near panic. Their only idea seemed to be to end it all. There were two approaches used in these cases. Firstly, they were asked to think of the worst scenario – and at first I had to make some suggestions. When they had an idea what was worst, then it was pointed out that these were worst scenarios. If this was the case, then there must be better ones. I would then suggest less bad, gruesome or painful situations. This got some acceptance, but they were still inclined to talk about suicide. My reaction was not to argue with them, as pressure could panic them. Instead, I said that suicide was a possibility, but I asked them to delay it for a day and we would speak over the phone. The next day I would speak and the agreement then struck that the suicide would be delayed for another day. The clients fairly soon came out of their highly anxious states.

It is worth noting that thoughts of suicide originate in individuals, but may be caused and reinforced by factors outside the person. Concern about AIDS was reflected in the extended families of clients, who sometimes would not let them into their houses. Clearly, information and support was required here. Most clients were injecting drug users and formed a subculture, where information was shared. It was important that what we thought was correct information was put into that subculture, to attempt to dispel what was a group sense of hopelessness.

Suicide and attempted suicide

Counsellors can sometimes get caught up trying to decide whether a client's behaviour constitutes attempted or actual suicide. This can conceal ideas such as client manipulation, and – what is sometimes omitted – the resentment by counsellors that they are being manipulated.

In practice, there is a whole range of behaviours. A few clients are manipulative, and this is their way of coping. We have to concentrate and help them look at what they do, and not attribute their behaviour to the "kind of persons they are". Instead, the interest is placed in the balancing of short- and long-term gains of their objectives.

Another aspect of suicidal clients is the degree of desperation they are feeling. What we find is not faulty thinking but extremist thinking; thinking in a panic. But to clients it all seems quite logical. Clients frame a solution, and then are accused of being irrational. Actually they are being quite rational, and the advantage is that we can use this rationality; we can get them to review their decisions and behaviour.

Counsellors might imagine that suicidal behaviour has some goal, and fail to appreciate the nature of suicidal thinking. This can range from the fully determined to the dissociated, when clients intend to kill themselves but also feel they are not part of what is happening. Some clients will put themselves in a lethal situation, and then what happens is what happens. They neither intend to kill themselves, nor intend not to kill themselves.

Counsellors can help by getting clients to identify their mode of thinking and take responsibility for it, even if the mode of thinking is not to take responsibility for anything.

Contributing factors to suicide

When trying to disentangle the fact of a suicide or attempted suicide, we will be given or obtain basic information as to when, where, in whose company, the lead up and any past pattern of similar behaviour occurred. Another factor to consider is the use of alcohol or drugs. Both, but especially alcohol, are related to suicidal thoughts as alcohol and some drugs are depressants. Coming down from other drugs can also produce depression. There is also the fact that depressants can release people's inhibitions so they are likely to act more impulsively. This does not take away responsibility, as no one physically forces a person to drink or take drugs.

The danger comes when drinking or taking drugs becomes a life pattern, and is used to deal with difficulties; used to cover up troubles. This takes away from the person's ability to cope with life and overcome its problems. However, the drinking or drug taking might in turn be related to underlying depression, so there are various strands to be sorted out.

Wider effects of depression in the family

Although depression and suicidal thoughts usually start with one person, they can affect the whole family, draining energy and affecting relationships. Guilt can arise, as others wonder whether they caused the client's behaviour. There can also be anxiety about the subject's future (Twigg and Atkin, 1993). Depression can extend to the whole family which can become depressed (Haas and Clarkin, 1988), affecting relationships both inside and outside the family. Thus consideration of the whole family is required, by both counsellor and client. Where there were family or marital problems before the advent of noticeable depression (Jacobson et al., 1991), family or marital work can be of use (Rounsaville et al., 1979), provided the depression is not severe (Beach et al., 1990).

Post-counselling

After counselling, one option is for clients to attend a self-help group for those with depression or those feeling suicidal. These groups should always be professionally facilitated, as there is the danger of individual depression and suicidal thinking becoming a group phenomenon. Another problem can be that those who are suicidal may have had problems in forming trusting relationships, and so will test out ongoing relationships in the group, and test out the facilitator by threatening to self-harm. This is done in the expectation of rejection, confirming the idea that the client is worthless, and worthy only of rejection. The facilitator or group worker will help the group look at what is going on, how the suicidal can feel and behave, and how others react to such behaviour (Comstock and McDermott, 1975).

The other task is that of repairing relationships in the family. The threat and fear of suicide can cast a shadow over everyone, and there can be a lot of unspoken anger because of the pressure felt from that fear and anger. The suicider can be judged inappropriately, in that he is viewed as acting inconsiderately, not thinking of anyone but himself. This fails to take on board that the thinking processes of the suicidal can differ; they can take a very different view on life. For instance, a person might attempt suicide out of the house "so the family won't be upset" or "so I am no longer a burden on them." It is not that they are inconsiderate; it is just that they do not appreciate what they are doing from the point of view of others. And that is itself a reflection on the view they hold of themselves in relation to others. As they are worthless, no one will miss them. Sometimes it is trying to grasp how someone could think this way that is difficult for the family.

The rest of the family, especially the potential suicider's partner, requires help. They will have their feelings, and it is not always easy to contain them. However, suicide is more likely if the client's spouse is seen as critical (Keitner et al., 1990).

Children and suicide

Depression and suicide can occur in children, usually after puberty. However, younger children might also feel suicidal, though whether they are depressed is difficult to know.

> *Annette*: "On the way back from Australia by ship I remember very clearly standing on the deck and watching the dolphins diving in the water. I wanted to be free like that, not trapped, so the idea of throwing myself off the ship came to me. I was five years old at the time."

At such an early age, we have to look to the child's background for possible causes. As children grow older, suicidal thinking is not uncommon. We have to be aware that thinking about death is part of growing up and being an adolescent. This might be due to the fact that adolescents are not just hormone driven but also still not capable of totally adult thinking.

Revenge

Although suicide has been a regular concern of counsellors as regards depression, the externalisation of anger has received less attention. This is often the case if depression follows personal violence, as in the case of physical abuse. Depression can be varied with feelings of sudden rage. This can be lessened by the rage being put into thoughts of revenge.

> *Eloise*: "I used to think of killing him, but killing him slowly. I would work out in my mind exactly how I would do it. Get him drunk and then stab him. Nothing ever came of it, but I used to enjoy thinking this way, thinking of getting my revenge."

It is pointless to tell clients not to think of revenge, as they will continue to do so. It can be a way of coping for them. We also have to appreciate that there can be good reasons for clients feeling as they do.

> *Jill*: "There was no way out, I could not escape him. He would follow me when he could. If I went out on my own, I would be cross-examined when I returned, have to account for every minute. At first I loved him; then came to finally hate him. I used to fantasize about killing him. Rather than get depressed, I would think about killing him."

It is better that the clients get rid of their anger, so getting them to punch a cushion and keep on doing that until they are tired can relieve some of the pressure. But people have to be helped to move on, and if they have been in a bad relationship, then continuing thoughts of revenge can just extend that relationship, even if it is merely a relationship in the client's mind. One method is to get the client to examine the face of the person to whom their hate is directed, to examine a photograph of him for several minutes. Clients do not always see the person, but see the image of the person in their head. When they actually look hard, then they begin to question the meaning of the relationship.

> *Jill*: "I saw him in town the other day, and it was like looking at a different person. He was no longer attractive. There was nothing about him. He was nothing to me. It was like looking with different eyes."

Some clients can get frightened of their anger, try to repress it. It can either simply grow and become more uncontrollable, and more frightening, or it is repressed but eats away at the client. It helps to normalise feelings of hate and anger, especially when there is good reason for such feelings. Then it is possible not just to express feelings but to talk about them.

> *Jill*: "I feel angry sometimes and I am frightened of scaring people."
> *Me*: "You think they could not take it?"
> *Jill*: "I'm afraid of what they would do."
> *Me*: "Is it how they would react or the fact of you being angry that worries you most?"
> *Jill*: "I think it is getting angry. That anger scares me, that and other people getting really angry."
> *Me*: "So it is the anger that worries you."
> *Jill*: "And being rejected. If I get angry they might reject me."

As we can see, feelings are rarely pure and simple, but complex; they may reflect other experiences. In the above example, rejection was a theme, and this was a major factor in her anger. Anger can reflect anxiety, fear, or can be a way of stopping statements or questions when they get too close to sensitive topics. And only the client knows the meaning of such anger.

Reprise

About half of those who commit suicide are later said to have been suffering from severe depression (Clayton, 1985). The number of those who attempt suicide and have depression is a very small percentage. Unfortunately, it is difficult to predict who will commit suicide after attempting to do so. What we do find is that the picture is complicated, as intervention changes what is likely to happen.

Chapter 12

Couples and Families

COUPLES

Partner and the role of self-help

The psychiatric approach to depression is based on the medical model, designed to help individuals with organic damage or infection. Little or no attention is given to the rest of the family. The partner and family can be totally excluded from the situation using the concept of medical confidentiality. They are given little help for themselves or to promote their competence (Goldstein, 1981). Couples are treated as two separate persons. Yet most couples stay together because they want to do so, because they care for each other, because they are a couple. Both counsellors and couples should accept this positive aspect and remember that being married can act as a buffer, resulting in the rate of depression being lower among married persons as compared with single persons (Gove et al., 1983).

Couples: introduction

Couples are affectively and cognitively involved, their behaviour intertwined. Depression that touches one will affect the other (Fadden et al., 1987). Equally, the indirect effect of depression on a partner will affect the depressive. Just as depression may be a closed book to the depressive, the same can well apply to the partner. The insidious onset means what is happening may be unknown to both parties. If the depressed member cuts off, this may be seen by the other partner as representing a worsening of their relationship (Walster and Berscheid, 1978), – one person is not pulling his or her weight. Yet usually nothing is said. Instead, all that seems to be occurring is that the relationship grows weaker, and two parties drift apart. So, members of couples withdraw from each other when they most need to be together and be mutually supportive (Dohrenwend and Dohrenwend, 1985). Rather than retreating, couples need to come together, and this will happen if members feel less under stress and have a greater control over their situation (Anderson, 1977). This requires that both do not contend for control of their mutual relationship but aim to exert control in the various specific areas of difficulty encountered (Sadowski and Blackwell, 1985). In reality, such control is not easily obtained.

Effects of depression on a couple

If the mutual relationship between the couple is good, then the partner is likely to notice at some time that things are not right, though there seems no reason for this. There is confusion as the partner tries to understand what is going on, such as the lack of warmth in the relationship. This may be interpreted as a normal cooling in a relationship, which happens over time, or there may be no obvious cause and is just something to be accepted. Alternatively, the partner tries to change the situation, to get the depressed person reacting normally – motivated, happy, interacting as before. But nothing seems to be effective. So the partner re-evaluates the situation.

Firstly, offers of help can be rebuffed, and this can be hurtful. But from the depressive client's point of view, it is difficult enough to deal with his or her own feelings, without having to deal with those of another person. What is worse, a partner might try to motivate or cheer the depressed person up. Not only is this almost certainly going to fail, but those depressed can feel worse in that they probably know what partners are trying to do and feel guilty simply because they cannot be cheerful. The main reason is the extreme lethargy; the client simply cannot be bothered with any personal interaction. It is difficult to describe this lethargy, except it is as if the brain has seized up and every mental operation is burdensome. Even thinking about doing something can prove too tiring.

In time, the partner may see a distancing of the relationship as a normal change to be expected over time, and so accepts the situation. Alternatively, the relationship can be judged to be not right, and the client, the partner or both are to blame. When blame enters the relationship then there can be action such as arguments or guilt and self-blame. The centre of attention then moves to this personal warfare and the couple get caught up in it, rather than the true cause – that of depression. What is true is that depression sets up strains in the relationship, and initial sympathy can turn to irritation if the depressed partner fails to recover.

Depression and marital disharmony

Difficulties occur even in good relationships when depression strikes, but they are greatly magnified if the relationship is poor. The depressive behaviour is not seen as inexplicable but as part of the ongoing marital discord. Detachment and distancing can be interpreted as deliberate ignoring of a partner, sulking or as interest being elsewhere. But, even worse, marital discord can itself lead to depression (Paykel et al., 1969), and is a significant factor for depression in both men and women (Weissman, 1987). Depression in one spouse is linked to marital discord in up to 30% of couples (Waring et al., 1990), and this is linked not merely with depressed behaviour but also the resultant communication problems, especially lack of self-disclosure (Biglan et al., 1985). The latter seem very important if the depressed person is a woman (Brown and Harris, 1978). What occurs is a vicious circle, as the interaction of poor marital relationships and depressive behaviour result in marital discord, which in turn promotes depression, and depression can then lead to marital discord (Claussen and Yarrow, 1955).

Partners and helping

To better understand the interactions of partners, one of whom is depressed, we have to have an idea of both depression and what it is like to live with someone who is depressed. The following are just some of the possible features:

- Anxiety, which might centre around concern for the depressed partner, about the family as a whole, about jobs, finance and the future
- Anger, which might proceed from the strained relationship with its unidirectional nature, the lack of the subject's sociability and feelings of exclusion, and a sense of loss over what might have been.
- Love is a feeling commonly overlooked, but it may underlie many partner relationships. However, there can be complications in that the partner may question who exactly is this subject, whether depression is an affliction or part of the person. There may even be feelings of being trapped living with the depressive.

Those who are depressed have to understand that their partners may have feelings about their relationship, some of which are connected to the episodes of depression. These feelings are best shared between subject and partner for maximum effect, though this is not necessarily the same as maximum benefit. Sometimes alleged expert advice warns against such a process, as the depressed person is likely to be upset and this might worsen the depression. This ignores the fact that clients can be well aware of the effects of depression on the relationship and partner. The thoughts and feelings stay in the mind; all that the silence does is to prevent a resolution of difficulties.

Ongoing good marital relationships and depression

In good relationships, strange or unusual depressive partner behaviour is not likely to be taken personally and seen as hostile. On the other hand, there is a loss, a lack of behaviour aimed to please the partner, especially by the depressed subject (Wills et al., 1974). From the other side, a good relationship is important as it can act as a buffer against the difficulties with the rest of the world. What is important is for partners to know what is happening. This may mean at the very minimum a diagnosis of depression, which can greatly diminish partner anxiety and fears about depression, their role, and their personal relationship. It can also give hope, in that the partner sees help as being given and is not alone in dealing with a depressed person.

This leads onto a further problem in that the non-depressed partner does not wish to aggravate matters and so may be unsure on how to proceed, what might upset the depressive and worsen the depression – such as warranted demands. This balance applies to people in general. We have to judge when and what to reveal to others (Rawlins, 1983). However, if a person is depressed, the situation becomes even more delicate. The result can be the partner speaks about what seems safe or what it seems the depressed partner wants to talk about. Communication can be uneven, very much partner-led, and negative – often focused on symptoms and distress (Hautzinger et al., 1982). Depressed clients tend to interpret communication negatively (Gotlib, 1983) and this is reinforced by the fact that in marital distress there is negative attribution; positive behaviour is seen as being due to the situation but negative behaviour is taken to be caused by the other person (Fincham and O'Leary, 1983). Sometimes it is best if the partner is just there for the depressed person. That in itself can be supportive and reassuring.

Action with partners

There is a danger that depressed subjects will act as if they are helpless and take up an ill role, putting their lack of action down to depression. However, it is not enough to suggest that they should think of others, as depression even in mild form can increase self-absorption and a disregard for others. My feeling is that clients have to make efforts to contribute positively to relationships.

They are helped both as individuals and in their relationships by taking a more positive role.

Couples are strengthened through better mutual communication. This can be divided into two aspects. Firstly, the depressive can individually practise communicating, and this means just getting into the habit of talking and listening, a task which they may have to force themselves to do. As communication becomes easier, so relationships can improve (Duran, 1983). This in turn allows couples to be honest and direct with each other.

But, as ever, it is all a matter of balance. There is little evidence that direct communication is always better than indirect communication between couples (Sillars et al., 1984). This is hardly surprising, as human communication is extremely complex (Montgomery, 1984). We can find communication varies, and the role of non-verbal language can become more important with depressed clients.

The other point for counsellors to remember is that couples who have been together for some time get to know the other person very well and rely on non-verbal language. But this can be a poor channel of communication, as depressed clients pick up signals poorly, and do not give out the usual ones.

So sometimes direct language may be more easily understood, and sometimes couples talking about their communication is needed. There has to be understanding and acceptance of depressed communication – from both parties. So couples know:

- When depressed, eye contact is reduced, attention is poor and concentration diminished.
- Depressed persons may not initiate conversations but can participate. However, there will be times when such conversation becomes positively painful and is avoided.
- Depressed persons react very poorly to negative comments. In fact, the best single predictor of relapse is the frequency of criticism from a depressed person's partner (Hooley et al., 1986).
- Depressed persons deal poorly with expressed emotions or to emotive issues.

The balance is for the client to try to deal with as much as possible, and for the partner to be aware of temporary limitations.

Marital therapy

It is not always easy to differentiate between depression that causes marital strain and conflict, and marital conflict that causes depression. What seems to be true is that help should be contemplated for both depression and marital difficulties. Certainly, for mild to moderate depression, marital work can be of help (Beach et al., 1990). In fact, women's recovery from depression often depends on their rating of the married relationship (Goering et al., 1992). It should be noted that marital work tends to help women more than men (Clarkin et al., 1990), but if the partner is seen as uncaring in the eyes of the depressed person, then outlook is poor (Hickie and Parker, 1992). What may be best is that attention is given according to the needs of the couple, whether depression or marital difficulties, or indeed both, need attention (Rounsaville et al., 1979).

Talking about relationships

The periods of non-depression may be used to talk. There is always the danger that once depression symptoms have gone, couples think that is the end. It is merely another stage, which can be used by clients to look back and describe how they felt then and how they feel now, what it is like to be depressed, and how difficulties can be overcome. The last is important, otherwise listing a catalogue of apparent difficulties may be merely imposing a burden on client partners. In addition, the partner's perspective and possible changes in roles might be discussed. The aim is agreement and mutual action, not imposition, guilt and uncertainty. The former can be obtained through talking about the relationship. This not merely maintains or repairs the relationship, but goes to deepen and strengthen it (Baxter and Bullis, 1986).

What can be said about such discussions is that the time is never right. There is never a perfect time to talk. But if matters are good between couples, then it is a good time. And if couples are in conflict, they are more likely to maintain a better relationship if they discuss it (Bernal and Baker, 1979). Combined with the fact that inaction allows matters to get worse, getting to grips with mutual communication as soon as possible is beneficial. It is worth remembering that people usually prefer that their partners initiate such discussions (Acitelli, 1986), so clients should not leave it to their partner to begin. And communication is a process, and should be spaced out to allow time for information processing (Dempster, 1988).

Any discussion should try to take time to centre on the relationship itself. This reminder is needed, as there does tend to be a gender difference. Men are more inclined to see relationships as a means to an end, a way of achieving certain goals, whereas women are more likely to see the relationship as an end in itself (Scott et al., 1991). Too often, debates can centre around who does what, or who is not doing what. This can lead to arguments, a charged atmosphere, and the expression of high emotion – unhelpful as regards possible depression (Asarnow et al., 1993). What is needed is more concentration on the here-and-now, and each person bringing about improvements in their behaviour and not telling the other what to do.

For couples, it is often important to ignore the content of talk or arguments, and concentrate on what is being communicated about the relationship (Watzlawick et al., 1967). This is usually covered by questions such as, "What is happening to us?" However, this question is likely to be one that is left unspoken. Couples tend to assume they agree, and this might not be the case; they can also assume they disagree, when in fact they agree (Kenny and Acitelli, 1989). Both have to realise that they need to check out each other's views.

Role changes in couples

As with any crisis, there are opportunities for change and progress. New roles may have to be taken up (Rosenbaum and Najenson, 1976), and this gives new opportunities. What has to be noted and mutually discussed is the development of all parties through new roles, and this means talking about expectations and possible changes in relationships (Parker, 1992).

Another role is that of prevention, and some of this rests with the depressive's partner, as often it is the partner who is first aware of another oncoming episode of depression. Some things that might be observed in the depressed person's behaviour are:

- Changes in usual behaviour.
- Lack of attention, such as not listening to what is being said.
- Sleeplessness.
- Change in eating habits.
- Depressive demeanour, such as slumped shoulders, little eye contact, and hands moving little.
- Drinking or increased drinking.
- Longer time spent in bed.
- Diminished sexual interest.

Signs of depression will vary, so it helps to ask partners what signs they saw in their partner's behaviour that can be put down to depression.

This does not mean partners have to take up a caring role. Depressed clients have to be responsible for themselves as much as possible.

FAMILIES

Introduction

Those who become depressed do so in a social context, usually that of their family. This means families have to deal with a depressed person and may react unhelpfully, making the situation worse for everyone. On the other hand, by increasing the self-esteem of the family, recovery is aided (Strupp, 1989). It is not just partners of depressed clients who are affected; children are also affected and this might continue into later life (Marsh et al., 1993). So help may be needed by the whole family.

Helping the family?

The family's need for help depends mainly on the extent of the person's depression, whether it is developing, whether there have been previous depressive episodes, and any identifiable cause of the depression. Initially, the policy of least intervention is best (Thompson, 1990), giving the family its opportunity to adjust and use its own resources (Lewis, 1989). We also have to consider whether over-helping may bring about negative effects (Carr, 1990). For instance, giving therapy to the whole family may be justified on the assumption that the whole family is ill or causing the depression (Bernheim, 1989), and is thereby labelled as dysfunctional.

Content of information for the family

For families to be helped, then they need information. They need to be aware of how depression affects the individual and also its interaction on the family.

- Gradual onset and compensation
- Lethargy and rationalisation
- Lack of control and hyper-control
- Lack of expressed affection and avoidance
- Poor communication and interpretation.

The above list gives just a few of the aspects of depression and possible family consequences. The gradual onset of depression may be marked by attempts not just by the client but the whole family to compensate for the situation. This can mean the evolution of new roles in the family and new alliances. It may mean the eldest child takes a near parental role, or becomes the support for the non-depressed parent.

The worsening of depression during the day can lead to the person being seen as "not an evening person", as someone getting old before his or her time, or as a lazy person. Lethargy can be interpreted as rejection, which can lead to resentment. This can feed back into the depression, and aggravate the family's situation.

The lack of control due to depression can lead to a sense by the partner of no support in dealing with the family, resulting in attempts at increased control. Or the depressed person is conscious of the lack and tries to compensate by being over-controlling, and relying on extremist thinking and not being relaxed about perceived unwanted behaviour.

Depression blunts affection and its expression, which can lead to avoidance by the depressed person of situations where a show of affection is expected. And poor communication leads to everyone having to try and interpret what is going on. Again, the slow onset of depression makes this a gradual process, so it is hardly noticed or seen as strange.

The information about depression is so often seen in individual terms that we fail to take account of its interactional nature in a fairly closed organisation such as the family. We fail to see other family members as being part of what is happening, as being affected by and affecting in turn the depression.

Family action

Other information given about depression is that of causes. These can be seen as genes, brain chemistry and stress. Genetic explanations may fail to address the unasked question as to whether the children are likely to grow up and become depressed. And if the question is asked, then a definite answer cannot be given – which is not reassuring if your family is involved. Brain chemistry and the role of serotonin at least give more definite answers and there are drugs to combat the depression. However, this places the problem very much in the hands of the depressed person, who themself is unable to help. The idea of stress does involve the family. But constantly having to watch oneself and not cause stress is likely to cause resentment in the long run, and can increase family stress.

Doctors and psychiatrists, using the medical model, are interested in causes, but these are not very useful as far as the family is concerned. They can become the silent grounds for blame and blaming. Rather than causes, families want to know what they can do to help. They want to be involved, and they are usually prevented from being involved.

In order to help, it is helpful to turn down the emotional intensity within the family, and use a neutral example to get members participating. We might get them to imagine someone in the family has broken a leg. How do members think that person would want them to react? Answers given to me have included:

- Taking exercise to strengthen the leg
- Not feeling guilty about resting the leg
- People should not keep on asking about it
- Accept that accidents happen
- Look forward to the day when the cast is taken off
- Say something to people who stare at the cast.

The counsellor can help members to picture various scenes and then ask them for their reactions. Then the scenario can be transferred to that of a person with depression, with discussion of the similarities and the differences.

Individual and family management

The active participation of the family is increased if they can understand that the depressed person has been attempting to manage on his or her own, and now agrees that some outside help is needed. This comes in part from the counsellor, but mostly from those around the depressed person. This management can include the use of alcohol; that is one way of coping, but now another way will be taken. Talking about what has happened can get rid of resentment and help depressed persons understand how they are viewed. For instance, a depressed father might drink to be able to cope with visitors to the house and to appear not depressed but happy.

To his wife the smell of alcohol about him is embarrassing, as is his over-jolly and somewhat uncontrolled behaviour. His young children are confused by his change in mood and him not seeming to be himself. To them he is becoming frightening. The counsellor has to be careful that the outcome is not that of the depressed person feeling guilty. There has to be movement to a situation where there is a greater satisfaction all round. So when clients say they are sorry about their drinking, my reaction is to tell them that the problem is not so much drink as poor coping, and this can come in part from not allowing others to help. And one aspect of depression is the narrowing of focus, the concentration on self and just not seeing and taking account of others. So what is required is action.

Everyone can act. This applies to the depressed person. This can be action through taking medication, which can in itself be seen as positive action; steps to improving the situation for the whole family. This applies whether or not the medication is effective. It shows that the depressed person is trying to help matters by taking the prescribed tablets.

Severe depression

The role of the family and the depressed person's partner or parents can become even more important in cases of severe depression. Such clients are restricted in ensuring their views are taken on board. They may be unassertive, uncommunicative, or unable to concentrate to be able to put their views across and unable to counter any argument. At this very time they need personal help for themselves; they are psychiatrised and left less, not more, powerful.

The role of the counsellor can be far from clear. Firstly, the client is likely to be the depressed person's partner or parent, and help can only be directed to that person, initially. And what is required is more power for the family, and that way the client can be helped. And the first task is for the family to register it has an interest in what is happening, an action which the counsellor supports. And in fairness, psychiatrists can react very positively to family interest. It is just that usually their training does not run to working in a family context. Once they see family members as allies rather than complicating factors, then everyone gains. This also requires that the family does not see the psychiatrist as the opposition, but as someone trying to help. Families should also realise that they may be the best conduits to the psychiatrist for what the client wants. When severely depressed, it is difficult to express oneself, but this can be done by a partner. The difficulty is knowing whether the partner is speaking for the clients, or for himself or herself.

Dynamics of the family

A person with depression takes up a sick role in the family, and this can have its own consequences. The first is that the role can be useful at first, but if taken too long, it locks the client into under-performing and is restrictive on the rest of the family. Another problem is that the sick role can become the centre of the family function. This gives undue power to the depressed person, a power that is misplaced as that person has cognitive and affective limitations. The result is that everyone does what fits in with the client, whether this is really beneficial or not. The other side of this is that members of the family can be overlooked. This is accepted as long as the client is ill, but changes when the symptoms of depression leave. This lifts the lid on the family's desires, expectations and frustrations. This means that at the very time the client is getting ready for ordinary life, the family suddenly dissolves in chaos. This in turn can put the client's progress at risk or make leaving the sick role seem less inviting.

FRIENDS

Introduction

In times of depression, friends can be helpful. They may act as a useful substitute for close relatives, who are seen by clients as being too involved and unable to view the situation calmly and unemotionally (Twigg and Atkin, 1993). Sometimes even the knowledge that there is someone at hand if required can be a boost (Sinclair, 1990). However, the family may wish to discourage outsiders, fearing they might bring stigma and disgrace on the family (Fisher et al., 1988). Friends are also often overlooked by professionals, whose training and practice makes them underestimate the help they can give (Heller, 1979). It has to be admitted that there may appear to be problems with confidential information, as it may be seen as alright to share it with family, but not close friends. On the other hand, we tend to have expectations that friends will stand by us, a judgment that rests on the person being a friend, and prior instances of support, loyalty and helping (Chelune et al., 1984).

Yet if a person is having difficulty in coping with life, then assistance is sought from family and friends rather than professional sources (Golan, 1981). In fact, many women value talk with best friends more than that with husbands, finding their self-esteem increases and they are then better able to deal with problems – including their spouse (Oliker, 1989). But it is not just that talking to friends makes people feel better. It can help with the expression of feelings and with the clarification of ideas (Becker, 1987); it decreases obsessional thinking (Wegner et al., 1987), and makes sense of what has happened (Silver and Wortman, 1980). Friends are not always going to prove to be of use. They are liable to pass on confidential information. Indeed, part of friendship can lie in the trading of such information or gossip. In addition, friends may think they have rights, such as being given information and their help and advice being taken (Rosen et al., 1987). Finally, friendships can end quite easily (Wiseman, 1986), and this can occur when parties move away, take new jobs, or take up new interests (Rawlins,

1994). This leaves open the question as to what then happens to any confidential information held by both parties.

On investigation, we find there is a difference between friends and close friends. With the latter there is more sharing of feelings, informality and relaxation (Planalp and Benson, 1992). The amount a person discloses depends in part on the closeness of the friend. In contrast, depressed clients are best using close friends for any possible disclosure about their condition. They should be wary of disclosing to friends first, even if they happen to be on hand and the subject's need to disclose is great. We should also get away from the stereotype of self-disclosure being about sitting down with another person to talk. Men tend to prefer doing things together rather than just talking (Caldwell and Peplau, 1982). From both the depressive's and the close friends' point of view, it might be easier to go out together, to doing things together and then disclose. Such aspects as shared fun and joking are important parts of friendship extension and maintenance (Jones, 1991). Close friends are more likely to be close to both the subject and the subject's family and other friends (Jerrome, 1984). When self-disclosing, the subject should be aware of what the person sees as confidentiality.

Obtaining support from friends

If subjects become depressed then their effective social skills are diminished. This makes them less attractive as friends and as objects of help, especially as they cannot reciprocate at the time the attention and help given to them (Pearson, 1990). In addition, people may feel asking for help or sharing difficulties is an admission of weakness or inadequacy (Fisher et al., 1988), and this lessens their self-esteem. This in turn makes them apologise and draw attention to their seeming inadequacies, which can be off-putting to friends. For some people, it can come as a shock to realise that some friendships will end once the fact of the subject's depression is known, but for some friends there is a fear of being lumped together with the depressed person or suffering contamination (Hirsch, 1979). It does help if the subject mentions that the depression is likely to be a passing episode and treatment has started. The subject should try to forget those who disengage themselves and appreciate those who stand by them and do offer help.

In fact, the process of soliciting help can be complex. Depressives might be reluctant to seek support from friends as their low self-esteem makes them fear rejection, so they have to assess those friends who are likely to be accepting and will stand by them (Boyce et al., 1988). With more severe depression, friends are more likely to be alienated and withdraw support (Froland et al.,

1979), partly because the demands on them can grow into dependency (Tolsdorf, 1976). Depressives are likely to have different needs at different times, so rather than use one friend, they use different friends at different times (Mitchell and Moos, 1984). Thus, when considering help to be gathered from friends, subjects should realise that there are inhibitions on both sides.

Social effects

One of the effects of depression is that it can bring stigma. The client can become known as "that person who suffers from depression" and even the family can be "the family where the father/mother is depressed". This can result in a loss of friends. It is said that such a crisis lets a person know who his or her true friends are. From the client's perspective, the outcome can be:

- A decrease in the size of the social network
- Less social contact
- More social activities in the home or immediate neighbourhood
- A decrease in the quality of interactions
- A restructuring of the social network to include those involved with similar health problems.

For the maximum recovery, social networks might have to be restored. In practice this is easier than it might seem. One problem is usually not the reactions of others but the depressive's fear of how others will react. Then they have to react in a social manner, which at times can mean putting up a front; pretending that they feel perfectly all right. Checking out how a person comes over can be done with the counsellor or in the family.

Bibliography

Abramson L, Seligman M and Teasdale J (1978). Learned helplessness in humans: critique and reformulation. *Journal of Abnormal Psychology*, 87: 49.

Abramson L, Metalsky G and Alloy L (1989). Hopelessness depression: a theory-based subtype of depression. *Psychological Review*, 96: 358.

Acitelli L (1986). When spouses talk to each other about their relationship. *Journal of Social and Personal Relationships*, 5: 185.

Alessi N (1991). Refractory childhood depressive disorders from a psychotherapeutic perspective. In Amsterdam J (Ed.) *Advances in Neuropsychiatry and Psychopharmocology*, Vol. 2. *Refractory Depression*. New York: Raven Press.

Alexopoulos G (1991). Biological correlates of late life depression. In *Abstracts of Consensus Developments Conference on the Diagnoses and Treatment of Depression in Later Life*. Washington, DC: National Institute of Health.

Alloy L and Abramson L (1988). Depressive realism: four theoretical perspectives. In Alloy L (Ed.) *Cognitive Processes in Depression*. New York: Guilford.

Alloy L, Kelly K, Mineka S and Clements C (1990). Co-morbidity in anxiety and depressive disorders: a helplessness\hopelessness perspective. In Maser J and Cloninger C (Eds) *Co-morbidity in Anxiety and Mood Disorders*. Washington, DC: American Psychiatric Press.

American Psychiatric Association (1993). *Practice Guidelines for Major Depressive Disorders in Adults*. Washington, DC: APA.

Anderson A (1982). Inoculation and counter-explanation: debiasing techniques in the perseverance of social theories. *Social Cognition*, 1: 126.

Anderson C (1977). Laws of control, coping behaviours and performance in a stress setting: a longitudinal study. *Journal of Applied Psychology*, 62: 446.

Anderson J, Williams S, McGere R and Silva P (1987). DSM-111 disorders in preadolescent children: prevalence in a large sample from the general population. *Archives of General Psychiatry*, 44: 69.

Aneshensel C, Frerichs R and Clark V (1981). Family roles and sex differences in depression. *Journal of Health and Social Behavior*, 22: 379.

Angst J and Dobler-Mikola A (1985). The Zurich study: VI. A continuum from depression to anxiety disorders? *European Archives of Psychiatry and Neuroscience*, 235: 179.

Arkin R and Baumgardner A (1985). Self-handicapping. In Harvey J and Weary G (Eds) *Attribution: Basic Issues and Applications*. New York: Academic Press.

Asarnow J, Goldstein M, Thompson M and Guthrie D (1993). One-year outcomes of depressive disorders – child psychiatric inpatients: evolution of the prognostic power of a brief measure of emotion. *Journal of Child Psychology and Psychiatry*, 34: 129.

Atkinson D, Worthington R, Dana D and Good G (1991). Etiology beliefs, preferences for counseling orientations and counseling effectiveness. *Journal of Counseling Psychology*, 38: 258.

Bagley C and Young L (1989). Depression, self-esteem, and suicidal behavior as sequels of sexual abuse in childhood: research and therapy. In Rothery M and Cameron G (Eds) *Childhood Maltreatment: Expanding our Concept of Healing*. Hillsdale NJ: Erlbaum.

Barnett P and Gotlib I (1988). Psychosocial functioning and depression: distinguishing between antecedents, concomitants, and consequences. *Psychological Bulletin*, 104: 97.

Barrett JE, Barrett JA, Oxman T and Gerber T (1988). The prevalence of psychiatric disorders in a primary care practice. *Archives of General Psychiatry*, 45: 1100.

Baumeister R (1990). Anxiety and deconstruction: on escaping the self. In Olson J and Zanna M (Eds) *Self-inference Processes: The Ontario Symposium*, Vol. 6. Hillsdale, NJ: Erlbaum; p. 259.

Baumgardner A, Lake E and Arkin R (1985). Claiming mood as self-handicap: the influence of spoiled and unspoiled public identities. *Personality and Social Psychology Bulletin*, 11: 349.

Baxter L and Bullis (1986). Turning points in developing romantic relationships. *Human Communication Research*, 12: 469.

Beach S, Sandeen E and O'Leary K (1990). *Depression in Marriage: A Model for Etiology and Treatment.* New York: Guilford.

Beaumont G (1996). The place of cloripramine in psychopharmacology. In Healy D (Ed.) *The Pharmacologists*, Vol. 1. London: Arnold; p. 309.

Bebbington P, Katz R, McGuffen P, Tennant C and Murray J (1989). The risk of minor depression before age 65: results from a community study. *Psychological Medicine*, 19: 393.

Beck A (1976). *Cognitive Theory and Emotional Disorders*. New York: International Universities Press.

Beck A, Rush A, Shaw B and Emery G (1979). *Cognitive Theory of Depression*. 302. New York: Guilford Press.

Beck A, Steer R, Kovacs M and Garrison B (1985). Hopelessness and eventual suicide: a 10 year prospective study of patients. *American Journal of Psychiatry*, 142: 559.

Beck A, Brown G, Berchick R, Stewart B and Steer R (1990). Relationship between hopelessness and ultimate suicide: a replication with psychiatric outpatients. *American Journal of Psychiatry*, 147: 190.

Beck A, Steer R, Beck J and Newman C (1993). Hopelessness, depression, suicidal ideation, and clinical diagnoses of depression. *Suicide and Life-threatening Behavior*, 23: 139.

Becker C (1987). Friendship between women: a phenomenological study of best friends. *Journal of Phenomenological Psychology*, 18: 59.

Beitchman J, Zucker K, Hood J, da Costa G, Akman D and Cassavia F (1992). A review of the long-term effects of child sexual abuse. *Child Abuse and Neglect*, 16: 101.

Belle D (1982). *Lives in Stress: Women and Depression*. Beverly Hills, CA: Sage.

Benson H (1976). *The Relaxation Response*. London: Collins.

Bernal G and Baker J (1979). Toward a metacommunicational framework of couple interaction. *Family Process*, 18: 273.

Bernheim K (1989). Psychologists and the families of the severely mentally ill: the role of the family consultation. *American Psychologist*, 44: 561.

Biglan A, Hops H, Sherman L, Friedman L, Arthur J and Osteen V (1985). Problem-solving interactions of depressed women and their husbands. *Behavior Therapy*, 16: 431.

Blaney P (1986). Affect and memory: a review. *Psychological Bulletin*, 99: 229.

Blashfield R and Livesley W (1991). Metaphorical analysis of psychiatric classification as a psychological test. *Journal of Abnormal Psychology*, 100: 262.

Blazer D, Hughes D and George L (1987). The epidemiology of depression in an elderly community population. *Gerontologist*, 27: 281.

Blehar M, Weissman M, Gershon E and Hirschfield R (1988). Family and genetic studies of affective disorders. *Archives of General Psychiatry*, 45: 289.

Bloor M and Horobin G (1975). Conflict and conflict-resolution in doctor\patient interactions. In Cox C and Mead A (Eds) *A Sociology of Medical Practice*. London: Collier-Macmillan.

Blumberg S and Hokansin J (1982). The effects of another person's response style on interpersonal behavior in depression. *Journal of Abnormal Psychology*, 92: 196.

Bongar B, Lomax J and Marmatz M (1992). Training and supervisory issues in the assessment and management of the suicidal patient. In Bongar B (Ed.) *Suicide: Guidelines for Assessment, Management, and Treatment*. New York: Oxford University Press.

Bosscher R (1993). Running and mixed exercises with depressed psychiatric patients. *International Journal of Sport Psychology*, 24: 170.

Boswell P and Murray E (1981). Depression, schizophrenia, and social attraction. *Journal of Consulting and Clinical Psychology*, 49: 641.

Boud D and Pascoe J (1978). *Experiential learning: developments in Australian post-secondary education. Sydney, Australia; Australian Consortium on Experiential Education.*

Bower G (1981). Mood and memory. *The American Psychologist*, 36: 129.

Boyce W, Kay M and Uitti C (1988). The taxonomy of social support: an ethnographic analysis among adolescent mothers. *Social Science and Medicine*, 26: 1079.

Brady F (1979). *Father's Days: A True Story of Incest*. New York: Dell.

Bridges K and Goldberg D (1985). Somatic presentation of DSM III psychiatric disorders in primary care. *Journal of Psychosomatic Research*, 29: 563.

Brown G (1991). Epidemiological studies of depression: definition and case finding. In Becker J and Kleinman A (Eds) *Psychosocial Aspects of Depression*. Hillsdale, NJ: Lawrence Erlbaum.

Brown G and Harris T (1978) Social origins of depression: a study of psychiatric disorders in women. Tavistock, London.

Brugha I and Bebbington P (1992). The under treatment of depression. *European Archives of Psychiatry and Clinical Neuroscience*. 242: 103.

Bruhn J, McCrady K and du Plessis A (1968). Evidence of emotional drain preceding death from myocardial infarction. *Psychiatric Digest*, 29: 34.

Buchan H, Johnstone E and McPherson K (1992). Who benefits from electroconvulsive therapy? Combined results of the Leicester and Northwick Park trials. *British Journal of Psychiatry*, 160: 355.

Burgoon J, Parrott R, LePoire B, Kelley D, Walther J and Perry D (1989). Maintaining and restoring privacy through communication in different types of relationships. *Journal of Social and Personal Relationships*, 6: 131.

Burke R (1984). The Type A experience: the occupational and life demands, satisfaction and wellbeing. In Burke R (Ed.) *Occupational Stress.* Toronto: York University.

Byrne A and Byrne D (1993). The effect of exercise on depression, anxiety and other mood states: a review. *Journal of Psychosomatic Research*, 37: 565.

Caldwell M and Peplau L (1982). Sex differences in same-sex friendships. *Sex Roles*, 8: 721.

Campbell J and Fehr B (1990). Self-esteem and perceptions of conveyed impressions: is negative affectivity associated with greater realism? *Journal of Personality and Social Psychology*, 58: 122.

Carlozzi A, Campbell N and Ward G (1982). Dogmatism and externality in locus of control as related to counsellor skill in facilitative responding. *Counsellor Education and Supervision*, 21: 227.

Carlson G and Kashani J (1988). Phenomenology of major depression from childhood through adulthood: analysis of three studies. *American Journal of Psychiatry*, 145: 1222.

Carr A (1990). Failures in family therapy: a catalogue of engagement mistakes. *Journal of Family Therapy*, 12: 371.

Carroll JF (1979). Staff burnout as a form of ecological dysfunction. *Contemporary Drug Problems*, Summer: 1.

Carroll JS (1978). The effect of imagining an event on expectation for the event: an interpretation in terms of the availability heuristic. *Journal of Experimental Social Psychology*, 24: 310.

Carver C and Scheier M (1990). Origins and functions of positive and negative affect: a control-process view. *Psychological Review*, 97: 19.

Casper R, Redmond E, Katz M, Schaffer C, Davis J and Koslow S (1985). Somatic symptoms in primary affective disorder: presence and relationship to the classification of depression. *Archives of General Psychiatry*, 42: 1098.

Chelune G, Robison J and Kammar M (1984). A cognitive interactional model of intimate relationships. In Derlega V (Ed.) *Communication, Intimacy, and Close Relationships.* New York: Academic Press.

Clark M, Milberg S and Ross J (1983). Arousal cues arousal-related material in memory: implications for understanding effects of mood on memory. *Journal of Verbal Learning and Verbal Behavior*, 22: 633.

Clark M and Williams G (1989). Moods and social judgments. In Wagner H and Monstead A (Eds) *Handbook of Psychophysiology: Emotion and Social Behavior.* Chichester: Wiley.

Clarkin J, Glick I and Haas G (1990). A randomised clinical trial of inpatient family intervention: results for affective disorders. *Journal of Affective Disorders*, 18: 17.

Claussen J and Yarrow M (1955). Introduction: mental illness and the family. *Journal of Social Issues*, 11: 3.

Clayton P (1985). Suicide. *Psychiatric Clinics of North America*, 8: 203.

Cobb S (1976). Social support as a moderator of life stress. *Psychosomatic Medicine*, 38: 300.

Cochrane N (1990). Physical contact experience and depression. *Acta Psychiatrica Scandinavica*, 82(Suppl. 357).

Colligan M and Murphy L (1979). Mass psychogenic illness in organizations: an overview. *Journal of Occupational Psychology*, 52: 77.

Comstock B and McDermott M (1975). Group therapy for patients who attempt suicide. *International Journal of Group Psychotherapy*, 25: 44.

Cooper J, Bloom F and Roth R (1991). *The Biochemical Basis of Neuropharmacology*. New York: Oxford University Press.

Coppen A, Metcalfe M and Wood K (1982). Lithium. In Paykel E (Ed.) *Handbook of Affective Disorders*. New York: Guilford.

Cordle C and Prettyman R (1994). A two-year follow-up of women who have experienced early miscarriage. *Journal of Reproductive and Infant Psychology*, 12: 37.

Coryell W, Lowry M and Wasek P (1980). Diagnostic instability and depression. *American Journal of Psychiatry*, 137: 48.

Coryell W, Scheftner W, Keller M, Endicott J, Maser J and Klerman G (1993). The enduring psychosocial consequences of mania and depression. *American Journal of Psychiatry*, 150: 720.

Costello C (1993). *Symptoms of Depression*. New York: Wiley.

Coyne J (1976). Depression and the response of others. *Journal of Abnormal Psychology*, 85: 186.

Coyne J and Gotlib I (1983). The role of cognition in depression: a critical appraisal. *Psychological Bulletin*, 94: 472.

Coyne J, Wortman C and Lehman D (1988). The other side of support: emotional overinvolvement and miscarried helping. In Gottlieb B (Ed.) *Marshaling Support: Formats, Processes and Effects*. Newbury Park, CA: Sage.

Craighead W, Hickey K and DeMonbreun B (1979). Distortion of perception and recall of neutral feedback in depression. *Cognitive Theory and Research*, 3: 291.

Cullberg J, Wasserman D and Stefansson C (1988). Who commits suicide after a suicide attempt? An 8–10 year follow-up in a suburban catchment area. *Acta Scandinavica*, 77: 598.

Cutrona C (1982). Non-psychotic post-partum depression: a review of recent research. *Clinical Psychology Review*, 2: 487.

Davidson R and Ekman P (1994). Afterword: what are the minimal cognitive prerequisites for emotion? In Ekman P and Davidson R (Eds) *The Nature of Emotion: Fundamental Questions*. New York: Oxford University Press.

Dean C, Surtees P and Sashidharan S (1983). Comparison of research diagnostic systems in an Edinburgh community sample. *British Journal of Psychiatry*, 142: 247.

DeFrank R and Cooper C (1987). Worksite stress management interventions: their effectiveness and conceptualization. *Journal of Managerial Psychology*, 2: 4.

Dempster F (1988). The spacing effect: a case study in the failure to apply the results of psychological research. *American Psychologist*, 43: 627.

Depression Guideline Panel (1993). *Depression in primary care: Volume 1 Detection and diagnosis AHCPR Publication 93-0550*. Rockville, MD: US Department of Health and Human Services.

Depue R and Spoont M (1986). Conceptualising a serotonin trait as a behavioral dimension of constraint. In Mann J and Stanley M (Eds) *Psychobiology of Suicidal Behavior*. New York: New York Academy of Sciences.

DiMascio A, Weissman M, Prusoff R, Carlos N, Zwillig M and Klerman H (1987). Differential symptom reduction by drugs and psychotherapy in acute depression. *Archives of General Psychiatry*, 31: 1450.

Dimond R and Havens R (1975). Restructuring psychotherapy: towards a prescriptive eclecticism. *Professional Psychology*, May: 193.

Doherty M, Mynatt C, Tweney R and Schiavo M (1979). Pseudodiagnosticity. *Acta Psychologica*, 43: 111.

Dohrenwend B, Shrout P, Martin J and Skodol A (1986). Overview and initial results from a risk-factor study of depression and schizophrenia. In Barrett J (Ed.) *Mental Disorder in the Community: Progress and Challenges*. New York: Guildford Press.

Dohrenwend BS and Dohrenwend BP (1985). *Stressful Life Events and their Contents.* New York: Neale Watson.

Dubovsky S and Thomas M (1995). Beyond specificity: effects of serotonin and serotonergic treatments on psychobiological dysfunction. *Journal of Psychosomatic Research*, 39: 429.

Dunner D and Schmaling K (1994). Treatment of dysthymia: fluoxetine versus cognitive therapy. *Presented at the XIXth Collegium Internationale Neuro-Psychopharmacologium Congress, Washington, DC. Neuropsychopharmacology*, 10: 35.

Dunning D and Parpil M (1989). Mental addition versus mental subtraction in counterfactual reasoning. *Journal of Personality and Social Psychology*, 61: 521.

Duran R (1983). Communication adaptability: a measure of social communication competence. *Communication*, Quarterly 31: 320.

Dyer J and Kreitman N (1984). Hopelessness, depression and suicidal intent in parasuicide. *British Journal of Psychiatry*, 144: 127.

Edwards D (1990). Cognitive therapy and the restructuring of early memories through guided imagery. *Journal of Cognitive Psychotherapy*, 4: 33.

Ehrenrich B and English D (1978). *For Her Own Good: 150 Years of the Expert's Advice to Women*. New York: Anchor\Doubleday.

Elkin I, Shea M, Watkins J, Imber S, Sotsky S, Collins J, Glass R, Pikonis P, Leber W, Docherty J, Fiester S and Parloff M (1989). National Institute of Medical Health treatment of depression. Collaborative Research Program. *Archives of General Psychiatry* 46: 971.

Elmes E and Bjork R (1975). The interaction of encoding and rehearsal processes in the recall of repeated and non-repeated items. *Journal of Verbal Learning and Verbal Behavior*, 14: 30.

Epley S (1974). Reduction of the behavorial effects of aversive stimulation by the presence of companions. *Psychological Bulletin*, 81: 271.

Epstein W (1995). *The Illusion of Psychotherapy*. London: Transaction Publishers.

Evans J, Barston J, Pollard P and Byrne R (1983). On the conflict between logic and belief in syllogistic reasoning. *Memory and Cognition,* 11: 295.

Fadden G, Bebbington P and Kuipers L (1987). Caring and its burdens: a study of the spouses of depressed patients. *British Journal of Psychiatry*, 151: 660.

Fava G, Munari F, Pavan L and Kellner R (1981). Life events and depression: a replication. *Journal of Affective Disorders*, 3: 159.

Fava M and Kaji J (1994). Continuation and maintenance treatments of major depressive disorder. *Psychiatric Annals*, 24: 281.

Fawcett J (1988). Predictors of early suicide: identification and appropriate intervention. *Journal of Clinical Psychiatry*, 49(Suppl. 10): 7.

Fawcett J, Scheftner W, Fogg L, Clark D, Young M, Hedeker D and Gibbons R (1990). Time-related predictors of suicide in major depressive disorders. *American Journal of Psychiatry*, 147: 1189.

Federoff J, Sarkstein S, Parikh R, Price I and Robinson R (1991). Are depressive symptoms non-specific in patients with acute stroke? *American Journal of Psychiatry*, 148: 1172.

Feifel H and Nagy V (1980). Death orientation and life-threatening behavior. *Journal of Abnormal Psychology*, 89: 38.

Feighner J, Robins E, Guze S, Woodruffe R, Winokur G and Munoz R (1972). Diagnostic criteria for use in psychiatric research. *Archives of General Psychiatry*, 26: 57.

Fiedler K (1988). Emotional mood, cognitive style, and behavior regulation. In Fiedler K and Forgas J (Eds) *Affect, Cognition, and Social Behavior*. Toronto, Canada: Hogrefe.

Fieve R, Go R, Dunn D and Elston R (1984). Search for biologic\genetic markers in a longterm epidemiological and morbid risk survey of affective disorders. *Journal of Psychiatric Research*, 18: 425.

Fincham F and O'Leary K (1983). Causal inferences for spouse behavior in maritally distressed and non-distressed couples. *Journal of Social and Clinical Psychology*, 1: 42.

Finlay-Jones R and Brown G (1981). Types of stressful life-event and onset of anxiety and depressive disorders. *Psychological Medicine*, 11: 803.

Fishbein M and Laird J (1979). Concealment and disclosure: some effects of information control on the person who controls. *Journal of Experimental Social Psychology*, 15: 114.

Fisher J, Nadler A and Whitcher-Alagna S (1982). Recipient reaction to aid. *Psychological Bulletin*, 91: 27.

Fisher J, Goff B, Nadler A and Chinsky J (1988). Social psychological influences on help seeking and support from peers. In Gottlieb B (Ed.) *Marshaling Social Support: Formats, Processes, and Effects*. Newbury Park, CA: Sage.

Fisher S and Greenberg R (1989). A second opinion: rethinking the claims of biological psychiatry. In Fisher S and Greenberg R (Eds) *The Limits of Biological Treatments for Psychological Distress*. Hillsdale, NJ: Erlbaum.

Fleming J, Offord D and Boyle M (1989). Prevalence of childhood and adolescent depression in the community: Ontario Child Health Study. *British Journal of Psychiatry*, 155: 647.

Folkman S and Lazarus R (1986). Stress process and depressive symptomology. *Journal of Abnormal Psychology*, 95: 107.

Fong G, Krantz D and Nisbett R (1986). The effects of statistical training on thinking about everyday problems. *Cognitive Psychology*, 18: 253.

Forgas J, Bower G and Krantz S (1984). The influence of mood on perceptions of social interactions. *Journal of Experimental Social Psychology*, 20: 497.

Forgas J, Bower G and Moylan S (1990). Praise or blame? Affective influences on attributions for achievement. *Journal of Personality and Social Psychology*, 59: 809.

Freeman T, Clothier J, Pazzaglia P, Lesen M and Swann A (1992). A double-blind comparison of valproate and lithium in the treatment of acute mania. *American Journal of Psychiatry*, 149: 108.

Freud S (1917). *Mourning and Melancholia, in Collected Papers.* Vol. 4. London: Hogarth Press and the Institute of Psycho-analysis 1956; p. 152.

Froland C, Brodsky G, Olson M and Stewart L (1979). Social support and social adjustment: implications for mental health professionals. *Community Mental Health Journal*, 15: 82.

Furnham A and Capon M (1983). Social skills and self-monitoring processes. *Personality and Individual Differences*, 4: 171.

Garber J and Hollon S (1980). Universal versus personal helplessness in depression: belief in uncontrollability or incompetence. *Journal of Abnormal Psychology*, 89: 56.

Garrison C, Addy C, Jackson K, McKeown R and Walker J (1991). The CES-D as a screen for depression and other psychiatric disorders in adolescents. *Journal of the American Academy of Child and Adolescent Psychiatry*, 30: 636.

Gerner R (1993). The new mood stabilisers. *Audio-Digest Psychiatry*, 22(13).

Gershon E, Hamevit J and Guroff J (1982). A family study of schizoaffective bipolar 1, bipolar 11, unipolar, and normal probands. *Archives of General Psychiatry*, 39: 1157.

Gibbons F, Smith T, Ingram R, Pearce K, Brehm S and Shroeder D (1985). Self-awareness and self-confrontation: effects of self-focused attention on members of a clinical population. *Journal of Personality and Social Psychology*, 48: 662.

Gilbody S and Song F (2000). Publication bias and the integrity of psychiatry research. *Psychological Medicine*, 30: 253.

Goering P, Lancee W and Freeman J (1992). Marital support and recovery from depression. *British Journal of Psychiatry*, 160: 76.

Golan N (1981). *Passing Through Transitions: A Guide for Practitioners.* New York: Free Press.

Goldstein F (1981). Promoting competence in the families of psychiatric patients. In Maluccio N (Ed.) *Promoting Competence in Clients: A New\Old Approach to Social Work Practice.* New York: Free Press.

Goodwin F (1994). Treatment-resistant bipolar patients. *Audio-Digest, Family Practice*, 23\17.

Goodwin F and Jamison K (1990). Suicide. In Roy A (Ed.) *Manic Depression*. Baltimore MD: Williams and Wilkins.

Gotlib I (1982). Self-reinforcement and depression in interpersonal interaction: the role of performance level. *Journal of Abnormal Psychology*, 91: 3.

Gotlib I (1983). Perceptions and recall of interpersonal feedback: negative bias in depression. *Cognitive Therapy and Research*, 7: 399.

Gotlib I and Robinson L (1982). Responses to depressed individuals: discrepancies between self-report and observer-related behavior. *Journal of Abnormal Psychology*, 91: 231.

Gotlib I, Whiffen V, Mount J, Milne K and Cordy N (1989). Prevalence rates and demographic characteristics associated with depression in pregnancy and the postpartum. *Journal of Consulting and Clinical Psychology*, 57: 269.

Gove W (1975). The relationship between sex roles, marital status, and mental illness. *Social Forces*, 51: 34.

Gove W, Hughes M and Style C (1983). Does marriage have positive effects on the psychological well-being of the individual? *Journal of Health and Social Behavior*, 24: 122.

Greenberg J and Pyszcynski T (1986). Persistent high self-focus after failure and low self-focus after success: the depressive self-focusing style. *Journal of Personality and Social Psychology*, 50: 1039.

Greenberg L and Safran J (1989). Emotion in psychotherapy. *American Psychologist*, 44: 19.

Greenberg R and Fisher S (1989). Examining anti-depressant effectiveness: findings, ambiguities, and some vexing problems. In Fisher S and Greenberg R (Eds) *The Limits of Biological Treatments for Psychological Distress*. Hillsdale, NJ: Erlbaum.

Gregory W, Cialdini R and Carpenter K (1982). Self-relevant scenarios as mediators of likelihood estimates and compliance. Does imagining make it so? *Journal of Experimental Social Psychology*, 43: 89.

Griest H, Klein M, Eischens R and Faris J (1978). Anti-depressant running. *Behavioral Medicine*, 5(6): 19.

Haaga D, Dyck S and Ernst D (1991). Empirical status of cognitive theory of depression. *Psychological Bulletin*, 110: 215.

Haas G and Clarkin J (1988). Affective disorders and the family context. In Clarkin J, Haas G and Glick I (Eds) *Affective Disorders and the Family*. New York: Guilford.

Hafner R, Badenoch A and Fisher J (1983). Spouse-aided versus individual therapy in persisting psychiatric disorders: systematic comparison. *Family Process*, 22: 385.

Hall L and LLoyd S (1990). *Surviving Child Sexual Abuse: A Handbook for Helping Women Challenge their Past*. Basingstoke: Falmer Press.

Hall R, Beresford T and Quinones J (1987). Grief following spontaneous abortion. *Psychiatric Clinics of North America*, 10: 405.

Hamilton M (1968). Development of a rating scale for primary depressive illness. *British Journal of Social and Clinical Psychology*, 6: 278.

Hamilton M (1976). Clinical evaluation of depressions: clinical criteria and rating scales, including a Guttman scale. In Gallant D and Simpson G (Eds) *Depression: Behavioral, Biochemical, Diagnostic and Treatment Concepts*. Spectrum Books.

Hammen C (1981). Assessment: a clinical and cognitive emphasis. In Rehm L (Ed.) *Behavior Therapy for Depression: Present Status and Future Directions*. New York: Academic Press.

Hammen C (1991). Generation of stress in the course of unipolar depression. *Journal of Abnormal Psychology*, 100: 555.

Hammen C (1992). Life events and depression: the plot thickens. *American Journal of Community Psychology*, 20: 179.

Hammen C and Peters S (1978). Interpersonal consequences of depression: responses to men and women enacting a depressed role. *Journal of Abnormal Psychology*, 87: 322.

Hampson S and Dawson W (1985). Whatever happened to Pollyanna? The effects of evaluative congruence on speed of trait inference. *Personality and Social Psychology Bulletin*, 11: 106.

Hanh N (1993). *The Blooming of the Lotus*. Boston: Beacon.

Hautzinger M, Linden M and Hoffman N (1982). Distressed couples with and without a depressed partner: an analysis of their verbal interaction. *Journal of Behavior Therapy and Experimental Psychiatry*, 13: 307.

Healy D (1991). The marketing of 5HT: depression or anxiety. *British Journal of Psychiatry*, 158: 737.

Heckhausen H (1977). Achievement motivation and its construct: a cognitive model. *Motivation and Emotion*, 1: 283.

Heller K (1979). The effects of social support: prevention and treatment replications. In Goldstein A and Kanfer F (Eds) *Maximising Treatment Gains: Transfer Enhancement in Psychotherapy*. New York: Academic Press.

Herrick N and Maccoby M (1975). Humanizing work: a priority goal of the 1970's. In Davis L and Herns A (Eds) *The Quality of Working Life*. New York: Free Press.

Herz E (1983). Psychological repercussions of pregnancy loss. In Dennerstein L and de Senarchdeny M (Eds) *The Young Woman: Psychosomatic Aspects of Obstetrics and Gynaecology*. Amsterdam: Excerpta Medica.

Hickie I and Parker G (1992). The impact of an uncaring partner on improvement in non-melancholic depression. *Journal of Affective Disorders*, 25: 147.

Higley J, Mehlman P, Taub D, Higley S, Suomi S, Linnoila M and Vickers J (1992). Cerebrospinal fluid monoamine and adrenal correlates of aggression in free-ranging rhesus monkeys. *Archives of General Psychiatry*, 49: 436.

Hirsch B (1979). Psychological dimensions of social networks: a method of analysis. *American Journal of Community Psychology*, 7: 263.

Holister L (1994). New psychotherapeutic drugs. *Journal of Clinical Psychopharmacology*, 14: 50.

Hollon S and Beck A (1979). Cognitive theory of depression. In Kendall P and Hollon S (Eds) *Cognitive-Behavioral Interactions: Theory, Research and Procedures*. New York: Academic Press.

Hooley J and Teasdale J (1989). Predictors of relapse in depressives: expressed emotion, marital distress, and perceived criticism. *Journal of Abnormal Psychology*, 98: 229.

Hooley J, Orley J and Teasdale J (1986). Levels of expressed emotion and relapse in depressed patients. *British Journal of Psychiatry*, 148: 642.

Horne J (1993). Human sleep loss and behavior implications for the prefrontal cortex and psychiatric disorder. *British Journal of Psychiatry*, 162: 413.

Imber S, Pilkonis P, Sotsky S, Elkin I, Watkins J, Collins J, Shea T, Weber W and Glass D (1990). Mode-specific effects among three treatments for depression. *Journal of Consulting and Clinical Psychology*, 58: 352.

Ingram R, Smith T and Brehm S (1983). Depression and information processing: self-schemata and the encoding of self-referent information. *Journal of Personality and Social Psychology*, 45: 412.

Isaacson G, Bergman V and Rich C (1996). Epidemiological data suggest antidepressants reduce suicide risk among depressives. *Journal of Affective Disorders*, 41: 1.

Jackson S (1985). Acedia the sin. In Kleinman A and Good B (Eds) *Culture and Depression*. CA: University of California Press.

Jackson S (1986). *Melancholia and Depression from Hippocratic Times to Modern Times*. New Haven: Yale University Press.

Jacobs B (1991). Serotonin and behavior: emphasis on motor control. *Journal of Clinical Psychiatry*, 52: 17.

Jacobson N, Dobson K and Fruzetti A (1991). Marital therapy as a treatment for depression. *Journal of Consulting and Clinical Psychology*, 59: 547.

Jerrome D (1984). Good company: the sociological implications of friendship. *Sociological Review*, 32: 696.

Johnson-Laird P and Byrne R (1991). *Deduction*. Hove: Lawrence Erlbaum.

Joiner Jr T (1997). Shyness and low social support as interactive diathesis: with loneliness as mediator testing an interpersonal-personality view of vulnerability to depressive symptoms. *Journal of Abnormal Psychology*, 106: 386.

Joffe R, Levitt J, Bagby R, MacDonald C and Singer W (1993). Predictors of response to lithium and triiodothyronine augmentation of antidepressants in tricyclic non-responders. *British Journal of Psychiatry*, 163: 574.

Johnson E and Tversky A (1983). Affect generalisation and the perception of risk. *Journal of Personality and Social Psychology*, 45: 20.

Jones D (1991). Friendship satisfaction and gender: an examination of sex differences in contributor to friendship satisfaction. *Journal of Social and Personal Relationships*, 8: 167.

Jones E and Baumeister R (1976). The self-monitor looks at the ingratiator. *Journal of Personality*, 44: 654.

Jones W and Withington E (trans) (1923). *Works of Hippocrates*, Vol. 1. Cambridge: Harvard University Press; p. 263.

Joyce P (1985). Illness behaviour and rehospitalisation in bipolar affective disorder. *Psychological Medicine*, 15: 521.

Kanner A, Coyne J, Schaefer C and Lazarus S (1981). Comparison of two modes of stress measurement: daily hassles and uplifts versus major life events. *Journal of Behavioral Medicine*, 4: 1.

Karabenick S and Knapp J (1988). Effects of computer privacy on help-seeking. *Journal of Applied Social Psychology*, 18: 461.

Karasek R (1979). Job demands, job decision latitude, and mental strain: implications for job redesign. *Administrative Science Quarterly*, 24: 285.

Kashani J, Babero G and Bolande F (1981). Depression in hospitalised pediatric patients. *Journal of the American Academy of Child and Adolescent Psychiatry*, 20: 123.

Katon W and Sullivan M (1990). Depression and chronic medical illness. *Journal of Clinical Psychiatry*, 51: 3.

Katon W, Kleinman A and Rosen G (1982). Depression and somatization. Part 1 *American Journal of Medicine*, 72: 127.

Kavanagh D and Bower G (1983). Mood and self-efficacy: input of joy and sadness on perceived capacities. *Cognitive Therapy and Research*, 9: 507.

Keitman N and Casey P (1988). Repetition of parasuicide: an epidemiological and clinical study. *British Journal of Psychiatry*, 153: 792.

Keitner G, Ryan C and Miller I (1990). Family functioning, social adjustment, and reoccurrence of suicidality. *Psychiatry*, 53: 17.

Keller M, Beardslee W, Dorer D, Lavori P, Samuelson M and Klerman G (1987). Impact of severity and chronicity of parental affective illness on adaptive functioning and psychopathology in children. *Archives of General Psychiatry*, 43: 930.

Kelvin P (1977). Predictability, power and vulnerability in interpersonal attraction. In Duck S (Ed.) *Theory and Practice in Interpersonal Attraction*. NY: Academic Press.

Kendall P (1987). Cognitive processes and procedures in behavior therapy. In Wilson G, Franks I, Kendall P and Foreyt J (Eds) *Review of Behavior Therapy, Theory and Practice*, Vol. 11. New York: Guilford Press.

Kendell R (1988). What is a case? Food for thought for epidemiologists. *Archives of General Psychiatry*, 45: 374.

Kenny D and Acitelli L (1989). The role of the relationship in marital decision-making. In Brinberg D and Jaccard J (Eds) *Dyadic Decision Making*. New York: Springer Verlag.

Kermani K (1992). *Autogenic Training: The Effective Way to Conquer Stress*. London: Thorsons.

Kessler R, McGonagle K, Zhao S, Nelson C, Hughes M, Eshleman S, Wittchen H and Kendler K (1994). Lifetime and 12-month prevalence of DSM-111-R psychiatric disorders in the United States: results from the National Co-morbidity Survey. *Archives of General Psychiatry*, 51: 8.

Kiloh L, Andrews G and Neilson N (1988). The long-term outcome of depressive illness. *British Journal of Psychiatry*, 153: 752.

Kirmayer L, Robbins J and Paris J (1994). Somatised disorders, personality and the social matrix of somatic distress. *Journal of Abnormal Psychology*, 103: 125.

Kirschenbaum D, Tomarken A and Humphrey L (1985). Affect and adult self-regulation. *Journal of Personality and Social Psychology*, 48: 509.

Klerman G (1989). Psychiatric diagnostic categories: issues of validity and measurement – an invited comment on Mirowsky and Ross. *Journal of Health and Social Behavior*, 30: 26.

Klerman G and Weissman M (1980). Depression among women: their nature and causes. In Guttentag M, Salasin S and Belle D (Eds) *The Mental Health of Women*. New York: Academic Press.

Koenig H, George L and Siegler I (1988). The use of religion and other emotion-regulating coping strategies among older adults. *Gerontologist*, 28: 303.

Kovacs M and Beck A (1978). Maladaptive cognitive structures in depression. *American Journal of Psychiatry*, 135: 525.

Kovacs M, Feinberg T, Crouse-Novak M, Paulauskas S, Pollock M and Finkelkstein R (1984). Depressive disorders in children. II. A longitudinal study of the risk for a subsequent major depression. *Archives of General Psychiatry*, 41: 643.

Krause N and Stryker S (1984). Stress and well-being: buffering role of control beliefs. *Social Science and Medicine*, 18: 783.

Kroll J, Linde P, Habenicht M, Chan S, Yan G, Van G, Souvannasoth L, Nguyen J, Ly T and Nguyen H (1990). Medical compliance, antidepressant blood levels, and side -effects in Southeast Asian patients. *Journal of Clinical Psychopharmacology*, 10: 279.

Kuhara-Kojima K and Hatano G (1991). Contribution of content knowledge and learning ability to the learning of facts. *Journal of Educational Psychology*, 83: 253.

Kupfer D, Frank F and Perel J (1989). The advantage of early treatment intervention in recurrent depression. *Archives of General Psychiatry*, 46: 771.

Kupfer D, Frank E, Perel J, Cornes C, Malinger A, Thase M, McEachran M and Grochocinski V (1992). Five year outcome for maintenance therapies in recurrent depression. *Archives of General Psychiatry*, 49: 769.

Lacks P (1987). *Behavioral Treatment of Persistent Insomnia*. New York: Pergammon Press.

Lago D, Connell C and Knight B (1983). A companion animal program. In Smyer M and Gatz M (Eds) *Mental Health and Aging*. Beverly Hills, CA: Sage.

Laird J (1984). The real role of facial response in experience of emotion – a reply to Tourangeau, Ellsworth, and others. *Journal of Personality and Social Psychology*, 47: 909.

Laird J, Wagener J, Hahal M and Szegda M (1982). Remembering what you feel: the effects of emotion on memory. *Journal of Personality and Social Psychology*, 42: 646.

Landy S, Montgomery J and Walsh S (1989). Post-partum depression: a clinical view. *Maternal-Child Nursing Journal*, 18: 1.

Lazarus R (1991). *Emotion and Adaptation*. New York: Oxford University Press.

Lazarus R and Folkman S (1984). *Stress Appraisal, and Coping*. New York: Springer.

Leary M (1986). The impact of interactional impediments on social anxiety and self-presentation. *Journal of Experimental Social Psychology*, 22: 122.

Lee A and Murray R (1988). The long-term outcome of Maudsley depressives. *British Journal of Psychiatry*, 153: 741.

Lefley H (1989). Family burden and family stigma in major mental illness. *American Psychologist*, 44: 556.

Lesse S (1983). The masked depression syndrome – results of a seventeen-year clinical study. *American Journal of Psychotherapy*, 37: 456.

Lewinsohn P (1986). A behavioral approach to depression. In Coyne J (Ed.) *Essential Papers on Depression*. New York: New York University.

Lewinsohn P, Mischel W, Chaplin W and Barton R (1980). Social competence and derision: the role of illusory self-perceptions. *Journal of Abnormal Psychology*, 89: 203.

Lewinsohn P, Steinmetz J, Larson D and Franklin J (1981). Depression-related cognitions: antecedent or consequence? *Journal of Abnormal Psychology*, 90: 213.

Lewinsohn P, Munoz R, Youngren M and Zeiss A (1986). *Control Your Depression*. New York: Fireside.

Lewinsohn P, Hoberman H and Rosenbaum M (1988). A prospective study of risk factors for unipolar depression. *Journal of Abnormal Psychology*, 97: 251.

Lewinsohn P, Zeiss A and Duncan E (1989). Probability of relapse after recovery from an episode of depression. *Journal of Abnormal Psychology*, 98(2): 107.

Lewis M (1992). *Shame: The Exposed Self*. New York: The Free Press.

Lewis W (1989). How not to engage a family in therapy. *Journal of Strategic and Systemic Therapies*, 8: 50.

Lewy A (1994). Ordering sleep. *Audio-Digest Family Practice*, 23(14).

Lindberg F and Dinstad L (1985). Survival responses to incest: adolescents in crisis. *Child Abuse and Neglect*, 9: 521.

Linehan M (1981). A social-behavioral analysis of suicide and parasuicide: implications for clinical assessment and treatment. In Clarkin J and Glazer H (Eds) *Depression: Behavioral and Directive Intervention Strategies*. New York: Garland Press.

Loring M and Powell B (1986). Gender, race, and DSM-III: a study of the objectivity of psychiatric diagnostic behavior. *Journal of Health and Social Behavior*, 29: 1.

McCauley E, Mitchell J, Burke P and Moss P (1988). Cognitive attributes of depression in children and adolescents. *Journal of Consulting and Clinical Psychology*, 14: 903.

McGrath E, Keita G, Strickland B and Russo N (1990). Women and depression: risk factors and treatment issues. *Final Report of the American Psychological Association Task Force on Women and Depression*. Washington, DC: American Psychological Association.

McIntosh J, Hubbard R and Santos J (1985). Suicide facts and myths. *Death Studies*, 9: 267.

MacKinnon D and Farberow N (1975). An assessment of the utility of suicide prediction. *Suicide and Life-threatening Behavior*, 6: 86.

McLeroy K, Green L, Mullen K and Foshee V (1984). Assessing the effects of health promotion in worksites: a review of the stress program evaluations. *Health Education Quarterly*, 11: 379.

MacLeod A, Williams J and Bekerian D (1991). Worry is reasonable: the role of explanations in pessimism about future personal events. *Journal of Abnormal Psychology*, 100: 478.

MacPhillamy D and Lewinsohn P (1982). The Pleasant Events Schedule and studies on reliability, validity, and scale intercorrelations. *Journal of Consulting and Clinical Psychology*, 50: 363.

Marsella A (1979). Depressive experience and disorder across cultures. In Triandis H and Draguns J (Eds) *Handbook of Cross-cultural Psychology*, Vol. 6. *Psychopathology*. Boston: Allyn and Bacon.

Marsh D (1992). *Families and Mental Illness: New Directions in Professional Practice*. New York: Praeger.

Marsh D, Dickens R, Yackovitch N, Wilson J, Leichliter J and MacQuillis V (1993). Troubled journey: siblings and children of people with mental illness. *Innovations and Research*, 2: 17.

Matinsen E and Medhus A (1989). Adherence to exercise and patients' evaluation of physical exercise in a comprehensive treatment programme for depression. *Nordisk Psykiatrisk Tiddskrift*, 43: 411.

Matlin M and Stang D (1978). *The Pollyanna Principle*. Cambridge, MA: Schenkman.

Matt G, Vazquez C and Campbell K (1992). Mood congruent recall of affectively toned stimuli: a meta-analytic review. *Clinical Psychology*, 12: 227.

Mayo V and Tanaka-Matsumi J (1996). Thinking aloud statements and solutions of dysphoric persons on a social problem-solving task. *Cognitive Therapy and Research*, 20: 97.

Mechanic D (1967). Some factors in identifying and defining mental illness. In Scheff T *Mental Illness and Social Processes*. London: Harper and Row.

Meichenbaum D (1977). *Cognitive Behavior Modification: An Integrative Approach*. New York: Plenum Press.

Millar M and Wilcox B (1984). Perceived hassles and uplifts among nursing home residents. *Psychological Reports*, 55: 277.

Miller I, Norman W, Keitner G, Bishop S and Dow M (1989). Cognitive-behavioral treatment of depressed inpatients. *Behavior Therapy*, 230: 25.

Mirowsky J and Ross C (1989). Psychiatric diagnosis as reified measurement. *Journal of Health and Social Behavior*, 30: 11.

Mitchell P, Parker G, Jamieson K and Wilhelm K (1992). Are there any differences between bipolar and unipolar melancholia. *Journal of Affective Disorders*, 25: 97.

Mitchell R and Moos R (1984). Deficiencies in social support among depressed patients: antecedents or consequences of stress? *Journal of Health and Social Behavior*, 25: 438.

Montgomery B (1984). Communication in intimate relationships: a research challenge. *Communication Quarterly*, 32: 318.

Moos R (1992). Understanding individuals' life contexts: implications for stress reduction and prevention. In Kessler M, Goldstein S and Joffe J (Eds) *The Present and Future of Preventative Research*. Newbury Park, CA: Sage.

Morgan H, Barton J, Pottle S, Pocock H and Burns-Cox C (1976). Deliberate self-harm: a follow-up study of 279 patients. *British Journal of Psychiatry*, 28: 261.

Murphy E (1982). Social origins of depression in old age. *British Journal of Psychiatry*, 141: 135.

Murphy G (1975). The physician's responsibility for suicide. II Errors of omission. *Annals of Internal Medicine*, 82: 305.

Murphy G (1984). The prediction of suicide: Why is it so difficult? *American Journal of Psychotherapy*, 38: 241.

Myers D and Neal C (1978). Suicide in psychiatric patients. *British Journal of Psychiatry*, 133: 34.

Nadler A, Mayseless O, Peri N and Chemerinski A (1985). Effects of opportunity to reciprocate and self-esteem on help-seeking behavior. *Journal of Personality*, 53: 23.

Newman J, Engel R and Jensen J (1991). Age differences in depressive symptom experiences. *Journals of Gerontology: Psychological Sciences*, 46: 224.

Nierenberg A (1995). Overcoming treatment-resistant depression. *Audio-Digest, Psychiatry*, 24(14).

Nofzinger E, Thase M, Reynolds C, Himmelhoch J, Mallinger A, Houck P and Kupfer D (1991). Hypersomnia in bipolar depression: a comparison with narcolepsy using the multiple sleep latency test. *American Journal of Psychiatry*, 148: 1177.

Nolan S, Roberts J and Gotlib I (1998). Ruminative response style and vulnerability to episodes of dysphoria: gender, neuroticism, and episode duration. *Cognitive Theory and Research*, 22: 445.

Nolen-Hoeksama (1987). Sex differences in unipolar depression: evidence and theory. *Psychological Bulletin*, 101: 259.

O'Brien M, Petrie K and Raeburn J (1992). Adherence to medication regimens: updating a complex medical issue. *Medical Care Review*, 49: 435.

Ofshe R and Watters E (1995). Making monsters: false memories, psychotherapy and sexual hysteria. *Andre Deutsch* (Chapter 10).

Oliker S (1989). *Best Friends and Marriage: Exchange Among Women*. Berkeley, CA: University of California Press.

Ontiveros A, Fontaine R and Elie R (1991). Refractory depression: the addition of lithium to fluoxetine or desipramine. *Acta Psychiatrica Scandinavica*, 83: 188.

Pallak M, Mueller M, Dollar K and Pallak J (1972). Effectiveness of commitment on responsiveness to an extreme consonant communication. *Journal of Personality and Social Psychology*, 23: 429.

Palmore E and Kivett V (1977). Changes in life satisfaction: a longitudinal study of persons aged 46–70. *Journal of Gerontology*, 32: 311.

Parducci A (1968). The relativism of absolute judgments. *Scientific American*, 19: 84.

Parker G (1992). *With this Body: Caring and Disability in Marriage*. Milton Keynes: Open University Press.

Parmalee P, Katz I and Lawton M (1991). The relationship of pain to depression in institutionalized aged. *Journals of Gerontology: Psychological Sciences*, 46: 15.

Patton G (1993). Eating problems. In Costello C (Ed.) *Symptoms of Depression*. New York: Wiley.

Paykel E, Myers J, Dienelt M, Klerman G, Lindenthal J and Pepper M (1969). Life events and depression: a controlled study. *Archives of General Psychiatry*, 21: 753.

Pearlin L (1983). Role strains and personal stress. In Kaplan H (Ed.) *Psychosocial Stress: Trends in Theory and Research*. New York: Academic Press.

Pearson R (1990). *Counseling and Social Support*. London: Sage.

Pennebaker J and Beall S (1986). Cognitive, emotional, and physiological components of confiding: behavioral inhibition and disease. *Journal of Abnormal Psychology*, 95: 274.

Pennebaker J and Francis M (1996). Cognitive, emotional, and language processes in disclosure. *Cognition and Emotion*, 10(6): 601.

Pennebaker J and O'Heeron R (1984). Confiding in others and illness rate among spouses of suicide and accidental death victims. *Journal of Abnormal Psychology*, 93: 473.

Pennebaker J, Hughes C and O'Heeron R (1987). The psychophysiology of confession linking inhibitory and psychosomatic processes. *Journal of Personality and Social Psychology*, 52: 781.

Perkins D, Farady M and Bushey B (1991). Everyman reasoning and the roots of intelligence. In Voss J, Perkins D and Segal J (Eds) *Informal Reasoning and Education*. Hillsdale, NJ: Lawrence Erlbaum.

Perris C (1992). Bipolar-unipolar distinction. In Paykel E (Ed.) *Handbook of Affective Disorders*. New York: Guilford Press.

Peterson C and Seligman M (1984). Causal explanations as a risk factor for depression: theory and evidence. *Psychological Review*, 91: 347.

Pitt B (1973). Maternity blues. *British Journal of Psychiatry*, 122: 431.

Planalp S and Benson A (1992). Friends' and acquaintances' conversations: perceived differences. *Journal of Social and Personal Relationships*, 9: 483.

Quinnett P (1987). *Suicide: The Forever Decision*. New York: Crossroad Publishing.

Rachman S (1984). Agoraphobia: a safety-signal perspective. *Behaviour Research and Therapy*, 22: 59.

Rapp S, Parisi S, Walsh D and Wallace C (1988). Detecting depression in elderly medical inpatients. *Journal of Consulting and Clinical Psychology*, 56: 509.

Rawlins W (1983). Openness as problematic in ongoing friendships: two conversational dilemmas. *Communication Monographs*, No 50: 1.

Rawlins W (1994). Being there and growing apart: sustaining friendships through adulthood. In Canary D and Stafford L (Eds) *Communication and Relational Maintenance*. New York: Academic Press.

Rehm L, Kaslow N and Rabin A (1987). Cognitive and behavioral targets in a self-control therapy program for depression. *Journal of Consulting and Clinical Psychology*, 55: 60.

Rhodewalt F and Agustsdottir S (1986). Effects of self-presentation on the phenomenal self. *Journal of Personality and Social Psychology*, 50: 47.

Rie H (1966). Depression in childhood: a survey of some pertinent contributors. *Journal of the American Academy of Child and Adolescent Psychiatry*, 5: 653.

Robins E (1981). The Final Months: A Study of the Lives of 134 Persons Who Committed Suicide. London: Oxford University Press.

Robins L, Helzer J, Croughan J and Ratcliff K (1981). National Institute Mental Health Diagnostic Interview Schedule. *Archives of General Psychiatry*, 38: 381.

Robinson G, Stirtzinger R and Stewart D (1994). Psychological reaction in women followed for one year after miscarriage. *Journal of Reproductive and Infant Psychology*, 12: 31.

Rodger C, Scott A and Walley L (1994). Is there any delay in the onset of the anti-depressant effect of electro-convulsive therapy? *British Journal of Psychiatry*, 164: 106.

Rosen S, Mickler S and Colins J (1987). Reactions of would-be helpers whose offer of help is spurned. *Journal of Personality and Social Psychology*, 53: 288.

Rosenbaum M and Najenson T (1976). Changes in life-patterns and symptoms of low mood as reported by wives of severely brain-injured soldiers. *Journal of Consulting and Clinical Psychology*, 44: 881.

Rosenblatt P (1988). The social context of private feelings. *The Journal of Social Issues*, 44: 67.

Rosenblatt A and Greenberg J (1991). Examining the world of the depressed: do depressed people prefer others who are depressed? *Journal of Personality and Social Psychology*, 60: 620.

Rosenman R, Friedman M, Straus R, Wurm M, Kositchel R, Haan W and Werthessen N (1964). *A Predictive Study of Coronary Heart Disease: The Western Collaborative Group Study*. Basel: Karg.

Rosenthal N (1989). Light therapy. In Karasu T (Ed.) *Treatment of Psychiatric Disorders. A Task Force Report for the American Psychiatric Association*, Vol. 3. Washington, DC: American Psychiatric Association; p. 1890.

Ross S, Ross D and Vesta F (1976). Oral summary as a review strategy enhancing recall of textual material. *Journal of Educational Psychology*, 68: 689.

Rounsaville B, Weissman M and Prusoff B (1979). Process of psychotherapy among depressed women with marital disputes. *American Journal of Orthopsychiatry*, 49: 505.

Rush A, Ermin M, Giles D, Schlesser M, Carpenter G, Vasavada N and Roffwarg H (1986). Polysomnographic findings in recently drug-free and technically remitted patients. *Archives of General Psychiatry*, 43: 878.

Rutter M, Cox A, Tupling C, Berger M and Yule W (1975). Attainment and adjustment in two geographical areas: 1. The prevalence of psychiatric disorder. *British Journal of Psychiatry*, 126: 493.

Ryan N, Puig-Antich J, Ambrosini P, Rabinovich H, Robinson D, Nelson B and Twomey J (1987). The clinical picture of major depression in children and adolescents. *Archives of General Psychiatry*, 44: 854.

Sackheim H (1989). The efficacy of electroconvulsive therapy in the treatment of major depressive disorder. In Fisher S and Greenberg R (Eds) *The Limits of Biological Treatments for Psychological Distress*. Hillsdale, NJ: Erlbaum.

Sackheim H, Decina P and Prohovnik I (1987). Seizure threshold in electroconvulsive therapy. Effects of sex, age, electrode placement, and number of treatments. *Archives of General Psychiatry*, 44: 355.

Sadowski C and Blackwell M (1985). Locus of control and perceived stress among student teachers. *Psychological Reports*, 56: 723.

Salzman C (1993). New developments in treating depression. *Audio-Digest, Psychiatry*, 22(07).

Saper Z and Forest J (1992). Effects of types of instruction on solution of psychological self-help problems. *Psychological Reports*, 70: 1095.

Schildkraut J (1965). The catecholamine hypothesis of affective disorders: a review of supporting evidence. *American Journal of Psychiatry*, 122: 509.

Schlieffelin E (1985). The cultural analysis of depressive effect: example from New Guinea. In Kleinman A and Good B (Eds) *Culture and Depression*. London: University of California Press.

Schouten P and Handelsman M (1987). Social basis of self-handicapping: the case of depression. *Personality and Social Psychology Bulletin*, 13: 103.

Schwartz N and Clore G (1983). Mood, misattribution, and judgements of well-being: informative and directive functions of affective states. *Journal of Personality and Social Psychology*, 45: 513.

Scott C, Fuhrman R and Wyer R (1991). Information processing in close relationships. In Fletcher G and Fincham F (Eds) *Cognition in Close Relationships*. Hillsdale, NJ: Erlbaum.

Seligman M (1975). *Helplessness: On Depression, Development and Death*. San Francisco: Freemen.

Siegman A (1993). Cardiovascular consequences of expressing, experiencing and repressing anger. *Journal of Behavioral Medicine*, 16: 539.

Sillars A, Pike G, Jones T and Murphy M (1984). Communication and understanding in marriage. *Human Communication Research*, 10: 153.

Silver R and Wortman I (1980). Coping with undesirable life-events. In Garber J and Seligman E (Eds) *Human Helplessness: Theory and Applications*. New York: Academic Press.

Simons A, Garfield S and Murphy G (1984). The process of change in cognitive therapy and pharmacotherapy for depression: changes in mood and cognition. *Archives of General Psychiatry*, 41: 45.

Sinclair I (1990). Carers: their contribution and quality of life. In Sinclair I, Parker R, Leat D and Williams J (Eds) *The Kaleidoscope of Care: A Review of Research of Welfare Provision for Elderly People*. London: HMSO.

Smith T and Allred K (1989). Anxiety and future loss, depressive reaction to past loss. In Kendall P and Watson D (Eds) *Anxiety and Depression: Distinctive and Overlapping Features*. San Diego, CA: Academic Press.

Smith T, Synder C and Handelsman M (1982). On the self-serving function of an academic wooden leg: test anxiety as a self-handicapping strategy. *Journal of Personality and Social Psychology*, 42: 314.

Snider J, Davis M and Brown R (1984). Effects of self tape-recording on self-awareness in a context of self-counseling. 54: 311.

Spitzer R, Endicott J and Robins E (1978). Research diagnostic criteria: rationale and reliability. *Archives of General Psychiatry*, 35: 773.

Strack S, Blaney P and Gschneidinger R (1985). Pessimistic preoccupation, performance deficits and depression. *Journal of Personality and Social Psychology*, 49: 1076.

Strike K and Posner G (1992). A revisionist theory of conceptual change. In Huston W, Duschl R and Hamilton R (Eds) Philosophy of Science, Cognitive Psychology and Educational Theory and Practice. Albany, NY: SUNY.

Strube M and Roemmele L (1985). Self-enhancement, self-assessment, and self-evaluative task choice. *Journal of Personality and Social Psychology*, 49: 981.

Strupp H (1989). Psychotherapy: can the practitioner learn from the researcher? *American Psychologist*, 41: 717.

Szasz T (1974). *The Myth of Mental Illness*. New York: Harper and Row.

Szasz T (1987). *Insanity*. Chichester: John Wiley.

Taylor S and Brown J (1988). Illusion and well-being: a social psychological perspective on mental health. *Psychological Bulletin*, 103: 193.

Teasdale J (1983). Negative thinking in depression: cause, affect, or reciprocal relationship. *Advances in Behaviour Research and Therapy*, 5: 3.

Teasdale J (1988). Cognitive vulnerability to persistent depression. *Cognition and Emotion*, 2: 247.

Thase M and Kupfer D (1987). Current status of EEG sleep in the assessment and treatment of depression. In Burrows G and Werry J (Eds) *Advances in Human Psychopharmacology*, Vol. 4. Greenwich, CT: JAI Press; p. 93.

Thirkettle J and Knight R (1985). The psychological precipitants of transient postpartum depression: a review. *Current Psychological Research and Reviews*, 4: 143.

Thoits P (1983). Dimensions of life events that influence psychological distress. In Kaplan H (Ed.) *Psychosocial Distress: Trends in Theory and Research*. New York: Academic Press.

Thompson A (1990). *Guide to Ethical Practice in Psychotherapy*. New York: Wiley.

Tjosvold D and Field R (1987). Effect of concurrence, controversy and consensus in group decision making. *Journal of Social Psychology*, 125: 355.

Tolsdorf C (1976). Social networks, support, and coping: an exploratory study. *Family Process*, 15: 407.

Tsuang M and Faraone S (1990). *The Genetics of Mood Disorder*. Baltimore: John Hopkins University.

Tversky A and Kahneman D (1982). Judgments under uncertainty: heuristics and biases. *Science*, 185: 1124.

Twigg J and Atkin K (1993). *Policy and Practice in Informal Care*. Milton Keynes: Open University Press.

van Praag H (1980). Central monoamine metabolism in depressions: 11 Catecholamines and related compounds. *Comprehensive Psychiatry*, 21: 315.

Walster E and Berscheid E (1978). *Equity: Theory and Research*. Boston: Allyn and Bacon.

Waring E, Patton D and Wister A (1990). The etiology of nine psychotic emotional illnesses. *Canadian Journal of Psychiatry*, 35: 50.

Watzlawick P, Beavin J and Jackson D (1967). *Pragmatics of Human Communication: A Study of Interactional Patterns, Pathologies and Paradoxes*. New York: Norton.

Waxer P (1976). Non-verbal cues for depth of depression. *Journal of Consulting and Clinical Psychology*, 44: 493.

Wegner D, Schneider D, Carter S and White T (1987). Paradoxical effects of thought suppression. *Journal of Personality and Social Psychology*, 53: 5.

Weiman C (1977). A study of occupational stressors and the incidence of disease risks. *Journal of Occupational Medicine*, 19: 119.

Weissman M (1987). Advances in psychiatric epidemiology: risks and rates for major depression. *American Journal of Public Health*, 77: 445.

Weissman M and Myers J (1978). Affective disorders in a US urban community: the application of research diagnostic criteria in an epidemiologic study. *Archives of General Psychiatry*, 35: 1304.

Weissman M, Leaf P, Ischler G, Blazer D, Karno M, Bruce M and Florio L (1988). Affective disorders in five United States communities. *Psychological Medicine*, 18: 141.

Wells K (1985). *Depression as a Tracer Condition for the National Study of Medical Care Outcomes: Background Review*. Santa Monica, CA: RAND.

Wenzlaff R, Wegner D and Roper D (1987). Depression and mental control: the resurgence of uninvited negative thoughts. *Journal of Personality and Social Psychology*, 55: 862.

Wesner R and Winokur G (1990). Genetics of affective disorders. In Wolman B and Stricker G (Eds) *Depressive Disorders: Facts, Theories, and Treatment Methods*. New York: Wiley.

Wilkinson J and Canter S (1983). *Social Skills Training Manual: Assessment, Programme Design, and Management of Training*. Chichester: Wiley.

Williams J (1992). *The Psychological Treatment of Depression*. London: Routledge.

Williamson G and Schultz R (1992). Physical illness and symptoms of depression among elderly outpatients. *Psychology and Aging*, 7: 343.

Willner P (1984). Cognitive functioning in depression: a review of theory and research. *Psychological Medicine*, 14: 807.

Wills T, Weiss R and Patterson G (1974). A behavioral analysis of the determinants of married satisfaction. *Journal of Consulting and Clinical Psychology*, 42: 802.

Wiseman J (1986). Friendship: bonds and binds in a voluntary relationship. *Journal of Personal and Social Relationships*, 3: 191.

Wolpe J and Lazarus A (1966). *Behavior Therapy Techniques*. New York: Pergamon.

Zetin M, Sklanky G and Cramer M (1984). Sex differences in inpatients with major depression. *Journal of Clinical Psychiatry*, 45: 257.

Zoega T, Barr C and Barsky A (1991). Prediction of compliance with medication and follow-up appointments. *Nordisk Psykiatrisk Tidsskrift*, 45: 27.

Zola I (1973). Pathways to the doctor – from person to patient. *Social Science*.

Index